Hunters, Gatherers, and Practitioners of Powerlessness

European Anthropology in Translation
Published in Association with the Society for the Anthropology of
Europe (AAA)
General Editor: **Nicolette Makovicky**, Oxford School of Global and Area
Studies

This new series introduces English-language versions of significant works
on the Anthropology of Europe that were originally published in other
languages. These include books produced recently by a new generation
of scholars as well as older works that have not previously appeared in
English.

Hunters, Gatherers, and Practitioners of Powerlessness

An Ethnography of the Degraded in Postsocialist Poland

Tomasz Rakowski

Translated by
Søren Gauger

berghahn
NEW YORK · OXFORD
www.berghahnbooks.com

Published in 2016 by
Berghahn Books
www.berghahnbooks.com

English-language edition
© 2016, 2019 Tomasz Rakowski
First paperback edition published in 2019

Polish-language edition
© 2009 Słowo/obraz terytoria
Łowcy, zbieracze, praktycy niemocy
By Tomasz Rakowski

The translation of the book has been completed thanks to the funding support
received from the Polish Ministry of Labour and Social Policy as part of the 2010
European Year for Combating Poverty and Social Exclusion programme.

Library of Congress Cataloging in Publication Data

Names: Rakowski, Tomasz.
Title: Hunters, gatherers, and practitioners of powerlessness : an ethnography of
   the degraded in postsocialist Poland / Tomasz Rakowski ; translated by Soren
   Gauger.
Other titles: Łowcy, zbieracze, praktycy niemocy. English
Description: New York : Berghahn Books, 2016. | Series: European anthropology
   in translation ; volume 6 | Translation of: Łowcy, zbieracze, praktycy niemocy.
   Gdańsk : Wydawnictwo słowo/obraz terytoria, 2009. | Includes bibliographical
   references and index.
Identifiers: LCCN 2016025119 | ISBN 9781785332401 (hardback : alk. paper)
Subjects: LCSH: Poverty—Poland. | Unemployment—Poland. | Poland—Social
   conditions—21st century. | Post-communism—Poland.
Classification: LCC HC340.3.Z9 P625513 2016 | DDC 331.13/709438—dc23
LC record available at https://lccn.loc.gov/2016025119

British Library Cataloguing-in-Publication Data

A catalogue record for this book is available from the British Library

All photographs are © Paweł Pałgan.

ISBN 978-1-78533-240-1 hardback
ISBN 978-1-78920-534-3 paperback
ISBN 978-1-78533-241-8 ebook

Contents

Foreword

The fall of communism and the post-communist transformations has captivated the attention of social scientists from all disciplines. Economists have focused on various types of economic strategies, their implementation and outcomes (paying special attention to the realization of "neoliberal blueprint"); political scientists have been studying new forms of political life and their (dis)functions; sociologists have engaged in producing large panoramas of changing social structures and cultures. It has been left to anthropologists to delve into the minutiae of everyday life, show how people cope with the often dramatic changes in the institutional environment, and (re)construct their lives in the situations that often have the nature of quick sands.

Anthropologists, by and large, have been faithful to the creed of their profession and concentrated their efforts on studying the fate of the "weak," those who have suffered most after the 1989 regime change. While never short on compassion, they have not been always able to produce deep and nuanced portrayals of lives turned upside down. Perhaps, it was inevitable that it would take a Polish anthropologist/ethnographer to write an authoritative study of the postcommunist condition. Two giants, Bronisław Malinowski and Florian Znaniecki, crafted the foundational intellectual code of that country's distinct social scientific tradition. The former invented the method of participant observation (and, as a consequence, modern empirical anthropology); the latter taught us to study social reality with the "humanistic coefficient" (thus contributing to the formation of the Chicago School of sociology). Znaniecki, arguably, is the actual inventor of the Thomas Theorem: "If men define situations as real, they are real in their consequences." Rakowski, an heir to this tradition, takes it to a new level, enriching it not only with the results of his own trail-blazing ethnographic work, but also with novel interpretive threads, taken for example from Marleau-Ponty's phenomenology. As a result we get Znaniecki's attention to actors' own understandings of the situation enhanced with Rakowski's efforts to reconstruct and render narratively extra-verbal, "bodily" experiences that are so fundamental for human existence in Marleau-Ponty's thought.

Rakowski does not reconstruct the totality of the postcommunist condition. As an apparent practitioner of what Sherry Ortner has recently called "dark anthropology",[1] he studies its most tragic dimension, by immersing himself in the lives of those who experienced the total, if temporary, collapse of the economic and social foundations of their existence. Many anthropologists have worked among the "losers" of postcommunist transformations and produced effective portrayals of their suffering, resilience, and ingenuity. In those portrayals, the main culprit is usually neoliberalism, an economic program accepted at the urging of such international institutions as the IMF and the World Bank and implemented by the governments seemingly insensitive to the plight of the "average" people. These people, whose lives are often tragically impacted by the reforms entailing plant closings and massive unemployment, are not necessarily portrayed as passive victims, but we rarely get deeply textured depictions of their lives and efforts to come to terms with the world turned upside down. This study is different, as Rakowski produces three nuanced ethnographies of social and economic resilience in the face of not just an economic collapse but also a cultural catastrophe. It is hard to find a better ethnographic example of the work that is "ontological" in its spirit. What we get is not just a picture of the attempts to rebuild economic layer of existence; we get a comprehensive portrait of dealing with the total collapse of the world, as its economic foundation is gone, its social anchoring lost, and its cultural scaffold dismantled.

Yet, as Rakowski shows, people do not give up and work creatively to put back their "worlds." Their ability to re-construct an economically, socially, and culturally viable existence after they experienced a catastrophic collapse of the taken-for-granted reality depends on the material resources, social networks and cultural codes they can access and employ. The simplistic renditions of the post-communist transformations present them almost only as total economic catastrophes engendering massive suffering and social malaise (vide: Naomi Klein). The actual situation is more complex, as different groups of people have managed to reorient their lives differently, depending, of course, on their (uneven) access to various resources (such as economic, political, social or cultural capitals). Some immediately found their way in the "private" world of the market economy (and those are not only the scheming "oligarchs"), some found employment in the reinvigorated state bureaucracy or newly created municipal and regional administrations, some ended up on welfare rolls. Rakowski studies individuals and communities for whom none of these three options was available. As he writes: "One might say that beyond the "private," "state," and "welfare" Polands, there existed another, fourth dimension of making do in the new reality—"ecological" strategies and activities or, to phrase it differently, "hunter/gatherer" Poland".[2]

After experiencing the collapse of taken-for-granted social worlds embedded in the state socialist economy, modern Polish "hunters and gatherers" left almost completely to their own devices, had to build their lives anew. Rakowski carefully reconstructs not just three different strategies of survival, but much more comprehensive efforts to put the "reality" back together. For him the first goal of the ethnographic method is a deep immersion into the "alien" world, the world created by the people pushed outside of the "mainstream," whose rules do not apply anymore. Such immersion is not sufficient to faithfully reproduce this world, but the attempt is nonetheless made "in good faith," not least to show respect for the cultures that are sui generis, and need to be understood on their own terms. Rakowski shows that such cultures are not ad hoc constructions, a mere adaptive responses by the people who are barely making it, hanging on by a threat. They are, instead, fully-fledged cultural systems with their own rules and codes, often built on the traditions (or their fragments) of concrete communities. These rules and codes are not easily translatable to an idiom of ethnographic writing and Rakowski—working in a manner familiar to the proponents of the ontological turn in anthropology—produces nuanced literary approximations of three specific worlds of precarious existence albeit each constructed differently, according to the cultural codes of three distinct local knowledges. The text is a complex and tantalizing mélange of his own descriptions of personages, situations, performances and gestures; his "natives'" own stories; and useful theoretical leads, coming, for example, from Freud or Melanie Klein. Being aware that an accurate translation from one culture to another is impossible, Rakowski composes a text that very imaginatively exploits tensions and contradictions between the terms of "their" culture and the conceptual apparatus of modern anthropology. By doing so he puts into great use the principles of ethnographic theory, as set forth, for example, by the important journal of new anthropological thinking, HAU.

For the non-Polish audience, the work has also other benefits. For example, it introduces and critically re-evaluates the long and rich Polish sociological tradition of studying poverty. Rakowski reviews this literature and is thus able to situate the post-communist poverty in the context of its "predecessors": the poverty of the interwar period (1918–39) and the poverty that existed under state socialism. Consistent with

Znaniecki's principles, poverty is often studied in the Polish traditions as a condition that cannot be reduced to economic or material deprivation. It is a specific, usually complete mode of existence in the world, with its own social configurations and cultural scripts that are often completely incomprehensible in terms of categories derived from the "mainstream." This exoticism of poverty makes ethnographic immersion the only method that can help us *try* to grasp its profundity. By taking an "ethnographic path" (author's own term), Rakowski contributes in an original way to the recently fashionable theme of resilience, particularly resilience of both individuals and communities subjected to the often-misconceived economic experiments designed and implemented in the name of neoliberalism. Again, his originality comes from adopting a very comprehensive economic-and-social-and cultural approach to the studied reality.

Rakowski tackles also the ambivalent legacy of state socialism rarely discussed in the anthropological literature. On the one had it was a system of specific enslavement (as it curtailed people's basic civic and political rights) but on the other it produced considerable improvement in the material conditions of life for millions of people and gave them certain level of economic stability and predictability. The post-1989 changes restored basic political and civic freedoms while exposing people to the economic forces of market economy (often entailing dislocations and unemployment), built according to the precepts of neoliberalism. While some people experienced the elation associated with "liberation" and the tragedy of social and economic degradation simultaneously, many have had hard time enjoying "freedom" as their lives collapsed, if only temporarily. This new social reality—whose ambivalence or contradictoriness is quite difficult to grasp, as Rakowski astutely notes—has been rarely illuminated in a more nuanced manner than in this work.

Jan Kubik
School of Slavonic and East European Studies
University College London

Notes

1. Ortner, Sherry B. 2016. "Dark anthropology and its others Theory since the eighties." *Hau: Journal of Ethnographic Theory* 6 (1): 47–73. ISSN 2049-1115 (Online). DOI: http://dx.doi.org/10.14318/hau6.1.004.
2. Ibid., 38.

Acknowledgments

I would like to express my gratitude to all those who helped bring this book to completion. I thank my interlocutors and associates in the field, and the impoverished people who, while dealing with the challenges of their difficult situations, still took the time to share part of their lives with me. These include the diggers, bootleg miners, scrap collectors, and former miners of the Wałbrzych area; the scrap collectors and the impoverished farmers of the areas around the Bełchatów Mine; the residents of the villages and the gatherers and farmers near Szydłowiec and Przysucha. I thank those who accepted my associates and me; I thank those who spent entire days with us, talking, sharing their experiences, and inviting us into their homes.

I affectionately thank my teachers and supervisors, Professor Roch Sulima and Professor Anna Zadrożyńska, masters at perceiving the most important ethnographic sources, the most private and fully fledged experiences of other people. I thank those who taught and inspired my thinking: Elżbieta Tarkowska, Agata Bielik-Robson, Andrzej Mencwel, Andrzej Leder, Grzegorz Godlewski, Paweł Rodak, Wojciech Pieniążek, and many other outstanding humanists. I thank the community from which I came, and from where my knowledge derives, and my colleagues from the Warsaw University Institute of Polish Culture. I also thank my colleagues from the Warsaw University Institute of Ethnology and Cultural Anthropology, and my colleagues from the 'Op. cit.' Editorial Board.

I would also like to thank my splendid reviewers and wonderful scholars: Professor Katarzyna Kaniowska and Professor Michał Buchowski. Their work on the original version of this book was an honor and great support for me.

I thank the students who accompanied me on my research and recorded the findings. Their ability to create a sensitive, committed ethnography helped me find my way. I thank Weronika Plińska, Dorota Murzynowska, Krystyna Mogilnicka, Emil Zubelewicz, and all the wonderful participants in the ethnographic workshops I ran at the Warsaw University Institute of Polish Culture, and the participants in the laboratories that took place at the Warsaw University Institute of Ethnology and Cultural Anthropology. They opened my eyes to things that had previously seemed "imperceptible."

I also thank my research companion, photographer Paweł Pałgan, for his many years of devotion to the field work.

I would like to thank all those who helped me prepare the English edition of the book. I am very grateful to Jaro Stacul, who encouraged me to work on this edition, to Soren Gauger for his thoughtful translation, and to Inga Michalewska-Cześnik for her scrupulous work and support in editing the final English version of the text.

With all my heart, I thank my family: my resourceful wife, my children, parents, brother, and friends, who all withstood my periods of temporary "isolation" and helped me carry on with my work, my research, and my writing.

Preface

The liquidation of large postsocialist industrial factories occurred in many places in Poland during the 1990s. This caused workers to be dismissed on a mass scale, as a result of their suddenly being made redundant. At the same time, the state-owned farms (PGRs) were being closed in the countryside, which also added to the growth of unemployment, and farming practically ceased to be profitable. This was how whole 'new poverty' regions came about, primarily as the result of the transformations that followed the system change.

It was the following years, 2001–2006, however, that emerged as the time of the country's most profound collapse and crisis. This was a period when the society experienced great regression, mass unemployment, and often, the conclusive liquidation of survival skills that the population had known. The unemployment rate reached its highest in the postwar era.

Today all this is history, though perhaps it has only been partially examined and recorded. In 2007, at any rate, unemployment in Poland began to drop sharply, clearly diminishing with the passing of every month, along with the scope of poverty, as the unemployed were finding whatever work was available in the European Union, and then leaving at once, thus improving Labor Bureau statistics. Yet the consequences of this abrupt poverty and collapse of farmsteads will continue to be felt in many places, much as the memory of this difficult time will linger.

My work and my research took place during the period of the greatest collapse—the years 2002–2006. The language of the description conforms to the events and is mostly maintained in the present tense, in order to relate an ongoing ethnographic reality. My sense was that this was the best way to render the atmospheres and behavior I encountered. It has also allowed me to hold the anthropological narrative in the immediate form in which it occurred.[1]

Notes

1. For methodological advice in making this decision, I owe my gratitude to Dr. Zuzanna Grębecka of the University of Warsaw, Institute of Polish Culture.

Introduction

The Anthropologist as a Poverty Inspector

An Anthropological Shift in Perspective

The "Culture of Poverty": Getting Beyond the Concept

The demands of anthropological work in the Trobriand Islands (Malinowski 2002 [1922]) postulated the longest possible stay in the area, in order to experience life as the residents there experienced it. However, this was practically an impossibility from the standpoint of my research on poverty and sudden impoverishment. This basic foundation of ethnographic description—the authority of first-hand experience (Clifford 1988a)—would seem particularly risky here, placing me, the researcher, in the middle of ethical complications. It should seem apparent from either side of the fence that the ethnographer will eventually return home with his or her tape recordings and memories, and the consciousness of this fact destroys any hope of real participation. The metaphor of the sudden appearance of the White Man, Foreigner, or Traveler is entirely justified here, and differences in ways of being, moving about, or the "colonization of the future" (Giddens 1991: 86) are visible at once. Crossing into the sphere of poverty and misery, ethnographers immediately note their difference, much as Marcel Griaule once did when beginning his research on Sudanese villagers in the 1930s: "Hundreds of eyes follow us. We are in full view of the village; in every crack in the wall, behind every granary, an eye is attentive" (quoted in Clifford 1988b: 70). As the inevitable Foreigner, the researcher is condemned to being a poverty inspector, always on a temporary stay.

Foreign realities of being are often found in remote places, or at least have always had a certain spatial dimension. Marcel Mauss, for instance, was fond of observing loaves of bread in European bakery displays. This allowed him to develop the premises of his idea on the scope of Celtic civilization, and at the same time to construct a theory of encountering cultural otherness from observing facts in their full scope. In the tradition of searching for "patterns of culture" initiated by Ruth Benedict, otherness took the form of a socioeducational complex that forms the cultural shape of the individual and his or her psyche ("culture and personality school"). Much has been written, therefore, on the impact of generally acknowledged values on the shaping of a mental life (while recognizing all its complexity as revealed through psychoanalysis), on the impact of education and reigning norms, on the categories of time and space, the notion of prestige, the symbolic universe, the body, or on gender. This made the inert power of "cultural reality" visible: patterns of emotion or of precise thinking underwent a dramatic change, establishing and conditioning the behaviors of individuals, conditioning the whole.

Oscar Lewis's research into the impoverished slums of New York and San Juan (1968; 1970), which allowed him to create the paradigmatic concept of the "culture of poverty," mainly adopted this psychocultural tradition. In a brief summary of his many years of research, Lewis stated that his "culture of poverty" not only represents, but above all perpetuates a sort of order. Time, space, the body, work, and money have set forms here. The phenomenon Lewis describes thus takes on clear and set attributes, including a lack of participation in greater social structures, a particular form of organization with the evident erosion of community ties, the deprival of a childhood, a tendency to live for the moment, the immediate present, and, most importantly, a "weakness of the structure of the ego," a resignation and a fatalism (Lewis 1968: xlii–lii). Categories of this sort give the "culture" being researched—or more accurately, its representatives—certain relatively stable attributes, i.e., settled and socially stimulated "biopsychological dispositions" that are typically found in representatives of the "culture of poverty." This image of the culturally shaped psychosocial pattern was carried further, however, which is why it has appeared in subsequent concepts of the culture of poverty. This was the case with the controversial theory of the "underclass," initially based on the purely structural stratifying categorization by Gunnar Myrdal (1962; see also Aponte 1990), in which the tradition of thinking in categories of the "culture of poverty" was assigned negative, stigmatizing connotations. It was given attributes of powerlessness, inertia (the perpetuation of "bad" patterns), and disintegration (of social and family ties); its emblem became the clever and insolent man who was unemployed, lived in temporary relationships, and neglected his family. Trapped in a circle of poverty, criminality, and the habitual inaccessibility of employment, this image created the basis for the investigation of a culture of "social defectiveness," a culture of social aid dependants and the redistribution of benefits—a "parasitical culture." This caused the paradigm of the mental constitution of the individual in society to hover perpetually over consecutive theoretical descriptions of spheres of poverty—the cliché of the "defective" or "maladjusted" social character. This is also the point where the critique of the concept of "culture of poverty" has started and caused so much debate (Leacock 1971; Valentine 1968; see also Aponte 1990) and where the critique of the myth of "dependency culture" has also emerged (Dean and Taylor-Gooby 1992).[1]

To my mind, the problem equally derives from the fact that the whole image of the reproducibility of "patterns of culture" originally pertained to other foreign cultures whose attributes were mutually non-transferrable, such as the cultures of the North American Indigenous People described by Ruth Benedict. In the "culture of poverty" or the "underclass," on the other hand, this reproducibility was chiefly meant to concern "our" familiar culture, existing within the sphere of the local social structure, which evolved, or became visible in a particular historical moment, when cities, agglomerations, and stable groupings of people emerged. This time marked the birth of sociology. The metaphors of the terminology describing poverty thus pertain to the order of signifiers of the imagined society "in general," first of all to "our" European societies, certain historically located specific structures with all their philosophical bases, such as the post-Enlightenment ability to model reality and to make it operative. This is also the background of the concepts of economic, definitional, and existential effectiveness. Oscar Lewis's "culture of poverty," therefore, clearly bears upon this "local" sociological model of culture and society. At one point Lewis writes of the "adaptive" property of the culture of the slums, using the categories of "efficiency/non-efficiency" (1968: xlii–lii). From this perspective—that of a culture as a properly functioning organism—we can see why, for Oscar Lewis, the powerful ties that bind social groups, like those that exist in rural societies or any kind of developed sociocultural organization, are precisely what defer the creation of a "culture of poverty," safeguarding people against the disintegration and deprivation of "culture." As such, this model *a priori* includes a package of values characteristic for the imagined well-developed societies such as work, co-citizenship, good social bonds, and civic participation, which later became the basis for the reconstruction of poor people's world view. At this point something paradoxical takes place: the norms of "our" society begin to serve the description of an entirely *different* social environment, an other and incomprehensible culture (Valentine 1968: 113–120). Then we also see that a model of "culture of poverty" described in this manner, its loss

and its "lack," is none other than the flip side of "our" culture; as Charles
Valentine has phrased it (1968: 116–117), it is the picture of an "unpatterned social existence." In this book I am going to follow this particular
element of critique and attempt to build my own way of getting beyond
this powerful image.

Social Trauma and Dependency: Shift in Perspective

The "culture of dependency," of people reliant on social aid (receiving
welfare, long-term deprivation of work and earnings), has almost always
been a bone of contention in public statements on poverty, both in the
Enlightenment discussion on the "Poor Law" (Patrick Colquhoun was
most clearly using the term "dependency" in a negative sense in 1815)
and in the storm of public opinion spurred on by the Thatcher program
carried out in Great Britain. On the basis of research concerning British
social assistance, the authors of *Dependency Culture: The Explosion of a
Myth* (Dean and Taylor-Gooby 1992) revealed the circulation of signifiers in the theoretical and administrative description of a group of social
assistance clients in Kent and London. It turned out that in the everyday
emic experiences of social care clients, the official terms were still inev-
itably associated with notions of criminality, demoralization, calculating opportunism, and turns of phrase like "cancer," "defect," "loss," and
"parasitical behavior." The linguistic and definitional backdrop of social
assistance in practice—in spite of all intentions—thus utilized symbolic
Foucauldian discourse mechanisms that form the social image of "wild
poverty," following the path of least resistance. This practice brought
along the discursive, symbolic imperative to work and to be independent, which was in turn confronted by the reality of unemployment and
dependency. In this fashion, dependency unambiguously came to be a
defect and a weakness—this may be precisely the reason why stress is
placed on social assistance symbolically "making clients independent,"
emphasizing their opportunities to make their own decisions. This may
also be the reason for social aid strategies in which the "assistance" of
clients has some effect on the decisions being made, such as the choice
of the branch they use, or the selection of magazines or other goods they
order.

Similarly, to translate this image into Polish circumstances, one often
reads that long-term unemployment and reliance on welfare or social
assistance creates an analogous "culture of dependency" over time. In
fact, it creates something called a "culture of unemployment," a culture
of "living on welfare" (Marody 2002), a culture of "systemic helplessness" (Giza-Poleszczuk, Marody, and Rychard 2000: 85) and "learned
helplessness" (Sztompka 2000: 58, 106–107; Zinserling 2002). It has

also been suggested that the ex-miners, ex-workers, and, above all, the rural folk create a "systemic residue" (on the polemic surrounding the use of this term with regards to rural folk, see Szafraniec 2002). The terminology alone demonstrates these groups' evident failure in dealing with the post-transformation reality. As such, all of these terms create a picture of social isolation and social passivity, of an inability to be in and adapt to civilization, of social groups who require ongoing assistance and *activation* (see, for example, European Social Fund, Polish Ministry of Labour and Social Policy documents, years 2007–2013, priority I, measures 1.1, 1.5, and 1.6). They remain outside of the main drift of social development—outside of the positively or normatively understood transformation from the People's Republic (PRL) socialism to a democratic state.

This perspective is particularly visible in the context of the transformation that occurred in Poland in 1989. The violent impact of the system change brought the experiences of unemployment, degradation, and sudden impoverishment to many people and to many social and professional groups. It also ushered in new images of reality—many began to have the impression of submerging into dangerous and uncontrolled chaos (Tarkowska 1993a: 90–91; Szpakowska 2003: 18). Piotr Sztompka (2000; 2004) later named this phenomenon the "trauma of the great change." "Social trauma" is a term that, to some degree, encompasses the social experiences of which I write, i.e., the sudden and unexpected arrival of unemployment, poverty, and painful degradation for many groups of people. Moreover, this occurrence was essentially external, unanticipated, "swift and sudden," and consumed all of social life. What happens in a society under such circumstances? Piotr Sztompka demonstrates that particular forms of response emerged. When faced with trauma (the incomprehensible reality of the transformations), we see the emergence of certain typical make-do strategies, originally described by Robert Merton in his *Social Theory and Social Structure* (1968), a book devoted to American social responses to the experience of financial crisis. First of all, the inability to reach goals (cultural goals, such as a certain level of affluence in American culture) prompts the innovation of strategies that are carried out in a new, criminal fashion, often in defiance of norms. Secondly, there are conformist strategies, a total yield to change, without "sticking one's neck out." Third, there are strategies of ritualizing life, compulsively repeating established ways of being in the world. Fourth is a regressive response, a flight "into another world," or even the creation of private "rituals of regression" (Sulima 2003). Fifth is a revolt strategy. In the context of the Polish trauma of the 1990s, as Sztompka writes, these sorts of coping strategies emerged.

Here, however, these strategies took on a special aspect, as the result of a trauma. One example of these experiences might be behavior that appeared in many post-transformation societies, independently recorded by various researchers, and marked by an aspect of "resignation" (in a sense, this is a Mertonian strategy of "retreat," or a "ritual of retreat"). This includes practices of complaints, grumbling, and declarations of resignation within closed groups, something commonly known as "village grumbling" within rural communities (Kędziorek 1996), or, elsewhere, the language of the "poor mouth" (Buchowski 1996: 60), social "grief" (Rakowski 2006a; 2006b), and "complaints" (Bruczkowska 2004). "They laid it all out, they laid it out.... What'll happen next, that I don't want to know." "It's all done for, I'm through looking ahead, there's nothing—there's nothing here, and nothing's how it's going to stay." "What could there be here—there's not going to be anything, I tell you." These monotonously repeated phrases were present in almost every ethnographic conversation in the Polish countryside. The unemployed in the former mining town of Nowa Ruda provided similar statements: "Things'll only get worse and worse, going downhill, and nobody wants to say a word ... and why should they? There's nothing to talk about." Piotr Kędziorek splendidly captured this kind of ritual denigration of one's position (1996): "We're mute, we're stupid. Why ask us any questions? We don't know anything round here."

Some might claim that all these examples, revealing social trauma, are symptoms of regression—of disadvantageous and ineffective changes—and bear testimony to an "incapacity to exist." From the resulting perspective we are dealing with a "nonadaptation," or, to borrow a phrase from William Ogburn (1964: 86–95), a "cultural lag" (the notion used by Ogburn to capture certain slowness in culture while facing rapid change, coming from the external world—social, technological, knowledge based, etc.). One example of such a lag is when certain behavior remains the same, despite changing socioeconomic conditions. We might cite social demands or incessant lamentation as examples. These societies are portrayed as lacking in initiative, as "passive subjects" undergoing the trauma of transformation. Polish sociologist Piotr Sztompka (2000: 20) has even written about their "pathology of agency." Nonetheless, it is abundantly visible that a certain world of the values of mainstream society—of Polish society, or, more broadly speaking, of "Euro-American societies" (such values as active social participation, subjectivity, self-aware entrepreneurship, a task-based approach, the ability to plan one's future, and so forth)—is implicit in this concept. It is only against this yardstick, through contrast, that one sees this as "cultural incompetence" or "cultural lag." Through the inappropriateness of the griping and grumbling and all manner of grudges, it is apparent to many people that these things bear testimony to a lack of constructive social behavior (cf. Buchowski 2003: 114–119).

And yet, here we find something entirely different. The recurrence of this behavior, and its constant presence, allows us to confirm that it is a certain form of social communication and a way of grasping experiences, albeit an entirely incomprehensible one—the exact reverse, it would seem, of the popular "keep smiling." How are we to perceive this phenomenon? From the perspective of the theory of great transformation, this grumbling is doubtless a symptom of this social trauma, an example of "cultural lag," passivity, resignation, or "learned helplessness" (or even perhaps—inertly—"systemic helplessness"). At this point, however, I would like to execute an *anthropological shift* in perspective. All these complaints and accusations, the grief and the laments, can then be treated in opposite fashion, as testimonies of cultural activity, as testimony to the many people who have experienced a great deal of tension since 1989, and have lived through it in a way that suits their culture. The complaints, resignation, and laments are thus, to my mind, a fully fledged mode of communication that includes various manifestations of personal regression and degradation, the social theatre of the "losers" of the transformation (Sulima 2003). This is an inner-cultural framework for surviving a situation. Here we cross beyond the nonanthropological tradition of remaining in "our" society. It is an ongoing attempt to cross beyond the categories of thought in "mainstream society."

Hermeneutics and Anthropology

We might say that the premises of cultural theories often create at least two different perspectives: of culture as a functioning model and of culture as a mode of behavior and being in the world. In the first case, concepts and key words are operationalized and employed, as a project of modern, functional social sciences. Then a negative image of a "culture of complaint," or in general of culture as modifying and distorting functional or economic behavior (what are called "cultural factors"), is created. Then too, "independence" or "social subjectivity" becomes positive and unconditionally desired; it becomes a manner of perceiving culture that presumes that any incomprehensible and uneconomical behavior is merely a "cultural factor" (a kind of distortion). Then, through this language, there also arises a constant imperative to become independent, both in an economic and a physical sense, prompting a rejection of the inexpressibility and radical alienation of the experience of poverty and degradation.

However, from another perspective—the point of view taken in my research—all forms of "culture of complaint" (and thus of "cultural lag") are words and behavior that express dependency. In this sense, they are not symptoms of trauma or "responses to change," attempts to adapt or to tune in. They begin from an adamant, unmodified level of culture, even its "rock-hard core," as it was posed by Gordon Mathews (2000: 11–17), and their correlation with the reality of the events transpiring, however this might be understood, is obscure, and filled with researchers' misconceptions. They are the axis of an oralized knowledge, or a social experience—a "folklore" (Tokarska-Bakir 2000: 380–381) that is, for instance, the expression of an ongoing (social and existential) dependency, a prereflexive structure of being that is, in part, shaped through history. One might trace its genealogy to show this "culture of complaint" to be an inertia, a Braudelian (1982) structure of "longue durée," tied to the rural memory of centuries-long, almost sacral dependency, or, in workers' environments, to a structure that forbids stepping out of the group or other ways of life, achieving success and "putting on airs" instead (Hoggart 2009). As such, these are ways of being in the world that are utterly incomprehensible in the contemporary language I use, in which we may find deeply embedded notions of effectiveness.[2] This is why, from the anthropological perspective I have adopted (my "anthropological shift"), they are perpetually present as hardly comprehensible and very silent "aspects of culture," which always leave behind an inexplicable residue of behavior. This is why an encounter with being in a culture of the other often ends in the annoyance, failure, and, as Joanna Tokarska-Bakir (1996) has written in her article devoted to the field specifics of an anthropologist's experience, irritation of certain deep cultural knowings, prejudgments, in Gadamer's sense of the word, such as those that concern the specific European sense of independent subjects, or their entrepreneurial/economic motives for action.

From this perspective, we cannot speak exclusively of cultural conditions that predispose people to behavior that is not outwardly economical, or that is outright uneconomical (radically other), that predisposes them to resignation and complaints. The practice of "social grumbling" is not, therefore, merely an external cultural factor (though we can speak of cultural conditions); it is a sphere in which we come to apprehend the radical difference (given that they take on the whole mainstream structure of the world), and incomprehensibility, to a large extent, of those who engage in it. In other words, hearing their regrets and complaints, maintaining their incomprehensibility and full otherness (autonomy, fully fledged culture), we ought rather to treat them as "folklore," a knowledge or cultural experience ("lore") making itself known. These lamentations and complaints enclose the speakers, after all, in the space of dramatic, though simultaneously commonplace (as in the grumbling, for instance), decisions; the exhaustion and using up of words, and their rhythm and recurrence, are highly significant here (Tokarska-Bakir 2000: 13–16). As Roch Sulima has stated (1992a), these are composed of screams and silence: a scream is a sign of contact with the world, while silence expresses the opposite, showing its strength in "insistent silence," in a ritual lack of words in conversation, in statements like "there's nothing to be said." "This makes way for conducting anthropology/folklore studies in existential categories," Sulima wrote two decades ago (1995). In existential categories, the statements, complaints, and moaning gathered by ethnographers demonstrate the constant, unrelenting, and unmodified nature of the reality of culture.

Consequently, the hermeneutic project of apprehending the impoverished, socially and economically degraded human being is an attempt to bridge contact with a way of being in the world (and a creation of a separate "culture of powerlessness") that is geographically near (the reality of "our" society). Yet, it is absolutely different in terms of culture, and not entirely comprehensible. The culture of the losers of the transformation, of complaints, moaning, even resignation and regression, passivity and fatalism, Oscar Lewis wrote about for years, is, to my mind, a fully fledged testimony of culture. Though it is a testimony that sometimes declares itself with great suddenness, when combined with the terminological whole of the mainstream culture it allows some people (as is the case with criminal environments) to think that this is "not culture, but rather a lack thereof" (Hernas 1976: 475). Research experience as hermeneutic experience therefore has little in common with an experimental approach. It neither checks nor verifies the previously anticipated reality, more resembling Hans-Georg Gadamer's notion of "negative experience" (2004: 350), i.e., that which "thwarts expectations." It is a kind of research in which the "tests" and "facts" of culture refuse to submit to increasingly sophisticated interpretations. Every encounter involves taking up a kind of challenge: it is an anthropological attempt to contact an utterly alien reality. The anthropological perspective I take and its value reveals itself in the flip side of culture, a testimony of dependency and powerlessness, in such words as "helplessness," "impotence," and "passivity," as well as "shrewdness" and "canniness." In sum, this generally concerns a certain concept of the people upon whom my research is focused.

How are we, therefore, to deal with other notions of the culture of poverty, the culture of dependency, and ultimately of those degraded during the period of the transformation in Poland? Within these notions, their culture, labeled a "culture of dependency" or a "culture of poverty," signifies a lack or a shortcoming, and not a presence. As Charles Valentine once wondered, "Is Culture not a Culture?" (1968: 113–120). I would like to stress that it is not my intention to criticize the values or the attributes of mainstream culture. I am not denying the positive attributes of entrepreneurship and independence, nor of "civic attitudes" or being geared toward taking on challenges—a forward-thinking attitude. I, myself, participate in this world, which is undoubtedly my cultural *shikata ga nai*—a Japanese expression for "it can't be helped" (Mathews 2000: 14). Furthermore, the impoverished, poverty-stricken, socially degraded and the chronic welfare receivers also participate in it and "dream" of it, a fact to which their complaints and grief would seem to testify (Dean and Taylor-Gooby 1992: 135). I am not of the opinion, therefore, that descriptions of social change showing the "inability to exist" in the new conditions, an incapacity to "take advantage of the transformation," vulnerability to social trauma (Sztompka, 2000) and phobias (Kocik, 2001: 97–103, cf. 88–90), or images of change expressed in sociological variables (such as attitudes toward pro-market changes, the structure of a farm's expenditures, opinions on the "state of Polish farming," the presence of optimism or hope, or even lifestyle indicators such as diet, dental care, or the habit of eating in restaurants) portray the phenomena accompanying the transformation in Poland in an *appropriate* and significant fashion. They describe them in a manner appropriate to their method and their paradigm. Nor am I trying to suggest that I find the practices of complaints or any sort of illegal or socially unstable odd jobs (or sometimes even semicriminal earning strategies) appropriate or lucrative in either a social or an economic sense. I am writing, after all, about impoverished and degraded people who are eagerly awaiting some form of work and livelihood—and one that is legal and fully acknowledged.

There is no getting around it—this is an anthropological dimension of sympathy, if only by dint of the fact that anthropology is, in essence, professional empathy. In this case, however, this empathy holds an entirely different meaning than it does in its colloquial use, and is doubtless incomprehensible to many. Empathy takes on a different form here, and is not, as Joanna Tokarska-Bakir phrased it (1999b), an attempt at common consolation, or a shared desire for things to improve. Nor does empathy mean that someone who knows the cause of a "bad situation" carries a functional social lesson in his head, along with a design to "solve the problem." Empathy is in itself a kind of renunciation of action (ibid.); a person who empathizes remains in the world of those with whom he empathizes, though he is merely visiting them. He records all the grief and the laments, trying neither to conquer nor to invalidate them, not trying to create a more functional reality, crossing into the social sphere of dependency. This "anthropological shift"—the anthropological inspection of the world of the degraded human—allows one to recognize at once, through "nonaction" and this special kind of empathetic thinking, that these worlds are by no means "empty." It allows us to recognize this other, alien manner of functioning in the world with all seriousness (and attention), for all its tensions, anxieties, and social phobias as an existence *par excellence*. Finally, it allows us to describe, as Valentine once urged (1968: 120), impoverished people's fully fledged experiences and ways of being, i.e., to describe the internal, cultural world of the degraded.

Toward a Method

Maurice Merleau-Ponty—The "Patron Saint" of the Present Ethnography

As an anthropologist, I am always shifting my focus of attention from the social events currently transpiring in more visible processes, after which I turn my gaze further still—to the social experience of participation in these processes, to the interior world of the person I have met. This "shift in the ... centre of gravity," as a Polish anthropologist Katarzyna Kaniowska has phrased it (1994: 24), travels "from cultural objects (phenomena, norms, customs and so forth) to the cultural subjects that make use of them." I have tried to capture this dimension in my research, and a certain self-referential aspect is visible in the objects of my investigation and of my research. Social experience is always joined to a way of being, to activity and to one's impact on events. The shaping of experience itself is therefore affected by the socially manufactured conditions in which it is acquired (Berger and Luckmann 1967). As such, the creation of social representations makes the society itself, including the anthropologists, function differently; this fact is not unfamiliar, for, as Paul Rabinow has stated (1996), representations are "social facts."

In a sense, however, this shift extends significantly further and is difficult to perceive clearly. It would seem to be evident that anthropology cannot precisely explain processes or the "facts" of history (though this is precisely upon what it remains based). It often only reports their significance, what is said, thought, and perceived about these facts and events. As a Polish historian Małgorzata Szpakowska has noted (2003: 11), the transformations an anthropologist studies, and the significance thereof, take place "not only in a quantifiable sphere, but also (and primarily) in the sphere of the consciousness." Yet, how are we to delve into the sphere of the consciousness of the people we study, that is, of my interlocutors and partners? How, from the point of view of the anthropologist, can one speak of another person's experience of "cultural existence"? The custom in anthropology is to try to extract these things from widely differing materials, from tape-recorded statements, from opinions that are jotted down, from filmed events and from many other media—from various records of the reality being researched. These latter materials form the basis for ethnographic texts, in which events are constantly transforming into meaningful content. According to Paul Ricoeur's hermeneutics (1981), when situated in an ethnographic reality, Clifford Geertz's "thick description" (1973; see also Clifford 1988a: 37–41), these texts begin to bear within them a certain cultural "world," though one with no direct indicators. This is, therefore, a sphere of indirect ("nonostensive") references, in which meanings are always precipitating from events, a dialectic of events and meanings (Ricoeur 1981: 205). On every occasion there occurs a step beyond the framework of knowledge inhabited by the discourse participants, the knowledge that indicates "me," "you," "the environment," etc. As Ricoeur writes (1981: 202), these are "non-situational references which outlive the effacement of the [world]."

We might say, however, that this knowledge is only a fragmentary version of reality, which, in many respects, turns it into elaborated stories, fiction revealing the ethnographic content (Clifford 1988a; 1988b). Moreover, the very ethnographic authority that stands behind this knowledge is a kind of covert poetics of the ethnographer's text (ibid.). It thus turns out that written ethnography that records other people's realities is always an arbitrary step in writing. This was, after all, what gave birth to the crisis of representation and the literary turn in anthropological methodology. What, therefore, is the relationship between the reality encountered in the field and the manner in which it is recorded and represented? What is the relationship between the discourse, the material of events and instances that take place, to use Emil Beneviste's definition of "instance of discourse" (see Clifford 1988a; see also Ricoeur 1981: 198), and the ethnographic knowledge presented? Such questions have begun to be asked in ethnography, leading to the discovery of the strategy and inevitable necessity of *textualizing* other people's realities in ethnography, which appears with each new paragraph (Clifford 1988a). James Clifford writes that textualization is the process of extracting a text from a fluctuating and dynamic situation, i.e., from discourse, conversation, from the incidents and events of life, from "being there." Ethnographic writing about others, about their internal cultural worlds and their internal expression, is thus a kind of action whose main onus rests upon the writer, the anthropologist who inscribes the meaning for good.

Some ethnographers have decided, however, to reverse this relationship, to give the right to action and to creating the text in part (or perhaps mainly) back to the people being encountered and described. Famously, Kevin Dwyer based his *Moroccan Dialogues: Anthropology in Question* (1982) on conversations he held with Faquir Muhammad, his Moroccan interlocutor, using numerous interspersions in an attempt to show an impromptu and "decentralized" process of creating ethnographic knowledge. To Dwyer's mind, the other person, the ethnographic interlocutor, has more knowledge of "what is being talked about," more than the ethnographer, or at least the possibility should exist to negotiate the meanings of words and behavior. Then the ethnographic interlocutor is able to create his or her own fiction, rupturing the textualized images, the "textures" in which the ethnographer is continually trying to "clothe" them (ibid.: 275–276). This awareness of the "vulnerability" to wounding or to "breaking" the line of thought then becomes a method of practicing ethnography.[3]

I cannot fully agree, however, with the vision of humanity or the subject of the ethnographic research, presented before us here. From this perspective, after all, the ethnographic interlocutor, whose statements and way of being in the world the ethnographer attempts to grasp and collect, is a person who, to some degree, tries to "play" and "negotiate" with his or her cultural knowledge, building its narratives, images, and approximations. At any rate, this vision keeps both the ethnographer and the interlocutor within the sphere of the "discourses" and "texts" they create—and this is precisely the perspective of textual anthropology, or the "reality of the text." Then, however, the "discourse" or "real-life situation" in which everything an ethnographer sees, hears, and feels is a fiction created by the native information source, a fiction of the world in which they live, not unlike the other fiction ethnographers create in tandem: the fiction of the other ("ethnographic fiction") and the fiction of themselves—i.e., of the ethnographer—becomes the "fiction of ethnography" (Clifford 1988b: 80). Consequently, this is a perspective in which both people seem to have their cultural equipment at the ready, and given that this is a certain linguistic world, they can choose whether to make it accessible to the other (Burszta 1992: 127–128). At any rate, the natives manage this knowledge themselves, or at least they are conscious of the fact that they can be "making it accessible" (and, to some degree, indeed they can); this concerns knowledge concealed from strangers, though in a way that concurs with an unconscious cultural *praxis*. Another consequence follows: the world presented by the other person becomes, from this perspective, a creation (as opposed to a work), and in this way it departs from reality itself. As Wojciech Burszta argues, "discourse in a sense 'evades' reality's control, as the world created in its framework is one possible world, an imagined one" (1993: 195). I do not believe, however, that this is the case. "Imagined" cultural knowledge does not, in the majority of cases, forfeit its reality. It generally appears only at the moment of movement, at the moment when this cultural world is "set in motion," and particularly in the case of the most internal, reflexive actions. As Gordon Mathews has phrased it (2000: 13), this serves as its invisible and very real "bedrock basis," or, as Naomi Quinn and Dorothy Holland similarly opine, it is what one sees *with*, but seldom what one sees (quoted in Hastrup 1995: 51). Our most internal, idiosyncratic behavior can be said to act in reality, though it does often remain invisible. "No one ever actually *saw* a social relation, a kinship system or a cosmology," Hastrup writes (1995: 48), to which we might add that these things do, after all, form the trajectories of our lives, our struggles, our successes, and our tragedies as well. This is why, on a certain level of cultural behavior, it is not true that this internal world of cultural actions severs itself from reality—or at least not in the environments where I conducted my research. Nor was the ethnography that came about there an unconstrained "knowledge" of any sort. As Rabinow has written, transparent ethnographies do not exist.

In her anthropological study of self-awareness of customs (based on the analysis of letters, diaries, and other written testimonies), Małgorzata Szpakowska (2003: 12–13) writes that she is incapable of accessing the "internal realities" of her research subjects as "a subject among subjects." After all, subjects do participate in a shared world of "views, perceptions, opinions and convictions," which leads them to develop designed or created images of the world and themselves. A moment later, however, she adds that the statements she collected "were always formulated in a code of sorts, and did not necessarily match the author's intention (to say nothing of their adherence to the facts)" (ibid.). This is linked to what Georg Simmel once demonstrated, Szpakowska (ibid.: 13) writes further, that often what others say is not the same as their "inner reality"—what they say is only a "transformed," "teleologically directed, reduced, and recomposed" version of this "inner reality" (Simmel 1964: 312). To my mind, this is a key point. On the basis of my ethnographic practice I have adopted the notion, like Simmel, or like Maurice Bloch, Madagascar ethnographer and author of *How Do We Think They Think? Anthropological Approaches to Cognition, Memory and Literacy* (1998), that what people say is quite often a fairly inadequate key to how they think and live (ibid., particularly the chapter entitled "Language, Anthropology and Cognitive Science"), which means that a culture's inner world does not hold easy equivalents in words, declarations, and behavior. To a substantial degree, this is a kind of "silent" or "wordless" knowledge with no explicit definition (ibid.; see also the chapter "What Goes Without Saying: The Conceptualization of Zafimaniry Society"). As we all know, however, this invisible reality and cultural knowledge does exist, and it shapes our behavior, our way of being, and our perception in a very real way. This is another reason why the "transformed," "reduced," and "recomposed" version of this reality is not merely a negative value, or a "curtain." I would say it stands as more of a challenge, to look at the world of culture in a way that allows us to perceive the reality that is actually transpiring, a reality whose words and declarations are often merely distant relatives. I would say that this reality is at the very least "perceptible," and that the texts and fictions of both the ethnographer and the subject of his or her research change very little.

But why, indeed, is it "perceptible"? I would say it is because the subjects of the statements or the cultural behavior, much like the ethnographer, are people of "flesh and blood," and they are continually interested in the processes going on all around them, as, for example, that the sun is "very hot today out in the fields." Put simply, they have real bodies and no less real worlds. This is a foundation for my ethnographic knowledge, an ethnography based on perceiving the horizon of the body (and the world). This is even the primary condition that allows one to encounter another, different person at all. This is not my own observation, of course, but rather an idea imported from the phenomenological "patron saint" of the present work, Maurice Merleau-Ponty. The social phenomenology of Merleau-Ponty has been most perceptively outlined against the backdrop of phenomenological traditions in the social sciences by Herman Coenen (1989), and then as part of the anthropology of Thomas Csordas (1990; 2001a [1994]). Coenen has shown that, as compared to the classical social phenomenology of Alfred Schütz, Merleau-Ponty went further: insofar as the I-Other relationship in Schütz does not result in any real knowledge of subjects, the latter's work provides room for the body, and a shared orientation toward the world, some form of understanding and coexistence (Coenen 1979). A communication of sorts therefore transpires through the body. Subjects see the world with a certain anonymity of seeing in the backs of their minds; this facilitates the act of seeing, but in itself it is impossible to comprehend, as one cannot, after all, "see from everywhere" (see Merleau-Ponty 2002: 79). The world is thus a constant derivative of interwoven (ibid.: 171) and returning acts of perception and expression (Merleau-Ponty 1973). In and through the horizon of its anonymity, it is always simultaneously assigned to a concrete subject, and only his or her perspective allows for its existence and its confrontation with another person's view. In short, seeing and being in the world are always tied to a particular body, and they are always "somebody's."

In this way, Merleau-Ponty delves into a preverbal, vital level of being in the world where everything is confronted anew. One might also say that he delves into a level of abrupt, spontaneous movement of the cognitive/experiential world, toward "untamed" or "undomesticated thoughts." As Polish philosopher Stanisław Cichowicz writes, these "reside in the heart of the human *praxis*," a "landscape of data for exploring and reshaping that emerges from unprocessed being" (1999: 11). As such, this is also an archaic source of Claude Lévi-Strauss's search for the roots of ethnographic knowledge about the world. It was this dynamic image of phenomenological "savage perception," as Merleau-Ponty himself called it, that lit the way for Lévi-Strauss in the latter's research; *The Savage Mind* (1994 [1964]) was even dedicated to the memory of Maurice Merleau-Ponty. In his famous essay "The Science of the Concrete," he wrote of a moving, sensory (physical) field, within which these internal worlds of culture, forms of bricolage, of "speaking with reality," were continually being produced. In similar fashion, Merleau-Ponty wrote, "just as nature finds its way to the core of my personal life and becomes inextricably linked with it, so behavior patterns setle into that nature, being deposited in the form of a cultural world" (2002: 405). But what significance does this have for the anthropology of culture and for my subject, the experience of social degradation, and for the social being as such?

The significance of this hermeneutics of the body and world is simply vast for the practice of ethnography. Firstly, it is possible to situate this primary communication, this largely preverbal *praxis*, in the sphere of field events and other people's ways of living, the worlds in which they live. The coexistence of the ethnographer and other people in the center of a field of practices is somewhat in opposition to the notion of an ethnography of "subjects struggling against one another," which, to a large degree, excludes such communication (in the pretextual sphere). Instead of a perspective of mutual suspension of the subjects' consciousness, their mutual "annihilation" to allow only one of them to exist (the "either you or I" strategy, existence through negation, as Sartre presented it), phenomenology extracts a world in which the "I" meets another person. As a result, their worlds coexist, even if they clash. How is this possible? Merleau-Ponty says that when the "I" encounters a "you," the world is equipped with a "shift." This shift takes place in either cooperation or counteraction. Encountering another person thus entails a reorganization of the world; it forces us to apprehend, and makes our apprehension adopt a new way of being toward its objects, forcing the entire field to "shift." As such, encountering another world is also a form of knowledge of this shift, while the whole phenomenological *inter-monde* facilitates this (lack of) knowledge—another person truly becomes the "other" when, as Merleau-Ponty writes, they become what they are: themselves—i.e., "unlimited" beings, "an outrage for objective thought" (2002: 406).

This allows the inclusion of those "incomprehensible" structures of cultural being in ethnographic reflections, it allows me to note the enormous role played by the practice of moaning and sorrow at the collapsing, "sickly" world (Rakowski 2006b), and to grasp the local manner of using certain key words, such as "nerves" (Low 2001 [1994]). These led me to a nonverbal lived experience, and, at the same time, to a nonlinguistic "world."[4] At this juncture, however, it is primarily the incomprehensible inner universe of culture that emerges, incomprehensible because of its new image of indirect, nonostensive references to the "world in which people live." As I have said, this "world" and all its images go hand in hand with a "vulnerability"; its presence and foreignness, after all, force a reorganization of "my" world and simultaneously reveal parts of the world of "others." Such ethnographic knowledge is, therefore, constantly giving way under the pressure of the other world, in which I participate as an ethnographer. It is constantly "trembling," "left open," it is veiled, then revealed—it is "practically invisible" (Merleau-Ponty 1973). One might say, in sum, that in order to be "vulnerable to wounding," one has to have a body.

Secondly, the process of accessing this "internal reality" looks entirely different. Here I must return once more to Merleau-Ponty. He demonstrates that a field exists between subjects that comes before texts or any other kinds of "permanent expression" (Dilthey). This is a position of an "anonymous life" (see Merleau-Ponty 2002: 404), a horizon filled with quiet activity, where the experience of what is found in the outside world is located. Only then does an orientation and dependency on the world or, in other words, on the body (the experience of pain, for instance), appear between these subjects. The lion's share of this "reality" is, therefore, in itself preverbal and prelinguistic, and this very reshaping—as per the phenomenological description— is "merged and reshaped" in a way that allows all sorts of "ruptures" and "incomprehension." This sphere is accessible, but never in full. It always remains open. The ethnographer's role is that of the constant

observer, ready for anything. This observer creates a description of the
world, which is less given (*dany*) than assigned (*za-dany*) (Tokarska-
Bakir 1995: 14), and through the "shifting" of this world sees the results in his or her observations themselves. I should like to emphasize,
however, that this world is neither their "presentation" nor their "representation." It does not resemble a foundation, but is "merely an attempt
to describe" (Migasiński 1995), dependent on the situation and on the
concrete subjects, which are always different.

We might, therefore, state that ethnography is a record of a mutual
cultural "cultivation" of the body and the world, an experience ever
present in the transformations of the world, and simultaneously in the
subjects' "internal reality."[5] This is a description of a cultural landscape
that incorporates all its "past actions" (Ingold, 1992), one might say,
the experience of the body, or its "earlier" form of speech; it takes place
through action, through being in the world, or indeed, in the material world, in things. After all, things change alongside experience. We
might take, for example, a candle flame that, when a child touches it,
literally becomes "burning"—it becomes another being (Merleau-Ponty
2002: 60). In contemporary ethnography, research has begun on certain
silent physical acts that contain the most vital social experiences, giving
a significance to events that have never been acknowledged, creating
a "vacuum" in the historical sciences (Bloch 1998: 67–70). This is a
silent oral history, one that exists beyond rulers' projects and decisions,
beyond the central facts in the history of events (Thompson 2000: 3–8).
As such, this is a history which serves people standing in the wings of
crucial political events and decisions, very often so "voiceless" people—
the poor and the socially degraded (ibid.: 109; Tarkowska 2000a: 30–
31; Buchowski 2003: 119).

Method: (Lack of) Ethnographic Knowledge

What, then, is my subject? What kind of reality am I trying to render? I
shall try to respond to these questions once again, this time shifting the
response to the field of (ethnographic) research. As Florian Znaniecki
has noted (1973: 28), this is, above all, "someone else's" reality, not mine,
and is, therefore, always the experience of concrete subjects (Merleau-
Ponty). As an anthropologist, it is precisely this sphere of culture I seek
to research. True, this is a sphere that exists, to some degree, nowhere
and everywhere; it is found, as is customary to say, at the "crossroads
between worlds," i.e., that of researchers and their subjects, their interlocutors (Kubiak 1997: 11; Zimniak-Hałajko 2000: 111). As I have
mentioned, it is a participation in the oral substance of someone's life "as
it happens," and a participation in the social process of creating another

person's experience. To my mind, however, owing to its very nature, this sphere has very seldom been compellingly communicated, which is partly why I have chosen to call it the territory of anthropological/ethnographic (lack of) professional knowledge. This knowledge or, plainly speaking, ethnographic experience, has often been the subject of reflection, though it has continually been bypassed and pushed into the sphere of wordless practices. These experiences are, in fact, often extra-verbal, practical, and intuitive, precisely the kind that cannot be written down, but can only be applied.

I will try, therefore, to present the premises of my methodology, and at the same time, the "cosmology" of the following research, the special character of the reality that was encountered in this fashion, a reality that had experienced the "great change" and post-transformation degradation. This is precisely the level of professional lack of knowledge, a sphere of experience that is most difficult to communicate. It is the ability to conduct an ethnographic conversation or interview, the ability to create a delicate and impromptu set of questions, evasions, new encounters, the ability to understand knowing silences, or when to drop or pursue a topic, and so forth. As such, it is a level of knowledge that remains hidden and silent; for indeed, how is one to speak of it? Precisely—at times it cannot be expressed.[6] I do believe, however, that the value of the existence of beings of ethnographic knowledge should not be denied simply because it cannot be communicated. After all, there does exist something like an *ethnographic experience*. In speaking of experience, I do not have in mind a quasi-biographical reflection on the anthropologist's private emotions, anxieties, or moods, which emerge during the course of the field research. Nor am I speaking of an autoethnography or ethnographic self-analysis/self-reflection (on self-conscious, reflexive ethnography). By *ethnographic experience* I am referring to something far more straightforward. I mean experience conceived as a certain practical ability, a skillful practice, that is, what we are thinking about when we say that we have had some kind of experience from having accomplished a task. As an anthropologist, I believe that I begin to have experiences when I spend time in another person's reality.

Therefore, contrary to recent belief, it is research experience, and not "the act of writing" (the anthropologist is "one who writes"—see Geertz 1973: 35), that marks the identity of the anthropologist. This was a fundamental discovery for me: conducting ethnography is, to some degree, tied to its prior absence and then, a certain presence. This comes from the fact that beginning every research means setting off on a long and winding road, and what we anticipate might not turn out to be there at all. Often—at least when the ethnography is truly interesting—it is not there. The subject of ethnography is, therefore, such that it is always being created, it is evolving in time. This is the basic attribute of anthropological work, of the anthropological experience. How, then, does this subject come to be? How does anthropology create its subject? This is a question posed by Johannes Fabian in his well-known book *Time and the Other: How Anthropology Makes Its Object* (1983), devoted to temporality and the process of ethnography. At one point he writes, "Fieldwork, demanding personal presence and involving several learning processes, has a certain time-economy" (ibid.: 89). In the creation of ethnography, there is, consequently, a certain tension in time—and on a range of different levels.

I would now like to recall some of my own research: I was conducting research in a place where people were occupied with and interested in "digging holes." In the former mining town of Wałbrzych, a city with tremendously high unemployment, several thousand jobless men worked through the entire year digging surface coal in what are called "bootleg mines" (the Polish *biedaszyb* literally means "poverty shaft") in order to support themselves and their families. Here is an extract from my research experiences.

On the first day of my research, before I had seen the bootleg mines, two men covered in coal dust carrying picks and mining helmets passed me in a lush meadow on the edge of town. They looked utterly bizarre, I would even say unreal. A few days later, after I had got to know them and was returning with them through the fields to their homes, I realized that the coal dust signified an active, working bootleg miner. The people we passed immediately recognized this, and stopped to ask them about coal, and to strike up deals for sales and delivery. I then started observing this more closely. It turned out, for instance, that private city transport did not charge the diggers, and their only proof of their occupation was the coal dust covering their bodies and clothing. It also turned out that the diggers were not allowed to sit down on the buses if they were riding "dirty." Some time later, I heard many stories from them about the St. Barbara's Day festivities in the bootleg mines: on that day, the diggers go "clean," as they say, spread a table with a clean tablecloth, and then drink a few toasts to each other's health. But it was only a half year later, when we met for St. Barbara's Day, that I truly understood what it meant to go "clean"—they were all scrubbed, their hair combed and their clothing clean and pressed. This created a tremendous contrast with the black and "dirty" bootleg mines where they worked on a daily basis. From then on, I began to turn my attention to this: after their workday was finished, the diggers turned into very clean people, and took very good care of themselves.

A few weeks later I started speaking with the diggers' wives as well. The wives of the teams with whom I worked kept their distance from the bootleg mines. "My woman wouldn't come here," one of the diggers told me, "not for all the money on earth. She doesn't even want to hear me talk about it. When I come back from digging holes, she always says [laughs]: 'Don't kiss me, you're all dirty.'" As it turned out, however, during the time I lived there, she cleaned his work clothes, soaking his black, sooty clothing in the attic of their old building, and then washing them in an old-fashioned machine. Her husband was not allowed to enter the flat in his dirty clothes. Every day after work he left everything on the doorstep and entered the home wearing little more than his underwear. These actions took on a certain changeless, even ritualized order.

Then I recalled the decades when these people worked in the Wałbrzych mines, recalled the shower rooms, in which they invariably washed themselves before returning clean to the buses, to the town, to their families. It occurred to me that the shower room marked a boundary between, on the one hand, the dirt and the mine, and the cleanliness and life outside the mine on the other. The division between life before the shower room (in the mine everyone addressed each other in the familiar form, regardless of age or position) and after the shower room (when they returned once more to the formal form of address) was clear. There was a sharp rift between the work in the black depths and the clean world outside of the mine. Now this mine had risen to the surface. For when the shower rooms ceased to be, the dirt of the mine, the black coal dust, spread far and wide, along with its strength as a signifier, and in this new environment, powerful and mutually contradictory meanings began to multiply.

Pretextual Ethnography

This is a certain fragment of the ethnographic knowledge I gained during the course of my research. How did this knowledge occur? How is ethnography created? What was the process of its origin? How is its subject created? We shall look into this process in a few consecutive stages.

(1) As I have stated, ethnography comes from a special kind of absence. What does this mean? I went to the Polish countryside during the time of the great change because I (the ethnographer) had never been there, nor had my ethnography of this place (or perhaps, of this event) previously existed. But this also means that after a few days, as bootleg mines became everyday reality and lost all trace of the "exotic," they began to "bore" me. The work of these people became no more than hard work. I kept asking myself whether there

was anything anthropological in what I was seeing. Were my activities there, in fact, anthropology? At that moment, it was impossible to say what was part of the knowledge being acquired and what was not, impossible to discern what should really be of interest to me. The result was a certain fear of the void, an anxiety born from lack of knowledge. I worked as the diggers did, trying to understand how their work affected their place in the local society, trying to understand how they spoke of it, seeing neither the dirt, nor what they did with it. Only later did I recall how, in the first days of my research, I wanted to help work in the bootleg mine, and it was decided that it would be better if I refrained from going along, because I would get dirty. Someone even said contemptuously: "The hell he's going to, just wait and see, *he'll get all dirty* [emphasis mine]". I also recalled how, in some holes, a number of the diggers removed their outer layers and gave them to me, so that I could go down wearing something "dirty," as they put it. At the time, I paid little attention to this.

(2) The result of all this is an ethnographic way of looking—and in tandem an ethnography, as such. This means that after some time one's perception becomes attuned to hearing essential things. After all, one's way of seeing and observing things, of hearing voices and understanding them, changes from one day to the next. I initially took no notice of the hygienic practices in the diggers' homes, and only later did I begin to observe them carefully, from a special perspective. As I gained knowledge, I learned to hear and see in a more observant manner. "One time I was visiting my neighbor," a digger told me. "I was dressed up, all clean, and I asked him if maybe he wanted to make a bit of money." This sentence stuck with me, particularly the phrase "all clean." Then I knew that my perception was changing and that I was learning something. After a few weeks of research I had acquired new cognitive skills, i.e., I had begun paying attention to things that had earlier seemed irrelevant, or that I simply had not noticed. Beforehand, I had been looking and I had seen practically nothing, I had heard what my companions in the bootleg mines were saying, allowing the most important things to slip by unnoticed, perhaps a fairly frequent experience among anthropologists.

(3) The problem was that I made some decisions and picked up on some things, while hundreds of other possibilities kept presenting themselves, to acknowledge other elements as vital and "significant." For instance, while working at the bootleg mine, I realized the great significance of hearing/physical practice or knowledge that

was involved in doing this sort of work, and to what extent it could become routine and entirely unremarkable. As one digger put it in an unsolicited statement, "I know that already—you've got to understand, I've got feelers like an animal … the structure gives the signals … if it all goes to shit, well, that's that." Let us take a look at one more fragment (a statement from another digger): "Birch tends to snap like matchsticks, but the spruce generally creaks. I've got an allergy to birch. … It just snaps right away, it's dangerous, while spruce just cracks a bit at a time … it gives you signals, and then you don't just sit there and wait, you know you've got to beat it. … Recently I was sitting there and I heard the spruce crack, so I picked up a roof timber, punched it in, made some supports … and it's all still standing there to this day." Soon thereafter, I discovered that they used only "quiet" manual equipment (picks, saws, shovels, hoists, cradles, sieves, sieve stands); there was even a cult of manual work, in part associated with the danger of the police or city patrol hearing the noise from the machinery. Diggers increasingly did their work by night because bootleg mines are essentially illegal. At the same time, diggers were capable of spending hours discussing their self-made constructions for sifting coal, the equipment's virtues and new ideas for improving it. At this point the fear of there being no substance for ethnography was suddenly replaced by an overabundance of associations, an overabundance of potential knowledge. Then what the researcher has originally encountered as a void becomes an ethnographic swamp that pours in from all sides.

(4) Yet things are even more complicated. Numerous inconsistencies and sudden accelerations appear in fieldwork, such as unexpected "twists" in the way things are seen and apprehended. When I attended some St. Barbara's Day celebrations, suddenly, as if touched by a magic wand, I gleaned all the ethnographic "facts" concerning the dirt in their full scope and total contrast, and then I understood a great deal more than what I had known to date. I had the impression that curtains had parted, revealing knowledge that had been concealed from me. Another moment when "the curtains parted" occurred when I lived with a digger's family in an old building in Boguszów-Gorce. It was during one chance evening that I noticed something that had totally escaped me before—the pile of dirty clothes, covered in coal dust, lying right in front of the doorway.

I shall attempt to make a summary. I perceived many silent and heterogeneous processes of gaining knowledge, which were difficult to communicate. Firstly, the subject of my ethnography was noticed and captured, thus leaving behind the seeming impression of the nonexistence of the explored reality, i.e., in some way, I perceived something essential. Secondly, a dynamic and fluctuating, yet operative, cognitive competence, a certain professional concentration (or sensitivity), emerged. Thirdly, a process occurred whereby the strands and elements deserving attention multiplied, causing a spontaneous selection of field observations, opening an attempt to harness the chaos of the various research paths. Fourthly, as a researcher I am constantly dealing with a (cultural) reality in which there are sudden and accidental plot twists, whereby things are unexpectedly revealed, taking the form of a temporal event.

This bears testimony to the idea that ethnography is a long-term process, a kind of event that has a "time economy." On the one hand, it is made up of more or less conscious research steps, on the other, of unpredictable plot twists, of unexpected discoveries and associations that have a real effect on the progress of the ethnography being created. During this process an operative knowledge, an ability, develops. How is one to pass on this knowledge? How to write about it? The problem is that this knowledge originates in the event, implying, as Johannes Fabian (1983) demonstrates in his book, a certain "coevalness" of being between the anthropologist and his or her subjects. Only from this original encounter do the subsequent rungs of the typical ethnographic distance emerge, such as Geertz's (1988a) "being there" and "writing here," or perhaps "being then" and "writing now," which are integrated later on in the ethnographic, present-tense description. Thus, the grammatical tense used in ethnographic writing bears this complicated time reference to the real research subject (discourse events, for example). The result is a suppression and hiding under the "ethnographic present" the processual aspect of fieldwork—the temporal and noncoherent aspect of field events, filled with ruptures and accelerations, is then buried beneath the ethnographic message. However, it is only when the perspective includes decision-making, plot twists, and learning processes (the perception of such things as coal dirt) that this layer of functioning and practical, unspoken knowledge, of ethnographic experience, begins to be visible.

The process of acquiring ethnographic experience is also made visible in the practice of taking field notes. This action is directly linked with the creation of written (i.e., materialized) ethnographic knowledge, which might be why this unvoiced process becomes apparent in it. Field notes, after all, are not merely revealed knowledge, or knowledge that is written and textual. As Roger Sanjek observes in his introduction to the excellent *Field Notes: The Makings of Anthropology* (1990a), notes (the silent voice of anthropology) are a fragment of an exceptionally embarrassing and privatized professional knowledge (Kaniowska 1999: 49–50; Rabinow 1996: 28–58; Zimniak-Hałajko 2000: 115). Moreover, this process of jotting down notes is further complicated by the fact that one must oscillate between various processes (temporalizations)—the writing itself, in which we keep a distance from the subject, and full participation in a given event. According to Rena Lederman, author of the outstanding *Pre-texts for Ethnography: On Reading Field Notes,* notes thus become dangerous, as they are "challenges to the memory" (1990: 73). This less concerns recollections, as such, than the particular temporal process of creating knowledge in use, in practice, in a word, in the field. Spread out over time, notes are constantly selecting from shifting conclusions, separating the most correct conclusions from momentary phantasmagoria, shuffling the order of various elements. Where should the focus be? What should be remembered? What should be written down?

In the form of field notes, ethnography thus slips out from the sphere of the written text. Notes are a pretext, a documentation of the pretextual sphere of ethnography. The "headnotes"[7] that Simon Ottenberg (1990: 144–146) describes are of this very nature. These "thick notations," arising in the head of the researcher like mnemonic knots where they lead their own strange lives, sometimes for several years at a stretch, remain in the ethnographic memory and are supplemented with written notes. They are entirely private, intuitive, and almost subconscious; and they record a reality with no concrete reference point, something Fabian, in one of his lectures, called ethnographic "non-referential memory." This is a kind of spontaneity that can be entirely incomprehensible for the writer himself. In my own notes, for instance, I found the note "Junk and cascades!" and to this day, I cannot decipher what I might have had in mind. A note also contains a condensed version of the knowledge acquired. It is a moment in which the text is in the process of being created, is emerging, and, to some extent, is still in the realm of the unwritten text—that of the events in the field and the roles being played out. It is ethnography that comes about from these half-chaotic, half-precise movements—first as a process, then as a path, *The Ethnographer's Path* (Sanjek 1990b: 398–400), and only then as a closed description, a closed text. As such, there is a certain continuum from pretext to text. As James Clifford precisely phrased it (1990: 51–52), the first thing to appear is the "inscription," which is fairly fleeting and pretextual, then the "transcription," which is distanced and temporalized, and finally the "description," a product that is often final. This process of recording ethnographic knowledge is at least potentially unending. It splendidly depicts the layer of professional ethnographic (lack of) knowledge, the pretextual element of the discipline. As such, ethnography is more an art of remembering and of perceiving than an art of writing culture (Kaniowska 1999: 53–57). It records the mysterious process by which pretextual human activity crosses beyond individual events and begins to mean something on the outside (Ricoeur 1981; 1989), albeit in an utterly fragile and phantasmagoric way. Nonetheless, it does have some significance—and this means it is worth recording.

We are sketching out a tension between the position of ethnographers as researchers who carry some experience inside of themselves, and ethnographers as writers who carry in themselves texts, textual statements. I believe that, in the latter case, the identity of the professional ethnographer is clearly assimilated by the act of writing. Supporters of the "Writing Culture" paradigm (Crapanzano, Tyler, also Dwyer) make a passionate appeal for the ethnographic text as a lively echo for the preservation of field dialogues and heteroglossia. By the same token, however, they approach ethnography as a discipline that quite naturally includes the art of writing, devoting all their energies to writing; in a sense they are graphocentric or scriptocentric (see Clifford and Marcus 1986). Stephen Tyler attempted to take notice of these writerly efforts of postmodern ethnography in his well-known text, *Post-Modern Ethnography: From the Document of the Occult to the Occult Document* (1986). Therein Tyler proposes a range of practices for writing ethnography in which no kind of closed text ought ever to arise. He wages a war on all representations implanting themselves into written anthropology, and he broadens the ethnographic "crisis of representation" on all sides. He attempts to shift all representation into evocation, thus focusing attention on the vocal act of ethnographic writing. As such, he creates a kind of performance that disrupts all sense of professionalism and security and opposes all records of experience (ibid.: 137–138), all mimesis, evading all the traps of textualization in advance. I dare say that, according to Tyler, ethnography is a certain postmodern exorcism conducted upon the textualized product of an ethnography that remains modernist. It is an attempt to animate a living, many-voiced field experience in the moment of writing—albeit after the text. One might say that it is post-textual ethnography. What if we were to attempt to go even further back? What is the source of this whole situation of conversation or living discourse, I wonder? Along with the whole process of negotiating and creating significance, the process of creating the field of the text (filled with momentary relationships of domination and servitude), all the attempts made by works called "Writing Culture," I should like to stress, aim at restoring an immediate dialogue. How are we, therefore, to cross from discourse (the discursive event) to text without the discourse adopting a petrified form filled with "hidden authority"? This was one of the chief tasks of the ethnographic avant-garde. What if we were to attempt to go even further back? What is the source of this whole situation of conversation or living discourse, I wonder? How did the authors of the ethnographies even end up there? What were their courses through the field, what were their concepts and their chaotic notes? With what ethnographic pretexts did they come in contact, and with which did they become so well acquainted that they ceased to notice them? I have nothing against writing anthropologists—it is, after all, a splendid thing to be able to write an anthropology, or to write about the writing of anthropology; and were it not for their texts, I myself would scarcely be capable of writing today. I would, however, like to delve further within the field marking the identity of the discipline, into my ethnographic (lack of) professional knowledge—a knowledge most difficult to relate. The silent path of the ethnography that thus evolves, the professional lack of knowledge, *The Makings of Anthropology*, is, I believe, my primary anthropological experience and my primary skill. Alongside the occultization and mobilization of the lifeless ethnographic text (the lifeless document) proposed by Stephen Tyler, I propose the notion of the mobilization, the animation, and perhaps even the occultization of the silent, nonverbal, and pretextual practice of professional lack of knowledge in the field, of ethnographic experience. It awaits its explorers and its most difficult language, which may, perhaps, enable it to communicate this world.

The Most Bitter Side of the Polish Transformation: Fields of Research

The "New Poverty"

Looking back, we can see quite clearly that the system change that began following 1989, apart from its good sides, had the effect of bringing sudden poverty and economic collapse to many social groups. The change—i.e., the shift from People's Republic (PRL) socialism (1952–1989) to a democratic state, from a centrally driven economy to a market economy—ushered in new and largely unforeseeable social and economic processes, and an entirely new reality along with them.

We might say that the transformation that occurred was accompanied by an unpredictable effect. There appeared an entirely new world with new regulations (such as the experience of the free market economy), one that was incomprehensible to many. Most social groups continued to live according to the old reality, and thus came clashing up against the new and (subjectively speaking) unpredictable post-transformation reality (Tarkowska 1993a: 88–89; Sztompka 2000; Szpakowska 2003: 18). Many people had difficulty finding their feet in this new situation. For many this process quite unexpectedly brought unemployment and resulted in poverty. A new social experience emerged: the coming of an unforeseen change, a "bad change" from the outside, creating a certain "temporal dimension" of the social transformations (Tarkowska 1993a). State factories, an enormous network of state-owned farms, and many other socialized village factories (sewing shops, dairies, tanneries, etc.) were liquidated as part of the broadly defined deindustrialization of whole regions. To these experiences we ought to add the economic collapse of the countryside, which shouldered the heaviest costs of the transformation (Kocik 2001; Szafraniec 2002). It was in the countryside that a severe economic recession set in, a sharp dip in the viability of (mainly small and medium-sized) farms, and an end to all centralized regulations, guaranteed purchases, and ensured farm viability, be it for larger or smaller amounts. This resulted in new, sprawling regions of unemployment, poverty, and want. This phenomenon was called the "new poverty" (Tarkowska 2000c: 54–59); it came about in the sphere of a newly democratic state, and was all the more striking in that it was taking place across a vast area (Beskid 1999; Golinowska 1997) and in full view (Tarkowska 2000a). Piotr Sztompka (2000) has referred to this widespread social experience as the "trauma of the Great Change."

The experience of sudden impoverishment and the existence of poverty are not, of course, devoid of historical background, and are partly rooted in the processes of the previous decades, or even of previous centuries. As many authors have demonstrated (Tarkowska 2000a: 9–12; see also Beskid 1992; 1999), there were entire spheres of poverty in the PRL years, though these were kept invisible (and still are, to speak from today's perspective), which is why the contemporary phenomenon of poverty among certain groups stands out so clearly. Poverty and social inequality were imperceptible during the PRL period for a number of reasons. Firstly, there was the centralized policy of almost compulsory employment and various other social benefits, bonuses, coupons, factory vacations, credit relief, and so on (Tarkowska 2000a: 11), as well as the guaranteed purchase and pick-up of farm crops. Secondly, owing to the principle that poverty could not exist in a socialist state, the topic of the phenomenon itself was made a political taboo. The few sociological works on the subject were never published (ibid.: 9); moreover, the word *poverty* had no right to exist in the public language, as Elżbieta Tarkowska writes further. Various euphemisms were used, however, to speak of the poor, such as "insufficiency" or "people with limited powers of consumption" (Czechoslovakia). Meanwhile, poverty did, of course, exist in the PRL—and above all, it touched retirees, pensioners, unqualified laborers, families with many children, families with problems of alcoholism, and single mothers (Gliński, quoted in Tarkowska 2000c: 53–54). The scope of poverty increased in the 1980s, and when the society of the People's Poland entered the transformation period, a substantial portion was already hovering on the verge of poverty (Golinowska 1997: 311–312; Tarkowska 2000c: 54).

There is, however, a certain continuity of experiences and spheres of poverty, deriving from pre- and postwar Poland. Poverty is, after all, a phenomenon present in various states and in various epochs (Tarkowska 2000c: 49; Geremek 1989; Szytełło 1992), while the creation of modern-day spheres of poverty, it turns out, is often largely derived from many previous relationships. In prewar Poland poverty touched a vast portion of the society. Somewhere around one million citizens lived in a state of deprivation, almost below biological capacity for survival (Żarnowski 1992). Though mainly concentrated in overpopulated, work-deprived villages, this deprivation was also present in the industrialized cities, above all during the crisis of the 1930s.[8] Furthermore, people also remembered the poverty and unemployment in the Great Crisis (1929–1935), which produced profound social trauma (Sztompka 2000: 162). One description of these social experiences can be found in the work of Florian Znaniecki (Thomas and Znaniecki 2010), in his (and Thomas's) work on groups of peasant emigrants from overpopulated villages, and in studies on the psychosocial effects of unemployment in city environments and factory housing estates (Zawadzki and Lazarsfeld 1993). A second unrecognized and underexamined wave of unemployment appeared in the 1950s (Tarkowska 2000a: 12), further increasing the postwar level of poverty. As such, various spheres of postwar poverty and shortage had existed long before in Polish society. As Małgorzata Szpakowska has written (analyzing first-hand written social sources, such as reports contained in letters and diaries), it was a time when "shortage and widespread indigence" (2003: 33–39) were experienced. The modernization of living conditions and widespread migration to cities for factory labor during the PRL era (see, among others, Czechowski and Stelmachowski 1990; Czerwiński 1975; Gołębiowski 1990; Kaczyńska 1999; Styk 1994; Marody 1991b: 231–234; Szczepański 1973; Szpakowska 2003: 14–15; Tarkowska Tarkowski 1994: 276; J. Wasilewski 1986; Wódz 1989: 76–79) were thus a natural response to this widespread postwar substandard existence of poverty and overpopulation of the countryside. However, they were also the result of the socialist propaganda of the "great construction," the building of the "new city," and the "new man." We ought also to add that in the Stalinist years, this propaganda was preceded by a rhetoric of "cleansing" and "drainage" of the suffocating old quarters of the cities—hotbeds of poverty and all that was "rotten," "diseased," and "tainted" (Tomasik 1999: 95–99).

In the social history of the Polish lands we can therefore trace a certain continuity in the creation of regions of poverty, shortage, and social isolation through the transformations that occurred, which can be translated into a map of these phenomena. The most susceptible are medium-sized cities and industrial monocultures, such as Wałbrzych, Nowa Ruda, Lubsko (Rakowski 2006a), and Żyrardów (Lipko, 2003), with factories that have monopolized the local labor market (Osińska and Śliwińska, quoted in Tarkowska 2000c: 58), and where massive unemployment appeared after the factories were liquidated in 1989. These phenomena took their toll on the old, postindustrial quarters of cities in Upper Silesia and in Łódź, where a great many people apparently lost their industrial jobs. At any rate, there are multiple studies about the poverty of these locations (on Łódź, see, among others, Golczyńska-Grondas 2004; Grotowska-Leder 1998; Warzywoda-Kruszyńska 1999; on Katowice and the Upper Silesian Industrial Region, see Wódz 1994). It is well known that the post-state farming societies, such as those scattered about the Recovered Territories, particularly in Pomerania, Warmia, and Mazury, in the wildernesses of Bieszczady and the Low Beskids, as well as in many other regions of Poland, also experienced poverty and unemployment after 1989 (Tarkowska 2000e: 90–117), when factory workers were suddenly stripped of their employment. Another poverty-stricken region was the villages of the "Eastern wall" and the lands of the onetime peasant/worker villages, such as the vicinities of Szydłowiec and Skarżysko-Kamienna (the former Central Industrial District), which experienced a very high level of unemployment after the liquidation of heavy industry (Rosner 2002). The village areas in particular were places of invisible poverty and hidden unemployment, where poverty was often scattered over space and buried most deeply (Kocik 2001: 70–71; Tarkowska 2000c: 58–59).

Post-Transformation Social Degradation

This work therefore seeks to examine the social experience of swift impoverishment—a new, post-transformation poverty that, as Tarkowska has noted (2000c: 54), arrived suddenly and was dramatic in its effect. My work principally concentrates on the experiences of groups that were thrust into poverty in Poland after 1989. As I have already mentioned, this "bad change" came unannounced—nobody saw it coming. These groups initially expressed their approval of (or some relief at) the changes that occurred in the state-owned companies and farms (Tarkowska 2002: 100–101) or the Wałbrzych mines (see chapter 3). Nor was the "free" market feared in the countryside (on the villagers' attitude toward the centrally regulated prices of purchases in 1992 and 1999, see Kocik 2001: 75); later, however, a profound disappointment emerged. Unemployment and the humiliating necessity of relying on welfare (whose colloquial name in Poland derives from the name of Jacek Kuroń) appeared. Later came the loss of rights (the unemployed were prohibited from working off statutory hours, which was vital in gaining rights to welfare) and, finally, the unprofitability of work on many farms. The result was impoverishment and the loss of social security; and more blows followed hard on the heels of the poverty and unemployment, creating private and social trajectories of degradation.

The subject of study and the field of research are thus the experience of a changing reality that took place in these impoverished social groups, and of their ways of functioning in the new world, a world of unemployment and of financial incapacity, both personally and in the old institutions. The former, historically impaired social territories bereft of social capital do not always overlap with the places that experienced this poverty (Tarkowska 2000cd: 59, 66; see also a study on the continuing patterns of culture of prewar farming factories in state-farming societies: Palska 1998). Poverty is primarily represented here in the form of a transition from a person with a stable social status to the status of one who is unemployed, who suffers shortage (later poverty), and who participates in family, social, and private life. The experience of this "bad change" that comes from the outside world is thus, above all, the experience of social and biographical degradation. The world of the degraded after 1989 is the anthropological focus of the present work. Why is degradation the frame I have chosen for my field of study? After all, many methods of grasping and describing poverty, unemployment, and socioeconomic impairment, from quantitative socioeconomic indicators (Golinowska 1997: 19–30) to the most subtle, theoretical concepts of the social and political sciences (in terms of the strategy of approach as well, i.e., the prevention of poverty; see Lister 2004; Lepianka 2002: 5–7) can be listed. In the history of research on poverty the consecutive theoretical concepts mark out a definable course. This begins with Oscar Lewis's "culture of poverty" (1968; 1970), through the notion of the "underclass" (Domański 2002: 24–25; Gans 1996; Katz 1999), "dependency culture" (Dean and Taylor-Gooby 1992), the concepts of marginalization, social exclusion (Frieske 1999; Kowalak 1998; Lepianka 2002; Washington, Paylor, and Harris 2000), and social isolation (Wilson 1987; Lepianka 2002: 18), and proceeds to entirely new strategies of researching and conceptualizing poverty, shifting the responsibility for its definition onto the shoulders of the research subjects themselves, thus granting them terminological subjectivity (Lister and Beresford 2000; Lister 2004). All these concepts form a certain continuity of change and reorientation, overlapping in various ways and serving different perspectives in describing poverty. They have often been applied in researching impoverished regions in Poland, particularly the concept of the underclass (Golczyńska-Grondas 2004: 38–39; Warzywoda-Kruszyńska 1998; Wódz 1994; Tarkowska 2000e: 116–117). It ought to be added that some of these, particularly the concepts of marginalization and social exclusion, function differently, depending on the research context and specifics (regional, ethnic, national), and so on (Lepianka 2002: 18). In turn, by thinking mainly through concepts of social exclusion and marginalization, and, to some degree, of the underclass (Gans 1996), other thinkers prefer to emphasize the processual nature of the phenomenon of poverty and the dynamics of its transformations, as poverty can then be regarded as a consequence of social changes.

In this study I have chosen the term *degradation* as a way of defining my field of research, as it gains its significance first of all through the temporal perspective: the perspective of impoverishment, the abrupt appearance of unemployment, and the associated loss of social status. Therefore, the temporal dimension is crucial here. It is directly related to the condition of wider economic transition and social change, which started in Poland in 1989. What is more, this notion is both related to individual, biographical perspective and to the wider, or even massive, social experience. Thus, degradation is about facing a certain "external" socioeconomic process, a kind of fate, and about particular reactions to this situation developed along the way. By using this term I am able to capture a certain moment in time and space, the chronotope for the described process and experience. Thus the impoverishment of various groups and field sites, also related to the specific time of transformation, is the main feature of the notion. This gives an important specificity and serves it more appropriately than the notions of social exclusion, marginalization, or "dependency culture," and it is also more specific than the new concepts of conceptualizing poverty. In a work devoted to the general issues of poverty, we may find a few moments when the temporal dimension of the experience of poverty is framing the knowledge; it is usually about the temporality of the everyday experience of poverty. There is also an important reference to the societies of Central and Eastern Europe, where the process of income decline took place on a massive scale and where it was particularly hard to capture poverty even by such measurement tools as relative poverty lines (Lister 2004: 41–42).

Therefore, there is something very specific in the dynamic, temporal dimension of getting under the new socioeconomic conditions in Central and Eastern Europe: the impoverishment, the sudden experience of poverty, the situation of degradation. Using the term *degradation,* I tried to give a clear description of some new conditions and experiences occurring in time—as Dorota Lepianka writes, "the painful degradation processes" (2002: 16). Most importantly, I tried to capture here both changes to the external (social, economic, political) and the internal (psychological, behavioral) reality, to describe methods of social survival (cf. Tarkowska 2000b: 32).

Postsocialism: History and Experience

The experience of unemployment, generally after many years of steady work, was of tremendous significance for my research. The experience of degradation thus goes hand in hand with the capacity to hold down a job, and the associated (self-)expression of one's social (professional, economic, etc.) status. Indeed, it is not only unemployment that signifies degradation and social exclusion (particularly in Western Europe). Often, it is even enough to do work that is below one's qualifications or "under the table," or to do "one-off" jobs and to be poorly remunerated (making it impossible to satisfy personal and family needs) for social exclusion and marginalization to occur (Lepianka 2002: 17). In these circumstances of transformation and abrupt change in Polish reality, both unemployment and the new replacement jobs, often informal and very poorly paid—i.e., the "working poor" type (see Tarkowska 2000b: 37; see also Stanaszek 2004)—were the central causes of poverty and social degradation. In fact, they created the "new poverty" (Tarkowska 2000c: 56–57; cf. Golczyńska-Grondas 2004: 31). Social degradation is thus quite naturally tied to the past. This is why degraded societies are less often groups impoverished and socially impaired from the outset than groups formerly functioning with some capability and financial stability, with families, with a feeling of security ensured by the socialist state, and with sizeable (perhaps even oversized) social status.

Work and life in the PRL period thus become a stable point of reference, and present-day social experiences are closely tied to the past, having the structure of a "changing reality" (Tarkowska 1993b). The past very often becomes the degraded person's "point of departure" (here I am dealing with a narrative, a mythologized rendering, which is, of course, not the same as inauthentic). In such situations, I always encountered a researcher's dilemma: it is extraordinarily difficult to make a uniform picture or "recreation" of the past or a historical reality, as the PRL modernization of the country is, to my mind, an essentially ambiv-

alent phenomenon. On the one hand, it led to the socioeconomic tragedy of loss of freedom under slogans and appearances of progress; on the
other, this was a time when stable living conditions were created, a time
of progress and education for several generations. In Małgorzata Szpakowska's research on lifestyles and customs, for instance (2003: 33), we
can see that in spite of everything, the standard of living, at least tech-
nically speaking, increased during the PRL period (Szpakowska writes
that a certain "material and civilizational advance" took place). For me
as a researcher, this contradiction between the everyday, accustomed life
within the People's Republic and its tragic consequences, both during
those years and afterwards (Giza-Poleszczuk, Marody, and Rychard 2000:
17–20), is utterly irreconcilable. This ambivalence about the changes of
the PRL period, particularly when apprehended alongside the current
changes, is a cognitive threshold I am incapable of crossing. By the same
token, it cannot be merely overlooked, and the ever-present "point of
departure" or the experiences I have recorded is the inseparable background of these people.[9]

Social degradation as a social experience, the experience of functioning in new and often incomprehensible circumstances, is thus the
groundwork of my research (researching the social cost of the system
change). In this way, my work falls in line with multidimensional phenomena whose scope goes well beyond Poland, touching the whole of
the postcommunist Central and Eastern European bloc, and further
still, into the countries that once made up the former Soviet Union
(USSR); and it generally fits in with the context of anthropological research on postsocialism (Dunn 2004; Hann 2002a; Humphrey 2002;
Schäuble, Rakowski, and Pessel 2006; Kőresaar 2003; Verdery 1996).
In the new postsocialist circumstances (during the transformation and
with the simultaneous rise of information and globalization), many social labor groups were stripped of almost all their symbolic capital and
found themselves at the bottom of the social structure, with no access to
material, social, and symbolic goods. In his research in Romania/Tran-
sylvania, David Kideckel (2002; 2008) has shown, for example, that the
disintegration of the status of workers as a class functioning in the communist era caused this group to shoulder the whole brunt of the recession and the collapse of the socialist economy (2002: 115–116; see also
Hann 2002b: 4). This sudden deprivation of goods and privileges from
whole social groups is quite characteristic of Central and Eastern Europe
as a whole. These groups experienced disorientation on many levels: an
incomprehension of the source of their work and their unemployment,
an ignorance of the processes of privatization, and, as such, an increased
dependency on the unregulated, capitalist market, or even the black

market (Kideckel 2002: 119; Hann 2002b: 11). From this perspective we see entirely new modes of existence in the postsocialist world, modes that became incomprehensible to these groups, in which something was suddenly expected from them (the intentions of these expectations vary) that differed from what had come before, i.e., being socially, economically, and sometimes even politically active. They were also expected to participate in what were often neocapitalist structures (Hann 2002b; Kideckel 2002: 116–118; cf. Domański 2002), for which they possessed neither the requisite knowledge nor the skills. In these new conditions they had to actively attend to their own interests, or hold themselves responsible for their lack of success. This reliance on themselves or on blind fate, in comparison with the former governments that had once organized their lives and employment, makes for a postsocialist "condemnation to freedom," which has been described many times (Giza-Poleszczuk, Marody and Rychard 2000; Rychard and Federowicz 1993; cf. Sztompka 2000: 56–57).

As a subject for anthropological research, the world of postsocialism is thus an extraordinarily complex reality, though it does often betray certain shared attributes in many areas. There is no way to describe these changes without reference to the experiences of the former, socialist system, as many phenomena are organically tied to those of the previous, widely understood social and cultural practices, if only in terms of an "informal economy" or a strategy of "constant camouflage" of personal opinions and the private "I" (Szarota 1995: 210; cf. Tarkowska and Tarkowski 1994: 267). Nor can these changes be described without reference to the former way of being and acting in the socialist state—even if this was acting against the system (see Giza-Poleszczuk, Marody, and Rychard 2000: 18–19). One example here is the research into the postsocialist economic relationships in local societies, where an informal "grey" economy continues to be present in some places, as is a familiar relationship with bureaucrats, decision-makers, and an economy based on customs, rituals, games, and barter, or on "talking people around" (Hann 2002b: 9–10; see also Humphrey 2002; Ledeneva 1998). Nonetheless, the post-transformation and postsocialist changes cannot be described through reference to the social practices of the socialist state. Through their dynamic, they are, to some extent, unpredictable, as they have their own disarming sense of process (Giza-Poleszczuk, Marody, and Rychard 2000: 16–19). Though the heritage of socialism still exits somewhere beneath the transformations, it is primarily a current of grassroots, noninstitutionalized behavior that moves along its own winding trajectory. Suddenly impoverished and disoriented social groups appeared everywhere, finding themselves in the foreign landscape of the free market and politics, a free social discourse and a free narrative, both in terms of the collective and of themselves. As Anna Giza-Poleszczuk, Mirosława Marody, and Andrzej Rychard claim outright (2000: 19), there is no way to treat these postsocialist transformations in a channeled or teleological fashion; there was no single "real" transformation, for it ran its course in various manners, and is seen differently from different perspectives. It is a crucible of grassroots and institutional transformations combined (though the grassroots perspective is of particular significance here).

The experience of social degradation—the liquidation of factories and a secure farming existence, unemployment, the devaluation of possessions, the necessity of suffering poverty—is one of the private, noninstitutional dimensions of the transformation, and one that is very complex and difficult to describe. It contains many instinctive throwbacks to the "old" structure of the world, to tried-and-true methods of dealing with reality, which are utterly ineffective in the current circumstances. Many of my interlocutors functioned and built their world in the phantasmagoric structure of the socialist economy, and, in a sense of daily practice, *believed* in the system (Hann 2002b: 11); what later transpired was for them a "vacuum" of sorts, an incomprehensible and terrifying process. The disintegration of an old world so deeply rooted in the previous economic system of some social groups (laborers, working villagers, state-farm workers, independent farmers) triggered unpredictable social processes and unanticipated phenomena. We are still trying to grasp these processes, to assign them their sociological or historical significance, given that history follows its own course and bypasses people's experience. Meanwhile, a great deal has occurred there. These people have lived from day to day and have made an ongoing effort, if not only to gain a better tomorrow or to survive, then at least to comprehend, and to find an answer to a question: How is it that things changed so much? How is it that things are the way they are?

The Studied Phenomena

From 2001 to 2006 I conducted my research in Poland among the social groups that were struck by poverty after 1989.[10] The situation of these groups was almost always tied to the liquidation of former workplaces, factories, or mines, or to the loss of farming subsidies and purchase guarantees. At the same time, this research concerns people who were abruptly made impoverished, who were often drawing social welfare payments, living off their own pensions or those of their parents, and also off many informal methods of acquiring sustenance, though these seldom sufficed to provide for themselves and their families. Tarkowska (2000c: 56) notes that for the poverty-stricken in Poland during the transformation period, the following attributes or "factors increasing the probability of being impoverished" were typical: (1) youth, (2) unemployment, often long-term, (3) large families, (4) a low level of education, (5) residence in a small town or a village. She continues, "the unemployed and those involved in farming are over-represented among the poor populations" (ibid.). My research concerns the unemployed workers of closed factories and impoverished farmers—in short, poor people. The profile of my interlocutors differs slightly, however, as a result of the fact that the focus of my research is the processes of impoverishment and social degradation, of the people who experienced the transformation in the most painful fashion. We might, therefore, say that the typical representative of my "research group"—my "subject"—is a poor person who has been unemployed for years (generally since the early to mid-1990s), or is working illegally or at odd jobs (taking advantage of various "ecological niches," such as collecting forest berries). Generally, this person is between the ages of thirty and sixty (more often a man than a woman, as statements from men were the substantial majority), recalling his or her employment in the PRL period (or in the early years of the transformation) and the path to his or her unemployment. It is often a person with a trade- or elementary-school education, from a deindustrialized region, a small or medium-sized town, or a village. The experience of degradation and impoverishment was, therefore, decisive in my choice of interlocutors, my research subjects, and the cocreators of my text.

As I have said, my anthropological interlocutors were experiencing the harshest aspects of the Polish system change—"the other side of the transformation," as *Kultura i Społeczeństwo* journal phrased it (2002, no. 4). The path they walked went from adapting to and acting within the socialist system (while often quite aware of its violence) to exploring the incomprehensible limits of the daily existence they had once forged for themselves.

In describing the structure of the Polish transformation, Marody (2002) has shown that, following 1989, we were dealing with three "streams" of adaptation to the new circumstances. She isolated "privatized" Poland, i.e., the workers in the dynamic commercial companies, generally holding high qualifications, taking risks, and earning substantially; then "state" Poland, i.e., the workers in the "public sector," or the state institutions, the bureaucracy who earned less but who held regular employment and a stable social position (a full-time contract); and finally, "welfare" Poland, i.e., those who received pensions or welfare money. This final category covered people who were receiving and supporting themselves off of social assistance, welfare, family pensions, unemployment insurance, and social aid, all of which could be seen as characteristic of my field of research (cf. Golczyńska-Grondas 2004: 30–32). There are also many unemployed who take farming and construction jobs in the EU countries. I would like to point out, however, a second dimension to the existence of this collectivity, i.e., the sphere of generally invisible actions. In fact, many of these people did work, though as part of a "grey economy." They earned their pay and other direct goods through informal, hidden ("transient"), often semi-legal labor, work that made use of the remains of socialist industry or, one might say, the new "ecological niches," to reference Justyna Laskowska-Otwinowska's remarks on strategies of these sorts practiced by impoverished Polish Roma (2002: 228–229). These activities have already been described or mentioned by researchers from both Poland and abroad (Golczyńska-Grondas 2004: 75–76, 123–124; Sikorska 1999: 117; and Sławomir Piotrowski's 2004 article on the collectors of scrap from military training areas), and both Chris Hann (2002b) and Francis Pine (2002) have called attention to the practice as well. The present book carefully describes informal methods of earning money and acquiring goods, including all forms of scrap collecting and demolition of old buildings (infrastructures): gathering scrap metal and bricks, digging coal in bootleg mines, gathering mushrooms, berries, and wild herbs, wood, and pine branches, using industrial rubbish tips (scrap, nonferrous metals, synthetic materials, clothing and chemicals—whatever might come in handy), and poaching. An enormous wave of these phenomena flooded Poland in the years 2002–2005. Their scope and various incarnations are noted in many press articles of the period (Danilewicz 2006; Bakoś and Ryciak 2004; Lipko 2003; 2004; Trusewicz 2004, as well as numerous series of articles in the local press concerning scrap collectors and scrap thieves, particularly in the spring of 2004). This world of unending work and hunting for means of survival is the third element of my field of research. One might say that beyond the "private," "state," and "welfare" Polands, there existed another, fourth dimension of making do in the new reality—"ecological" strategies and activities, or, to phrase it differently, "hunter/gatherer" Poland.[11]

The Field Research

In this way I tried to record a fragment of a concealed history that had taken place over the last few years—a history that was still undergoing change, and for this very reason required special observation and careful recording (see Tarkowska 2000b: 28–31). I conducted my research, therefore, in places where this "flip side" of the Polish transformation had played itself out in a particular fashion. There were three such regions:

(1) the poverty-stricken, jobless villages of the Świętokrzyskie Foothills, the vicinity of Przysucha and Szydłowiec; (2) the deindustrialized former mining town of Wałbrzych, a city of vast unemployment, as well as its satellite, the town of Boguszów-Gorce; and (3) the villages surrounding the enormous exposed brown coal mine in Bełchatów (mainly in the wealthy municipality of Kleszczów, some of whose inhabitants are nonetheless very poor).

In each of the fields I have presented, my research involved many hours of ethnographic conversation: listening to spontaneous narratives, conversing in groups, and observing the participants. It was based on maximum contact with my subjects and on observations of those on the sidelines. I managed to tape-record the majority of the conversations, and later to write them out, though a substantial part of my material came about through making field notes and recording the statements I had heard, which is an obvious necessity in ethnographic research in environments of this sort. I also made use of interviews recorded and transcribed by my students and I am citing them in the following parts of the book. In just my own recordings—not counting the recordings and transcriptions of my students—I gathered around two hundred hours of tape; altogether this adds up to the considerable sum of several hundred pages of materials. I also attempted to keep a research diary, which is an extremely important source of ethnographic knowledge; in turn, my colleague Paweł Pałgan took several hundred photographs, which had enormous significance for my interpretations.

In some cases I managed to live and spend longer periods of time in the homes and farmsteads of my interlocutors (as did my students and colleagues). For several days at a time I lived with them and spent time with them, and later, in the years that followed, I returned more than once. None of this altered the fact that I remained a stranger among them, though they knew me and were accustomed to me. To some extent, I occupied the position of the "accepted ignoramus," a "marginal position" on the borderline between the role of a "distanced" ethnographer and one who had "gone native" (Hammerslcy and Atkinson 2007: 78–84; see also Mosse 2006). I often spent time in the field when I was a complete stranger as well, wandering about and observing behavior, conversations, objects, and everything that occurred all around me. I was often treated with suspicion, sometimes with indifference, but most frequently I managed to forge close bonds and kindly relations, though these were still full of mistrust.

On every occasion, however, this fieldwork was very difficult and filled with awkwardness (as well as a constant sense of unrest), as it was research on people who were suffering poverty and social degradation.

Notes

1. It is true that one theory aiming to change our research perspective on poverty is the theory of social marginalization (see Frieske 1999; Kowalak 1998; Lister 2004). Within its scope, a research phenomenon crosses beyond narrow cultural horizons, is closely tied to a whole network of social relationships, and contains multiple strategies—addressing space, education, and health. This theory avoids the standard messages of philosophical anthropology: class determinism (Marxism) or individualism (neoliberalism). I fear, however, that the conceptual network of marginalization, to some degree, also brings about symbolic systems, succeeded by the terminology of relevance/irrelevance. Having his say in the debate on the "underclass," Herbert Gans (1996) expressly warned against further categories and key words appearing in conceptualizations of poverty.

2. According to the authors of *Dependency Culture,* the word used by British unemployed for assistance payments or the right to receive them is 'dole' (Dean and Taylor-Gooby 1992). In conversation, however, it kept acquiring odd shades of significance, expressing a permanent and unchanging relationship, and when repeated multiple times, it turned into a sort of lament (the administrative term thus undergoing a shift in meaning). It then pertained more to the ontological sense of being as a dependency, in which such a thing as independence or full subjectivity is a delusion (a text in another language). It is a word that materializes the full power of the condition of dependency, and simultaneously, a monthly payment of benefits—the "dole," or allotted portion, takes the form of a Heideggerian *das Geschick*: participation and fate.

3. This gives rise to a situation where the reality of being in a culture is co-negotiated or disrupted, a form of ruptures, questions, and answers as opposed to a textualizing description. Then, too, stress is placed on the fully fledged rendering of another subject, on his or her words that "break" the ethnographer's statement, and on his or her impromptu generations of meaning. These errors and elements of "discord" (with various "facts," for instance) then become of the utmost importance (Dwyer 1982: 269–270)—all "miscommunications" between ethnographer and interlocutor take center stage in this new anthropological knowledge (Rabinow 1977: 154; cf. Dwyer 1982: 281–285). Ethnography thus becomes more of a field for an interactive game, where the I-you differences are made increasingly distinct. As such, it finally discards the long Western tradition, stripping it of its "Archimedean point" (Dwyer 1982: 281), in which the foreigner and his or her cultural knowledge are constantly misrepresented, depending on the present requirements.

4. Joanna Tokarska-Bakir (see 1997; 2000: 13–14) has recently written in similar fashion about the analysis of "reciting prayers" and "demented repetition."

5. Roland Barthes has written remarkable passages on such 'early' body language, outside of 'identity' and 'self-consciousness', in his essay on Phillippe Sollers's drama, in which he compares it to speech at the moment of awakening, even before a man confronts his own identity. Identity, he writes, can be imagined "like a predacious bird who flies high over our dreams in which we are deeply engaged in our life, our serious history; and when we wake, when the bird falls down on us, only then, before he touches us, we have to overtake, and begin to speak" (Barthes 1965: 599).

6. My experience tied to running ethnography workshops for students of the Warsaw University Polish Culture Institute, during which we did field research in Wałbrzych, had a great impact on the creation of this text. I then recognized that knowledge

I knew all too well from the field and research practice, and so anticipated by my students, was almost impossible to communicate directly—I was often forced into "silence" or "circling around" something. Moreover, I realized that the ideas I have formulated, to some extent, coincide with the views of Kirsten Hastrup in her outstanding article "The Empirical Foundation: On the Grounding of Worlds" (1995).

7. Kirsten Hastrup mentions the sort of "rich headnotes" described by Simon Ottenberg (Hastrup 1995: 56).

8. This historical context is also created by phenomena shaping the social map in the time of the partitions, and in earlier centuries: the reality of the impoverished and overpopulated Galician villages (S. Szczepanowski's *Nędza Galicji* ... [The Misery of Galicia ...]), or the post-manumission reality, with the difficulty of managing the peasants of the Russian partition / Congress Poland (Łukasiewicz 1992). Moreover, it concerns all of the urban poverty, the "street people," the poor workers, the urban rejects, derelicts, the "rogues, harlots and evil-doers," "people of easy virtue," the "tavern folk," and so forth. Elżbieta Tarkowska (2000b: 49–52) places the trajectory of various impoverished groups in prewar Poland and previous centuries in a continuity, summoning a synthetic rendering of history (in particular, the collective work edited by Jan Szytełło 1992).

9. Polish anthropological attempts to describe the reality of the People's Republic have been made several times (Robotycki 2001), both by historians (including Szarota 1995) and cultural historians (Bednarek 1997; 2000). They have also been picked up in increasing numbers of source-based works, largely written by historians and sociologists (such as Szpakowska 2003; Mazurek 2005; Szpak 2005). Of course, there are also many works undertaking a retrospective attempt to grasp the social condition of Poland during the PRL and on the threshold of the transformation (Beskid 1992; Marody 1991). As far as is possible, I provide mention of works on the PRL history in the various research areas (Wałbrzych, in particular) in the relevant chapters.

10. During my research, unemployment was at its highest in the history of post-transformation Poland, i.e., after 1989. According to the Central Statistical Office of Poland, the registered unemployment levels in the subsequent years were as follows (January statistics): 0.3 percent in 1990, 6.6 in 1991, 12.1 in 1992, 14.2 in 1993, 16.7 in 1994, 16.1 in 1995, 15.4 in 1996, 13.1 in 1997, 10.7 in 1998, 11.4 in 1999, 13.7 in 2000, 15.7 in 2001, 20.1 in 2002, 20.6 in 2003, 20.6 in 2004, 19.4 in 2005, 18.0 in 2006, and 15.7 in July 2006.

11. "Hunters and Gatherers" is the title of a text I published in 2004 (in *Op. cit.* journal). The term "hunter/wheeler-dealer" was used by Agnieszka Golczyńska-Grondas to define a type of man from an enclave of poverty in Łódź who "concentrates on organising living space and bringing home all kinds of 'loot'" (2004: 75). In turn, Hanna Palska and Joanna Sikorska, in their study of a poor family (2000: 254), wrote of a "gatherer" method of acquiring the essentials. Sławomir Piotrowski has written of "scrap gatherers" in the countryside after the state farms were dissolved (2004). Furthermore, Artur Bakoś and Igor Ryciak (2004) used the term "hunter/ gatherers" to define poor people supporting themselves by collecting undergrowth and scrap.

Chapter 1

The Szydłowiec and Przysucha Environs— The Świętokrzyskie Foothills

A World Full of Adversities

Unemployment and the Farming Recession

In the Polish countryside during the time of the great change, we might say that the experience of the recession, the breakdown of farming, and a sharp drop in living standards went beyond the local. With the afore-mentioned collapse of the centralized social economic system, combined with the collapse of mandatory crop purchases and fertilizer allotments and the cancellation of the credit system for farmers, unpredictable and alarming things started to occur. After 1989, a time of free market and new trading practices emerged, a time of pressure in a self-shaping world. At the same time, prices for farming products became unstable and began to topple, and there followed the constant necessity of counting and recounting "costs" and "profits." The farms were clearly becoming impoverished (Kocik 2001: 70); they had lost their clients—the state-run agencies—and then their very existence, too, hung in the balance. In such a climate, many farms lost their economic security and the chance they once had for contract purchases; and the constant, prescribed demand came to an end (Bukraba-Rylska and Rosner 2001; Pieniążek and Jaworska 1995; Rosner 2002). Furthermore, there was the irreversible imperative to become competitive and the necessity to adapt constantly to the unpredictable rules of the market, while simultaneously bearing the constraint of having to adapt to ever-new farming technologies (modern machinery, fertilizers, and pesticide sprays) to maximize crops. Thus new and unbridled forces emerged—economic forces.

In the years 1995–1996, when I conducted research in the Lublin Province, this "bad change" was perceived as taking place in a way that was both "subterranean" and irreversible. The experiences of the farmers (chiefly those on small and medium-sized farmlands), in their steady impoverishment, began to be reflected in their closest vicinities, the ones most familiar to them—in their farmers' observations concerning agriculture. "At one time," it was said, "there weren't all these pests—now we got trade, the bloody free market, and then here comes these pests, damn it to hell. And if you spray, then you get the worms, little holes everywhere. The flu used to last three days, now it stays for seven. Because all that poison's in the system, all kinds of AIDS running about, and I'll tell you, we're all gonna die out.... They say three power stations are about to blow their tops in Russia" (TR/LB/1). Statements and predictions thus created a framework for more, resilient tales about the approaching end of the world, and all the harbingers that foretold it (cf. Tokarska-Bakir 2000: 101, 102; Zowczak 1993). A special kind of "ecological" consciousness arose, one that shared nothing in common with today's ecological consciousness, in the colloquial sense of the term. In these conversations the theme of the visible poisoning and contamination of nature was forever recurring. There was talk of the pollution of the earth, the poisoning of the air, of the cattle, the grain, the crops, of all of nature. In the field lands outside of Lublin they spoke with particular unease of how the niter (saltpeter), the sprays, the protein concentrates, the vitamin fodder, and other chemical crop agents would stay in the earth "for always." To their way of thinking, the earth had begun to submit to the laws of a "vicious circle"—through the constant fertilization and processing it would become polluted, and would thus need more fertilizer. "Now," people said, "they'll always have to fertilize, otherwise nothing more will grow" (TR/LB/4), while theretofore "everything had grown." They also said, "Yes, once everything used to grow, now hardly anything grows, the soil is ruined now" (TR/LB/3). "The earth used to be more fertile, and not polluted" (TR/LB/4), "now not much of anything grows; the soil is saturated with sprays and nitrogen" (TR/LB/6). New economics and unfamiliar processes went beyond everyday experiences, creating a "deformation." Abnormal events in the social process of forging reality thus became normal and visible (Berger and Luckmann 1967); knowledge of the new market economy, upon which the farmers were dependent, was translated into everyday reality, and images focused around it (Pieniążek and Jaworska 1995: 9–10).

This was the method of grasping the most unsettling harbingers of change. Through technological change and the introduction of chemical agents to increase crop yield, the fear lurking deep within every

experience of change in the countryside embraced the *whole* of the surrounding world. Everything all around—the air, land, vegetables, grain,
and meat—seemed contaminated, poisoned; it was a forecast of the ultimately tragic transformations occurring in the outside world, a sign of
a "violated reality." "There used to be no plagues in the world," said one
farmer, "now everything in the earth has sunk, the stink has descended.
... Potatoes just used to grow, now they're spray-grown ... nothing
grows without [the spray]. ... There used to be less of the potato bugs ...
now they've come to Poland to stay" (TR/LB/3). "Sprays, stink, poison,
the potatoes stink after you boil them, they have black spots, the trees
dry up. ... It'll bring sickness, cancer ... cancer in every tree. ... Who's
ever heard of such a thing?" (TR/LB/3). "The potatoes aren't even good
for fodder ... all those pests came imported from England ... some kind
of crap fodder ... and now you've got rabies" (TR/LB/10). "Everything's
poisoned I tell you, there used to be bees, and now I can't keep them
for the third time running" (TR/LB/9); "it must be from the air, maybe
from Chernobyl ... the potato bugs are going nuts, there's strange sicknesses" (TR/LB/3). In these images/signs[1] we can see an attempt to con-
dense all of reality, to grasp the entirety of the "bad change" underway.
The harbingers of "bad change" are present in the attributes of organic
matter (the crops, the meat, the food), and are visible in the air and in
the earth. Whereas once these concerns pertained to the unpredictability of weather and "natural" cataclysms (air, famine, fire, and war), they
now pertain to economic/market dependencies (Kocik 2001: 43).

     In this chapter, I would like to examine how this experience of "bad
change" is present among the inhabitants of the villages of the Świętokrzyskie foothills, the vicinity of Szydłowiec and Przysucha, where I
conducted my research from 2003 to 2006. Previously, those who had
small farms combined with income from working in steel and rolling
mills got along quite well; I was often told that in the years of the People's Republic, "every farm had at least one guy who worked in a factory." These were generally very small farms in the border regions of the
Świętokrzyskie Plains, with degraded or medium-fertile soil, particularly
poor for tilling. In turn, the inhabitants of the villages to the north
of the forest line (the Gielniów-Przysucha-Chlewiska-Szydłowiec line)[2]
had slightly larger farms, and better-quality soil. These northern farms
were previously villages where farming was done for both personal and
commercial needs.[3] At any rate, the combination of farming with factory work granted a more stable, predictable income and created a kind
of economic freedom, supporting new housing, the modernization of
old huts, and the installation of bathrooms and kitchens (particularly
in the 1970s). Moreover, farmers could purchase farming machinery,

and even luxury items such as furniture or automobiles. According to both official records (i.e., statistics counted according to the listings of people registered at the Labor Bureau) and unofficial accounts (those unemployed and unregistered), the liquidation of the majority of the surrounding factories in the 1990s created an extremely high level of unemployment. This was the standard fate of overpopulated villages composed of small, self-sufficient farms (Frenkel 2001; Kocik 2001: 67–72; Łapińska-Tyszka 1995; Rosner 2000b). By now, the level of unemployment on a nationwide scale in the Szydłowiec region (according to the Regional Labor Bureau in Szydłowiec) is very high, reaching up to 42 percent (29 percent in 2001, 42 percent in 2004, 39 percent in 2005). According to the Regional Labor Bureau in Przysucha, it is lower in that region, reaching up to 29 percent (21 percent in 2001, 29 percent in 2004, 27 percent in 2005). However, this only covers the official unemployment levels; the hidden unemployment there is massive (70–80 percent). According to some estimates, it almost doubles the official unemployment statistics (Frenkel 2001; Kocik 2001: 67–71; Rosner 2000b: 95). The hidden unemployment is linked to the large number of people considered dispensable in the purely economic sense, e.g., those who are not legally employed, perhaps working on the farm for fewer than twenty days a year (Kocik 2001: 68–69). This is a process of "absorbing" unemployment, a trait peculiar to the countryside, incorporating dispensable and jobless people in its own fashion (Szafraniec 2002: 84). Furthermore, there has been a drastic drop in the profitability of farming, particularly on small-area and low-yield farms (precisely the kind predominant in this area). The majority of these, producing on small, degraded patches of soil, plowed by horse or sometimes by farming machinery, have practically no significant value on the present-day market (many people do not even try to cultivate fewer than two hectares of land, so as to retain their rights to benefits). Thus, these villages, for the most part, are comprised of the unemployed and impoverished; almost all of my interlocutors received unemployment benefits in the 1990s, and most went at least episodically to social services for assistance. Presently, most of the villages described are filled with kilometers on end of abandoned, uncultivated fields, all gone to seed. "It doesn't pay," I was generally told. (Only in the vicinities of Ostałówek and Ostałów did the landscape change a bit, and tilled farmland came into view.)

Things are much the same in the western part of the region, in the Przysucha vicinity, in villages like Zawada, Lipno, Mariówka, and Smogorzów, where rows of withered fruit orchards, and raspberry and currant bushes stretch for kilometers, delivering a striking impression (observations made from 2002 to 2005). Until recently, these areas comprised a rich orchard center—in nearby Skrzyńsko, from spring to autumn, a gigantic Hortex (fruit juice) factory bought huge quantities of fruits and vegetables, everything that could be collected, from the local farms. Kilometer-long rows of currant bushes were planted to supply the factory, as were orchards of apple and pear trees; the fields were full of workers, and the roads were full of trucks hauling the collected fruit. At present the Hortex factory is still cutting back on production, and has suspended the purchase of local fruit almost entirely, accepting only tart apples in the fall. The impoverishment of these regions thus results from the simultaneous liquidation of the industry—and of the many thousands of jobs in the area—and the deep farming crisis. The consequences of the previous modernization of the People's Republic, for farmers and workers alike, are visible in the creation of new farming and industry structures in the countryside. Following 1989, the entire postcommunist network of steel mills, rolling mills, and many other sideline factories was almost entirely shut down. The result in terms of earning a living, of calculating an income, and of the whole socially manufactured way of life (including its cultural dimension), was an abrupt deindustrialization of both the farming and the factory regions. Before the transformation, the residents of Budki, Aleksandrów, Majdanki, Borki, Huta, Zaława, Cukrówka, Ostałówek, and Ostałów in the Chlewiska commune, of Niekłań and Furmanów in the Stąporków commune, and of Mechlin, Gałki, and Stoczki in the Gielniów commune worked simultaneously on their farms and in factories as laborers. As the inhabitants recall, buses drove from the factories through the villages, generally from the steel and rolling mills in Stąporków, Suchedniów, Skarżysk-Kamienna, and Rzucaw, collecting workers from right outside their farms. Moreover, there were many other factories running in the region: sewing workshops and cement plants in Gielniów, Skłoby, and Gałki (the Postęp sewing workshop), the Rozmet factory in Chlewiska, the Profel military electronics factory in Szydłowiec, the Skalbud stone masonry, and others. An employee at the Regional Social Aid Centre in Stąpoków, formerly on staff at a foundry, recalled that during communist times, there were always a hundred more job openings than people looking to work. Finding enough workers was an enormous difficulty. Following 1993–1994 (our conversation took place in 2004), hundreds of unemployed began turning up at the center, and she still had difficulty assigning them regional intervention labor. For the time being—i.e., for the past dozen or so years, as it is generally said—"there's nothing left" in the local area.

A Community of the Unemployed:
Immobility, Odd Jobs, and "Tragic Scarring"

In these areas many people are still occupied with working in their own backyards—tidying homes, sheds, stables, putting up fences, cleaning old paint and grime off window frames, then painting them once more. This is something that the visitor finds striking after some time. In the majority of these unemployed villages one sees how whole families—often with the help of neighbors—are hard at work repairing, renovating, and painting their properties. This is often piecemeal work, i.e., patching a broken fence, painting a metal gate, repairing and replacing parts of roofs on wooden huts a few decades old, etc. In addition, the men are always "wheeling and dealing," making "work" arrangements, often going to their neighbors in groups of three or four to "do some work," to cement a well or to lay drains for a septic tank. Unemployed men often treat the conversations I initiate as a prelude to a job offer (most often in construction). I am regarded either as someone with whom it "makes sense to speak," or with whom it "is pointless speaking" (as they say). A great lack of trust is visible here because, as I was later informed, they return from many such "under-the-table" jobs without payment, or with only partial payment. However, the public visibility of these collaborating groups leads me to see this as a striking reversal of the previous situation from the 1980s and earlier, when the villages cleared out on the weekdays, and everyone went to work in the factories or the fields. In these typical linear villages, which are built along the road, one can see who is doing what; and "what one is doing" at present in these circumstances of general unemployment is of enormous significance. The road thus becomes a "social bulletin-board" (or "social procession")—the residents of the towns, sitting on their front lawns, get their information about what's happening around them from the road: who's working where. One could say, of course, that the road has already served such a function, as everybody can see which machines are driving off into the fields and what they are hauling back. But now, as a result of unemployment and the frequent presence at home, in the domicile, in the village (not at work), this function has intensified. Thus, a community of village unemployment has evolved, built from the necessity of enduring unemployment, and also of a certain social observation regarding what work might "need doing," who "was doing" what, or who was not doing anything. These phrases are in constant circulation, as in: who has been seen carrying berries, who has "left to do some construction outside Warsaw," and who is "sitting and minding the rabbits." Unemployment has thus become socially transparent; and apart from the excess of time, there has emerged what I might call an excess of presence. Therefore, the villages' so-called invisible unemployment is seen by one and all, in this socially visible phenomenon of "excess of time" or "hanging around the house" (cf. Tarkowska 1997; Kalbarczyk 2002).

Moreover, a small number of mobile shops have begun to circulate around the villages. These are generally old, rusted Polonez pick-ups whose drivers sell bread, oil, flour, and "chemical supplies"; after some time, these "shops" have begun stopping in front of all the properties. Eventually, almost none of the villagers buy at the marketplaces, although—as I have been told—things are "better and cheaper" in town. In this way the villagers save money they would have otherwise spent on their trips to market; shopping at the marketplace has become a local sign of affluence. The mobile shop proprietors sell cheaper items (and of poorer quality, eg. in Mechlin and Zaława), and also more readily give credit (or as they say, "a tab") than do the local store owners (who might have had more difficulty collecting debts). In the microscale of the village, such a purchase thus stands as a public testimonial of economic inactivity, or at any rate, a daily-renewed message that is carefully observed and analyzed. I have often been told which neighbors bought from the mobile shop the day before ("I saw him buy potatoes from the guy who comes round after one o'clock," Mechlin) and who was "buying on" ("Those guys get their bread from the car that comes round," Zaława). Having means of sustenance, we should add, has both an economic and an axiological dimension in village cultures, and a few decades ago on the majority of Polish farms, buying extra food with cash was a certain shameful necessity (Laskowska-Otwinowska 1998: 24–25; Pieniążek 1995: 33). The unemployed village, we might say, has thus become an "itinerant village"; there has simultaneously emerged an experience of open nonproductiveness of the farms, and the immobility of its inhabitants. Villages of this sort (described by Jan S. Bystroń at the opening of the twentieth century, when there were traveling salesmen with devotional goods and other items) are still visited by shops of various specialities, by various specialists, by people selling whole sacks of carrots, onions, and potatoes, and by companies offering loans and credit, and elsewhere still, by vehicles collecting scrap metal (old farming machinery, barrels, trash), and by vehicles collecting waste of all description.

In this way a local commonality develops in the experience of unemployment, and a commonality in the breakdown of active farming. How has this process happened? How is this change experienced and received inside these societies? If it is visible and cannot be denied, then almost every conversation begins with an attempt to define what is happening in the area, and what is happening in the nearby villages. Every conversation is for them, the unemployed villagers (my interlocutors), a forced confrontation (with themselves); they then go beyond an informative language, stating certain pat phrases, which they repeat a few times, recalling the complaints collected by Piotr Kędziorek (1996). One might say that they are unable to get across what has happened to make this profound change "for the worse." These conversations often involve repeating this irreducible fact, the general lack of work, and the uncultivated fields that stretch on all sides. "I have no work ... I have no job offers," the unemployed from the village of Majdanki repeat. "There's no work," they add in a similar vein, "it's one big zero ... zero work ... zero crops." "Now it's every man for himself. ... How are you going to find work? Go up and ask the mayor?" (TR/PŚ/17). In another village, Cukrówka, things are much the same: "Here, you see, there's no work. ... Let's not kid ourselves. ... I tell you, there used to be footwear, metal, transport [factories]. ... There's nothing to be done. ... It used to be here, and so what?" (TR/PŚ/26). "Everything's collapsed, everything, they've destroyed everything, there used to be a dairy, now they destroyed it. ... There used to be factories." "They closed down the factories ... closed them down ... what's to be done? ... Think how many factories there used to be! They didn't want to let go!" (TR/PŚ/10). These rhythmic statements thus keep on returning, and more words appear after them, frequently showing aggression (toward themselves as well); there are also often questions directed at me concerning work, though these were not meant to be answered—they were what Kędziorek has called "vain questions" (1996: 119). "There's no work here ... you have work ... what are we going to do ... there's nothing ... just nothing." "What do you suggest I do, tell me? I'm out of work, and now what? Hard times, and now what? Can you suggest something? You can see there's nothing here. ... Maybe you'd like to hire me?" (TR/PŚ/2). In this way, this experience becomes an inseparable part of the communicative situation—the appearance of shame, which here is chiefly present in the public sphere, visible to all, is an act of social visibility—and as such, becomes manifested (cf. Giddens 1991: 95–96). The very act of being in the village, near the house, sends out a message, and this manifold and ever-present transparency of being dispensable grows all the more aggressive and demonstrative as a communicative message. Thus arise statements that derive a certain satisfaction from what is happening all around, and directed toward the speakers themselves (autoaggression). "The bushes are growing up round the hut, but they won't make it, because we'll soon be dead and gone" (TR/PŚ/10). "These houses still hold retirees, pensioners, but soon they'll plow everything down, and then they'll be gone" (TR/PŚ/17). "When a child's born round here they ask if the grandparents are still alive [as a source of pension], because if they aren't, what's the good in the child being born?" (TR/PŚ/12).

These complaints are all characteristic of the statements I heard. In these quoted complaints, work is generally presented as unproductive and absurd. It forever carries the image of that implacable "bad change," the imagined insolubility of farming. Furthermore, it is at once relentless and futile (Tomicka and Tomicki 1975: 124–125). "And what are you supposed to grow here? You take a tractor, take some fertilizer— then collect the crops and bring them back. Where does it get you?" (TR/PŚ/4). "But what's it all for? You take a horse, get to work, plow, once, twice, cart the manure. ... You've got to work, dig, carry, and then what have you got to show for it?" (TR/PŚ/10). "And you pay for the wood for the hut and then haul it, and chop it, and haul it some more, and there you go—you've got nothing" (TR/PŚ/10). "But what kind of work is that ... you go gather some berries, and they last one evening, then you're out ... then you've got to go out again" (TR/PŚ/19). "My goddamn village. ... Do they ever work here? Who works here? A little job here, a little job there ... just odds and ends. Then he goes to buy some wine and presto—it's all gone" (TR/PŚ/34). I get the impression that the idea is to keep stressing the "meagerness" of a day's work, of the gathering of herbs, berries, and "undergrowth" of all sorts, of one-off construction jobs. All occasional forms of replacing regular income are in themselves worth a pittance in these statements, as they are neither farming nor industrial work. Thus, the money they bring is also "meager," just "enough for a bottle of wine," "as much as you spend in the morning"; "you dig, cut, dry [spices]—and you've got enough for one beer" (TR/PŚ/10). There is also visible shame associated with gathering work, given that it does not involve farming, and so is not perceived as labor: "Nobody does anything 'round here. ... People gather berries and herbs ... they don't do nothing" (TR/PŚ/15). I have generally been told in conversation that people started gathering reluctantly and "entirely by chance": "I have some friends in Huta, they talked me into it, but I just do a bit of gathering" (TR/PŚ/6). Odd jobs, firstly, deprive villagers of their sense of agency (on this point, see Kocik 2000: 51–60; Olędzki 1971: 214; cf. Thomas and Znaniecki 2010). Secondly, this is deindustrialized work, unrelated to any industry, which was so overevaluated and mythologized in the period of the People's Republic—and as such, it is no work at all. There is a constant contrast between gathering and odd jobs and the image of "industrial work"—as solid, almost economical, and providing tangible results: "There were so many factories! ... I rigged machines, screwed in the parts. ... Now they've cut back, all right" (TR/PŚ/10). "What can he do ... if a man worked on steel and in the rolling mills, what's he supposed to do now!" (TR/PŚ/4). "There used to be metal factories, people had money, and these days—he [the farmer] sells things, or he don't" (TR/PŚ/26). Industrial labor, then, according to these statements, has a socially acknowledged, particularly solid quality, unlike something that will "vanish at once," like income from gathering work, odd jobs, hired labor of all sorts. The principle of symmetry comes into effect here: meager work equals meager wages, frittered away on wine or spent on "food, bread—and by the afternoon it's all gone." This "meager" work thus has a wider and more general reference—it is, I repeat, ineffectual, the money earned from it is a "straw fire": "it's gone by the morning," "I drink a bottle of wine and it's gone."

This "bad change" in the world is equally visible in the manner of speaking about the earth and the surroundings—these are very powerful and emotional images. The transformation of fields into fallow lands is irreversible, and the change that has taken place has a lethal dimension (Kędziorek 1996; Kocik 2001). These statements contain signs of what I might call adynamia and stoppage—an immobility. Just as everything once "was running"—the factories were running, the depots were running—now one hears that "everything's stopped." "It was all running, everything was running, raspberries and strawberries were picked, the cars were made one after another, fabrics were produced, clothing.... Has a hole opened up or what? Everything's stopped.... Now nothing is running" (TR/PŚ/38). "There was a tannery, a co-op, that's how it was ... now they just sit there." "There was so much ... so much of everything ... everything just sits there now ... the earth sits there" (TR/PŚ/26). "There you have it—the fields sit there.... They sit there far as you can see.... In Broniów they sit there, in Pawłów they sit there, in Cukrówka they sit there" (TR/PŚ/13). "Everything went," they told me in Ostałów, "cauliflower, carrots, beans, they lined up to the morning. ... *It was never ending* ... [emphasis mine], then everything started to go wrong" (TR/PŚ/7). These concerns take their toll on a whole worldview. Statements continually contain images of a "frozen" world that is "sitting there," and often instead of the world, we have an imagined condensation: "the earth." "Now everything sits there, wherever you look it's fallow ground" (TR/PŚ/10). "The earth sits there.... Now you can't do anything.... There's only rocks ... that grow here" (TR/PŚ/4). They speak of the ubiquity of fallow with evident concern. The "earth" is spoken of, in many statements, as constantly becoming overgrown; one might say it is a certain collective imagining of a "returning, overgrowing forest." One forever hears that the "forest is returning": "The fallow fields are sitting there.... Once it used to be quite a ways to the forest, and now the forest comes right up to the village!" (TR/PŚ/6). "There's nothing here.... What can you do here when there's nothing around, everything's been overgrown, everything's been overgrown" (TR/PŚ/ 26). "The forest's coming back!" (TR/PŚ/27). "Now there's nothing, and everything's a forest" (TR/PŚ/33). These fields, we should add, were mostly "taken" from the nearby primeval forest (the Świętokrzyskie Forest), some not too long ago (forty to fifty years back), and laboriously cleared—these fields were founded almost "from the wilderness." There thus exists a collective memory of clearing and fighting for the earth; this memory explains this greater significance of "the return of the forest" ("the tragedy of overgrowth").

Here we start to sketch a clear panorama of an intensive and internal "cultivation of the world," though in this case, on the most immediate level, we are dealing with more its noncultivation, a general dread, a collective eschatology of unemployed and impoverished farmers—my interlocutors. "Everything's overgrown, it's the end.... There are insects, vipers" (TR/PŚ/4). "The vipers lie there and come at you wild.... They always used to come, but not this way! My neighbor just had a viper" (TR/PŚ/12). "The fallow fields sit there.... It's just a matter of time till the famine comes" (TR/PŚ/24). The retreat and return of the forest is particularly significant here, as it cannot be stopped; it also affects the transformation of the earth itself, a change in its utility: "There's nothing here.... Now it's too late for anything" (TR/PŚ/33). "The earth won't produce! There's no people.... They just sit there" (TR/PŚ/16). The very earth has become indisposed and hostile, and rhythmic phrases keep recurring in the people's statements: "Now we have to clear, protect, and fertilize, and work all the while," "And take the fertilizer, and gather it, and haul all that." The resulting motif is one of laborious blundering, of illogical action without end. It is as if the earth itself sucks energy. "It's been so long since anything's been done, there are no machines—this field here would devour me" (TR/PŚ/16), an unemployed father of five (working temporarily in Szydłowiec) told me in one village.

Motionless Orchards, Motionless Fields: Failure

To extend the running interpretation of the experience of village failure, I will draw from the important ethnographic dimension of the "survived world," from the notion of security created and incarnated as a community. Practically everything—fragments of dishes and fabrics, all the nets and fish-pots—everything that finds its way into the hands of the resilient ethnographer/collector, once had a developed and familiar shape in village cultures. Forged in a set and established way, a tool worked effectively, with every movement, with every chop. Every blow of the axe, every fish disentangled from a net, every beam in a framework built a sense of normalcy, a certainty that time was flowing "as it always had." Cultural researchers have generally concentrated on everyday actions that are renewed within a community, ones as familiar to the natives as the backs of their hands. The immortal ethnographer/collector Oskar Kolberg (1962) created a multivolume collection of "folk items," enumerating in his work the articles that comprised the world he encountered. For Kolberg, "folk" was a sprawling space that wove together customs, ways of life, speech, legends, proverbs, ceremonies, witchcraft, games, songs, music, and dance. Contemporary history, under the term *"Annales,"* opened wide to everyday activities, details of clothing, and hygiene rituals. It discovered age-old social structures, and carted all the world's poverty on stage, a "beggar's opera" of impoverished peasant and townsfolk homes. The pages of history made room for a world of ordinary and natural behavior, ways of working, walking, and washing, of making hay, of building and of living—a world built laboriously, and laboriously survived.

It is a pat phrase that the body is a measure of all things. It provides a measurement of cloth (the ell, taken from the elbow) and the sum of twelve inches (one foot); and even the alchemist's constellation of the organs (the microcosmos) is contained in the body (cf. Libera 1997). To provide an example: lunch is a meal eaten at high noon, a time when life comes to a standstill, and when, as ethnographic texts reveal, apparitions appear, headaches crop up, when fats and honey (i.e., an abundant meal) are necessary for time to continue its course (Brzozowska-Krajka 1994: 151). Hunger thus marks noontime, and the body and its needs mark out the hour. The time of the zenith and phase of fatigue are one and the same. One of my interlocutors—a farmer from just outside Przysucha—said that ever since the fields had been vacated and lay there unplowed, people had begun to lose their sense of time; they felt as though lunchtime and its accompanying hunger had passed them by (TR/PŚ/36). Working alone, she said, hunger and noontime could be substantially delayed—"lunch is like mass," as the proverb goes. Lunch concerns the renewal of culture. Lunchtime, initiated by a general sense of hunger, begins when everyone leaves the fields—but who leaves first? Where does the hunger come from? Perhaps part of the catastrophe of the farming recession I would like to describe is in the fact that the body no longer indicates time, and time does not indicate the body.

In his book devoted to the identity of the late-modern epoch, Anthony Giddens (1991) draws from this basic experience of corporeal being, and formulates the related notion of "ontological security." In a sense, this precisely concerns behavior that proceeds according to the body, which always expands a "tried and tested" zone. The foundation for fields of security and normalcy is thus, to a large extent, created by what allows those actions to be performed "as usual"; everything down to everyday gestures—the way one opens a door, for instance—structures and sets reality. In late modernity, however, this basic security is largely ensured not through activities themselves, but through institutions that work almost imperceptibly, due to a socially manufactured "trust": plumbing, water, and food supply, public sanitation systems, all sorts of cultural infrastructure. Thus, this "expansion" of security fields also encompasses issues that are entirely abstract and severed from the present experience, those issues requiring "expertise," such as the risk of environmental catastrophe or heart attack prevention. In this way, this constant monitoring of certain future points, and the projection of uncertain points creates, as Giddens puts it, something that recalls a "colonization" of future events, the constant projection of that normalcy. This can be expressed in a popular diet plan, in eating habits that obsessively ensure against future mishap and ward off potential illness. However, this constant estimate of risk paradoxically increases the sense of danger hovering over late modernity like a phantom, making itself felt in every morsel of food, in every habit we pick up. Giddens writes, "The point … is not that day-to-day life is inherently more risky than was the case in prior eras. It is rather that, in conditions of modernity, for lay actors as well as experts in specific fields, thinking in terms of risk and risk assessment is a more or less ever-present exercise, of a partly imponderable character" (ibid.: 123–124).

How is the world made secure in the Szydłowiec and Przysucha areas? The issues I am addressing here concern both the flow of daily affairs and the impoverished farmers', fruit growers', and workers' and villagers' sense of being at risk. In this space, a space decidedly "non-ecological," having absorbed the metalized sacks of the nearby processing plants, and having also absorbed, where possible, whatever quantities of fertilizers, spraying agents, and detergents (a fact that stands in no contradiction to the lament for the poisoned world), this "ensuring of the world" generally reveals itself through *ecological* statements. I am using the term *ecological* as a way of being, a state of "feeling at home" in the world; *eco*, from the Greek *oikos*, means household, a domesticated space (Michera 1994: 89; Robotycki 1998: 154). In the villages I describe during the time of the crisis, the time of economic stagnation found its expression in statements on physicality and ecology. "The body," wrote Maurice Merleau-Ponty, "in so far as it has 'behavior patterns,' is that strange object which uses its own parts as a general system of symbols for the world" (2002: 275). Thus the body is an experimental space that is cursed and marked anew every day through our favorite "hideouts" and "foodstuffs," which are constantly revealing a new and changing world.

"My brother was working, I was working, everyone was working, so many years of working, and now they just sit there, this guy sits there, the other guy sits there, and gets tired out, everyone's tired … because there's no work to be done" (TR/PŚ/36). Stories about work perhaps best relate this sort of "domestication," and as we can see, nearly the same images of unemployment are forever recurring. A lack of work begets an unhappiness that is understood almost organically: it brings disease, it shatters the order of the world and of the body. Then this body is *superimposed* onto the rest of the world, and stamped onto a sprawling horizon: "The water's gone cloudy, turned all yellow, some kind of sand's got into it? Some kind of rust? I mean, it used to be clear, you know, crystal clear as rubbing alcohol. … Now look at it [This is a region of surface lime rock strata—there are problems with the water, it is often cloudy, the wells dry up]" (TR/PŚ/39). "Where are you sick?" one hears, "I've got an earache. Where does it hurt? My head. What have you got? Cancer. Well, if it's cancer, it must be the chemicals …, the chemicals—you know, all this fancy stuff" (OST/1). "What will grow here now. … All the droughts we've had, the weather right now, and three years of the same. Drought, drought, drought, and then wet, wet, wet, yeah, it alternates—and so it all sits there, everything rots into the earth, it rots, because *something's* [emphasis mine] going on" (TR/PŚ/38). "Something" is happening to make these times bad ones, times of stagnation, and in the consecutive statements those above-described motifs of chaos and standstill are forever recurring. As I have already demonstrated, work is similarly described by the attributes of the world of chaos; it is a physical ailment, a state full of anguish, an unnecessary and draining activity.

> You toil and toil, then plant, what kind of work is that? Then you go out there, you fertilize, you gather stuff—and you take what you get, and if it all rots? And how do I know it won't rot? Now when you gather the crops they're sometimes rotten already, and then what? You've got nothing. And if instead of planting all that, you just went and bought food, you'd have the same as what you planted in the ground. … Where's the sense in that? If you're picking apples, there's so much work there, you have to bend over, two or three people go at a time. … You break your back … and nothing's what you've got to show for it … nothing. … They pay you eight grosze. … Then I spend it all on transport. (TR/PŚ/37)

In general, we might say that the tones of apples and pears that sit there (which bring in a negative economic value if collected) are a central motif in conversations in the Przysucha area. And indeed—what kind of ecology is this?

Dependency and Irreversibility: A Reproof at the World

We might cautiously suggest that we are describing a certain "apocalyptic mindset" that has appeared in these unemployed and impoverished villages. An "apocalyptic mindset," outlined by Pitirim Sorokin (1943), is a modus for apprehending history (Tarkowska 1993a: 92) in times of war, famine, and severe economic crisis. Then, as Sorokin writes (1943: 27–28), an increasing sensitivity appears, extremes become perceptible, and in particular, a sense of a lethal outside force develops, one that is often transformed into all manners of the catastrophic, magical thinking and fantastic associations of the most diverse ideas (ibid.: 35, 38). The apocalyptic mindset is also based on an experience of the cyclical nature of time, reshaped to a large degree through Christianity. What I have in mind here, as Aron Guriewicz demonstrates (1976: 105–120), is the cyclical mythical/ritual structure stretched across a line that ends with a point of destination, a line that forms the basis for the experience of time in Christianity (Brzozowska-Krajka 1994: 16–17). This transitoriness is thus linked with a shift on a cosmic scale. The Apocalypse is absolute time breaking through, changing the face of the world. Thus, the eternally green forests will wither, the most enduring institutions will be consumed by chaos and decay, and signs on the earth and in the heavens will pronounce doomsday—the end of the world. One might thus say that the elements of this transitoriness go together with the reutilization of history to create a societal sense of "collapse" or "renewal," so clearly present in the communication practices of the interior of Europe. Moreover, this is also a grammatical reality, expressed as the march of time (represented as a straight line) in European languages, where everything is constantly advancing, and every event brings irreversible change. In this cosmology, God can turn back the clock, but the changes that have taken place cannot be reversed (Eco 1992). This significance of change (as catastrophe) is thus deeply rooted in the language itself, in European grammars (ibid.). On the very level of language, the approaching change prompted by the economic recession or the catastrophic mood of (late) modernity described by Giddens (1990; 1991) is created by specifically "local" European eschatologies.

The experience of "bad transformation," ever-present in imaginations and repeated full force in the unemployed, post-transformation countryside once dominated by peasants/laborers, thus holds true to the structures of "long durée." We still find the overriding conviction, so prevalent in the countryside and generally articulated in then/now comparisons, that things will continue to change for the worse (Kędziorek 1996; Kocik 2001; Rakowski 2006b; Sulima 2003). The stable and correct world of the past is forever being contrasted with the dramatic, incomprehensible changes in the present/future (ibid.), in the present slipping into the future. Something else occurs here: in this way of experiencing life, change is revealed as an ontology that typifies these communities or, perhaps, as a "villager's philosophical anthropology" (Kędziorek 1996: 120), and a profound apathy sets in toward external processes, or toward the external world. "I told you, they want to hang us by the book. So they're hanging us. They've hung us, and they'll hang us some more. Because we stand no chance of picking ourselves up" (OST 1). "Things are dire here. And they won't get any better. Nothing's going to get any better" (TR/PŚ/26). In these reports the world is perceived as an incomprehensible and indomitable force.[4] "At 'Rozmet' I worked as a driver. ... I broke my contract and lost my rights to welfare ... end of story. I gave up. I worked in Chlewiska. ... There was lots of work, plenty of factories, the foundry in Rzucawa, there was also a co-op, and all those factories. ... Now there's nothing" (TR/PŚ/23). This was a statement from an unemployed man from Zaława. Here, such a depiction of one's own path, an inevitable path that runs "off course" or "all on its own," is extraordinarily significant: both work (what it is and who organizes it "isn't worth asking," "doesn't need to be mentioned") and dismissal from work come from the outside. Moreover, the fields become overgrown here as well—just as the factories were (or became) closed and "unemployment came along." One is forever hearing: "it sits there—it doesn't pay"; this involved a natural relinquishment. "And oaks are growing here on the fallow fields. ... Those ones are State-owned. ... I don't know what the community council will do with it ... they pay pensions ... and it sits there, it just sits there—what do I care" (TR/PŚ/5). As such, the fallow fields are an image of the shabbiness of all there is, and also of the society's powerlessness; they bear testimony to social regression.

This world is hence potentially *uncontrolled,* and as such, it begins—"on its own"—to drift irreversibly toward collapse, it starts to become "overgrown." Of course, such a picture is substantially derived from the "folk vision of the world." Here is a world constantly hovering on the brink of catastrophe, where all attempts to stop its decline, from scrubbing floors to participating in the flowery, decorative rituals of Easter Week, end in vain (see, among others, Tomicka and Tomicki 1975; and Andrzej Różycki's excellent film *Turki*). Such an approach to the outside world is most difficult to understand, however, as it is both total dependency on the world and—symmetrically, as it were—a duty to have an absolute impact on it, making for a peculiar and incomprehensible ontology, indeed. "Were it not for the actions of people," Joanna Tomicka and Ryszard Tomicki write, "the existence of the world would be threatened, or even impossible" (ibid.: 148). A certain continuity is visible here, creating a situation in which the world is constantly being *tended to,* in which person (the peasant) only "stands guard" over existence (Wojciech Pieniążek's phrase). He or she does not process the world in the sense of *creatio ex nihilo,* but only "manages" it, and with all power. Thus the world is controlled to the extent, one might say, as it depends on a human, and simultaneously, as a human depends on it; then it is controlled in a *total* fashion. This is a situation in which events transpire independently, and yet simultaneously require titanic labor (the principle of noncontradiction notwithstanding). "There appears to be," Wojciech Pieniążek and Grażyna Jaworska write, "the imminent threat of the existence of the world drifting into chaos. One must constantly try to maintain order [i.e., the experienced and created world]" (1995: 39). In this way a certain model of the human/world relationship (the "benevolent host" model), one that presumes all this necessity of *total* control over the world, is revealed and becomes comprehensible (ibid.: 37). The model of this relationship is profoundly present, I believe, in the above-described experiences of the unemployed villagers. However, this less signifies an acceptance of a worldview than it testifies to the internal chaos over which proper (i.e., full) control unfolds (and which then becomes particularly dangerous), which is why a force is needed to maintain order in the world. The unpredictability and inevitability of phenomena in the local reality of nature ("air, famine, fire, and war"), or currently, of that restless reality of the free market economy, are so mighty that only a total and omnipotent (despised, yet stable) power could grasp them. We are now able to understand that this world vision, this ontology, merges with the need for a centrally guided economy, a firm, outside hand supporting the world (at least, the "world of farming prices"), an all-overseeing host, or, to borrow Elżbieta Tarkowska and Jacek Tarkowski's phrase, a "Great Redistributor" (1994: 273–274). "If there were a host, this would all be different." You can still hear, "there's no host here" (also in the Bełchatów region, see TR/BŁ/22), "because the host's no good here—that's what I say" (TR/PŚ/37). These phrases can be heard in almost the opening words, as a matter of priority, the "host" being at once a bureaucrat, previously a party bureaucrat, and presently, perhaps, a council member. Lucjan Kocik (2001: 66) and Jerzy Wilkin (2000: 135) say without hedging that this is the "paradox of the Polish transformation." Kocik writes, "Most farmers prefer the visible, powerful ... hand of the State to the invisible and *unpredictable* [emphasis mine] hand of the market" (ibid.). "If only the prices were controlled by the government," Pieniążek and Jaworska's interlocutors were forever saying (1995). "There has to be stability for the farmer"; "There have to be ensured prices"; "There has to be regular credit, so that I can be sure" (OST/1, among others). "For grain, livestock, and potatoes there should be one price across the country" (Lublin Province, quoted from Pieniążek and Jaworska 1995: 34). This may not result from the helplessness of farmers against the market (or attempts to "force" an economic position, to limit the risk of the producer), it more likely derives from this permanent state of dependency; the enduring cultural experience is a profound sense of debility (Tarkowska and Tarkowski 1994: 275).

This has still more consequences—a visible mistrust appears in statements concerning non-State-run, private work institutions. The statement that one is "working for a private guy" is always said with reluctance. Compared to unemployment, it is only the lesser evil. "No jobs around—now you can only find private work" (TR/PŚ/26). "They're working with those private guys ... they've got workshops ... when it's the right season, you work, when it's off-season, guess what [no work]. ... There used to be so many [State-run] factories here" (TR/PŚ/10). "There were so many [State-run] factories, he worked, and he worked, and then what ... they fired him.... Now there's no factories, you've got no companies here, just the private ones, and what good's that.... Here today, gone tomorrow, or in two months!" (TR/PŚ/26). "My son's ... working privately now" (OST/1). "Those two only work under the table, for a private guy.... There used to be factories.... What are they living off of now? They're trying to pick up work [odd jobs, private work], grasping at straws" (TR/PŚ/7). And so we see a deep conviction of the negative value of "private" factories, "[private] factories, middlemen—they'll do us in" (TR/PŚ/7); of the fact that "private factories" are "bushes" (found everywhere), unlike the stable, "constructive" industrial or State-run factories. Some economic perspectives are also revealed here—an image of the entrepreneur who "buys" the farmer's labor, and thus earns money dishonestly ("The tradesmen earn there. He buys here, and travels there, wherever it's more expensive. And the people [the farmers] just look on and lose what's theirs," Lublin; Pieniążek and Jaworska 1995: 34). This concept is also tied to George Foster's well-known description of the peasant societies' image of goods being limited in the world (1965), which was applied by Tarkowska and Tarkowski in interpreting the Polish social reality of the 1980s (1994: 272–273). This is an ontological image whereby the "quantity of goods"—as a being of sorts—is constant and forms a "closed structure." It may be for this reason that a sudden rise in the prosperity of a neighboring village, or of a private entrepreneur (or tradesperson), or, ultimately, a general, sudden modernization, creates the (compensatory) impression of the local area's impoverishment (or even "destruction"; cf. chapter 3). Similarly, when an area suffers violent impoverishment, there must also be an imagined "criminal" excess in other people's hands, i.e., in the hands of the entrepreneurs, managers, authorities, government, or "foreign capital." This might also explain the constant association of entrepreneurs, tradespeople, or the wealthy with diabolical attributes: "The devils rock rich men to sleep," "The rich man's even happy in Hell," "The master gets richer off the sweat of the servant's back," etc. (an analysis of sayings, Marmuszewski 1998: 121).

And yet, something more is revealed in these images. The processes of economic activation, modernization, and entrepreneurship bring self-negating results—in the form of this "bad change." It is, in effect, entrepreneurship and enterprise that have come to accompany recession (incomprehensible as this may seem to us), becoming its flip side. "Enterprise" (*przedsiębranie*) is performed here by an ungoverned conversion of the world, the very Polish prefix (*przedsię-*) suggesting that the world has become a modern object, a "barrier," an imperative for people to be manipulative. "We had swimming holes, the boys swam there till October. ... Hortex started rinsing their apples there, and everyone rinsed them, all those substances started coming off. ... We'll have to fill them in with rocks" (TR/PŚ/38). "There was one private guy who set up a tannery, filled in the wells, filled in the drainage. ... Everything was all right as it was ... they shouldn't have messed with anything. ... The Health Department came out here once and couldn't unplug them, so they made them off limits. ... We had to pour stones in the wells. ... Now it all just sits there" (TR/PŚ/38). "There's nothing here any more ... only private guys. ... Everything lies fallow ... the earth just sits there" (TR/PŚ/38). The motif of "stopping" and "overgrowing" appears, paradoxically, right alongside the words "private guy." A chain of associations is thus formed: private employer–entrepreneur–object–stopped time–stagnation–chaos. "This month I got 50 grosze from the private guy!" one farmer said, "and next month it'll be 35 grosze! One carton of milk! How does that grab you?" (OST/1). "You can take it or leave it, the middlemen tell me. The same milk used to fetch 90 grosze, now it's 43 grosze—how can that be? I ask you. I don't know. Did the milk get dirty? Did the interest rate fall? It's just the middlemen getting rich off of our backs. And swindling us" (OST/1). There are similar statements in Pieniążek and Jaworska's research: "If only the middleman didn't make so much. ... The middleman does as he pleases ... , I've got no control over what he does" (1995: 30). According to this vision of the world,

free market is thus deeply distressing, or at the very least "unethical"—
"it promotes shrewdness or even trickery instead of hard work" (ibid.:
37). But how do this economic stagnation, this water contamination—
catastrophes of all description—absurd, arduous labor (chaos), this "private" entrepreneurship and modernization (the cosmos) add up to a
single conglomerate, to one body? I get the distinct impression that in
these pictures (in these accumulated social experiences), the state of the
ideal economy is the reverse of the "private" economy. Rather, it is a
state of an externally regulated reality, given that the model ruling "good
host" is omniscient and has *total* control over everything, no matter how
minute. In one village the "privately owned" shop was forever treated as
dubious: "He'll raise the prices on you," we were warned, while all the
men gathered at the old shop, the "State-owned" one, which had worse
supplies. Here we see a symmetry between omnipotence, the world, and
its overseer—the host (Pieniążek and Jaworska 1995: 38).

In the context of what we have said, the phenomena of the villagers'
passivity and resignation toward the world (Szafraniec 2002: 93–96),
of disheartenment (Wilkin 1988), of "the trauma of the Polish countryside" (Kocik 2001), or ultimately even "learned helplessness" (Zinserling 2002) take on entirely new significance. These attitudes became
visible during the transformation years of the 1990s. They are normally
perceived as a negative phenomenon, as a "civilizational incompetence"
(Sztompka 2000) or even a "societal phobia" (Kocik 2001) that creates
"cultural backwardness." "There's no work," complained the unemployed
in Ostałówek, "even though they guaranteed there would be … I signed
a paper" (TR/PŚ/17). "There would be [State-intervention] work—that
would clean up those forests [overgrown fields]" (TR/PŚ/17). "There
used to be work … they cleared the forests … there were potatoes here
… but it's all overgrown anyway … because after all, if there was work,
it wouldn't have got all overgrown" (TR/PŚ/17). We might therefore
say that in Poland the socialist, centrally governed economy was a component of the villagers' ontological structure and corresponded with its
internal code (Kocik 2001: 40–41), and against its internal economic
autonomy. "This is where they gather herbs," said an unemployed man
from Zaława, "we do the collecting … he [like the majority of our subjects, they did not know the name and the origins of the depot owner]
shows us what to get. … If something happens, *he* comes and we go out
[gathering]" (TR/PŚ/23). Here we can shift our analysis of the "bad
change" to the level of the most internal experience of the impoverished
countryside (the level of the incomprehensible, mysterious "idiocy of
rural life," to borrow Marx's famous expression from *The Communist
Manifesto,* 2004). Inside this particular sphere, relations with the outside

world are perceived as a constant risk, and every action that affects the outside world (using tools, collecting goods, drawing water from the well, building a hut, plowing) bears the stamp of this unease. "Each of these actions, though for us instrumental," write Joanna Tomicka and Ryszard Tomicki (1975: 149), "was composed of two layers—the rational and the irrational ..., expressing the deep conviction that man's every action in the world *disturbs the natural order* [emphasis mine]." Actions hold the whole rural culture of *survival,* and carry the sometimes obsessive baggage of "magical" or "ritual" acts, filled with pleading expressions of gratitude, at other times full of terror and dread (Olędzki 1999: 184, 186–189).

This human-world relationship is inscrutable. On the one hand, it is a culture of constant dependency, constant threat, and subordination of the world: "What can we do, sir?" (Biebrza vicinity, 1991–1993, quoted from Kędziorek 1996); "We've hit rock bottom, sir!" (Szydłowiec vicinity, 2005, TR/PŚ/26), "I believe that someone's in charge of this world, but now it must be the demons in charge, the devils in charge ..., because we're headed for the end" (Roztocze region, 2001, quoted from Bruczkowska 2004). "The land sits there. ... Everything's stopped" (Pawłów village, 2004). On the other hand, it is quite the opposite—an act full of tension, a constant "resurrection" of the earth (the springtime rites of revivification, the wallowing in the dry earth), actions as powerful and all encompassing as the dependency is. This is therefore an expression of "harsh destiny" (partly in the sense of Martin Heidegger's *das Geschick,* 1997, as furnished in the glossary), and simultaneously of the necessity to be forever grappling with the world, the necessity of this omnipotent control ("If only there were a host here. ... Someone who would finally deal with all of this," Majdanki village, 2004), to take preventive action, and only as such, the necessity of living in the looming shadow of failure. This is the basis of the experience of the countryside's culture of survival, as opposed to "survival strategies" themselves. As a result, this "prevention" encompasses the whole internal world, a world of nonadaptation and incomprehension.

This reality—the "survived world"—is, however, socially internalized, before forms of internal experience are found on the outside. In this way, experiential self-contained wholes are created—spheres of an intensively "cultivated" world, images of "overgrowth," "stoppage," and "contamination," in which physical, meteorological, technological, and economic phenomena are made fully *visual.* Insofar as the external world is deaf to the subjects' real actions, one might say that it sets itself in motion, becoming expressive and animate. James Frazer (1993) has created an "ecological compendium," detailing attempts to curse and beg the unbridled elements—"the perforation of huts," "the plowing of rain," the bridling of "the wind—the breath of twins." Now social phenomena occupy the place of natural phenomena; much as hailstorms and lighting once evoked terror (and still do), economic forces introducing "bad change" now bring a sense of menace, owing to their unpredictability. In the post-transformation village—as Lucjan Kocik writes—it is less "fear of the natural elements than of the effects of market games that weigh most heavily" (2001: 43). And much as villagers furiously lashed a river after a flood that swamped their homes and fields (from a statement by Wiesław Myśliwski, *Myśmy ustanowili przyrodę* 1994: 135), now the transformation has inscribed itself within this world, bringing catastrophic harbingers of "poisoning," "contamination," "overgrowth," and finally, "private business." One might say it is a local version of "the tragedy of development" (Berman 1983). This is a constant, engrossing being with the outside world—with what comes from the outside. It is a world upon which, despite all appearances, they *strongly depend,* and to which they pay unwavering attention.

Second-String Ecology

The experience of the recession (the "bad change") thus transpires through the cultivation of the body and the world (ecology). It is a certain existential style that is difficult to isolate; thus conceived, it is none other than a space of *normalcy*—of ontological security. The outside world works much as the body does; it occurs invisibly, through gestures and everyday rituals, in the use of the cultural infrastructures we do not always acknowledge (electricity, antibiotics). To unearth this world, I have invoked the way the villagers' daily rituals from the early twentieth century "cultivated the world." These include the turning points of dawn and high noon, and common rituals, or, more properly, rites (*obrządki*): washing, working, eating, removing garbage, saying everyday things.[5] The word *rite* here indicates, as in Polish linguistic custom, both ritual (ceremony) and cleaning, as in throwing out rubbish, or doing a range of other chores around the house.

As it is in this kind of imagination (Brzozowska-Krajka 1994): when the day begins, before the first rays of sunlight, the villager bends down, cups water in his or her hands, washes the face, eyes, and eyebrows, and takes water to his mouth. The use of water suggests awakening, the cutting of one's ties with sleep, which, as they say, is "a brother to death" (Pokropek 1993). Water opened up a new time, and *mobilized* the villager—after all, cold, "rousing" water was used in specially dosed showers to discipline soldiers, and even whole armies of "good-for-nothing layabouts" (Vigarello 2008). Nonetheless, water has equally often been

perceived as a poison that seeps into the pores and infects the internal
structure of the body ("dry hygiene"—dirt removed with a clean cloth—
is used to this day) (ibid.). The power of water is quite ambivalent, much
like a morning's ablutions; these are meant to close the nighttime state,
but for this to occur, time must rely on the power of the previous connection, or the resolution of what exists. The element of water is therefore a subtraction (–) state. A range of associations drifts from the night,
through the chill, the darkness, and the boundlessness of water, to the
sea—a motionless and amorphous being. Taking water into the mouth,
an act so typical for morning rites, can also be understood as growing
silent and "coming to a standstill," as the performance of a duty.

After washing, splashing water into the eyes, and spitting on the floor
came the real activity of the morning rites (Brzozowska-Krajka 1994:
78, and elsewhere). All the rubbish and dirt had to be cleared before the
sun reared its head. As converted substances, now used up and worthless, the status of dirt and rubbish is again a vague one, to say the least.
In folk tales it is before sunrise that refuse transforms into gold and
sparkling jewels (the chief concern with the overproduction of rubbish
is the waste of nitrogen, i.e., the "loss of a treasure"). Similarly, ordinary
water, collected from plant stalks "just before sunrise" and drunk drop
by drop, transformed into a marvelous substance that cured inflamma-
tion of the lungs.

Such transformations also took place during another daytime turning point, during the "culmination of the day," at noon. It was believed
that workers who did not pause in their labors in the field, who did not
return to their huts, would certainly lose their way, risking an encounter
with ghostly specters (the Polish *południca* actually derives from *połud-
nie,* the word for noontime) that ask bizarre questions and draw the respondent into absurd brainteasers (Brzozowska-Krajka 1994: 145–148;
for more on the meaning of folk brainteasers, see Tokarska, Wasilewski,
and Zmysłowska 1982: 86–87). Such riddles often made the respondent
choose between refuse and jewels. It generally turned out that the refuse
was the correct choice: excrement transformed into a swarm of bees or
a pancake with butter, i.e., into extensions of life, whereas the jewels
changed into extensions of death and loss, such as a venomous viper
(Brzozowska-Krajka 1994: 156–159). This transformation, this inevitable decision, correct only when it defied logic and all obvious instincts,
unveils the special nature of this being in the world—a position of irreversible dependency (Leder 2002). After all, the wrong answer to the
riddle immediately concluded with a cruel death—a bite of the viper.
The noontime culmination once again takes the form of an absurd, in-
human necessity. At dawn, the responses to the first greeting of "How's

it going?" are: "Well, you know," "It goes three ways: bad, not good, and rotten days," "You learn from your bruises" (Brzozowska-Krajka 1994: 96–97). A range of contradictory meanings and actions, of uncertain and random statements, thus obsessively filled the void (*horror vacui*) revealed at the turning point, though not just in order to fill it.

In light of this, recalling the menace in the dawn and noontime rites, brought on by the reality of the turning point, the everyday ecology of these impoverished villages takes on added significance. The daily rites—the two turning points of the day's cycle we are considering—are based on the lurking menace of an unfilled nothingness, on a sense of the permanent fragility of the world. If the rite was not concluded, it could cause the disintegration of the world or the course of affairs, not because the magic formula or rite "did not work," but because the world is essentially menacing and merciless. For this reason, all attempts are made to support the world, lest it should even slightly tilt out of balance—through the noncompletion of some rite, the contamination of water with detergent, through the emergence of "toxic dirt" generated by dangerous and destructive forces. This is a world of a dynamized equilibrium; a world, one might say, of "magical automatism," in which an incomplete rite brings a terrible punishment. Unemployment engenders the "tragedy of overgrowth," the use of chemical agents in the fields yields poisoning, and contamination and entrepreneurship must cause the whole area to fall into a recession. Just as sleeping through the dawn brings misfortune, and much like the work of modernization depicted in Edward Redliński's *Konopielka* (1975), these activities release invisible and immobilizing forces. "The rivers will come to a halt, the mills won't turn!" foretold the wandering old man in Redliński's book. "The birds will freeze in time and hang in mid-air! The trees won't grow! The hare will stop in mid-leap, and the wolf will stand behind him with jaws agape! Everything will freeze" (ibid.: 40). The menace of transformation, as a menace of a subtraction (–) state, thus reveals an absurd dependency on the world. "Everything sits there," an unemployed fruit grower from near Przysucha told me, "the Hortex plant sits there, only the devils mill about and do their work. Nothing, nothing changes, because it has no right to. There's not the slightest movement" (TR/PŚ/37).

* * *

The everyday activities in the village (established movements, morning curses, fattening lunches) that oppose the world of death/necessity are simultaneously focused on the latter's existence with all their might. As I have shown, the turning point is primarily a subtraction (–) phase, a stasis, a moment wherein being is suspended (Wasilewski 1989: 255–256). This dying time, this temporal inertia, is indirectly reminiscent of a study of rites of passage by Arnold van Gennep (1961)—a study of immobility. *Rites de passage* (turning points with a - sign) are an extremely powerful structure in the sphere of customs and in the sphere of tradition. With regard to the societies of "late modernity," we would rather speak of Anthony Giddens's "fateful moments," which are loaded with a risk.

As Giddens writes (1991), the sphere of the above-described ontological security is marked by an absurdity that creeps into its menace. With all their prosody, the body language, the freedom of movement, gestures, and gesticulations testify to the fact that "nothing is really wrong," that a physical environment and style of interaction are being maintained. However, the development and maintenance of such a "style" does take a great deal of energy, and encompasses most of the activities in cultures where the turning moments in contemporary life are designed down to the finest detail. This causes a situation wherein a very small disruption to the maintenance system reveals the momentary uncertainty of the "surroundings," the familiar and natural world swiftly turns fragile and alien—here Giddens writes of the unsettling thought of what might happen if "something went awry" in modern times. On the one hand, this might be a case of simply tripping, especially in a place that is particularly culturally "secure" (e.g., an exclusive event); on the other, it might be the sight of a lethal accident on the road we take to drive home every day. The sphere of normalcy and security is ruptured for a few moments.

The sphere of normalcy (Giddens's "protective cocoon") of everyday life in central Poland in the 1990s, a sphere of flowing time, when trucks of apples and black currants streamed by, and of limitless work in factories and farmers' depots, was interrupted by the laws of some ruthless mechanism, hitting this sphere in the underbelly—in the very heart of the *rites de passage*. This nightmarish "rupture" to the Świętokrzyskie lands reinforced the old-world beliefs of the villagers—that the demons of everyday behavior and daily ecology sprout from the earth. The three-pronged menace of change with its indirect zero-gravity point emanates from every action, and most of all, from every statement. One manifestation of this state was a social impulse ("Nothing, nothing changes, because it has no right to change. There's not the slightest movement" [TR/PŚ/37, among others])—an involuntary gesture, something called the "resignation response" (Wilkin 1988).

Through this rupture of normalcy, through the coming of the recession, which will not, after all, last eternally, there shines an entirely incomprehensible world—words reach us of a world filled with the constant renewal of menace, an incessant lament (the "tragedy of overgrowth"). The misfortune in no way disrupts the presecured and "imperceptibly" cultivated world of late modernity. It is not by accident that through "culture," this world is full of "existential security"—order, repetition, predictability, and continuity (what "human nature values," as Piotr Sztompka writes [2000: 27]). As an experience of a turning point and change, misfortune is paralyzing in its irrevocability. Whatever the attempt is meant to affect, trying to exert *influence* on the course of events is tied to an enormous fear. The start of day in the morning, the first gestures (cleaning, uttering first words), reveals an incomprehensible wound and an existential impasse. The turning of the world around the Przysucha orchards, the motionless fields and orchards, is a movement inside an incomprehensible, archaic culture. It is a world both ruthless and absurd, ever on the verge of falling inert, a world that requires morning riddles, face-washing, a filling lunch at high noon; one that requires a body to continue walking its course.

The New Face of the Jobless Village

Gatherers of Wild Herbs and Undergrowth, Gatherers of Fir Wood

An intensive "cultivation" of the surrounding world has become particularly visible in these regions, though it has been cultivated through the experience of its inevitability, its twilight, with the creation of new images of "overgrowth" (the "return/break-out of the forest"), a social poetics of forced change. We might say that this world has not disappeared at all, however, that it continues to be intensively "cultivated" and "experienced," that there is no complete "turning one's back to it": "I may well turn away from it," to borrow Merleau-Ponty's phrase, "but not cease to be situated relatively to it" (2002: 424)

In my research environment there is always invisible activity, resulting from the constant attention focused on a world in which even a refusal to communicate (silence and reluctance) is an intense form of communication (ibid.). It is particularly in times of rural economic degradation and in jobless villages that such things come to light: deeply buried, internal, cultural mechanisms for surviving the economic recession and the "bad change." This is a new environmental management, acting within entirely new conditions, operating on many levels and in various second-string ecologies.

Nonetheless, entirely new economic niches and new activities, what one might call "ecological" professions (to cite Laskowska-Otwinowska

2002: 228–228), have appeared in these regions of rural unemployment and poverty. These include every temporary manner of earning money and supporting a household in circumstances of impoverishment and unemployment. As I have already pointed out, many residents of these villages largely maintain their livelihood through gathering berries and herbs (both medicinal and edible); and elsewhere, through gathering fir tree branches (for garlands, wreaths, etc.). This gathering has become an almost universal source of income, and I have observed its scope increase from year to year in the various villages. For example, in the farming and nongathering village of Ostałówek, two women worked at gathering herbs in 2005; but by the next year, four families were at it, and their gathering took them far beyond the cultivated fields. In the Świętokrzyskie foothills, where I conducted my research, and particularly in the villages by the forests (Borków, Budki, Huta, Aleksandrów, and Majdanki), women and children carry buckets filled with wild blueberries in the months of June, July, and August. They freely speak of how their hands are "purple and scratched" through all these months (people will often show me their hands in conversations during this time). They generally go into the forests in the morning around 7:00 AM, and return more or less around 12:00 PM. Then vehicles drive around the fields purchasing wild blueberries (paying from six to nine zloty a kilogram, or more); as such, everyone is always bidding, determining who the best customers are and who is paying most at a given time. After that, some return to the forest around 4:00 PM and sell what they have collected on the following day—wild mushrooms, blueberries, raspberries, and sometimes blackberries are gathered and sold in similar fashion; some places have even opened up private depots attached to homes.

Collecting herbs and other forest plants is also on the rise. In the above-mentioned villages, whole families gather plants throughout most of the year—oak bark, alder buckthorn (illegally), birch tree leaves, about a dozen varieties of herbs, and other plants. The history of this gathering, we must add, is strictly tied to the collapse of farming. These circumstances, as we know, led to almost all the fields going fallow and overgrown, most over the course of ten or fifteen years, though some of the fields outside the forests, which were difficult to plow, had gone fallow prior to 1989, after having been given to the state for rent. Presently there stretch kilometers of fallow, thickly overgrown fields, with small birches and oaks sprouting up as well. After some time, people realized that many herbs and medicinal plants were growing in those overgrown fields; advised by people who buy herbs, they began gathering them to sell by weight. In such villages as Zaława, Cukrówka, Broniów, Ostałówek, Budki, Borki, Majdanki, and Huta, many people, primarily unemployed or retired women, and sometimes children (on the feminization of this sort of work, see Tarkowska 2003: 10, among others) collect enormous quantities of medicinal plants and herbs. Herbs in abundance included field horsetail, golden rod, tancy, coltsfoot, St. John's wort, medicinal valerian, oak bark, alder buckthorn, birch leaves, blackberries, linden flowers, yarrow, and many others that the collectors themselves are incapable of naming. Department vehicles drive there with buyers from "Herbapol" and other herb companies, and purchase herbs in increasing quantities. In Zaława, for example, there are at least two "herb man" vehicles making the rounds: the "Monday one," which collects sun-dried herbs, and the "one every two weeks," which collects more costly herbs dried in the shade. It is a subject of heated debate as to whom it is preferable to sell. This is, therefore, a very visible phenomenon, seen almost everywhere from May to September. Passing through the gathering villages, one sees bunches of herbs set out to dry, spread out on plastic on the roofs of houses, and whole families at work sifting through their gatherings.[6] Elsewhere, one sees piles of freshly stripped alder buckthorn branches, or people returning from the fallow fields carrying bunches of plants. This gathering is constantly and quietly discussed and arranged by the residents: who gathers how much, and to whom they are selling. This creates a socially controlled internal image of gathering, although as an attribute of the village society, it is associated with shame; many people at first reject this work, claiming to have only tried gathering once or twice. Later in a conversation, it emerges that this is an important part of their income.

Many people in other regions more to the west, such as the vicinities of Gałek, Stoczków, and Mechlina, have also begun gathering fir branches, which they refer to as "roaming for fir branches," a practice known since the communist era. These branches from the green firs that grow in the area are broken all the way up to the "crown" (which, as one of the residents of Stoczków puts it, makes the trees resemble something like a "Polish palm tree"). They are then bound in parcels and carried home, either on the gatherers' backs, or sometimes in a horse-drawn cart (or only occasionally by a tractor, as they prefer to go unheard). Later, the branches are collected and sold to florists in Łódź. They are most frequently used in making wreaths (although this gathering reaches its peak two weeks before All Souls' Day, when the demand is the highest, it goes on all year round, even through the winter). In the villages and the farmsteads that neighbor the forests you can sometimes spot whole families with children carting home tied bundles of fir branches, sometimes two or three at a time (one bundle weighs about ten pounds). The gatherers say it is getting harder to collect fir branches, and one has to wander farther and farther into the forest to find a good, "unpicked" fir tree. "Nowadays," says one young gatherer, "you can't get much from one fir tree … five or six bundles and that's that. … It's not like a fir in the old days! I remember tossing down fifteen bundles or more" (TR/PŚ/31–32). I should mention one more gathering practice here: the illegal gathering of kindling (in villages near forests), which was another source of income a few years ago.[7] Many people now take wood directly from wooded fields and—more to the north—from rural forests. "You can tell a rural forest—it's always picked through and thinned out, they go out to whatever forest they can find, and steal whatever's sticking out of the ground," an unemployed man from Zaława told me candidly. "Everyone does it," an unemployed resident of Cukrówka said. "They cut the birch trees to have fuel to burn. … People take it—because what else are they supposed to steal? Should they break into their neighbors' houses? … So if something is just growing there, and no one knows whose it is, they just take it" (TR/PŚ/21). Since the fields have been overgrown with birch saplings and oaks, there are more and more trees to cut down, and no one pays particular attention to whose land they are growing on. Some cut down slender birches only four or five years old.

To provide the full picture of how people earn money in these lands, I shall only add that many of the unemployed in these villages also take farming and construction jobs abroad, in the EU countries. Of course, there is also a seasonal job migration that occurs, which generally means trips to Germany, and sometimes to France, Spain, and Scandinavia for farm work (gathering cucumbers, fruit, etc.), and work for women in Italy as household helpers, though the latter return home to their families, children, or husband after stays of only a few months. Herb, blueberry, and fir-branch gatherers also try to find seasonal work, but this often meets with failure (such was the story of some gatherer women from Cukrówka and from Zaława), as they bring home only modest sums. Some of the inhabitants of these villages go to the Grójec area to do poorly paid apple picking, or to just outside of Warsaw, to do heavy, poorly paid construction work. I have noticed that many people also work for their neighbors who receive pensions, doing one-off jobs, running shops, or finding some decent seasonal work, and thus are able to put some money aside for later.

The "New Ecology": The Convertibility of the Environment

This gathering and exploitation of hidden "niches" in the environment is a social experience of inestimable importance. It is another invisible sphere of "cultivating the world," of remaining in constant contact (in a relationship) with the nearby surroundings. The "world where people live" is revealed here, but as a dynamic picture that shows us what is happening in the experience of "external" changes. It is a world based upon the appearance of impoverishment, unemployment, and the new gathering practices that have come as a result (much as previously, village poverty was everywhere accompanied by gathering kindling for private use, often from state forests). What course does this ecological record of the "transformation" take? All these quiet practices occur imperceptibly, I would even say in a prereflexive fashion, as a constant attachment to the environment—in this way, the environment also participates in the gatherers' internal narratives. This is a relationship between the memory of one's activities in an environment and repeated actions, and a new sense of orientation in one's surroundings, so that different aspects suddenly spring into view. The world is then perceived anew—the weeds ("for the fire") turn into herbs, and are elevated to become valuable medicinal plants ("horsetail—we gather it all 'round"). How can this be?

These herbs are gathered in these villages to be sold, but this gathering alone sets in motion new activities, even before independent knowledge is created. This is nonetheless a practical activity that quickly becomes highly skilled, physical, nonverbal recollection that is entwined in movements, gestures, and images, bypassing any expected "knowledge formula," any kind of "herbal knowledge." For example, through demonstration, I was often shown how "rootlets" (cinquefoil, tormentil) are picked. I was also told how easily they are picked when dry, in which forests and fields they grow, and in what kinds of soil. In more forested villages, such as Skłoby, I saw homemade hoes for digging them up (TR/PŚ/27). "We went gathering," I heard, "we gathered golden rod … they've got these little white leaves" (TR/PŚ/23). "Now these little rootlets are sprouting … these bunches of yellow flowers … and those you collect, you pluck the little ones and tear the fat ones in half. … I'd have to show you; then you shake the sand from the bag, and spread it out" (TR/PŚ/27). This knowledge is practical in nature, unlike knowledge that sets things in order, and it includes many pragmatic/applied details; this is knowledge "in motion," always restoring a concrete active situation ("It blossomed nicely here, big flowers, but no rootlets" [TR/PŚ/27]). It also combines counting with estimation: what is "easily" gathered, and what is harder to gather, what the weight of items is and what the depot rates are. The same goes for the wild blueberries and the fir branches—these are generally "numbers in motion," tending to take the form of price lists per kilogram, how these prices fluctuate, what is worth picking and what is "going strong." In this way, whole reams of numbers and calculations come about, sometimes compared in a very haphazard fashion. "Those blue ones—they were there, they gathered them for two złoty.... It used to be less, but now they pay more"; "Alder buckthorn 2 to 2.40 last year"; "Now you get 20, 14, 7 for wild mushrooms ... you can take them in"; "The little blue flowers come in spring and apparently they take them" (TR/PŚ/23). "You know—the ones with little yellow balls, they take those ones, and they pay four or five złoty for them." As we can see, it is not so much the names of the herbs that count—these are frequently not known, or forgotten—as the "recollection of activity," the "recollection of numbers" or "collection of numbers," and their constant comparison.

In this way, alongside the nonverbal knowledge of plants appears a special kind of reacquaintance with long-familiar terrain: "The one with white blossoms—it grows along the ditches, what's it called? ... Coltsfoot, we know it now, it grows outside of Pawłów under the bushes ... that must be good land" (TR/PŚ/27). "It has dark leaves like potatoes, and you have to know where to pull it out" (TR/PŚ/27). Furthermore, the long-internalized space of the village, the space of the cultivated fields, underwent an almost complete blurring. The gatherers know perfectly where the plots of herbs stretch; but it turns out that they often cannot recall either who owns the land where they gather the herbs, or the layout of the fields and their borders from when they were still being plowed. Once fallen into disuse, this division ceased to hold: "Who knows, really. ... Those are peasants' fields, but further on? Who remembers where people had fields? It's all overgrown." And again: "Here, maybe the older people remember that this was once mine, and over there belonged to you. ... There past the fence maybe belonged to Grandma, that rings a bell, but those fields I don't know, maybe they were Uncle's?" (TR/PŚ/21).

Under the surface of the experiences of "overgrowth" and the "bad change" emerge new fields of ecological perception, filled with unrelenting recognition of things and properties. The environment thus becomes a modus of remembering space, and simultaneously a modus for forgetting it, bearing testimony of human existence in the world, of ongoing involvement. "The environment," as Tim Ingold writes, "as distinct from nature or the 'physical world,' is the same reality constituted in its relation to a subject, or group of subjects, in their active engagement with it" (1992: 48). Thus emerges the surface of a shared, newly apprehended world, theretofore imperceptible. Gathering became widespread in the villages, described in a sudden and unannounced fashion; it became a social fact, or even a matter of course ("Here everyone goes gathering ... there's about nine families that do nothing else"). Gathering skills appeared out of nowhere, and no one was able to say precisely how it had begun: "We found out about the herbs from our neighbors ... how long was it—two years back. ... Now everyone goes gathering round here" (TR/PŚ/23). "They told us three years back that there's herbs here that they go out picking ... so we picked them a bit as well. ... You've got to lay them out to dry, wrap them up" (TR/PŚ/12). The origins of herb gathering are therefore socially imperceptible (i.e., forgotten): "Everyone round here gathers them, but how it all started, who I found out from ... I don't know" is a recurring refrain. Moreover, no one had previously known or even thought that these herbs could be gathered. Mint and St. John's wort were sometimes gathered. Some elderly women recalled (though seldom) how other herbs were gathered; but in general these herbs went unnoticed: "Thistles, St. John's wort, horsetail—they were just weeds. You picked them off the potatoes and threw them in the fire, but now I think—hang on, I'm not throwing those out, I gather them up—it's money, after all" (TR/PŚ/21). And so a new form of activity evolved—and along with it, a new environment, though no one noticed its creation, no one managed to notice how a new world was appearing—a new landscape of being.

In this manner the herbs began to be *perceived*. This changed a great deal in terms of the "cultivation of the world," as it is not neutral objects we are dealing with, but rather our relationship to our surroundings, with objects, or, in a word, with the world (Merleau-Ponty 2002), creating certain fields of the environment (see Ingold 1992). The body and its actions (e.g., gathering, seeking out wild herbs) are then carried over to the surroundings, and the relationship with the environment thus becomes the whole of perception—the whole of being. The effect of perception is not merely a new form of physical observation, as Ingold writes (echoing James Gibson). It is "a new state of the perceiver" (Ingold 1992: 45), who begins to apprehend things differently. Herbs suddenly "crop up" on all sides, they become visible: "It's all there under your nose, you just don't know it. You can go out there and work, pick them ... you just go and gather them up, and gather them up. ... They might be growing right outside your door, and you don't even know it" (TR/PŚ/21). Thus there emerge new skills of perception that create the environment—they create certain *resources,* deriving them from a socially formed attentiveness, through the whole of the active, physical involvement. Gatherers coming across an object in their surroundings immediately orient themselves around it, and immediately see it as not only an object, but as a resource for sustenance, heating, etc., seeing not only a "plant or a weed," but "money" (TR/PŚ/21). As such, new fields of social memory came about alongside this new activity, a new landscape of being, as Ingold wrote (1992: 48): "[the environment] is not separately cognized, prior to action, for it is by their action in the world

that people know it, and come to perceive what it affords." In her article
"From the 'New Ecology' to the New Ecologies" (1999), Aletta Biersack
demonstrates that the space of shared activity—practical activities in
the environment—creates a certain historical ecology, concentrating a
knowledge of the objects of culture present in the landscape that cannot
be put into words, inscribing a memory of practical/perceptual actions
(ibid.).

This is how a new, more fluid image of reality comes to be, a way of
conceiving both one's surroundings and oneself. The unspoken "knowledge" of these societies derives from their involvement in gathering.
What emerges is a new environment, invalidating the previous, familiar
"subjective universe" (*Umwelt*, a concept of Jakob von Uexküll's, quoted
in Ingold 1992: 42), guiding what might be called "searchlights of attention" into entirely different realms. Then the arable fields cease to be
arable fields, or "soil," and fields of herbs are seen to stretch all around.
It is astonishing that this landscape appears so unexpectedly: "Herbs are
growing here everywhere now"; "Who would have thought that all this
would come in handy!" (TR/PŚ/21). As such, this is an offshoot of the
activity itself: "It grows like gangbusters in those places, you just go and
gather it up" (TR/PŚ/21). Depending on the gatherers' activities (and
their efficiency, such as the effectiveness of their digging and picking),
further "incarnations" become visible in the environment, and another
"living" attribute of the environment comes to be—its active resources
are created (see Ingold 1992: 45). The significance of these goods as
coming from somewhere outside is thus accentuated; sometimes their
remarkable abundance and self-evolution are also emphasized (providing an analogy to autogeny): "It all sows itself ... all by itself it's
sown. ... I've never seen the likes of it. Now it's growing everywhere";
"There's this over here and that over there ... it's all over the place!" (TR/
PŚ/21). "There's so much of it! Tons of people gather it up here. ... Everybody goes gathering. ... There's somebody gathering in almost every
backyard!" (TR/PŚ/27). Herb gathering did not happen gradually. In
general, as the ability to spot and dry the herbs increased, and the conviction spread that they were "valuable resources," it happened suddenly.
It seeped into the sphere of immediate perception in a startling manner,
coming "out into the open"—and in a sense, all by itself: "They were just
weeds, I never suspected they'd be good for anything. ... There's tons of
it here!" (TR/PŚ/21). Gathering fir branches is spoken of in terms of a
similar autogeny. Through an involved activity, it was as if a magic wand
made resources of fir branches appear all around, and again we have an
"imagined abundance": "You know—the forests can't be destroyed here
[speaking of the fir branches that are broken off]! ... The new growths

come so fast, that we'll have them next year already" (TR/PŚ/31–32). "It's all in the tree ... when you tear them off, you leave three or four branches, and then it grows like mad. ... You can't destroy a forest [my interlocutors claim that forests are only destroyed by 'chemicals'], because then the new growths sprout, and then it grows like mad, it's like an element, nothing withers up, it lives, it grows even more" (TR/PŚ/30). (Firs, of course, do often die from having their branches torn off.)

A characteristic sense of ease also appears in the manner of gaining these resources. "They sow themselves!" is forever being repeated, and there is a certain "imagined abundance": "You go, they grow like gangbusters, and you just gather them up" (TR/PŚ/21). "We have a spot where we know there's bark, and we can cart it off a few sacks at a time" (TR/PŚ/9). As I have said, this creates a new landscape. It is made through all these utilities, these practices of going to take what is just "sitting there." It is a transition toward a receiving, gathering economy, which is immanently rooted in the village culture, an economy that "absorbs" the surroundings ("Everyone will be brought to ruin, you might croak, but the forest will still be there! ... We just gather the branches, it doesn't make any difference. ... What else should we do? Stay at home? Gather nothing? And let it all *rot*!?" (i.e., "It will go to waste if no one takes advantage of it," not "Let it rot, it makes no difference to me") (TR/PŚ/31–32). "The paradox of ecology," writes Czesław Robotycki, "is that the concept of 'ecology,' presently understood as protection and shaping of the environment, comes from the Greek *oikos,* which in one of its basic definitions means 'home.' The environment is thus the home, which can be set up according to one's plan" (1998: 154). Here we come to another, complementary side of the village culture of survival—one showing less a passive or a helpless face than one of a special kind of activity that draws everything possible from the surrounding space. The constant exploitation of this world for all it has to offer is a notion deeply rooted in the village culture. "The peasant would happily domesticate every animal," Wiesław Myśliwski once said (Jackowski, Myśliwski, and Sulima 1994: 135), an astonishingly apt statement with regard to this culture. You can also see an axiological order at work— otherwise the sin of prodigality would be committed, since something is just "sitting there"—and an aesthetic order restored, since a "beautiful" forest is not a wild one, but a "purified" forest, with no "old trees." The old trees that "sit there" and "rot" in the nature reserves and national parks are incomprehensible in village culture, and foster resentment (see the work based on the research just outside the Białowieska Forest on the creation of the Białowieska National Park, Bąk and Kamińska 2005). A forest should be "planted in rows" just "like grain" (Olędzki

1971: 185; cf. Stomma 1986: 134). In village culture every thing, every fragment of the world is serviceable, and this state is a cultural injunction to create frameworks of security. Once more this reveals an overriding meaning for these goods that can and should be exploited, a sort of "internal economizing" in the village culture, an endless recycling that processes the whole of the surroundings. Gathering, acquiring goods and resources, is almost a metaphysical injunction in this case. "They drag the trees from the fields, they take the birch saplings. ... They've got kindling"; "Trees from the forest, from the field. ... You've got to drag it all in, there's no two ways about it!" (TR/PŚ/23); "Hares? There were heaps of them around—you just had to reach out and grab them, everyone did it" (TR/PŚ/40).

This is how a certain local mode of social (non)memory manifests itself, transforming the surroundings and inscribing itself into the active environment—"in collapsed acts" (see Ingold 1992: 50). This is a collective conversion of attention to the world (see Merleau-Ponty 2002), in which the change in one activity simultaneously brings about a shift in the whole structure of knowledge about the world (illuminated by a social "searchlight of attention"). This process was outlined by Claude Lévi-Strauss in a famous essay called "The Science of the Concrete," where he showed how the Indigenous use rhizomes, bark, and herbs that "jumped out at him" every other minute from the surroundings (1994: 4–14). This "knowledge of nature" ("science of the concrete") is indeed a changeable and dynamic processing of the environment (and at once, the structure), and a constant, imperceptible creation of new uses, and new meanings. This means a constant transformation in the significance of the environment, along with a changeability in "local knowledge." These cultures are often seen as conservative ("cold"), but, as Jack Goody has demonstrated, they are often capable of "conceal[ing] considerable shifts from one decade to the next, even though this ethnic way of labeling, of talking about things, *appears to assume a continuity, a homeostasis* [emphasis mine]" (1986: 6). This changeability, of course, is nothing new in local cultures (or folk-type culture, as I would sooner phrase it), in the villagers' culture. The term signifies an ongoing adaptation in the face of danger as a culture of survival, in which adaptation *itself* is suddenly the whole of cultural being-in-the-world. This also includes spheres of practice and communication/perspective that are *indistinguishable* (see Buchowski 1993: 31, 37–48; Olędzki 1971: 212; Tomicka and Tomicki 1975: 149). What is continually being revealed here is the remarkable dynamic of extraverbal, oral, action-based memory, in which there is a constant experience of the environment, and as a result, of the whole human world. It is where "human bodies are in constant contact with the environment throughout their lives," and where an ongoing, emotional "creation of space" within the culture is reached, a historical ecology, endlessly inscribing everything that "happens in the surroundings" (Biersack 1999). The fallow fields full of medicinal herbs are the clearest example of these transformations in a world that is both socially remembered and forgotten.[8]

In the culture of the jobless villages, full of reflexes and "imaginary threats" (of fatal transformations), this is perhaps yet another sphere of being in the environment—this time of active and practical ecology. It is this that reveals its ability to change, to cling on, and to adapt to new circumstances. This is an attitude of active involvement in the world, of delving into its every available fissure, of building new and "unnamed" skills. It is a world under constant observation.

Collection, Conversion, Transition

This unemployment, regardless of how it may look from the outside, is in no way "passivity." It is a constant relationship with the world upon which it depends, in spite of everything. In this world, those who experience "overgrowth" are not passive objects; they do not live in a cultural vacuum, but change their situation, grasping for new and imperceptibly "arising" methods of adaptation and "cultivation." This is a means of survival in conditions of regression and unemployment by returning to tried-and-true formulae.

In times of crisis hidden reflexes emerge in the villages to retreat to deeply buried forms of existence and farming behavior. Justyna Laskowska-Otwinowska (1998: 21–22, 31–32; see also Sikorska 1999: 127–142) writes that if a "bad time" came in the village of old, family and neighbor ties were strengthened at the beginning of the famine, and then became mutual "non-market protection." In the villages I researched, I noticed a similar phenomenon, albeit sometimes feigned; this showed itself primarily in neighbors hiring one another to work at jobs, sometimes not for payment, but as barter, a certain "closed" network of exchange of assistance, as Joanna Sikorska puts it (1999: 137–138). For instance, an herb gatherer from Cukrówka did her neighbor's sewing and ironing; the teenage son of an unemployed couple in Zaława and a young pensioner from across the street helped repair a neighbor's fence; and in Stoczki, a young, unemployed fir-bough collector helped his cousin in construction. Such work was very widespread, and, because of this mutual paid or bartered work, more than fonce I wasted days on end because, for example, I was unable to set a time for a conversation or a gathering excursion. The story of these internal neighborly services and their payment is, however, an extraordinarily vague one, since it is a touchy subject that is passed over in silence, a closed competition with a certain code of communication, and one that is generally hidden from outsiders such as myself. They do provide a certain security, however; a certainty that ultimately there will be "work of some kind."

Another sort of survival is the reduction of personal needs and a total reduction of the cost of living, down to the very limits. This generally occurs, as Kocik terms it, through "cultivating self-exploitation," concentrating on the internal circulation of materials and management of energy (2001: 36–37; see also Szafraniec 2002: 94), through creating frameworks of economic and even ontological self-sufficiency. This reveals a whole ecology of survival—an internal *autarkia* of poor households. What is its basis? In many locations—and this is the more frequent phenomenon—those unemployed in industry leave themselves only two hectares of land to cultivate for their own needs, in order to qualify for unemployment benefits (the same goes for retired farmers—the land allows them to receive their benefits). During times of unemployment and burgeoning village poverty, people live off their parents' farming or factory pensions, and also off their farms (on the statistical average of the "five-hectare household living off the pension of the elderly father," see W. Gadomski, quoted in Kocik 2001: 64; on the role of the pension and retirement in the village, see Korzeniowska 2002; Halamska and Maurel 1997; Laskowska-Otwinowska 1998: 29, also writes on pensioners as the "village bankers"; see ibid. 2000: 137; see also Rosner 2000a). "The farm," in Kocik's view (2001: 64), "then serves strictly as a source of nourishment and minimizes the social risk." As Maria Halamska and Marie-Claude Maurel indicate, the village in these sociological regions thus sets a trap for those who are not capable of "actively" participating in economic life, i.e., for what sociologists call representatives of "socially handicapped categories" (retirees, pensioners, and the unemployed). We can also follow Andrzej Rosner's lead and speak of the concentration of "village zones of progress barrier accumulations," such as the zone of the ex-COP (see Rosner 2002; cf. Kocik 2001: 65). Such farms provide means of *survival* with minimal cash inflow; the inhabitants are closed off and participate to a dwindling degree in monetary/goods exchange with the outside world (Halamska and Maurel 1997: 23; cf. Kocik 2001: 65; Laskowska-Otwinowska 1998: 24–25). In one such farmstead in Mechlin, three unemployed brothers lived off their mother's farming pension (around 500 zloty per quarter) and sometimes off one-time designated benefits. They plowed three-hectare fields with a horse and old machines, fertilized the soil with manure supplemented by only small quantities of niter, ate their own crops, and ground the grain for the poultry (though the village does have poor soil, multicrop farmsteads work quite adeptly with modern machinery). Things are much the same in agricultural Ostałówek, where the majority of farms produce for their own needs and for livestock feed, fertilizing with manure, sometimes with added niters, and sometimes with "Polifoska" (chemical fertilizer) when the farmer can afford it. The main plowing force in the village is the horses (there are around thirty of them). Few buy fertilizers from the outside, most burn cheap sawdust in the "*trociniaki*" (sawdust-fueled stoves), thus paying only for the electricity and a small tax on the land. There is no plumbing either, which means no payments (a few villagers deliver milk, and a few also sell grain or potatoes).

What we are therefore dealing with is only a minimal money-based circulation (see Laskowska-Otwinowska 1998: 25, 31). This shifting of existence to the lowest gears, where survival is possible almost "on its own accord," is clearly visible in particular in the poverty-stricken families with many children, supporting themselves on pensions, family/care benefits, and the men's poorly paid odd jobs. In one village (Gosań), a family living in an old hut with neither plumbing nor a washroom supported itself on the gatherings of the mother and children, and essentially focused on household activities (washing clothes, cooking, caring for children, etc.). The villagers perceived the family as social outcasts and non-independent. Observing how the family functioned and how it took its benefits, everyone said, "They make more off those benefits than the rest of us here put together." Things were much the same in Mechlin village. A very impoverished family (from which the parents had finished "special schools," and were under the constant supervision of social care workers) had found an old hut in which to live. They were given funds and felt upholstery to repair the holes in the roof. Here, the cost of living boils down to firewood payments (though they generally gather wood from the forest) and taxes; they live without electricity or plumbing, and make a little extra money collecting fir branches. In Ostałówek village a widow and her four children live in much the same way, in an old, draughty hut with sawdust heating and no plumbing; she cultivates a few rows of vegetables and this, she says, "keeps her going." In all these situations, where none of the villagers have arable land, the choice of residence is linked less with farming than with finding a place in a village, where the cost of living is minimal, and where they can practice an economic recycling that allows them to survive. In every other case the families came from a town, such as Szydłowiec, Kamienna, or Skarżysko. Elsewhere (in Cukrówka village, for one), I also came across young families that had moved from a larger town (Szydłowiec) to support themselves "more easily" (TR/PŚ/25). Katarzyna Osiadacz (2006), for instance, noting a similar phenomenon in northern Podlasie, describes a group of families returning from the cities to the village farmsteads (often inherited from parents or grandparents), not to cultivate the land, but to cut the cost of living. We have come to call this movement back to the cities in the 1960s and 1970s a "backlash" (Gilejko 2003: 15). There appeared an imagined limit to costs through "preventive conversion."

Other characteristic phenomena emerge here as well, blazing a new path of adaptation within the impoverished and degraded village. A village household is capable of absorbing large "excesses" of people, and also excesses of things, through replacement and conversion rituals (cf. Sulima 2000). By spring, I saw immediate results of work in many places. At the end of April, when the poplars growing alongside the roads in Ostałówek are pruned, villagers begin collecting whole piles and trailers full of thin and thick branches. The villagers are constantly converting this poplar wood for sale, saying it is "good for making boards," but they chiefly collect it for firewood. This is an example of a spontaneous collective need to convert the immediate surroundings into something useful, and also the need to stockpile. I kept seeing inhabitants who were busy collecting firewood: "Here you've got to gather firewood all year round for the winter," they said. Many people dragged trees (young birches) from the fields: "I dragged some trees from the fields," an unemployed man from Zaława told me. Yet, at the same time, I know that most of the households in Ostałówek use the cheapest kindling—i.e., sawdust—and burn it in sawdust stoves (one "cart" of sawdust is enough for the winter, and the cost of the material itself is around thirty zloty). In times of unemployment, many people busy themselves stockpiling wood, which visibly appears to be too much. This collecting, it seems, becomes more important than the actual need: it is an imperative to use what is all around, to manage things, to drag fallen poplars, to collect and convert objects, to create little piles of firewood from the saplings stripped of their bark. I believe all this springs more from carrying out an inner narrative (the "narrative of survival") than it serves to address real needs, since there is fairly little firewood to be had from the kindling. Drawing upon work by Rosner (2000b: 92—on the phenomenon of village unemployment), Kocik (2001: 56) writes, "The peasant understanding of 'spendthrift behavior' is unlike the concept of the market economy. It signifies a lack of wastage even when the cost of being thrifty with a given item is higher than the profits to be gained."

Materials and items are circulated to an increasing extent through this constant "working around the property." Things are forever stockpiled and converted or collected "out back." The most peculiar stockpiles can be found in yards, including rusted farm machinery (plows, seeders), sometimes weapon parts, but also tires, plastic bags, tiles, bricks, and cardboard. These things are often given the strangest applications, and are generally made to serve as provisional building materials. A sheet of rusted metal is attached alongside some coal—because "that's where it fit." These yards are constantly being converted, particularly in the villages that are still somewhat agricultural (Ostałówek, Mechlin), and you can see yards filled with the most varied objects constantly being converted, sometimes in quite imaginative ways. In Ostałówek the doors of the sheds and barns are often hung with various chains, ropes, and machine parts, as well as the license plates of motorcycles, cars, and tractors, both old and relatively new, creating a "gallery." One farmstead, inhabited by three unemployed brothers who did odd jobs, is filled with the typical array of junk. They have nine sacks of "magnesium fertilizer," and a "bench" (a black seat from a large vehicle, raised on small piles of breeze blocks and rubble). There are two or three large pieces of something unrecognizable (presumably parts of old, rusted vehicles, perhaps farming machinery), objects resembling rusted machine belts hanging on a log near the shed's entrance, tools, and a homemade hanger (Plińska 2006). At an afternoon meeting for coffee served at a "table," which resembles a stool with a strangely large seat, two stools are brought out, one of which also has an unusually large seat, "converted" out of very thin boards (ibid.). An object is not a finished product, one might say, but is always an object (at least in part) that can be used in a new, different way. When multiplied, this endless practice of converting things in these villages of jobless people with "excess time on their hands" (Tarkowska 1997) also lends more visibility to things, which causes them to circulate at an increased speed. They also start to "pile up," to borrow Roch Sulima's phrase (2005), to "boil over," to cross beyond the farmstead. This constant collection of goods and their continual conversion and supplementation, this reworking of the yards with disregard for real need, causes an "overproduction" of internal trash. This is less as a result of the civilization than of its inertia, of its imperative to be constantly converting things, heedless of the unemployment (Sulima 2000: 47–48). The final outcome is an invisible space of self-rationalizing behavior—a private "cultivation of the world"—in which a sense of "constant movement" (and thus constant [in]security) is forever present. This is capable of fitting or compacting the scope of materials and needs, and simultaneously, of granting a metaphysical sense of collecting, of converting, of "omni-circulation."

The status of these goods/objects during a time of shortage, with the threat of hunger and the lack of materials, firewood, etc., thus extends their applications, and suspends their characteristics. Then everything becomes useful, all material goods are weighed with the imperative to be used, so that nothing should "go to waste"; but because the application of goods is forever expanding, the majority of things are "potential goods." This is, therefore, a material world that undergoes proprietary transition. Special relationships to possessions emerge. Through these transitions, sole possession cannot be claimed by any single person or a defined institution; this is also why every public or private piece of property that is just "sitting there" is always a potential reservoir of valuable material and—perhaps—ought to be utilized. This is most probably why the social history of peasants constantly mentions their tendency toward theft and acquiring outside goods. It may also explain their tendency to use both the goods of the farm properties (Palska 1998) ("The lord's meadows," they once said, "bring sorrow when they're empty") and, during communist times, of the state farming organizations (ibid.; Tarkowska 2002: 92–93; see also Tarkowska and Tarkowski 1994: 276; Wasilewski 1986: 52), or even of their own internal farms, e.g., "finding" materials at their neighbor's house that could "come in handy."

This is also, I would argue, a silent and extraordinarily active "local knowledge," generally quasilegal (cf. Geertz 2005b), in which whatever lies there unused *must* be adapted or changed, its status becoming dissolved. A window shutter, for instance, can wind up in a village shed/ barn as a "handy" ledge or platform, or as a screen to seal off the pigpen. In one village I know near Chrzanów (Bolęcin), they collect less valuable pieces of equipment that might "come in handy." Such activities are described as "kidnapping"—as in the neighbor "kidnapped" the rake or "kidnapped" some good sacks, and the wronged individual swore that they would "kidnap" something else in return. In these places, mutual theft is a very active internal behavior—what the village "lives on"—that is invisible to outsiders. This has a peculiar status within the society. It is a silent, hidden knowledge or competition, something everyone knows about, but of which they cannot really speak, even behind closed doors. In Broniów, Cukrówka, and Zaława I was told that theft had become a "real plague" (TR/PŚ/44). Three cows had recently been stolen ("Only the chain was left"), as had a bicycle ("The guy who steals it only rides it out to the field … and leaves it there … and then comes back again for it the next morning"). A cement mixer ("Then it turned up just over the fence—in the neighbor's backyard") and a well pump ("The guy who borrowed it earlier stole it") had also gone missing. These may, of course, be to some degree spontaneous fabrications. Yet these statements are conscious of a certain "frivolousness" to the status of theft ("The bicycle—he just tossed it in the bushes"), and of the role that it has long played in village culture. These stolen objects are something akin to transitional or medial objects, and ultimately magical ones, crossing into folk myths, as for example, about the creation of man in the hands of the "creator's helper" (see Tomicka and Tomicki 1975; Wasilewski 1980). We can also see that this is a sphere that creates the "silent knowledge" of the village. Everyone knows "who steals," I was told on numerous occasions; if something disappears, almost "everybody" knows who took it. The same thing could be said for Ostałówek. When an aluminum pot was stolen from one housewife, she knew a minute later who had done it. She merely said, "I'll take care of this," which meant she would do it quietly, without admitting in public that something had been stolen. Another man responded in much the same way. When some machine parts—a bit of rubble, in fact—were stolen from his backyard, he knew at once who was responsible. He decided to tell no one it had happened, and he said a little while later that he would go over there during the night and "take it all back himself" (ibid.). All this took place in the presence of the ethnographer. In this way, theft becomes a silent social competition; but it reveals itself to be essential in the culture of survival, treating objects as transitory or fleeting, paired with the imperative to use and convert them. This "converting" inside the village culture, in the microcosmoses of the farmsteads, is thus capable of absorbing practically any quantity of "outside" material.

The "Culture of Survival"

In this way, we can create an inner-cultural picture where this internal reflex, this village "economizing," covers the cost of living (or provides imagined self-sufficiency). Of course, this is also a practical ability to get by at the limits of one's personal capabilities; then this internal circulation, or household recycling (Kocik 2000: 74–87) transpires almost unimpeded, becoming a socially generated picture of "effective conversion," an "internal metabolism" reduced to the minimum. "There's always something for the taking in the village, everything's yours—and so you can live," I was told repeatedly, even from those who were "migrants" to the villages around Bełchatów, in Rogowiec, and in Trząs (TR/BŁ/6, 10). What evolves is a conception of economic automation, a mechanism resembling a *perpetuum mobile*. In several places I heard, for instance, that poultry—hens and ducks—were "hatching like crazy." "It's mainly the little creatures, hens, geese, ducks … and other things, that can live off the earth" (OST/2). These creatures are born all on their own (cf. *Myśmy ustanowili przyrodę* 1994), and so the earth provides the life-giving basis for this "effective conversion," or even a certain notion of autogeny. This may also be why in Ostałówek the soil is mostly cultivated on the principle of inertia, to maintain the "economy" and the framework of security. "Here people really work the fields, because if they didn't … if they didn't work them, then we wouldn't have anything"; "All I hear 'round here is hold onto the land, hold onto the land, something might still be coming" (TR/PŚ/20). Here we can see both the pragmatic virtue of possession and an imagined "automation" ("autogeny"), and an "ensuring of existence," of working and collecting goods and keeping them in their yards, one that reaches back to their reflexes, to their peasant (farming) roots.

> Ethnographer: And if they stop collecting the milk … are you going to have to pour it out?
>
> Interlocutor in Ostałówek: We hold onto it!
>
> E: But you'll have to pour it out. …
>
> I: No! The hens will drink it! The hens will drink it. They won't catch any kind of bird flu. … End of discussion." (OST/1)

We can also perceive here how leaving impoverished women (social welfare receivers) in the sphere of household chores—laundry, sewing, gathering firewood, cooking, sometimes cultivating the garden—testifies less to a need for survival than to a necessity to create a minimal sense of security. "We live with the lowest expenditures, as cheap as possible" (TR/PŚ/3); "Things are terribly rough for us … we can't afford any of the payments … others here economize a bit … it's very hard for us to get by" (TR/PŚ/3). Here it becomes clear that this "circulation of materials" contains something significantly greater, that such economizing constantly incorporates the survived world, and this is where the unspoken life of impoverished village women takes place (Tarkowska 2003: 10–12). Any good seldom comes of collecting rubbish ("because it comes in handy"), of replacing old, worn parts of a fence (the "patch the patches" strategy), or of laboriously gathering branches and stripping their bark for kindling (the resulting firewood is not worth the effort, given the option of burning sawdust). This firmly rooted "thriftiness," this reflex to economize, often independent of its effects, now shifts into the foreground; and above all, it grants the opportunity to create an imagined "living security," "living for nothing," a security that takes the form of certain rural abilities (conversion, adaptation).

One such field of activity is, as I have already mentioned, the incessant (and in a sense, excessive) work on the farmstead, in the yard, which is no longer a yard for active farming. Therefore, this is a move toward a psychological "private garden," when participation in the old world, with its abundance of industrial labor and stable work, is no longer possible. "In those days, if they fired him, then they'd just take him the next day at Stąporków ... they were just waiting to hire him elsewhere" (TR/PŚ/24). During one of my conversations/interviews in Zaława, the fence was constantly being mended. A housewife, a young neighbor of the pensioner, and the eldest son of an unemployed married couple were working on the fence, exchanging old pickets for equally old ones, and using old, straightened nails that were soaked in oil before they were pounded in place. In Ostałówek I continually saw villagers paint and convert huts; and for days on end, I saw them inside their yards building fences of new boards from poplars cut down locally. In yet another village three men (one a pensioner, and all unemployed) painted their new fence with tar, spending the whole day on it: "We're tarring the fence ... we're making a fence. Well, you know ... everything's breaking down here ... what else is to be done?" (TR/PŚ/26). Things were much the same in the villages near the forests, as I have already stated, as during conversations they kept going to somebody's home to work on their well, or to strip old windows, paint fences, or repair a gate; they worked together, and thus filled up another day. This is a reflex to be constantly and forever at work, a ritualized "work around the yard"; except that this work results from a need to act that is tied to unemployment, and absorbs unemployment within itself (cf. Sikorska 1999: 127). This works in new, disquieting circumstances. Like a move to a large block of flats in a city, it gives a certain basis to an existence that is not necessarily material. This household self-employment, as Lucjan Kocik demonstrates (2000: 57), is a form of substitute activity in itself. "The farmyard," as Kocik writes, "has been a place where everyone can feel useful, even if his/her usefulness is not needed" (ibid.). The "non-productive existence" that came about in the once industrialized countryside, and the general experience of unemployment (the fear of being unnecessary) are reflected in these intensive activities. These images of constant "movement" or "circulation," create a "ritual of survival," a certain community of repairs, reconstruction, and labor, in a time when everything "is just sitting there" (Sulima 2000: 27). These are the alert reflexes of the old peasant instinct for prevention.

Notes

1. The signs of bad changes taking place in the world were often seemingly invisible—crops are harmful, though they might seem even too good, healthy, robust, "can't recognize them ..., they are poisoned, it [tomato] looks so fine from the outside, so red and round—but it's poisoned," "beets are huge" but they have a burning taste,

"tomato looks nice from the outside, but it's all green inside, food poisoning guaranteed" (TR/LB/10), "potatoes turn grey when mashed" (TR/LB/9).

2. In the villages of Budki, Borków, and Aleksandrów (the vicinity of the Chlewiska-
    Szydłowiec line), or Gałki and Mechlin (the vicinity of the Przysucha-Giełniów
    line), farmers generally possessed one or two hectares and produced food for their
    own consumption. Milk was put aside if it was to be sold, and animals were sold as
    well. Furthermore, these villagers carted off wood they found in the wilderness, often
    illegally gained, and sold it in the evenings in the farming villages to the north, or
    exchanged it for a wagonload of potatoes or grain. In such villages they said that the
    "*leśnioki*" (forest folk) had come with wood. "I still remember," said a farmer from
    Ostałówek, originally from nearby Jankowice, "how the *leśnioki* would come driving
    up with the wood. They always had strong, beautiful horses, and we always admired
    them" (TR/PŚ/20).

3. Grain, potatoes, and livestock were sold then at good, firm prices, and people trav-
    eled to the Main Square in Szydłowiec to get even better prices for their surplus
    goods. These villages were thus more agricultural, though the majority of villagers
    also worked in steel mills, rolling mills, and various factories (including military
    ones).

4. Such an image of the world is visible in rural laments on death (Kędziorek 1996:
    118), but also on those of catastrophe, epidemics, floods, and sometimes infertility
    and hunger (cf. Sulima 1992: 85). These are forms of "futile questions" in mourning.

5. I am borrowing heavily from a work by Anna Brzozowska-Krajka (1994).

6. The presence of these ways of life among the unemployed inhabitants of villages, as a
    certain acceptance of a natural order, is testified to by an article in the local "Biuletyn
    informacyjny" (news bulletin) of the Chlewisko District of June 2003. The article is
    devoted to the "burning of agricultural waste," but it mentions the widespread gath-
    ering of undergrowth and herbs. "In the spring and summer periods," writes an ed-
    itor, "gathering from the forest undergrowth (blueberries, blackberries, mushrooms)
    is often the sole, or an additional source of livelihood for many people, and even
    whole families, supporting their existence for months at a time. The burned areas
    thus limit their means of earning money, and we all know how difficult it can be to
    find work to bring in an income these days. Another source of income for the local
    inhabitants is gathering medicinal herbs, such as St John's wort, coltsfoot, valerian."

7. Cutting wood, particularly in the villages close to the primeval forests, is illegal.
    The period of their real "wood bonanza" ended over five years prior to writing (TR/
    PŚ/47).

8. It is, however, socially manufactured and recalled, a process of action. Like our per-
    ception of the world, we perceive it because someone is acting in it (Ingold 1992:
    42). It is, therefore, something akin to perception protention and retention, an envi-
    ronment organized around a subject that is behind (in time) and simultaneously in
    front.

Figure 1. The Szydłowiec and Przysucha Environs

Figure 2. "There's nothing around, everything's been overgrown ..."

Figure 3. "The Hortex plant sits there, everything sits there"

Figure 4. Orchards/Motionlessness

Figure 5. "They only accept tart apples in the fall"

Figure 6. Collecting, Conversion, Transition

Figure 7. "I dragged some trees from the fields ..."

Figure 8. "Thriftiness"

Chapter 2

Wałbrzych—Boguszów-Gorce

From Destruction to "Empty" Communication:
The Liquidation of the Coal Basin

The City and the Mine

Wałbrzych is a place that felt some of the most acute effects of the post-1989 transformations. Over the last dozen or so years the town has become a basin of illegal coal extracting practices. Wałbrzych bootleg mining ("holes" or "little mines") have been photographed and described in countless Polish and German newspapers under such eye-catching headlines as: "Silesian Moles," "Moles from the Bootleg Mines," and "Mole-Men." During communist times (or more precisely, since the early nineteenth century), Wałbrzych was a mighty center of the coal industry. Though the surrounding areas do have a few other factories (ceramics, foodstuffs, machine, electrochemical, and textile branches), it was, in fact, a coal industry monoculture (Skiba 1997c; 1979). Wałbrzych mineral coal mines—the Wałbrzych, the Thorez, and the Victoria—began to be liquidated in the early 1990s as part of the "mining restructurization" (cf. Skiba 1997a; 1997b). Most of the people employed in the mines or in the institutions surrounding them (including daycares, preschools, and cultural centers) lost their jobs for good, while "job offer" ads through the Labor Bureau began to include the phrase "Miners and ex-convicts need not apply" (Urbanek 1998: 76).

Vast unemployment, the scale of which can only be estimated by the official indicators (for example, in the post-mining town of Boguszów outside of Wałbrzych, the estimates of the Labor Bureau register about 60 percent unemployment), thus resulted in Wałbrzych and its environs.[1] During the time of my research (again, according to the Labor Bureau in Wałbrzych), the unemployment rate reached 28–32 percent.

What did people start doing? Many ex-miners and workers began extracting coal from shafts that were only a few meters long. At first it was in the town itself and its environs that semi-open-cast mini-mines began appearing, initially in 1999–2000, and according to some, as early as 1997–1998 (Pawłowski 2004). Sometimes they were worked by over a dozen people, but chiefly by ex-miners whose social welfare and redundancy payments had been exhausted. Initially, they rented heavy gear to unearth coal deposits running close to the surface, extracting it straight from the uncovered vein. However, after a series of confiscations (mainly in 2002), the loss of this heavy gear meant that all the work had to be done by hand. The miners built mini-shafts, measuring from only a few to seventy meters in length, using a very ingenious and complicated strategy. It is hard to say precisely how and where it all began. Whenever I inquired as to where the bootleg mining in Wałbrzych had originated, I was told of a different region (Biały Kamień, the vicinity of the Barbara shaft, the Sportowa Street vicinity running toward Mount Chełmiec, and many others).[2] It would seem, therefore, that no one is able to pinpoint where coal was first illegally extracted; and often, particular groups of miners have their own stories about its beginnings. Numerous variants of the most diverse stories appear in various parts of Wałbrzych. At any rate, bootleg mines are seen all over Wałbrzych, and in many adjacent locations. For example, in a local press article, published in February 2004 (Smerd 2004: 10–11), seven different regions with bootleg mines were identified, and their number was found to be growing, not decreasing, as the mining spread onto the outskirts, into the depths of the province. The number of people working this way was estimated at from two to six thousand.[3]

Many ex-miners and industrial workers also collect scrap metal, which remains in vast quantities in the abandoned buildings and in the ground around the factories. The tales of my interlocutors indicate that the story of the bootleg mines began with the search for scrap and other resources, such as copper cables; this was when the idea came to dig up the surface coal. Hundreds or more are unemployed collecting scrap every day; it seems as though a "scrap metal fever" has taken hold of the town. Nearly everyone knows the prices and kinds of scrap, and knows the pros and cons of the various depots and scrap materials. Many people dig up old pipes, old copper cables, or try to cart off nuts, joiners, and metal rails of all kinds from the closed mines. This scavenging is often accompanied by a planned technological activity known as "plundering." For example, the diggers say that they plundered the rails after the Kopernik Mine closed, which meant brief legal employment in a firm that was being liquidated. The official liquidation of the mining infrastructure is often shrouded in secrecy and a certain amount of scandal. A onetime driver for a Wałbrzych mine told me a typical story of "wild liquidation": a heritage shaft tower from a mine had been sold for scrap for a sum several hundred times lower than the going price (TR/WB/37). This enormous unemployment in Wałbrzych is also accompanied by collecting in the dumping grounds and the old districts. People collect anything that might possibly have any kind of value (scrap metal, nonferrous metals, bottles, clothing, rags, waste paper). Some of the unemployed retrieve parts of wooden construction for firewood, some steal and cart off coal from the railway supply stock or freshly fired coke straight from the loading platform. At the same time, many go to work gathering berries, wild mushrooms, birch tree branches, alder bark, herbs, and everything that social workers disparagingly call "undergrowth." The post-mining towns, as one might call them, are floundering in general demolition and gathering (Bakoś and Ryciak 2004).

Among my interlocutors (generally ex-miners), all sources of social welfare and livelihood have been eliminated along with the liquidation of the mines and the end of the two-year cover period in which the mines paid social welfare (equivalent to 75 percent of salaries). For most, this period ended in 1996–1998, when many bootleg mines were born and began operating. In 1998 other forms of social coverage appeared, such as one-time redundancy payments (41,000 zloty gross), but few were entitled to collect it at the time. Only five hundred ex-miners received it in Wałbrzych. In Boguszów, proportionally speaking, one hundred families or fewer might have qualified.[4] Some miners lost their redundancy payment privileges because they had signed contracts with mines in the Czech Republic or in Hungary; soon afterward, they lost these jobs as well. Others, who were receiving disability benefits when the mines were liquidated, lost these benefits after 1997 when the definition of "unfit for labor" changed.[5] They were left from one day to the next with practically no means of existence and their disabilities, though many of them took to digging in bootleg mines and collecting scrap. This worst and most unjust of all paths—from legal work, with benefits and disability, to unemployment and work in bootleg mines—was traveled by several of my closest interlocutors.[6]

The diggers in the bootleg mines and the collectors of scrap and other goods are thus the long-term unemployed, long since without rights to benefits, meaning that since 1995/1996, none of them have worked the requisite hours for the status of unemployed and the right to receive benefits. In the 1990s they often worked for periods of several months in private firms, sometimes doing "intervention work," earning around five or six hundred zloty, which did not allow them to meet their families' requirements, or collect benefits (as this was temporary employment). The diggers and scrap collectors and their families (that I researched) suffered evident poverty and shortage. They generally inhabited old German buildings in various areas (such as Sobięcin, Biały Kamień, and Kuźnice Świdnickie, but chiefly in Boguszów-Gorce, where we, together with some students, shared living quarters with unemployed ex-mining families). These homes, once administered by the mines, and presently by the city council, were often in deplorable working condition.[7] Some of them, such as those in Wałbrzych's Sobięcin district, had to be evacuated and demolished. They were in danger of collapsing, in part because of all the illegal scavenging that had gone on in them.

For my interlocutors, surviving each new day is an issue—which means finding firewood: "The cold was making us weep when we carried the trees back from the forest. And we were scared the rangers would get us. But without it we wouldn't have survived" (TR/WB/35); and sustenance: "The people downstairs gave us bread and potatoes when we didn't have any, and then we gave them some when they were out." "I dream that one day our fridge might be full, that everyone could just take, that this constant guarding the fridge might end, because it has to be guarded.... Nobody can just take for himself" (TR/WB/35). I have also observed them reusing the same tea bag for multiple cups of tea. Paying the electricity bill is also a problem: "That was a terrible year when they cut off our electricity. First we used candles, then we stretched a cord from our neighbor's house ... and split the bill" (TR/WB/13); and it sometimes happens that evenings are spent in the dark, with only a candle being lit for guests, such as the researchers. Most families in these circumstances take advantage of social welfare assistance, though this is generally a small amount (one hundred zloty or less); and acquiring it means first gaining an "active job seeker" card. As proof of employment refusal, around ten company stamps are to be collected every month, which scarcely pays off, given the cost expenditures in traveling to these companies. Workers at the Social Assistance Center in Boguszów say that families generally stop coming after three months of benefits, and then reappear a month or two later (TR/WB/40).

In Wałbrzych I conducted my research primarily among the diggers and scrap collectors from the districts of the old Sobięcin (the Sportowa Street district) and the Biały Kamień environs, as far as the bootleg mining fields that stretch to the Thorez Mine. However, my main research was done in the forests surrounding the Victoria Mine of the Sztygarska Street district. After some time, I had made good acquaintances with diggers from a few teams, mainly working near the Victoria, and soon we had joined a group of students living with their families in old tenement houses in a town at the foot of the mountains (Boguszów-Gorce). And so I lived and stayed for some time in the homes of ex-miners. Andrzej Pietrzyk and Zbigniew Krycki, the residents of one home, introduced me to the local environment, which had theretofore been closed to me. As a result, they (particularly Andrzej Pietrzyk) guided me in my thoughts and in my mode of research. I was enlightened by many of their statements; and through them, I met other people (e.g., I participated in the bootleg miners' Barbórka [St. Barbara's Day celebration]), and I took part in their family/neighbor events and minor celebrations.

Andrzej Pietrzyk lived with his wife, their two sons, a daughter-in-law, and two grandchildren in a two-room flat near the mountains. This was an old flat, its walls covered in tattered wallpaper, equipped with a few old furnishings, a stove, a tile heater, and a washroom outside on the landing one floor below. All the men dug in the bootleg mines, sometimes collecting scrap as well, digging for "pipes." Andrzej's elder son had been applying for several years to work in the coke plant, where Bogdan Zawadzki, his father-in-law and my landlord and frequent interlocutor, was employed. When the mine was liquidated, Andrzej was living on benefits; in 1997 he had lost his pension, and for several years since had been digging in bootleg mines. He had made a fruitless attempt to have his pension restored (by appealing to ZUS health care services), and the family had appealed to Social Services a few times as well, but eventually grew discouraged. Digging in the bootleg mines, they earned twenty, thirty, even forty zloty in one day (from seven hundred to a thousand zloty monthly), though of course was dependent on demand, on finding good coal deposits, and on building a good bootleg mine. Sometimes, when the men earned a little extra during the nights, they stopped working during the day. Sometimes they became dependent on their middleman, who took their coal and paid them their daily wages; though previously, when they sought buyers themselves, they had not earned much more (the problem then was with demand).

The other digger, Zbigniew Krycki, lived with his wife, Krystyna, and his two children (an adult son from a previous marriage and a four-year-old daughter) in the attic, in one vertical line, in an equally small and leaky flat. All of their money came from Zbigniew's work in the bootleg mine; they, too, had repeatedly applied for welfare. Every penny was counted in this household, and every coming week meant a lack of money. They were barely able to afford firewood and sustenance, were over a dozen months behind on their rent, and often borrowed from their neighbors (generally retired miners), but also from "Provident" agents (an international financial institution, frequently criticized in Poland for charging very high interest rates). Zbigniew worked very hard all day, and usually came home and rested. His wife ran the house and took all her payment from him—as is typically the case in mining families (see, among others, Mrozek 1988: 106–107). The two families were very intimate with one another, drinking coffee together in the mornings, and lending one another firewood, potatoes or sugar in lean moments.

The next family I met, inhabiting the same block of flats, had nine children. This family lived in extreme poverty, with almost no income, apart from social welfare and the father's small earnings as a collector of scrap metal, mainly copper and nonferrous metals. Both digger families repeatedly helped this one, sharing their food, firewood, and helping take care of the children. These were the families I came to know the best, though I entered other homes of ex-miners, diggers, and scrap collectors; they all lived in similar tenement houses, but also in old German detached houses, in Boguszów-Gorce, Kuźnice Świdnickie, and Sobięcin. Zbigniew Krycki's extended family occupied one such detached house, for example, in a large, damp flat that was difficult to heat. For some time, a coke maker from the Victoria factory (related to the digger's family through marriage) and his family were also my hosts. He was just about the only person in the neighborhood who possessed a regular income from legal work.

The Highly Ambivalent Story of the Wałbrzych Basin

In the People's Republic, the Wałbrzych mines were among the worst in the country—their mining/geological conditions were extraordinarily harsh, prohibiting fully automated work and increasing the risks for the crews employed there (Skiba 1979; *Eksploatacja* ... 2000). Particularly in the years following the war, after the takeover of the badly exhausted mines and industrial factories,[8] work was exceptionally hard and dangerous. After a cursory training, incoming settlers worked there as miners, as did German forced labor prisoners, who to a large degree were specially "placed" by the managing specialists and technicians (Skiba 1979: 73); sometimes women also worked "down below" (*Eksploatacja* ... 2000: 87). Numerous accidents occurred at work,[9] more frequently than in other mining basins. The cause of this high accident rate was a chronic lack of investment in the Wałbrzych mines, which meant that in the 1950s (during the six-year plan) they had become exceptionally unsafe, and also inefficient (Skiba 1979: 108). Their input to coal production on a countywide scale remained small (ibid.: 131–132), as did investments, and the work and living conditions—including the miners' pay—were substantially worse than in the Upper Silesian Basin (see, for example, Mrozek 1987: 23–24; Skiba 1979: 131). The mines were liquidated because of the interplay of many factors, including the out-dated technology of the equipment, the dwindling coal resources (a con-troversial point), and the falling demand for coke coal, the Wałbrzych mines' main product (Wierzbicka 1999: 147; *Doświadczenia* 1999: 28; cf. Kłopot 1997: 63–87; *Eksploatacja* ... 2000).

For these few decades of the People's Republic, Wałbrzych existed as a massive organism, creating a totally different world for a signifi-cant part of the population.[10] The heterogeneous group of settlers[11] mi-grating to the post-German mining districts was shaping a new social "state." Workers with low qualifications—i.e., generally those with only elementary or vocational school education—could get hired there (for information on Wałbrzych's "plastic youth" of the 1950s, see, among others, Kłopot 1997: 78; Małkiewicz 1997: 140–141). Socialist, pa-tronal factory estates were created for them on the foundations of the largely intact post-German miners' housing estates to provide for all the workers' basic needs. Schools, preschools, daycares, medical clin-ics, sports clubs and stadiums, garden plots, special internal "G" shops, cultural centers, and more were created around the factories. A special, enclosed "social climate" was thus created in the newly emerged group of Wałbrzych miners, owing to their relatively high pay (as compared to other professional groups), their special social benefits, and a series of "invented traditions" (Hobsbawm and Ranger 1983), i.e., celebra-tions and rituals of prosperity such as *tablice piwne* (bar competitions), *babskie combry* (wild get-togethers of married women during carnival time), or Barbórka (St. Barbara's Day celebrations) (Kłopot 1997: 70). The mining industry guaranteed to provide everything for these people, from their homes to their leisure. Such testimonies of this state, though clearly quite fortified by the "recollection" mechanism, appeared in con-versation with the ex-directors of the mines, who often used the same phrases, such as "we created for them," "we ensured them," or "we took care of everything they needed." I also heard such statements from the other end, from the receivers, during practically every conversation I had with ex-miners and workers in industrial plants. "There used to be everything, everything. ... When kids came along there was a daycare, then a preschool. ... There were 'ołówkowe' for the children—just as long as you worked" (TR/WB/23); or "Then they built and divvied things up ... if you were working you deserved a flat, and that was it, pe-riod. ... Now just try and show me one company that promises flats to their workers, that has built anything at all. ... Back then, there was ev-erything" (TR/WB/23). This was therefore a complete social, economic, and cultural world that evolved over the course of less than three genera-tions. To a large degree, the notion of the "miner's status" corresponds to this, as an independently shaped and regulated "lifestyle" (Kłopot 1997: 70). One might say that the foundation of its consciousness was largely a sense of social security and a "greater significance" as compared to other groups of workers (Kłopot 1997: 73; see also Balcerowicz 1997: 328, 354).

However, this image becomes "doubled" (ambivalent) when we see it through the lens of the historical, political, and economic realities of the Wałbrzych coal industry. Though they had been exploited and over-used (owing to the hasty wartime production), the Wałbrzych mines and their accompanying factories were taken intact by the Soviets. According to the oral information I received from the ex-directors of the Wałbrzych mines, there was a great deal of plundering and devastation under Soviet Army supervision. The precise technical documentation obtained when the ex-German offices of the Mining Council were taken by the Soviet armies was burned by soldiers to heat their ovens. The Polish communist authorities' postwar use of the Wałbrzych mines also left much to be desired. They were hastily administered, and basic safety principles for workers and the environment were neglected. In order to "fill the mining quota," "shallow mines" were used, compromising the protective posts supporting the foundation. The working conditions were invariably severe, as were the living conditions. When the miners arrived to begin working they were settled in old German miners' housing estates. Practically no new estates were built until the 1970s,[12] while the old German estates remained under the administration of the mines and industrial factories. Apart from some token expenditure, these institutions proposed no renovations, preferring to invest their money in increasing productivity. The mine administration thus ensured everything that was needed to survive, including a place to live, but had little interest in repairs or renovations of the old tenement buildings; one might say that everything was kept going by its own momentum. This led to a socially accepted way of living in which it was sheer nonsense to use personal funds to repair homes and blocks of flats. The residential buildings—old, German mining constructions—were left in the state they were found, with neither private bathrooms nor full plumbing (only external riser pipes); they were cramped and heated in the traditional manner, with coal furnaces and stoves. Mining damage constantly occurred, but was perfunctorily eliminated; funds for repairing damage—as in the towns on Upper Silesia—were spent on token causes/propaganda (Kłopot 1997). We ought to point out that this is a very typical example of People's Poland centralized city-planning policies, and of the local authorities' policies, by extension. Prewar constructions, the majority of which were old, were almost strategically neglected.[13] Meanwhile, the whole impetus for construction, in particular during the Gierek era (the 1970s) of prefabricated buildings, shifted into the suburbs, into the open (to put it more vividly), boundless expanses where tenement buildings and combines sprang up (Dzięgiel 2001: 59–80). Most of the miners in Wałbrzych remained in the old German buildings.

We are thus dealing with a clearly ambivalent picture of the history of Wałbrzych mining during the communist era. On the one hand, it was a time when "there was everything, and everything worked," as most of my interlocutors claimed. Indeed, during this period miners and factory workers had a clear sense of social and financial stability. On the other hand, this was essentially a complex of mines with insufficient investment and antiquated technology, a steadily declining level of prosperity, and exceptionally difficult natural (geological) conditions, managed according to the centralized instructions of the communist authorities, in defiance of all market principles. The decision to liquidate the Wałbrzych mines was initially received with a certain relief (Wierzbicka 1999; Urbanek 1998). However, it left an enormous group of people—miners and workers in the factories adjacent to the mines (estimated at the end of the 1980s to be approximately twenty thousand workers)—facing an entirely new and incomprehensible situation. The mines had organized these people's entire lives and worlds for them. Now all of this had fallen into total disorganization and disintegration, or had simply ceased to exist.

* * *

There is an even broader context to this situation, a historical or even historiosophical one: the settlement or colonization of the previously German lands following the Second World War. This tied together two opposing processes. In the Western Lands of Poland, the territory gained by the war was simultaneously rebuilt and devastated. The rebuilding was linked to communist ideology's emphasis on revealing the ancient Polishness of these lands, simultaneously wiping away the "Germanic varnish." In addition, a colossal role was also played by their *modernizing significance.*[14] This sudden construction of the edifice of socialism, and the whole propaganda policy of raising estates and building daycares and hospitals by sheer force, was therefore particularly strong in the Western and Northern Lands. The Wałbrzych authorities' policies serve as a good example, as the old German mining estates were neglected, while a prefabricated housing estate for miners, the Piaskowa Góra Estate, sprang up.

In reality, however, this colonization of ex-German cities and properties was most frequently preceded by a semi-official devastation and plundering of ex-German holdings and the infrastructure of the cities. All German inscriptions and technical signage were destroyed (Grębowiec 2006), and the charming little towns of Lower Silesia, with their Renaissance market squares and gardens filled with roses, were thus turned into dilapidated, "unwanted towns" (Mach 1998). This is illustrated in the history of Lubomierz, written by Zdzisław Mach, wherein the elaborate plumbing system, with its German technical documentation, was demolished, the first thing to go. The postwar history of the Western Lands is generally filled with acts of destruction, of looting oak floors for firewood, of plundering bricks, of dismantling, destroying, and carting off "treasure" and "trophies" to the capital, to the "head office" (Mach 1998: 72; Kolbuszewski 1988: 74–75). Based on anthropological and historical/sociological work to date, we might tentatively claim that the postwar devastation of the ex-German lands was the result of various social attitudes and motivations. Examples of these attitudes and motivations include: the continued "celebration" of the war's end, which Halina Gerlich calls "Polish celebration" (1994: 44–46), and the destruction of ex-German things as a means of easing settlers' sense of alienation (Mach 1998: 75; Kolbuszewski 1988: 74–76). There was also the widespread conviction after the war that the Western Lands would only temporarily belong to Poland (Gerlich 1994: 32; Kolbuszewski 1988; 76). Ultimately, the devastation may also be blamed on the activities of the new, local communist powers, so often devoid of scruples (Grębowiec 2006; Kolbuszewski 1988: 74; and Mach 1998: 70–71), which condoned the plundering and destruction (Mach 1998: 89–90; Kolbuszewski 1988: 74; Trosiak 2000; 366–367).

It is therefore perhaps a matter of simple reciprocity. After the war, Soviet machines were installed into ready, abandoned factories and mines. Whole divisions of disoriented "Central Poles" and Poles from the eastern borderlands were hired from one day to the next. By the 1990s, when the factories came to a standstill and the mines were liquidated, the ex-miners and workers dismantled them almost to the last brick, to the last steel rail. In 2001–2005, in such cities as Lubsko, Ludwikowice Kłodzkie, Walim, Wałbrzych, and many others, the walls of factories were dismantled, steel rails and fixtures were pulled up, and machines that were bolted down were blown up. On the outskirts of old factories many ex-workers dug up old pipes, copper cables, and the old mechanisms of the pumping stations. Apart from Wałbrzych, the most marked example of these processes was the border town of Lubsko, where, following the liquidation of the local clothing industry (the Luwena factory) at the end of the 1990s, there was a spontaneous, collective act of destruction. For several months in 2003, ex-workers and

their whole families took down the walls of the factory and of the closed
railway building. Dismantling buildings for scrap and bricks, searching
for valuable junk and waste, or digging bootleg mines were neither new
nor incomprehensible activities in post-German Wałbrzych. As during
the postwar years, they started by scouring the cellars, the cubby-holes,
the gardens, by rifling through all the junk in the attics, searching for
things to sell, and only then did they begin tearing apart the buildings,
the industrial infrastructure, and the old mines. This history is quite
similar, then, or even repeated, and yet completely different. The historical and existential context of this behavior changed in a fundamental
way. Particularly in Wałbrzych, a mining town, but also in Lubsko, this
was a ritual message, a collective lament full of verbal aggression, repetition, and threat toward authority in whatever definition. It was an informal testimony to the liquidation of the past, renewed in an everyday
language.

Experience and Liquidation: Destruction—The City—The Body.
In Wałbrzych, Boguszów-Gorce and Lubsko ex-workers in the onetime
factories (mines, coke plants, clothing) are therefore constantly destroying and dismantling the remnants of their world—the same world once
inhabited by their parents and grandparents—disassembling and taking apart everything that can be traded for money or reused. What remained of the closed mines was devastated, followed by what was closest
at hand, i.e., people's private possessions (homes, furnishings, garage,
and shed equipment), from which many took whatever could be sold
at the scrap depot. In the old German buildings of the Sobięcin district
of Wałbrzych, some of the unemployed inhabitants began dismantling
their own staircases, carving up the oak stairs, salvaging fragments of
roof ridges, wooden pillars, and supports, dismantling whatever they
could. These houses threatened to collapse, either partially or entirely.
What statements accompany these actions? Over the course of my conversations something appeared from the first moment—what I would
call a collective sense of the *totality* of the destruction. This is a regular
facet of the local discourse, of the customary language: "This is just a
ruin, just one *big ruin*," say the Wałbrzych diggers, "it should be destroyed completely!" (TR/WB/18). "Look, *everything's* torn up, *everything's* destroyed" (TR/WB/18). "Look, over there, past the forest, they
ripped up the railway tracks, entire bridges, unscrewed *everything* [em-
phasis mine], there's nothing left" (TR/WB/19). "Now there, over by
the edge of the gas main, have a look at what's happening: the blocks
of flats are cracking, they'll crack, it's *all* going to burst, whole buildings are swaying.... At the Central [Train Station] there's nothing left,

absolutely nothing, they're just unscrewing scrap" (TR/WB/20). These things are said in a special manner—they are generally the first, spontaneous words, and are later repeated, spoken like a refrain. Combinations like "everything" versus "nothing" are particularly evident (Mogilnicka and Plińska 2005; WAŁB, 19). Let us look at the following fragment of a conversation/interview: the complaints concern the dismantling and devastation of the Barbara Shaft, a site powerfully inscribed in the local collective memory.[15]

> Informant: "Here, opposite this energy pole, that's where the Barbara was.... Now there's *nothing*.... Now there's *nothing*. Now there's *nothing*."
>
> Ethnographer: "Is there a signboard or something?"
>
> I: "What? Now there's *nothing*. Now there's absolutely *nothing*. There you can see a narrow stretch of road that runs uphill. And straight ahead, where that road ends, there used to be the reception, and the shaft was there. There was *everything*. Now there's *nothing*.... There were workshops, cloakrooms, a reception. There was *everything*. Now there's *nothing*.... They took it all apart."
>
> E: "And those materials? What are they? People—"
>
> I: "It used to be a company: they took apart the building, cleaned up the bricks, carted them off.... They carted off the rubble. Now there's *nothing*." (ibid.)

This message is also, to some extent, beyond expression in words, eluding the questions of the ethnographer. These collective complaints and declarations of resentment are filled with expressions such as "destroyed," "blew up," "tore up," alongside the characteristic "everything"— "they destroyed everything" and "they tore up everything" are remarkably common in Wałbrzych. This special Wałbrzych rhetoric, the tantalization of a phenomenon, manifests itself through the constant and general perception of the whole. "They're digging all 'round Wałbrzych, you can't see it, but have a look in the morning or at around two in the afternoon, when everything is flying out the holes" (TR/WB/17). "They're digging up all of Boguszów" (WAŁB 16). "Everything is taken apart here. Wałbrzych is totally taken apart. Wiktoria is totally taken apart" (WAŁB 1). "They're digging in Boguszów, they're digging in Gorce, they dig where they can, they're digging everywhere" (TR/WB/22). And at the same time: "Wałbrzych is one big ruin" (TR/WB/20). "The Germans could go ahead and take Wałbrzych back" (TR/WB/17); "Everything was plundered, robbed, there's nothing left to steal.... But you still have to pay the electricity bills.... They pull out all their junk, plunder the water pipes" (TR/WB/17). The experience of destruction ("ruins") is thus transposed, we might say, to the whole of the environment—to the whole of the perceived world: "There's just a ruin, just a ruin," "Everything was plundered, stolen," and "All of Wałbrzych has been dug up" can be heard in nearly every conversation.

Furthermore, the liquidation of the industrial world is accompanied by certain widespread catastrophic or even apocalyptic images of reality, including images that appear in the press. Although these are, to a large extent, journalistic creations, they surely render a general social atmosphere, one that emerges in tales of total destruction, demolition, and liquidation. "When Will Things Collapse?" (Palacz 2000: 3), "Catastrophe" (Smerd 2004: 10), and "Damnation of the Former Wealth" (Dwornik 2001: 3) screamed the headlines of these articles. "Our houses have been cracking for some time now. They were cracking before, *but not so quickly* [emphasis mine]," said one of the interviewees in a report (ibid.: 3). A journalist writes, "Destroyed houses, gas leaks, flooded buildings.... This might be the future of Wałbrzych" (Palacz 2000: 3). According to this scenario, the city and mines are to be consumed by a catastrophe within a few years. Water will flood entire squares and institutions, and gas (methane and carbon dioxide) pushed up onto the surface will cause a series of explosions.[16] "They'll flood Wałbrzych," said the diggers and the ex-miners, "The water doesn't have to look, it's not blind, you know.... Wałbrzych in a few years, I don't even want to talk about it.... It'll all be under water—the cellars, the pavements, everything will be covered in water" (TR/WB/17). "They should open the border and let us run away from here, because they've flooded the mines, but the mines are still sitting there, deeper and deeper" (TR/WB/22). "Boguszów will collapse—there's too many holes" (TR/WB/35).

Moreover, it is extremely characteristic that statements accentuating the destruction of the body imperceptibly join these images of environmental destruction. Much as with the descriptions of the "ruins" and "annihilation" of the city, now it is the ill health, the personal physical deterioration that is emphasized. "I work here [in the bootleg mine], but I'm a first-category invalid. I have no feeling in one leg" (TR/WB/25). "I've got nothing left to breathe with, by all rights I shouldn't be alive" (TR/WB/8). "I've got no lungs—where can I go to work if I haven't got my right lung?" (TR/WB/3). "But who gives a damn if my lungs are bursting.... I mean, I shouldn't even be walking" (TR/WB/8). One often then hears such phrases as "we've been cheated" or "someone's cheated us"; the subject of the miners' pensions being "taken away" is a recurring refrain, as is the miner/pensioners' "return to health" (as the diggers sarcastically put it). In these and many other statements bodies are mangled and destroyed—what Weronika Plińska described as the ever-suffering body: "the backbone hurts—he's come out of the mine," "the discs and the spine get just about everybody," "silicosis—that's the worst" (2005: 5). In these statements the body fills the role of the irreducible world. It is here (unlike in the social "forgetting") that everything settles, and the body is the first to file a complaint against the liquidation of the coal basin. "My lungs are all turned to mince, and I worked seventeen years down below" (TR/WB/12); "Plenty of folks didn't even make it to retirement as a reward for their ruined lives. ... He got out of there, and right afterwards came ... the shakes, the silicosis, the anthracosis, *we have every possible sort of disease* [emphasis mine]." (TR/WB/12). "By the time you get home the hands hurt, you don't know where to put them. They hurt and they hurt, there's no way to bear it. Everything hurts and hurts, you've done your bit at the mine, you're not young anymore—*it hurts* [emphasis mine]" (TR/WB/25). The body registers everything scrupulously.

We might also note that images of the destroyed city interweave, even overlap, with images of the destroyed body. The word *ruin*, for instance, is used as both an emblem of the city (postindustrial remains) and the dreadful state of the ex-miners dentition—the diggers often repeated that they now had "ruins" for teeth (Szanciło 2005; Zubelewicz 2005; WAŁB, 24). This shift from the body to reality (and back) testifies to an extraordinarily deep metaphorization of personal experience. The body is more than just a recording instrument in the literal sense of the word; it is a loom that incorporates both one's private experience and that of the collective. I must return once more to the works of Maurice Merleau-Ponty (1973; 2002; see also Csordas 1990; 1999; 2001a[1994]), and the concept that creates an "internal framework" for the present study. From this perspective, the body and the world, it should be said, less mutually overlap than constitute parts of one and the same dynamized experience. As Merleau-Ponty wrote, "External perception and perception of one's own body vary in conjunction because they are the *two facets of one and the same act* [emphasis mine]" (2002: 237). As a result, the world becomes one's blood relation—this is constantly replicated in the most varied cosmologies of experience, in which the world is "seated in" the body. This "destroyed" body, meanwhile, extends into the whole of the surrounding world, and is transferred onto the entire "external world." The experience of the destruction of the postindustrial remnants (i.e., of the undermining and annihilation of the former world) thus *spreads outwards*, and physical destruction is transferred onto the buildings, onto the city, and onto the whole environment. And much as the bodies of the diggers and the scrap-collectors are ruined and subjected to devastation, so too are the staircases, the crumbling elevations of the houses, and the half-dismantled industrial halls. This is how an internal picture of the survived world is created, is "registered" in the material closest at hand, i.e., in the bodies of the diggers, the collectors, the former miners, and by extension, in the landscape of the plundered and devastated mines—in the landscapes of "ruins."

Here we come to yet another component of this picture. This destruction chiefly applies to *the present moment*, to what takes place in the here and now. These experiences are being recalled only now, when there is no longer any active mining, and when the whole apparatus bureaucratically registering this devastation and professional ailments of all kinds is defunct. In short, it is only now that these bodies overburdened by labor have become all-significant, have come to acquire new meaning. "They've destroyed us" is the message, though in a certain sense we might say that they (the ex-miners) were less "destroyed" by work in the mines than by the exact opposite, i.e., the lack of work, and by the closure of the mines themselves. The negative attributes of their work (occupational illnesses, the miners' inevitable "early retirement") paradoxically become attributes of post-mining unemployment.[17] One gets the impression that, despite the systematic neglect and destruction of the old German buildings in the years of coal-mining prosperity, there was no destruction carried out in Wałbrzych during the communist period ("there used to be everything"). There was no place for such clearly exhibited feelings of devastation and threat, for descriptions of degeneration and accidents, though there were many of these (this was then a "state" death or illness [TR/WB/31]). This means that the devastation has taken place only now, during the course of the current events, i.e., the liquidation of the mines. Over those following years, the body and the whole environment took on this particular sense of "destruction," this record of their experiences, which were transferred freely from the body to the surroundings, and from the surroundings to the "I," and so forth, infinitely. Some diggers from the Sztygarska region told me, "Just look what's happening. ... This is ... our ecology ... the coke flies in the air, in the smoke ... you can't even breathe ... the coal cloud is floating in" (TR/WB/8). "Here they let it out like a gas chamber, it's such bad shit ... the birds fall from the sky," "The poverty is terrible, but it's going to get even worse before it gets better, because things can't go on like this. ... Look at how the climate's changing—the mountains are bald, the forests chopped down. ... Those chimneys ... go and look, look at Saint Joseph" (TR/WB/8). The environment itself, we should add, had undergone significant improvement since the liquidation of the coal basin. Even the miners noted considerable reductions in smoke and airborne ash, and remarked at the noticeable improvement in the cleanliness and whiteness of the snow in winter, as opposed to the dirty grey it had been while the mines were operative. Deer and goats, subjects of the diggers' jokes and amusement, are sometimes observed approaching the bootleg mines (TR/WB/25).

I repeat: the world underwent destruction in Wałbrzych and in Boguszów-Gorce only in the face of the *current events.*

How to Speak of Liquidation?
(Auto)aggression—Dialogue—Social Muteness

As we can see, destruction simultaneously translates into a clear social "mood of destruction"; what arises, therefore, are both statements (i.e., verbal expressions) of destruction and actual enactment of it, by dismantling and "tearing up" scrap. The above descriptions have shown that in places such as Wałbrzych or Lubsko, nearly everything that could be taken apart for profit has been destroyed and dismantled. In conversation, this experience of total demolition is often linked with a bitter, collective fatalism. I heard more than once that things had to stay as they were: "The Slavs are genetically programmed for devastation" (WAŁB 16), or "There won't be any changes here for the next fifty years—my grandchildren will be digging holes and pulling up scrap, you'll see" (TR/WB/22). Something more is happening here, however. These words were spoken by people who had worked for many years in these cities, people whose lives were tied to them, who had lived and settled down there. They could not, therefore, remain indifferent to the general destruction of the factories, the unearthing and theft of scrap, the plundering of mines or the digging of shafts. Something comes to light here, however, which allows us to look with new eyes at this general demolition of industrial remnants and the devastation of city spaces. When there is talk of the destruction, or the collecting of scrap and other "resources," it tends to be with a visible and incomprehensible satisfaction. "All this," they said, "is just waiting to be blown sky high!" "This has to be dynamited, and done so that you can't tell anything was ever here!" In Lubsko they said: "There used to be something out of nothing, now there's nothing out of something; it should all be covered in gas and torched!" (TR/LUB/1, 2, 4). "We've got the highest unemployment in all of Poland," said the diggers from Wałbrzych's Sobięcin; and in a similar vein: "It should be totally destroyed!" (TR/WB/8). "They should level it all to the ground and plant strawberry fields!" (Plińska 2005: 6). At the same time, demolition and devastation are presented in a remarkably compelling fashion: "Wałbrzych is a ruin, even the birds are turning away from here" (WAŁB 6). "Wałbrzych is simply extermination … it has to be said" (TR/WB/22). With bitter satisfaction, the unemployed scrap collectors in Lubsko called their town "Baghdad" (in reference to the US bombing of Baghdad at that time) or "Grozny" (which was being bombed by the Russians a few years ago). What emerged was an incomprehensible collective satisfaction from the destruction, from the liquidation of the coal basin.

The image of the body destroyed and subject to destruction is thus given a certain form of self-expression in these statements. These words reveal the present overexposure of the body endangered, exposed to injury or death. Death stamps the determination, the unrelenting work in the bootleg mines: "Let them [the city patrol, the police] come, let them tell us we're not allowed to dig. ... I'll just go right to the bottom, and we'll see if they come after me there. ... They can *shovel the dirt in right on top of me* ... what kind of life is this?" (TR/WB/3). "If nothing comes of it, I'll *blow myself up here*—and then let them try and do something" (TR/WB/36). "Now we're going to build [dig and build a bootleg mine] ... and then it's down into the ground, down into the ground" (WAŁB 2). "One by one to work, and if we fuck it up—That's that!" (TR/WB/17). Similarly, the tragic accidents that occurred during the wild demolitions are still being recalled: "Lots of people died here while they were tearing apart and demolishing"; "There were plenty of tragedies, there were accidents" (TR/LUB/1) they said in Lubsko. "Now here was a real accident. ... One guy went to demolish a place where there was electricity ... he got burnt, they took off his hand. ... This wall crushed another guy" (TR/LUB/6). These quotes show a consciousness of being subject to danger (most frequently while digging bootleg mines and "tearing up" scrap). There is something symmetrically equivalent here to the satisfaction we described from the destruction of buildings and the infrastructure. Much as a readiness to "complete" the act of the city's destruction and demolition is expressed, so too is there a social manifestation of a readiness to bear injury—or a manifestation of such a capability (cf. Arnold and Babiker 1997; Eckhardt 1994; not unlike the polygon steel scrap collectors' declarations of withstanding injury, described in Piotrowski 2004). "Yesterday a whole overhang collapsed on us—if it had come down, that would have been a shock! I guess that's that. ... Too bad it didn't bury us!" (TR/WB/8).

This "imagined self-destruction" (to allude to the term "imagined suicide"; Schaüble 2006), culminating in a readiness to accept death, lends these statements an entirely new significance. Death and danger are something more than merely the actual risk. They generally arise in the context of bootleg mines collapsing and burying the workers inside (there have been numerous small incidents and five fatalities over the course of almost six years), and in the context of dismantling buildings, and in breaking into old mining galleries and sewer tunnels.[18] However, the sense of danger derives from something else. The minor incidents and fatalities in the bootleg mines are in fact statistically less common than they were in the Wałbrzych mines during the communist period. This means that the real danger of accidents was greater for those working underground *before* the liquidation of the mines (back when these dangers had their "raison d'être," as I have shown).[19] This helps us see that the relationship between these statements and the reality is neither clear nor unambiguous, and that the complaints are not mere expressions of a factual situation, real risks, or actual threats. What, then, is the meaning of these statements?

I would say that these are recurring social complaints, forms of social communication, acts of autoaggression. These complaints, whose source is a relationship with the outside reality, are a point of departure for an aggression aimed at the surroundings. Outside forces and agents are blamed for the massive local unemployment, which brought poverty and economic powerlessness.[20] Obvious as it may sound, in the eyes of the unemployed this aggression is chiefly aimed toward people on the outside, in official posts, seen as those responsible for this dire situation. During the course of my research, my interlocutors' first words were generally harsh statements aimed at me as a representative of the world of decision makers, politicians, or at least the media, who are not hard to find in fieldwork. These statements pertained to society as such, from ordinary people (onlookers) to the government (bureaucrats and politicians), including "those" who needed to "do something about this," but who "do nothing." As Richard Hoggart (2009 [1957]) wrote a few decades ago on the British working class, the comments pertained to the functionaries of the police and the city patrol, the bureaucrats at town hall, and to the mayor of Wałbrzych.

These complaints and exclamations serve no informative function— they are more a refusal to communicate, and are sometimes accompanied by active aggression.[21] Wałbrzych demonstrations saw slogans like "We want to work, we want to live!" being chanted for hours. Above all, I feel that these are acts of communication reaching their intended targets through a sort of communicative absence, or in a feeling of their ineffectiveness in communicating and in all other regards. Expressions of threats, aggression, and autoaggression become empty gestures; carrying no "target" meanings they are more like a social ritual. To my mind, this means that the contents of these statements bear no relation to real solutions, which are in fact not even expected. This is more of a kind of "communication without information" (cf. Rothenbuhler 1998), which is by its very premise *ineffectual*. In more general terms, one might say that this is a manner of expression prevalent in the Polish culture of the word—a special sort of ritual communication, where it is the physical/emotional component that takes precedence over all conceptual and information structures (Rothenbuhler 1998; Sulima 2003). Roch Sulima has called this form of expression[22] social autocommunication, and has recognized it as, essentially, a "dramaturgical and symbolic form of regulating a crisis situation" (2003: 2). We now see the meaning of the "hidden" demands of the demonstrating miners, demands that are often unreal, such as the introduction of high wages (for whatever sort of work) for unemployed miners, or for the official legalization of bootleg mines. I believe there are neither real negotiations nor real accomplishments being demanded here. Rather, the miners' public behavior, often aggressive and autoaggressive (see Jarosz 2005: 77–85; cf. Faliszek, Łęcki, and Wódz 2001: 79–81), combine with the demonstrations of readiness to damage things and themselves to form a full picture, and, when interpreted in this fashion, become a special sort of collective (auto)announcement. The format of this announcement presupposes a certain dialogue: the complaints, the grudges, the slogans of self-destruction, and the unrealistic claims are a particular attempt to contact (and simultaneously, to refuse contact with) an inaccessible, unattainable sphere. Within this sphere, an imagined maker of economic "decisions" within the "ruling power" "turns a blind eye," "is pleased," and allows all this to happen.

These claims cease to be realistic; their expression of grief is more important than their content or the complaints being made, and their demands for immediate change become an "empty" ritual.

Externalized Shame: Empty Communication and Internal Spectacles
We see a clear desire to reveal or to demonstrate this aggressive and autoaggressive behavior; by its very nature, it is meant to be public. It is found in the very first statements, spoken outright, and then clearly overrepresented in conversation. It in no way belongs to a sphere of quiet or concealed content or of informal communication, such as a sphere of conscious social resistance, which generally creates artificial communication structures (see, among others, Scott 1990). Nor is there an arsenal of gestures, words, and meanings, wherein every sign refers to a whole background of "invisible" knowledge (ibid.). These acts are almost involuntarily externalized; the first words I heard, the ones that "disrupt" an ethnographic conversation, were precisely these "com-

plaints" and "grumblings." My interlocutors seemed either to be saying nothing or to be "saying the same thing over and over": they cursed, complained, and expressed their woes to the ethnographer.

In this fashion, the diggers and the scrap collectors externalize, in collective forms of expression and in solitude, the misery of their current situation. Yet this emphasis on how they earned a daily living and what was occurring all around them, on what hundreds of other unemployed were doing, was, I believe, something more—they were practically making a public demonstration of their sense of shame. It is with this that I associate their peculiar psychological satisfaction from verbal or physical acts of destruction. I understand the word *shame* to mean an experience of powerlessness, an inability to fulfill the once internalized status quo of the world (Giddens 1991: 67–68), an incapacity to be part of a previous, internally established way of living and working (in a mining town). The shame expressed thus concerns a sense of adequacy in a person operating within a culture. According to Anthony Giddens, who follows Gerhard Piers and Peter Singer, the moment when a goal or a cultural norm—which might also be called the execution of a pattern—remains unachieved, it creates an "insufficiency," and then a profound sense of shame emerges (ibid.: 67–68). Drawing from the work of Helen Lewis and Helen Lynd, Giddens adds that shame "cuts the roots of trust," i.e., it severs the narrative of identity, and simultaneously restores a primary sense of dread toward the world; we "become strangers in a world where we thought we were at home" (ibid.: 66). This alienation and personal inadequacy, compared to the miners' living, working, and wage-earning norms, or even compared to those of an individual, run very deep indeed, embracing the entire world of the ex-miners' everyday lives and their original sources of identity, their "archaic environment" (ibid.: 68).

The phenomenon of the demolition and dismantling of the postindustrial heritage, and the manner in which this action was communicated, thus record the experience of shame, the inevitable gap between the social(ized) "I" and the "I" of the present day. "Too bad they didn't bury us," as the diggers said, "then we'd stop being such a nuisance to them." "Violence (aggression)," writes James Gilligan, "speaks of an unbearable shame" (quoted in Plińska 2005: 6). This shamefulness occurs in a particular fashion, what I might call "externalized shame." What the Wałbrzych or Lubsko unemployed do in a recurring and persistent manner—destroying and dismantling their towns, and "themselves" as well—is an act of constant *externalization,* a constant social revealing of the fabric of shamelessness. In a way, this is a reversal of the process that, according to Norbert Elias (2000), took place in European civilization: the transition from shame as an external, manifested social reality to shame as a complex internalization of cultural norms (enculturation). To quote Helen Lewis, who distinguishes between external shame, which is "open and undifferentiated," and internalized shame, which is "stifled," in Wałbrzych, among the responses I have analyzed, the internal or "stifled" shame of the ex-miners, scrap salvagers, and diggers is permanently "open" and "revealed" (or "exposed"). This is tied to the manifestation of the external and visible fabric of social relations, where it is put "on view" as a form of shame, and simultaneously as a masked fear of degradation (Elias 2000). "The root meaning of the word 'shame,'" writes Ernest Kurtz, "implies this process to uncover, to expose, to wound" (2007: 28).

As I have already mentioned, however, this communication is unsuccessful, it is an ineffectual manifestation. These messages, these declarations of shame and autoaggression, not only fail to put across the desired information (argumentation), but also essentially alter nothing; the surroundings, the world all around, stays unchanged after these statements are made. The social world is, in a sense, *deaf* to all their complaints and dismay. The complaints, the declarations of shame and the autoaggression are aimed at *nowhere*—at the empty mine shafts, at their own dismantled homes, at the devastated factories, and ultimately at their own bodies, their own lives. There is no one and nothing at which to aim the complaints/aggression: there are no building or mining-office administrators, nor is there any organizational mechanism that hands out payments and provides a sense of social security. Their place has remained *empty* in both a metaphorical and a physical sense. An example that best encapsulates the annihilation of the old system is the director's office of the Victoria Mine, which the diggers call "Belweder": the floors are covered in piles of expired documents, the windows and doors have been dismantled, and scrap collectors still continue to wander through it. By manifesting their shame and "physical aggression" in their statements, the diggers and demolition participants create a dialogue of sorts between themselves and the absent "other side," a dialogue with a void where the listener should be, or, to use Roch Sulima's formulation, a "complaint to the void" (2003: 5).[23]

A futile and unsuccessful reception is inscribed into this communication: "Who cares now if my lungs cave in? Has one of those guys dropped by to see me ...? No one" (TR/WB/8). "I'm working here and I'll go on working, this is my job. I've got to bring home the bacon. I'd like to see the crooks responsible come here. They're pretending like nothing's happening here" (TR/WB/3). "Who should we turn to now? Who should we turn to? Where should we turn to?" (TR/WB/36). "We're no miners, we're just old men.... A guy worked himself half to

death in the mines ... they could have sent a card for St Barbara's Day
... but they didn't. That's what they give you ... for having ruined your
life" (TR/WB/25). As a consequence of this "lack" of active or purposefully informational speech, these statements truly become something
akin to social impotence; they are inept, aphasic communication, and
in this dialogue, the main problem is the *indeterminability* of the op-
ponent. On the one hand, these statements are meant to combat this
communicative powerlessness—after all, they show a certain sense of
destructive "potency"—and on the other hand, they constitute a dramatic vociferation.

Rituals of self-destruction are, therefore, the only means of explicat-
ing and materializing (or somatizing) these people's deepest experiences
(Arnold and Babiker 1997; Eckhardt 1994). This is, therefore, a situation that constantly demands communication or reception, though by
its very nature it presupposes its absence. At this point, the message
aimed at others (or at myself, the anthropologist) rebounds with equal
force toward the initial subject. Autoaggression and self-injury is a response basically aimed toward oneself, "and not primarily with the aim
of eliciting a response from others" (Arnold and Babiker 1997: 8); they
speak of "somatizing" or specify an unbearable (or rather, "unspeak-
able") pain, which again becomes "internalized shame" (ibid.: 68).

In this way, the experience of destruction takes place primarily within
the subjects, though it is aimed outwards, at the surrounding world.
As I have noted, my interlocutors purposefully reveal their injuries ("If
you've got no money left, then you can go out onto the street and kill
some guy or sell one of your kidneys—but who would buy it? It's a
wreck") and their unashamedness ("We're not miners, we're geriatrics"),
making them public, while simultaneously stressing their constant readiness for self-destruction ("But if nothing happens, I'll just blow myself
up here, and then we'll see what they do"). The particular relational
and dialogical nature of these statements is revealed here, which means
that the other side is projected to some degree. We might say the words
are "partly another's" (Clifford 1988a: 41–42). However, projections of
every sort of authority appear on the "other side" (the side of reception)—the local politicians or the directors of the mines, a more vague
and undefined "authority" (a collective perpetrator of the changes and
liquidations), or an undefined "Warsaw," a world that remains deaf. This
dialogue is therefore created not just between the "I" and the public
sphere, but also between "I" and a part of one's self, because this "I"
contains the public sphere. As a result, this is an internal sphere where the
"I" is in constant dialogue with the world, a sphere in which the diggers

and the scrap collectors place themselves on show. This internal, imagined "acting out" (Arnold and Babiker 1997; Turner 1988: 102–107) might also be called "acting in," as it is a self-destructive, imagined act performed for one's own benefit. "Let them [the police, the city patrol] come and try to stop me from digging. … I'll just climb to the very bottom and they can look for me there. … Let them try to *bury* me in here … because what kind of life is this?"

Facing Reality after the Mines (1)

We have seen a fragment of the most dramatic experiences of the ex-miners in Wałbrzych. To my way of thinking, a psychoanalytic perspective grants us special insight in this dark place. Psychoanalysis is a humanist perspective that reaches back to primary experiences of being in the world—to the very experience of physicality. One must admit, however, that in many anthropological strategies it has been purposefully avoided, its premises treated in opposition to anthropological discourse (Heald, Deluz, and Jacopin 1994: 1–9). There is an entire "history of difference" that exists between these two perspectives. To some degree, this is the difference between the narrative of the "I" as a psychological being, enclosed within his or her ego, and the experience of the "I" as a collectively shaped and strengthened being. The latter grasps for an "internal dynamic" of the socially created world, gravitating toward vague, internal processes and experiencing trauma via the collapse of a once familiar existence.

The cosmologies of locally developed forms of suffering (Lazar and Luse 2007) reveal a social perspective of existing. As Gananath Obeyesekere has written, "Psychoanalysis provides a much-needed corrective to a complacent worldview … by focusing on human suffering and pain and the roots of suffering in desire" (quoted in Heald, Deluz, and Jacopin 1994: 9). Let us consider what happened in a concentrated area in the post-mining societies of Wałbrzych and Boguszów during a sudden and generally incomprehensible experience of unemployment, with an outside factor doing the injury. What took place, in a sense, was an uncovering of this level of being in the world, i.e., the emergence of new relationships with the world in a crisis situation—an injury that comes "from the outside." The result, detailed in *Cultural Trauma and Collective Identity* (Alexander, Smelser, and Sztompka 2004), is a situation of "cultural trauma," which remains on the level of collective memory (Alexander 2004: 5), perception, and all affective receptacles of cultural praxis. Nonetheless, as Erik Erikson demonstrates, this happens slowly, in a manner that is initially imperceptible (from ibid.: 4).

In conditions of cultural trauma, these two levels, the psychological individual and the "socially created reality," create certain mutual fields.
Such moments reveal the internal, imperceptible reality of collective
"mental labor"—such as internal "acting out" behavior or, ultimately, all
imaginary and often preverbal methods of mental and collectively survived coping mechanisms with experience (ibid.: 47). The experience of
cultural trauma—in other words, of the very dynamic aspect of cultural
phenomena—thus pertains directly to the language and experience of
modern psychoanalysis.

The Wałbrzych experience of destruction and crisis was therefore one
of external damage, or to use Freudian terminology, the experience of
"working through" mourning and melancholia[24] as a collective, creating something like intensive internal "labor," what Obeyesekere (1990)
would call "the work of culture." "The causes of melancholia," Sigmund
Freud writes, "go beyond the clear case of loss through death [of a loved
one], and include all the situations of *insult, slight, setback and disappointment* [emphasis mine]" (2005: 211). Such an interpretation of the
Wałbrzych experiences seeks to expand the psychoanalytical "I." This is
another relationship that constitutes the fate of the ego in the wide space
of internalized social and cultural relations, in the manner of the classic
works of Talcott Parsons (2007), Erich Fromm (1994), or Erik Erikson
(1993) (on paths of psychoanalysis and anthropology, see also Heald
and Deluz 1994).

This perspective is particularly essential, I feel, in the case of these
complaints—the ex-miners' humiliation and self-accusations—or of the
local "poetic" of suffering. For one might also ask, what kind of message is this, what does it serve? Analyzing statements of crisis survivors,
Freud showed that a sort of game transpires. When responding to the
various questions, survivors spoke of something completely different. "It
is not crucially important," he writes, "whether the melancholic is being
accurate in his painful self-disparagement. ... It is more a question of
him providing an accurate description of his psychological situation. He
has lost his self-esteem, and must have a good reason for doing so." And
shortly thereafter: "[Melancholics'] laments [*Klagen*] are accusations
[*Anklagen*], in the old sense of the German word: *they are not ashamed,
they do not conceal themselves* [emphasis mine], because everything dis-
paraging that they express about themselves is basically being said about
someone else" (2005: 207–208). This makes one thing clear: complaints
and expressions of social unashamedness, the expressions of anger from
the Wałbrzych and Lubsko unemployed, the readiness to destroy, to
"blow up," and the feeling of humiliation essentially accuse the powers
and processes external to them.

The accusations of the Wałbrzych unemployed thus address a conflict with the outside world ("ruins," "crap," "our ecology"). Yet, they also freely apply to physical experience ("we have every possible sickness"), to the miners' sense of identity ("we're not miners any more, we're geriatrics"), and to internal value ("am I somehow retarded, am I somehow worthless?") (TR/WB/33). Almost everything becomes the subject of resentment and aggression.[25] This is the experience of a reality in which "everything is destroyed" and "nothing is guaranteed"; the diggers, the scrap collectors, the gatherers, all indirectly speak of their attempts to understand a world that cannot be understood. This is made clear, for example, by the story of one of my closest interlocutors, a miner named Andrzej Pietrzyk, who, after nearly ten years of receiving miner's benefits, lost his rights to collect them (he had worked seventeen years "down below"). In 1997, after they "cured him," as he puts it, his benefits were revoked; now he works in a bootleg mine (TR/WB/12, 23, 25). Everything in his home hinges on his productivity, the money he earns semilegally, which does not afford him much; at his house, periods of hunger and cold alternate with better periods of sufficiency (when he has enough for food and firewood). At the time of writing, his situation was in no way tied to his effort in life—he had worked hard, as had his wife, and when he discovered that he was to go on retirement, he accepted this without great enthusiasm. What was the cause all of these bad changes that came? How did it happen that a man ceased to be a retired miner? Everything just "turned out that way," as they say. "I myself," he sometimes said, "*can't believe* in what has happened" (TR/WB/12).

As I have stressed repeatedly, the crux of the problem is that all these experiences are fluid and constantly change, depending on the context—this whole fluctuating and dynamized perception of reality, this imagined destruction of the body and the city, are key points in this experience. A process emerges here which Sigmund Freud and Melanie Klein have referred to as *investigating reality* (Klein 1987). What does this mean? From a psychoanalytic perspective—and in particular from a perspective of the British object-relations theory school—the "I" of a person is compelled to understand "what the world is like" at the very beginning of his or her existence, right from the moment of birth. This marks the emergence of the first mental and somatic acts, which constitute this understanding (Klein 1987; Winnicott 1971; cf. Erikson 1993; Giddens 1991: 51–60); the child learns less about the world than about his or her relationship with the world ("investigating reality"). In this way we touch the post-mining relationship between the "I" and the outside world, a relationship that, to a large degree, exists through elements of primary, ontological trust. Anthony Giddens (1991: 54) follows Erik Erikson in writing of trust as the basic element in developing a faith in the "I" in reality. Yet in fact, this reality is acquired and relational. It is rather an unreality of sorts, based on a whole range of rules, cultural signifiers, customs, and laws that do not exist unto themselves, and which must be given the status of a (intersubjective) presence. In much the same way, a child uses his or her first experiences to create methods. Giddens (1991: 42–43) alludes to Wittgenstein in writing: "Rather, 'what cannot be put into words'—interchanges with persons and objects on the level of daily practice—forms the necessary condition of what can be said, and of the meanings involved in practical consciousness." And furthermore: "Learning the characteristics of absent persons and objects [existing, for example, as a social consensus]—accepting the real world as real—depends on the emotional [ontological] security that basic trust provides" (ibid.: 43). In the statements of the unemployed I have analyzed, this process is revealed, but it works backward, becoming increasingly primary. It becomes visible much as it does in a child, who confronts reality in various phases. According to Melanie Klein, these are the schizoid/paranoid phase (the internal world is simultaneously the external world) and the depressive phase (an attempt to differentiate and guard against the first experiences of reality) (1987; see also Sánchez-Pardo 2003; Heald, Deluz, and Jacopin 1994: 4–5). Analogously, but in another language of the development of "competence at being," one might say that the child goes through a phase of basic socialization; further along in his or her biography, according to Peter Berger and Thomas Luckmann, the child undergoes a second socialization (1967; see also Jacyno and Sulżycka 1999: 51–55). As such, the Wałbrzych experience is, to some degree, a return (repeated, recalled) path, which begins with the child's lack of ability to be, the child's fear of what the environment might create. A new experience of reality begins with this incomprehension. The situation of crisis and profound powerlessness against the external world disturbs the very bases of the former, primary "knowledge of the world."

During my research in Wałbrzych, I got the impression that a sense of reality "as such," had already to some extent developed and been disturbed, and that now this reality required reinvestigating, to ensure that it existed. "Everything's reversed, everything's turned upside-down. ... The world's done a 180-degree turn, and is headed downwards. ... That's how it changed" (TR/WB/12). "I can't understand any of it— have they cured us, then?" (TR/WB/8). "They're shipping coal from the Czech Republic—I don't get it" (TR/WB/25). "Who knows what it's all about!" (TR/WB/30). Internalized cultural knowledge, this "competence at being," albeit fragmentary, discontinuous, and incoherent, ceased to exist. "This is where you wound up? Fucking hell!" one of the diggers told students, "Can't imagine what you'd be looking for here! There's nothing here! There's nothing here!" (WAŁB 13). It was a recurring refrain that a great many could not "come to terms with what had happened after the transformation." But what exactly does this mean?

The experience of unemployment and the destruction of the postindustrial world are forms of psychosocial "loss" (or a process of "destitution"). It recalls and takes us back to the primary stage, of the infant's confrontation with the world, to this intensive investigation of reality. At this moment, when the rules and routines of Wałbrzych (or Lubsko) daily life violently collapsed (or were reimagined), the fears and questions analogous to those posed by children return. Picking up where Freud left off, Melanie Klein claims that at one point "the child goes through states of mind comparable to the mourning of the adult, or rather, that *this early mourning is revived whenever grief is experienced in later life* [my emphasis]" (1987: 147). And somewhat further on: "This is the state of mind in the baby which I termed the 'depressive position,' and I suggested that it is melancholia in *statu nascendi*" (ibid.: 148). What, then, is this "state of mind"? On its own, it is less an actual frustration than a withstanding of its social and narrative significance, and it is this precisely that leads to social/juvenile neurosis (Erikson 1993: 252; cf. Klein 1987: 150). What emerges, then, is a way in which the child's "I" or the affected "I" recreates the external world and its manner of experiencing it. Like someone suffering a personal loss (i.e., part of his or her world), the child restores quite primary and very dangerous defense mechanisms, much as when the Wałbrzych unemployed experience a collapse of the difference between the internal world (the body) and the external world or "socially created reality" (on "external 'doubles' of internal reality"; see also Klein 1987: 148), and the reverse, signs of "what's on the outside" shift into the interior, mental/corporeal world. But how does this actually transpire?

Complaints—Accusations—Triumphs

To my mind, there is tremendous significance in the fact that nobody and nothing finds itself on the other side of these events (of the liquidation of the Wałbrzych basin); this is a a world that refuses to listen. All the cries and complaints that I have described are desperate attempts at communication, but they encounter a vacuum as a response. "Who should we appeal to now? Who can we appeal to here? Where are we supposed to appeal?" "Who gives a damn if my lungs burst?" "Let the crooks come … They're pretending nothing's going on here!" As I have said, this is a dialogue with "empty space."

At one point, one of the miners with whom I became closest, Zbigniew Krycki, gave a spontaneous lament (to his closer and more distant relatives): "I can't cope, am I somehow retarded, am I worthless? I'm definitely worse. I think I might hang myself. My wife once said she was going to go hang herself. I started to tear up when I saw her sitting there pregnant on the windowsill, starving. But what can I do? … The boss [of a semi-legal construction/renovation company] doesn't pay you for the month you've worked, and then for another month. … And then I thought, what, should I hang myself?" (TR/WB/33). As we can see, the complaints of this digger, though aimed, of course, outwards, toward an imagined receiver, an institution responsible (the authorities, the state, and all their metonymies), are transformed by the experience of powerlessness and unemployment into *accusations* aimed at himself, though they, in fact, address someone else. They concern the fact that the world has suddenly become deaf (social powerlessness) and incomprehensible (the experience of unpredictable transformations that are incomprehensible in the emic mode). These declarations of readiness to "hang oneself" are a kind of social "call out to the deaf," even a refrain and—as analyses of the materials reveal—an almost general, (self-)rhetorical gesture. "I just dig, what do I have to steal? Let them take me away and do me in!" (TR/WB/2); "If nothing comes of it, I'll blow myself up here, and let them do as they please" (TR/WB/2); "I've got a neighbor who lost his pension, and he hasn't got any legs. He told me yesterday that he was going to hang himself" (TR/WB/8).

Freud has shown that the "I" (the miner's "I" in this case, with all his due privileges) unable to maintain a connection with an external object (in this case the institution of the mine/city, to which the subject was almost organically tied) creates a substitute object within him or herself. This object and this space—the post-mining "I"—become the addressees of these accusations, and consequently, the objects of substitute destruction. "Hatred goes to work on this substitute object," writes Freud in *Mourning and Melancholy*, "insulting it, humiliating it, making it suffer and deriving a sadistic satisfaction from that suffering" (2005: 211). This "sadistic satisfaction" is worth noting, as it concerns acts performed simultaneously in the external and the internal world. And here once more we come to the source of the changeability and fluctuation of the degraded world, to the earlier processes of nondistinction between the "internal and the external" (Erikson 1993: 258). For a secure internal world to exist, it requires constant confrontation and affirmation from the outside, and is therefore a profoundly relational structure. "The ensuing doubts, uncertainties and anxieties," Klein writes, "act as a continuous incentive to the young child to observe and make sure about the external object-world, from which this internal world springs, and by these means to understand the internal one better" (1987: 149). The miners respond to the outside world much as a child learns of the realities of his or her external existence. The world of operating mines and the whole network of social internalizations have ceased to exist, and there is no way to "be certain" of its existence (it is "empty," much like the Belweder building). At this point it slips out of control, freely shifting from the inside to the outside, from the body to the environment, from the environment to the body, from the body to its mental projections and back again, straight to organic destruction. Then, to speak in terms of the Kleinian psyche, there is a constant grappling and struggling with the world, a constant attempt to grasp it, to seize control of it. And then these objects both external and psychophysical (internal, "substitute" objects) can be controlled and put in their place, the post-miner's "I" finally triumphs and is omnipotent, at least for a few moments. This is the "desire to control the object," as Klein has written, "the sadistic gratification of overcoming and humiliating it, of getting the better of it, the *triumph* over it" (1987: 153). "Let them come and forbid me from digging.... I'll just go right to the bottom, and they can look for me there. ... They can *bury me* if they like." "One by one into the hole, and if we fuck things up, it's so long for us!" "Yesterday a whole overhang came tearing off ... too bad it didn't bury us!" "What, don't think I can handle it?!" Weronika Plińska (2005) also quotes some young diggers: "I'm going to work! They can do what they like to me, break my arms, break my legs, and I'll still go out to work!" Here we can see a momentary act of grasping this incomprehensible reality, an act of imagined total control. Autoaggression is thus a *total* sensation, much like a sense of helplessness is an experience of full power(lessness) toward the anticipated unemployment. Then the need for destruction returns time and again, shifting from the exterior to the interior and back again, affecting everything, appearing everywhere. This is an all-essential channel of communication between miners, which also runs internally. It existed in this fashion and was constantly audible during my research in the deindustrialized Wałbrzych and Boguszów-Gorce regions. It serves as a framework of sorts for these experiences, and, I believe, it is imperative that it be depicted.

A World Affected from the Outside

Bootleg Mines, Diggers, Skills: The Body's Active Knowledge

Work in the bootleg mines and collecting and demolition labor share a special characteristic. All these jobs—digging coal, demolition, and scrap and refuse collecting—require no technological assistance, only "a set of hands." Nor do they have the whole hierarchical and established organization that previously functioned in the mines and in the coke plants. Digging, collecting, scrap hunting, or wood gathering are activities that trace back to before the Industrial Era (one might say, to even before the epoch of settlements, before the "Neolithic Revolution"). In two senses, this allows us to take the perspective of anthropological research on a society violently stripped of its former industrial/administrative organization. Firstly, I understand this in a substantial sense, i.e., of prewar (German) and postwar (People's Republic) industrialization, and the whole planned organization ensuring employment, work, social insurance, education, "culture," health care, and leisure—in a word, everything. Secondly, I am thinking in terms of a certain manner of existence that allows for a planned, predictable way of treating time and events, creating a stable everyday life—and a stable image of the world. This whole technological, social, and economic construct, as well as people's outlooks, were liquidated over the course of the last dozen years or so.

Initially (and until 2002) the Wałbrzych bootleg mines were dug with heavy gear; however, after a series of confiscations, they were dug by hand, and then reinforced with wooden constructions. At any rate, from 2002–2005, three to eight or nine people generally worked a single Wałbrzych mine. The division of labor went as follows: one or two people worked at the bottom as hackers; then there was a chain of people passing along the takings and transporting them to the surface. At this point, other people, said to "sift" or "work the sifter," went through the coal and poured it into sacks. Still others, generally schoolboys, hauled off the sacks and piled them into small buses or Żuk or Nysa pickup trucks. Often the same people hacked the coal, built the reinforcing structures (roof timbers, rods, land tie bars), carried out the takings, sifted them, packed the coal into sacks, and carried the sacks to the vehicles. The experienced miners worked at building the reinforcements and chopping, while the younger and less experienced ones "sifted" and carried.[26]

"Experience" therefore plays a considerable role in the mine, and this "knowledge" is clearly stressed in conversations with bootleg miners. On the one hand, the young miners learn how to build from the elder ones: "They kept coming to the Barbara and saying, 'Marek, please build us one ... ,' and then they stopped. ... They slowly learned how to do it for themselves" (TR/WB/25). On the other hand, they are constantly accused of ignorance, which can cause lethal accidents to happen to the diggers. "It's not so easy to build one," said one of the diggers I knew most closely, "you have to know how to do everything, know the ins and outs. ... There are guys here who've never done this work ... but when it's just miners doing the job, then you don't get any accidents" (TR/ WB/25). Statements like "you've got to know what you're doing when you build one" cropped up very frequently, sometimes even punctuating conversations. The work of particular reinforcements was also described in a particular fashion, always depicted as active; I was shown how they "work" when something happens, and no static outline of these structures was provided. Work in the bootleg mines thus clearly involves oral communication, and also recollection, in almost direct accordance with the dynamic attributes of the oral manner of communication. Stories of technical procedures can be difficult for the anthropologist to follow, since they more often follow a situation of "doing something" than any kind of actual structure. For example, diggers from Sobięcin told me about "risers" and about how they were made. They described how they carried out their tasks and what tools they used when the work was harder; but when everything "went" more easily, they were incapable of explaining what, in the theoretical/spatial sense, this "riser" was. In much the same fashion, a coke man from the Victoria, who came from a family of diggers that I had met, always explained the functioning of the coke plant in motion, and less according to its function than according to his position and the work he performed:

> Question: This extinguisher vehicle you work on—does it cart the coal from the oven?
>
> Answer: Well, when there's a batch, then you go and get the batch, you see ... then you extinguish it, you go up the tower ... you go on the ramp—
>
> Q: But where does the batch come from?
>
> A: You do it on the machine ... you set it how and for what you want, and it comes churning out. The button has [garbled] tones. And that's the batch.
>
> Q: And then?
>
> A: Then the batch goes into the oven. The machine churns it out and the batch goes into the oven. (TR/WB/40)

He spoke in much the same way when I went with him to the coke plant; I had to wait until something started to happen, for example, until the coke was extinguished, and only then, in motion, did I hear how many minutes it would sit there. Afterward, when the vehicle moved toward the ramp, I heard: "Oh, look ... now it's moving ... you see ... it's moving." This knowledge is, to a large degree, verbalized, and closely tied to the performance of an activity, to a concrete situation, a "situation instead of an abstraction" (Ong 2002)—it is an action that is underway. In the miners' tales, various elements of the process (whether building the bootleg mine or burning the coke) are combined with regard to the action being performed ("You see ... it's moving"), and not with regard to their functions or the whole of the process ("This extinguisher vehicle—does it cart the coal from the oven?").

This means that, in the bootleg mines, knowledge is more a kind of ability, tied to practical motions of the body, proper blows or a way of gripping a pickaxe. The diggers immediately noticed all the mistakes I was making at work: my way of carrying tools, or striking or "breaking" the coal. "Sifting" the coal is also an activity in which the rhythm of swaying the body and holding the sifting crate are extremely important, as it is with work on self-made sifting equipment. These abilities in using the body—"techniques of the body," to refer to Marcel Mauss's classic essay (2006)—thus create a reservoir of post-mining knowledge. The bodily extensions of the workers—the tools they use—thus become "techniques of the body." In this way, the body fills the space between the intentional "I" and the world of material objects, and objects become a kind of prostheses or extension of the physically active body, which simultaneously generates significance (Attfield 2000: 238–239). As Judy Attfield demonstrates, among such "appendages to the body" are tools we know and see in shop displays, such as drills, brushes, hammers, screwdrivers, etc. (ibid.: 245). Digging coal, building bootleg mines, collecting scrap, unearthing pipes, and extracting metal parts from the infrastructure become a wide field giving rise to new methods of using body/tool combinations. Similarly, in building and running the bootleg mines, the miners are constantly analyzing the function and design of the reinforcements they have made, of the various coal walls and the paths of the veins. "Here it's hard [coal]. As it goes up it—oh, see how it goes up there—like I said, it'll start to move. Half a pickaxe will ... you've got to put up a *taczak* [a pillar], oh, see, right over here. But ... one roof timber in there, and then a second one here ... from that spot, where the clay was"; and a minute later, "we take the *taczak* and put it here, and you go on the right flank. ... How much wood ... makes a roof timber, tear up a bookcase, whack, whack" (TR/WB/23); and again, "Just a sec, Leon, let's set a *taczak,* four meters down. There's some rock there, and it goes in some more, and there also has to be a sill ... six more sacks, and that'll be it ... and we'll build that *taczak* right away ... maybe half an hour, two *taczaki* up above, two down below, and there you are" (TR/WB/25).

The result is that the temporary construction of the bootleg mine is a subject of ongoing discussion, a "private technology" that replaces other technological procedures applied in mines, closely tied to the verbalized knowledge, the knowledge of the body. Moreover, diggers often have one "preferred" tool and speak of it constantly. A pickaxe with a metal handle, for instance, was handed to me with something bordering on reverence when I was learning to chop coal (TR/WB/8, 23, 25); and they often speak of regretting that tools were buried underground. "Look, everything here should come out with a saw, and you're cutting with your hands" (TR/WB/8); "We used to have a wood saw, one that *went through everything* [emphasis mine], but now it's been buried" (TR/WB/23). It was imperative that these were "silent" tools that made no noise, and I was often told of their outstanding qualities for manual labor. "If you started in with a chainsaw here we'd have the cops after us in a second" (TR/WB/8) they said, evidently confirming that the quiet tools drew no one's attention. The "lightness" with which these manual tools work is also emphasized. For instance, I was told how diggers chiseled through a meter-thick layer of rock to a vein of coal: "The boys went through here to the vein, look, here's the rock. ... The boys went through two meters of rock ... they had a chisel, and chiseled their way ... whack, whack ... they worked slowly, working away ... and they got there" (TR/WB/12); or how that marvelous saw cut through a pine with just "a few strokes" (TR/WB/23). All the same, we ought to note that the city/forest patrols know all too well where this team digs. On chilly days they warmed themselves by burning wood in old barrels, and the smoke pointed precisely to the spot where they dug; moreover, the terrain around them was covered in stumps of fallen trees. What is the meaning of these "silent tools," then? As we can see, their importance is clearly overemphasized.

"Techniques of the body" knowledge was also a collectively heightened perception of what went on in the bootleg mine. The miners did all their work with keen attention—something they called "listening to the hole." In a sense of what was tangible/audible, they constantly monitored the state of the shaft in which they worked. They claimed that the most dangerous situations were abandoned, "unworked" shafts, because then their state—i.e., how they "worked" or "held" and when they crumbled—was unknown. The safe shafts were therefore the ones that were "worked"; we might say, these were felt as one's own body was felt. "I'll tell you how it is with a pit," a digger told me, "you've got to be listening to a pit. If you're listening, then nothing's going to happen to you" (Szanciło 2005; WAŁB 26). Elsewhere I heard: "The pit will give you a signal" (TR/WB/12). Let's look at one more fragment (a statement from another digger): "Birches are like that, they snap like matchsticks. But a pine tends to tremble. I'm wary with the birch trees ... they fall right away, it's dangerous, and the pine just cracks slowly, it gives you a signal, and then you don't sit there waiting, you know you've got to get away. ... Recently I was sitting there and I heard the cracking of pine, so I went to the roof timber and made supports, built under it ... and it's still holding out to this day" (TR/WB/35).

I slowly realized how this listening ability was a routine of sorts, and nothing out of the ordinary. Furthermore, it was a team effort, a kind of shared communication, and the diggers had to depend on one another. Every "movement" of the shaft had to be immediately communicated. "When we're digging, there's no two ways about it ... the whole time you've got to be looking, keeping your eyes peeled; and they're looking out for you, because on your own, you're a goner ... you don't stand a chance" (TR/WB/12). "Everyone's looking out for everyone else ... you can move in this direction or that. ... When the signal comes, all right, we pull out! If the wood breaks, the supports bend, like it suddenly went to shit, that'd be the end for us" (TR/WB/12). These statements were repeated practically every time the conversation turned to the subject of accidents and dangers at work. The diggers warned one another, using their senses of hearing, touch, sight, and smell. "Then it's just like down below ... in the mines ... everyone looks out for everybody else" (TR/WB/23); "But a guy doesn't even think about it ... you don't let anybody out of your sight, you're looking up, all around you, at everything" (TR/WB/25).

Quite frankly, there is a mutual kindness among the diggers and a "silent attention" shown for one another. This does not mean there is no animosity or competition. I came across more than one incident of competing digger groups filling in each other's shafts, though this could also have been associated with informal ties with coal clients or agents (this I was unable to ascertain). Nonetheless, in terms of behavior within a group and toward third parties, care and attention are deeply embodied in the sense of Maussian "techniques of the body" (2006), such behavior resulting from a work community. I noted these automatic reactions repeatedly, even when I greeted the diggers for the first time and went down into the shafts. The diggers often interrupted their work to make sure I didn't fall or hit my head, though there were no objective signs of this—I even got the impression I was being coddled. The observer is also astonished by the mutual aid they provide. For example, they help each other when they heft the sacks of coal onto their shoulders, when they scatter the earth and when they hammer in the props, advising each other how best to perform a certain action (digging involves solving many technical problems off the bat). This mutual kindness[27] is generally one of the first things one observes in an anthropological study of bootleg mines (Wagner 2003). This is often simply because a single family works in a bootleg mine; for instance, in a few teams I encountered a father working with his four or five sons, or perhaps their cousins. This is a custom inherited from working in the mines, where there was also a certain nonverbal system of communication and a developed trust in warning signals, where "everyone looked out for everyone else." This indicates a remarkable community among the men working in the mines, a community to some extent defined and sold as part of the poetics of socialist propaganda, which spread a cult of physical and manual labor, and an almost erotic intimacy among male workers (Tomasik 1999: 128). To some degree this existed in Wałbrzych's mines; I was told of intimacy and mutual care "down below" that was taken for granted. Weronika Plińska demonstrates that this intimacy also arose from the spatial restrictions. The miners undressed together, washed each other's backs in the showers and, out of necessity, relieved themselves "down below"; and when they traveled in the underground rail, they sat "thighs wedged between thighs" because of the lack of space (Plińska 2005).

The diggers' community is thus generally a small group put together in one or a few neighboring bootleg mines, and is a sense deeply rooted in the miners' mode of behavior—or in the "body's knowledge."[28] The field of experience in which knowledge and communication are formed has also been transferred; it creates a framework of inert and physical memory, and as such is more a structure of unconscious repetitions than a possession of concrete knowledge. We might therefore state that this memory preserves neither visible, technical, or abstract principles that can be pinned down, nor even "building" structures. It is more a memory of the overall reality of the bootleg mine; it maintains contact with the reality and daily life of digging, with danger that "cracks" or "trembles." In *How Societies Remember* (1989), Paul Connerton described such memory as an "incorporating practice," as opposed to "inscribing practice" or knowledge that is gathered systematically (1989: 72–73). The memory of knowledge passed on in the bootleg mines is therefore incorporated knowledge, a kind of verbomotor correlate of recollection (see Ong 2002). Work in the bootleg mines creates an internal inscription; it is an extension of applied knowledge and abilities, and also a memory of having lived through danger.

Rhythm, Jokes, Anecdotes: "Scoffing at the World"

The danger the diggers face is only somewhat tangible to the anthropologist. After all, the Labor Safety and Hygiene (BHP) regulations no longer apply in the bootleg mines. And yet, as one works in the bootleg mines, one thinks of safety at all times. Certain sequences exist in bootleg mine work: hacking coal, collecting the kibbles into cradle cars, transporting it outside, sifting it and packing it into sacks. Every once in a while, however, there is a short break of around ten minutes, after someone says "time for a smoke," which is a kind of internal command that signifies a break. This derives from the miners' work customs and the division of time into shifts. Some diggers perform certain actions in a certain order, which is also tied to the rhythm of work. Many who were reluctant to speak with me at work, even if merely waiting for enough coal to be collected and to lift it out, behaved entirely differently during their breaks, then telling me a great deal. Physical routine thus crosses beyond the custom of the body's technique to become the body's "contents" or "property," an incorporated memory, or a "habitual memory," to quote Connerton, in which "the past is, as it were, sedimented in the body" (1989: 72). In mining cultures this testifies, as Marian Gerlich (1989) and others have shown, less to custom and routine than it marks the unrelenting tension and constant sense of danger in the mining life. The day's schedule plays a similar function, giving the diggers a powerful foothold in an everyday life. Returning home from work, the miners always did all their activities in the same order: they undressed, performed their hygienic rituals, washed, left their black clothing by the door, and ate supper. All this created an enclosed rhythm that was also observed by their families (Zubelewicz 2005: 3).[29]

In the bootleg mines, as once in the ordinary mines, work goes on with a sense of danger that is partly under control, but never entirely so, as it has an aspect of blind chance. This is where humor comes in. The diggers seldom laugh or joke while at work (hacking coal, carrying sacks, or loading them), though many jokes are made during the breaks. A break in digging is generally announced, and usually consists of smoking and making quips, sometimes in a fairly unsophisticated and impromptu fashion. These are the legendary "miners' jokes" about which Dorota Simonides has written (see, among others, 1984; 1988b). These jokes and the "guffaws" resulting from the mediocre, fairly off-handed word plays that are, to be frank, less than humorous even to the bootleg miners, are mainly told down below, during breaks from the hacking.

The jokes and the guffaws are, I noticed, clearly rhythmic, occurring at concrete intervals—several of my closest interlocutors regularly burst out laughing at intervals of a few dozen seconds or so, mocking one another. A clear above/below division takes place. Above, at the mouth of the bootleg mine, fewer jokes are told, and the preference is for discussion of technical matters, the construction of the shaft and clients, while down below the jokes come in rapid succession, and sometimes fill the whole of the break. As Anna Szanciło has observed, the diggers say that "down below you tell jokes," while up above you "discuss serious subjects" (Szanciło 2005; WAŁB 26). The jokes told underground are also more mediocre, go on indefinitely and have a rhythm all their own. Where does this rhythm come from? We might say that this is a rhythm present in some social practices (ritual laughter, lamentation); it allows for unpredictable events to be grasped, captured and neutralized. Rhythm, as Paul Connerton notes in his analyses of social physical practices (1989: 76), has a way of allowing the unpredictable to be grasped. Through its structure, through the forced, compulsive repetition, it closes the path that is open to possibilities. We are therefore dealing with an internal impulse of rhythmic laughter.

In this way, the diggers are bound by an invisible thread to a reality that brooks no negotiation. They never know how their workday will finish, if danger will occur (a collapse of the wooden construction or a cave-in), or if they will receive money for the coal they have extracted. Laughter is thus located between constant threat, on the one hand, and its neutralization on the other. At any rate, this "in-between" location is tied to the very manner in which the miners joke, as well as its rhythm and relentlessness[30]; the jokes themselves, meanwhile, are fairly indifferent, and generally boil down to the men mocking one another. While a group with whom I was working was returning home, they began chatting up some diggers still at work in a neighboring shaft: "What are you doing there underground? Found some kind of treasure?" At this the others began to shout: "We have, we've got some dynamite! Now we're digging with dynamite.... We've struck it rich, you see" (TR/WB/27). The joke was humorous to neither the diggers nor myself, yet everyone responded with a short guffaw. After some time I realized that the use of dynamite in a joke might have been significant for the miners, for whom it (or explosives in general) was an everyday tool. It resonated with a certain subconscious significance—the significance of an explosion as danger or death. Death and danger thus came into the open, came unsealed through jokes. As Anthony Giddens has noted (1991: 111), the word *risqué* indicates a risk in French, while in English it denotes an unfriendly joke or an offensive quip. This facilitates a certain transitiveness in meaning: a joke is a risk/threat (moreover, the English "risk" was once written the same as the French, *risqué*). Nonetheless, the whole situation remains somehow frivolous and unfitting; death, as it were, is shifted into the background, somewhat "tested out," and the presentation of dynamite as treasure sets the framework of the absurd for a few seconds. This manner of joking is to some degree the flip side of an "imagined death." "One by one we go to work, and if someone fucks up, well, that's that" (TR/WB/43), they would laugh, for example, as they descended into the shaft. "Don't be afraid, if you fall way down there, we'll dig you out" (WAŁB 26), they would say, or "Look here," smiling and pointing toward one of the shaft tunnels, "this could be your grave" (WAŁB 26). Similarly, though no longer in jest, I heard the miners make the above-quoted statements about how, if someone forbade them from continuing to dig coal, as a final recourse they would climb down a shaft and "blow themselves up." Or, in an alternate version: "Then we'll go down there, to the very bottom, and they can bury us."

The jokes spread among the diggers irritated me; I was truly fed up with them. This was particularly true at the beginning of my research, when they were generally aimed at my awkwardness. They stressed my two left hands and my inability to grip a pickaxe, and commented on how the coal sprayed directly in my face when I chipped at it. It later turned out that this was their standard behavior toward newcomers—they "tested" other researchers (students) the same way, and I was similarly tested at Barbórka (St. Barbara's Day) festivities. Then the whole group ordered me to solve some puzzles. The puzzles often involved manual dexterity and were condemned to failure, and my inability to solve them was accompanied by bursts of laughter. Such ritualized hazings of the newcomer as a *fryc* (greenhorn) or *fuks* (beginner; also called a "cat" or a "wolf" in Polish) have been described as quite typical of rituals in other closed groups: rural and industrial workplaces, prisons, or army barracks (Tokarska, Wasilewski, and Zmysłowska 1982: 100–103), and particularly, in the sphere of the mining culture (Simonides 1988b). The diggers themselves explained the average jokes made down in the mines involved tying together trouser legs, or opening a valve to spray someone with oil. It is notable that all the while these jokes cropped up in the vicinity of danger (TR/WB/23). "But it wasn't done so that something would really happen. ... We laughed, but he wasn't offended." We find the motifs of absurdity and reversal, characteristic of a symbolic sense of death, the motif of the symbolic "death blow" to the new (Tokarska, Wasilewski, and Zmysłowska 1982: 98–106). In the Wałbrzych mines the youngsters were sent to fetch a key to the (coal) wall, or asked to sniff a lump of coal to determine whether "there wasn't methane (an odorless gas which signifies the danger of explosions and death) inside" (Plińska 2005). This is always, however, an "overblown" death, out of place and light-hearted; and though it did not take center stage, it was always present.

The subject of this mockery was their (the miners') organic deficiency (their neglect of hygiene owing to their present economic living standard). As Emil Zubelewicz (2005) has noted, this particularly concerns the diggers' dentition—many have lost some of their teeth, and this is clearly evident in this group (as it is among collectors of scrap or other refuse).[31] The diggers refer to their dental situation as a "ruin," and their teeth are a frequent pretext for mocking one another. These remarks, though light-hearted, are saddening, and increase the sense of degradation. One of my interlocutors said that his mouth was a "ruin" and told, in fits of laughter, how his false teeth had fallen out in various situations. "They flew up in the air," his wife chimed in, "and he flapped his arms trying to catch them. Then he picked them up and wrapped them in a handkerchief. He made quite the scene" (WAŁB 24).

Law and Lawlessness: Interior Spectacles

Since 2001/2002 diggers of bootleg mines have been persecuted by city security patrols, and sometimes by police or the forest inspectorate. The bootleg mines function lawlessly (Zubelewicz 2005), a fact that is constantly being reported by the local newspapers, as in the articles "War between Law and Lawlessness" (Szczurowska 2003) and "(Under) mining the Law" (Gołębiowska 2002), where we find such phrases as "lawless town," "lawlessness in the forests," "lawlessness in the streets," "Wild West," etc. "They break the law," the police stated in the press, "they have no permit to extract coal, they ravage the environment, and put themselves and others at risk" (Szczurowska 2003). Nonetheless, diggers almost gained official permission to dig for coal in bootleg mines in 2002. The mayor at the time presented a "bootleg mine legalization plan," and the commander of the Wałbrzych police force promised that "no one would bother their digging" if they refrained from using heavy gear (Gołębiowska 2002). The next mayor, however, placed an official ban on digging, and initiated an energetic fight against the illegal shafts, while city patrols began confiscating coal, shovels, and pickaxes, and spot-checking Żuk vehicles. This gave rise to a vague and undefined situation. In 2000/2001 the diggers were still working in the parks inside of town and in the meadows just on the outskirts, so that the City Hall employees could see them through their windows, yet no one paid them any mind (Teczka press materials). Some time later, it was decreed that they were breaking the law. In reality, there was no full agreement as to the status of the bootleg mines. For example, former mine supervisor Bogusław Dyszkiewicz told the newspaper *Gazeta Wrocławska*: "I've got nothing against these people, who often risk life and limb in their difficult work, struggling to support their families." However, he promptly added that "it would be impossible to legalize this sort of work" (*Gazeta Wrocławska,* Wałbrzych supplement, 247/2001, p. 3). One might say that these are borderline or threshold activities, which take on negative or positive connotations at various levels of social sentiment. On the one hand, the diggers have the permission of the ex-mayor (during several collective demonstrations, the diggers chanted slogans like "We're working, not stealing," and these were accompanied by a certain pride and collective conviction, and even a sense of external acceptance in the propriety of the position adopted). On the other hand, the police and city patrols persecute and punish them, treating them as criminals. As one team phrased it, "'Illegal' is just empty talk. We're digging legally because we want to support our families" (Zubelewicz 2005: 7). "Am I some sort of criminal," one digger complained, "because that's how it looks …, we have the city court after us …, deferred sentences for the next two years …, that's how it looks! I just think it's all funny … they took my mug shot … from the front and the side—just liked I'd murdered someone!" (TR/WB/23).

The diggers describe this vague and incomprehensible situation in their own fashion, with their jokes, and, I would say, process it in a special way. This takes place on a defined level of communication, on the level of mockery and jokes, which pulls free from individual actions and enters the sphere of the collective repertoire of responding, relating, and surviving (see Bogatiryev and Jakobson 1982[1929]). This fluidity of social status creates an empty space here—a gap in categories and verdicts. How might it be filled? Here I found the oddest of mining expressions (constructing bizarre images and relationships). As an example, I shall quote a fragment of casual conversation between some members of a team returning home from work: "We were once returning from the pits [the bootleg mines], and in Kuźnice, a retired old woman asked us, 'Excuse me, have you got some coal?' And we say, 'OK, but we'll only sell a tone.' 'A tone? But I haven't got enough for a tone.' … 'And when is your pension coming in?' 'In two days.' So all right, we pour her out a tone. And she was so happy. But there was maybe six hundred kilograms there, tops," he added, bursting with laughter. Then a second digger chimed in: "Give us a break, there was eight hundred." "OK, so maybe there was eight hundred," he responded (TR/WB/23). Other anecdotes followed: "Once there were some boys driving along with a bundle full of asphalt stones. A woman was standing there in front of her hut, and they yelled out 'Hey! We've got some coal!' 'How much?' They told her. 'For two tones?' She paid up. She got up the next morning and found asphalt! The next morning her husband asks her, 'What did you buy all that asphalt for?'" (TR/WB/23). The story was accompanied by laughter, though I was aware that everyone had heard it already. A moment later there came another anecdote: "During the night we went 'round to the parish priest. We begged him: 'Take some of this coal off us, we've been driving three days already!' He agreed. But we had cobblestones. In the morning the sacristan comes out and sees the pile of cobblestones in front of the cellar. 'What do you plan to do with these stones?' he asked the priest, and the priest rubbed his eyes. There was just stones, and not a bit of coal" (TR/WB/23). All of these stories were accompanied by peals of laughter.

I heard the preceding anecdotes in various versions. I was told for half an hour, for example, about swindles carried out with a tampered scale, or of lumps of fine coal and frozen water that were sold as coal. Listening to these stories, I increasingly realized that it was very hard to link them with factual experiences. The issues concerned the very fact of telling these jokes at the expense of other people, of their neighbors and representatives of the "outside world," i.e., priests and policemen. The diggers I worked with dug for coal every day, and seldom dealt with sales or searching for new clients; this only happened when there was real difficulty selling. If they did sell coal directly (something I repeatedly observed), they did this within their circle of neighbors and family, and they prided themselves on their honesty; this was a kind of mutual neighbor/family service. It may have occurred on a few occasions that they went about a village selling coal. This was not a daily occurrence, however, at least in the period I was there, when they were tied to their middlemen and clients under very unfavorable conditions. The middleman took the cargo and passed them their day's wages (a transaction I cannot say was always honest); and, though they spoke of this reluctantly, they were quite evidently exploited. I believe nonetheless that they never actually intended to cheat the local residents, or even villagers who lived further away, or the priest. It often occurred that the diggers valued a steady daily wage over a one-time lucky deal. These stories did, however, express a sense of freedom that was easily turned into a joke or a quip, though in either case we had the illusion of a devil-may-care spirit gaining the advantage over the opposition (the clients).

Things were strikingly similar when it came to the punitive consequences the police and city patrols levied against diggers. In the above-mentioned statements we have a certain devil-may-care attitude toward gaining control and deriding the forces of the law. The diggers built improvised story-pictures, which led to imaginary shifts in social relations. They concocted jokes and mockeries of functionaries that were often dialogue-based and situational. "The city patrol once stopped me," said one digger, "and asked: 'What's in the bundle?' So I told them: 'It's full of bees!' Those boys were struck dumb.... They were totally boggled!" (TR/WB/15). Another anecdote: "One of our guys was lugging snow in some sacks, and drove around so long loaded up that he got stopped ... the police ... 'You're carting coal!' they say. And he says, 'What do you mean, I'm just bringing some white snow for my kids to play with.' So they have a look—and the sacks are filled with white snow! And what happened then? They all laughed as hard as they could; they're still laughing today. And he was just bringing a little white snow for his kids, he said" (TR/WB/23).

This sort of story (told through jokes and quips) was an almost constant feature of miners' communication. I also heard anecdotes that explained how everyone all around (city patrol, police, neighbors) knew all too well what was in the back of a Żuk vehicle. Of course, it was coal they had dug up, and the police and the city patrol were pretending "they don't know what we're up to here." This endlessly repeated refrain was part of the permanent repertoire of the team I worked with. "They [the police, city patrol] are well acquainted with us here," I constantly heard the diggers say, "they know perfectly well where we are and what we're up to" (TR/WB/23). "If they wanted to, they could have cracked down on us long ago," they said. "They all know what we're doing and where" (TR/WB/41). I once heard: "A ranger came 'round here with his dog and said [looking at the stumps all around]: 'It's not the wood that's important, I don't know where you got it from, but just make sure you're building safely'" (TR/WB/23). I later heard similar stories in several variants. "A policeman came 'round here, and we ran off into the forest. ... But he says: 'Lads, I'd like a bit of coal for myself, for the home. I just need a bit of *groszek* [a kind of coal].' And he got his *groszek,* and some fine coal as well, because I just happened to have *groszek* with me" (TR/WB/23). These statements reveal a certain image of familiarity, an acquaintance with the functionaries, even a momentary alternate order, in which their activities are entirely accepted and understood by society (authority figures).

Of course, we can assume that these stories really did happen, for there did exist a "silent" local acceptance (even among the police and the city patrols) of digging in bootleg mines or extracting post-mining scrap from the ground. Nonetheless, there was a clear reservoir of stories that I heard over two years of these daily conversations, these daily opinions and anecdotes. This means that there is a collective affirmation of these tales. At one point these tales wrench free and begin to live their own lives, creating a framework of transferred knowledge, in which, as Pyotr Bagotiryev and Roman Jakobson have written on the creation of folklore, a certain collectivity was "both producer and recipient" (1982 [1929]). These stories are forever being repeated. To what do they refer? To what do they bear testimony? We are dealing with a particular sort of game that transforms meaning and designs a new and improvised sort of social relationship. These jokes and quips are, on the one hand, meant to prove access to authority and its representatives, and on the other, to emphasize the diggers' sense of distance from these acts of trickery, rearranging, and derision. This repetitive and scoffing formula, a kind of improvised folklore, creates an entirely unanticipated framework for post-mining communication. They speak laughingly of a "Wałbrzych tone," for everyone knows that this describes a weight much below an actual tone. What are these stories truly about? I would like to return at this point to that undefined space, the empty place in social relations and transactions, the vacuum that requires filling. I believe that this empty space in the post-mining world keeps the ex-miners in the bootleg mines from asking themselves and others the basic questions: Who are they? How could they have responded to this? Are they honest working men, or do they steal coal on a daily basis? Many of them dig by night so that they won't be seen, carting off the coal in their Żuk vehicles in the morning, and they live in constant fear of being called to court, of having their equipment confiscated. Many of them have been through city court and are on probation. And yet they are digging coal as ex-miners, in a professional manner, minding their work as best they can, working hard and honestly and, upon returning home, giving their earnings to their wives. Almost everyone, including the police or the forestry workers, understands and respects this situation, or takes it into account. Thus I repeat: What is the nature of their situation?

The diggers are incapable of giving a clear response to this situation. However, they are forced to make daily efforts to understand their actions (digging holes for over five years), essentially, to explain their actions to themselves. Life goes on its daily course and poses daily questions, and jokes are a form of response. Through scoffing anecdotes, they invent momentary responses that topple the norms of honesty, the hierarchies of power and social relations. These go from imaginary and almost carnivalesque play at swindling, to spectacles of sorts and bursts of laughter (much like at carnival or mid-Lent), scoffing at others who are swindled in a mocking and absurd fashion. If we may permit ourselves such an expression, then, this is an *internal* spectacle; the actors/diggers easily succumb to jokes and laughter during their unstable work, repeating this several times over the course of the day (see Turner 1982: 102–116). In this way, they create a mirror of sorts, allowing them to be constantly checking their own appearances; then an infinitely processed knowledge of themselves and the world (responses) moves from these quips and anecdotes to an imagined "ground zero" of social structure (Turner 1969; 1990: 8–14). At this point jokes and laughter cross over from one extreme to another, much like the danger of cave-ins. While laughing and joking underground, the diggers' laughter grasps for "imagined death" (the grave), thus neutralizing it momentarily. The jokes and quips aimed at the law grasp for an imaginary threshold, a collapse of laws and measurements (the "Wałbrzych tone"), hierarchies (mocking policemen with the snow-filled sacks), statuses (the ranger cautioning them to work safely), and strictures of honesty (the coal swindles). As I have shown, the illegal extraction of coal is full of internal contradictions.

They therefore create a projection of how they live and operate by the circuitous, misguided route of these responses. This process of mockery, laughter, and joking is, I would say, extraordinarily draining; the power of the rhythmic laughter testifies to this. It is a particular form of autocommunication, in which one limit after another of the post-miner's "I," the post-miner's world, is held up to ridicule. The laughter then travels both ways with remarkable ease, endlessly liberating one and the same road.

The Grey Market: Deal-Making and Resourcefulness

This internal manner of making light of the social world (and of oneself) is part of a larger context. These illegal and informal activities go beyond the miners, and in Wałbrzych this is a phenomenon almost universally known. I chiefly have in mind collecting scrap or semiprecious metals, chopping down and stealing trees (for the bootleg mines or for kindling), stealing coal or metal parts of the infrastructure, etc. This results in the creation of a social consensus, whereby these widespread activities, these everyday methods of gaining a livelihood (to survive) employed by the local inhabitants, including the active state functionaries (Zubelewicz 2005: 14–15), are seen as *natural*. Numerous buildings are being demolished, and the dismantling of steel building parts and brickwork often takes place alongside a protected and effectively managed terrain. In the vicinity of the Victoria coke plant, alongside the old, functioning halls and the coking furnaces, the old post-mining buildings are being dismantled; for the coke plant workers this adjacent informal demolition and scrap collecting is a natural, everyday occurrence. As another example, trucks illegally carting off scrap and bricks drive up outside the postindustrial fields in the vicinity of the Central Train Station and the former Wałbrzych Mine, among a few other places, practically right before pedestrians. To this we might add the numerous collectors pulling homemade carts piled high with scrap and other refuse (windows, embrasures, electronics, and bicycle parts). At any rate, the buildings being dismantled for their bricks are often in similar or even better condition than those that are still operative. Here, we might compare the dismantled buildings, former properties of the directors of the Victoria Mine, to the old coke plant constructions still in use by private companies. An example from outside of Wałbrzych is the old German brickyard in Lubsko, which has turned out to be more valuable than the bricks it once produced. This "grey market" of goods has become a widespread phenomenon in various parts of western Poland (the same goes for Lubsko, according to my own research). Yet, nobody, including the police functionaries, entirely knows how to qualify this practice: is this demolition/collecting theft, or should it be regarded as a means of ensuring a livelihood?

Here we ought to note that this behavior reveals a property of social life that was evident in Poland's communist era. Back then, a portion of the factory goods were designated as being "for the workers," and taking home some goods from the mine, for instance, was to some degree socially acceptable, particularly if these things were needed by the worker and were perceived as "dispensable objects" for the mine (Wódz 1989: 59–60). This sort of internally sanctioned theft of "state" property, and the accompanying "familiarity," understood as a communicative and organizational symptom, was in part described during research into semicriminal, informal groups of workers (known as "cliques") in large state corporations during the times of the People's Republic (Tymiński 2002: 123–126). These cliques committed petty and more serious financial crimes (theft, embezzlement, corruption), and were accompanied by a certain ideology of "resourcefulness" and internal tolerance. This phenomenon, described by Elżbieta Tarkowska and Jacek Tarkowski (1994), after Edward Banfield (1958), as "amoral familizm," an informal means of creating access to goods and privileges accepted in small groups (of family or acquaintances) through "deal-making" or "connections," and as rooted in a widespread sector of social life in communist Poland. This world of "resourcefulness" inside a group was generally aimed against the official social structures and institutions; it was a quiet way of maximizing one's family interests, with "the presumption that everyone behaves the same way" (Tarkowska and Tarkowski 1994: 270).

What seems imperative here is the clear satisfaction arising from the very (imagined) potential of taking advantage of this informal world, of the "hidden" access to certain goods, of this "grey market." By the same token, it is not my impression that we are dealing with mere satisfaction derived from access to a defined sphere of goods or sphere of privileges, for this knowledge is almost universal in neighbor/family circles. "Everybody here knows what to do and how to go about it," I heard endlessly repeated. "If a guy fills up his tank at the [Orlen] gas station, everyone here looks at him like he's gone crazy [the reference here was to the widespread usage of combustible oil, known as 'soda pop' or 'tomato juice,' instead of legal fuel]" (TR/WB/42). Everyone knows about the illegal extraction of coal, the illegal taking of scrap, and the practice of cutting trees in the forest for firewood. "Oh, look—that forest is getting thin, really thin," I was told in one of the diggers' houses, in a tone that was nearly prideful. "We've cut almost all of them down … they're almost all gone [taken for firewood]" (WAŁB 24). It seemed to me that there is a sense of resourcefulness, something I would call an experience of satisfactory "momentary profit." This temporary benefit is, to my mind, quite crucial, and provides something more than goods or privileges that are simply acquired in reality; what emerges is something like a socially imagined "resourcefulness" and "familiarity" from the fact that "everyone here digs" and "everyone knows how and what." This is a feeling of "momentary abundance," an imagined conviction of a socially produced world of "familizm" and "understanding" with the police. Of course, nothing is ever certain. Things can always end with a fine and harsh poverty for days to come, and, perhaps, might thus require a communicative ritual of sorts—a "ritual of resourcefulness" (this phrase has been applied by sociologists Anna Iwanowska, Michał Federowicz, and Tomasz Żukowski, quoted in Tymiński 2002: 124).

A careful look reveals something resembling an economic "short circuit," where barriers of accessibility to "goods" or "resources" are overcome. Something located beyond the material reach of my interlocutors suddenly became directly accessible through a shift to informal means. For instance, I was wondering out loud how to organize minibus transport for a group of students (my research companions), and the diggers told me that they knew a few people who had minibuses and who offered transport services. When we spoke of the price for the trip (Wałbrzych to Wrocław), they told me that they would "arrange things" so that it would not be expensive. "It won't cost you much, no problem, he'll pour in what's needed [i.e., the combustible oil] and that's that. … That's all you need" (TR/WB/42). In this statement I noted a sense of sudden "deal-making"—a service or a kind of good suddenly became accessible in a different fashion. Much as in the tales of intimacy with the police or city patrol, a stubborn reality kind of "collapsed." "Look," said one of the younger diggers to his workmate, "you just take these sacks (from the coal depot) and now they're *legally yours.*" Pouring coal into sacks from a legal coal depot meant that it became "legal" (nobody would then suspect that it had come from a "pit"), though in practice it made no real difference, because coal was generally transported in "illegal," unmarked sacks, anyway. What is the source of this unconcealed satisfaction in these statements, then? Perhaps the vital point is not only the avoidance of coal confiscation, but rather a communication of this "momentary advantage," an imagined "deal-making" or ability to "arrange things." There appears a feeling and an understanding of having crossed the barrier of the impossible, and a consciousness of "getting by." I would argue that this is the second world-creating function of familizm: a socially imagined "abundance" or inheritance of "economic resistance," in a situation where every day can conclude with the loss of the day's wages, a fine, a few days' poverty.

This communicated ability to get by, the sense that, to some degree, the world has become "easy," that the diggers are "getting by well" and that "things are somehow moving along," also appears in the verbal exchanges between close acquaintances in various teams of diggers. While returning home with one of the diggers, we came across a friend of his, who was also a digger: "Hey there.... What's this, are you off now?" "I'm off. We've got something to take care of, and anyway." "Oh, and what are you up to these days?" "Well, we've got a new spot, the *taczaki* are already up, the shelves are going in next." "Does that mean you're working nights?" "A bit, a bit. ... You gotta do something, right?" "Yeah, gotta keep things moving along" (TR/WB/12). What was particularly marked in this exchange of information was a shared knowledge that created access to a sense of particular resourcefulness, of being socially engaged in informal ways of "getting by." This exchange of opinions clearly gave the diggers pleasure, accompanied as it was by calm, lowered voices, smiles, and confidential gestures; the statements were curt, thus upholding the aura of "everybody knowing," "getting by," "you've got to get along somehow." This is a familiarized mode of coexistence, one that chiefly reveals itself in a noninformational form of communication (this is its phatic function). To my mind, such acts and declarations of "ease" are key in forming relations within this society. Calling the informal trade of the occupation period an "excluded economy," Kazimierz Wyka (1984) describes similar practices of constructing a sense of "getting by" within a society that take place during a time of constant threat and shortage. Such an evidently communicative/ritual dimension of the "grey market" is also stressed by Roch Sulima (with reference to Wyka's findings). Developing the notion of the "parallel economy," he emphasizes the significance of street trade and profiteering as a kind of "affirmation in the public space" (2003: 3).

What appears in this space is a "familiarity" that is communicated every day, an in-between area (within which everyone knows "what and how"). In the case of Wałbrzych, this situation is part of an even larger context, i.e., the diggers' and scrap collectors' above-described state of ambivalence in the eyes of the law; the ambiguity of this state comes to the fore in a multitude of ways, in declarations of "ease," "familiarity," and "intimacy." And though digging or collecting post-mining scrap are to some extent socially tolerated, they remain, as I have shown, sources of fear and unrest. The diggers take great liberties in establishing versions of the "facts" that suit them in arguments and negotiations, which do not always lead to a positive result (they often have outstanding fines or court trials). I am not, however, suggesting that the work of the diggers or the scrap collectors be situated exclusively on the axis of informal law (established orally, for instance, as opposed to formal law, which is generally established in writing). I am more concerned with demonstrating how a certain imagined social consensus emerged in all its splendor at a given moment, the point of its situational activation, and how it proffered a sense of "portable security," reaching back to deeply rooted work methods (cf. Tarkowska and Tarkowski 1994: 278). The "model of behavior" that developed this social consensus (an intricate world of meanings saturated with "social security," still functioning by reflex) is described by Terry N. Clark (1975: 322; quoted in Tarkowska and Tarkowski 1994: 278). In examining Chicago policemen of Irish extraction, he finds that their "most striking attribute … is the scope in which they depend on exchange of services in arranging matters. Even if there is a routine legal method of arranging something, one can be certain that the Irish Catholic policeman will prefer an informal means.… *They consciously cross beyond the formal system to arrange informal affairs* [emphasis mine]."

One example of this sphere of social life is a scene depicted in a documentary film on Wałbrzych diggers, *We're All Made of Coal* (filmed by Roman Janiszek, directed by Tomasz Wiśniewski). In one scene, a group of diggers transporting coal in their Żuk is stopped by a police patrol, and a quarrel ensues. The diggers demonstrate their sense of injustice and being wronged before the police and the camera ("power exists only 'on stage,'" Georges Balandier wrote, quoted in Herzfeld 2001: 126). They shout that they are working hard, and for this they are called thieves and offenders, but after some time they begin to treat the officers with more familiarity, and convince the officers to release them. The functionaries point toward the camera and say, "What, you expect me to strike a deal in front of the camera?" to which a (now self-confident) digger responds, "Ah, that camera will be gone in a moment," and makes a gesture signaling that the camera should be shut off, simultaneously resolving the whole business "from top to bottom." With this single gesture, it seems to me, he evokes this entire sphere of understanding, where many things are possible beyond the "letter of the law," beyond the written protocol. At that moment he creates a momentary communicative consensus, evoking an informal mode of operating, which is, of course, "known" to the functionaries. In fact, it is something "everybody knows"; and though no one speaks of it directly, it evokes a certain "local knowledge" that, as Clifford Geertz has described it, combines "what is" with "what should be"—i.e., "fact" with "law" (1983: 170-175). This sets in motion what Edward Hall (1976: 105–117) has called the high context (HC) of the communicative message: a certain intricate, internalized knowledge of social actors in the practice of social life, of what "everybody knows" and needs no definition, inscription, or description. All these statements and gestures speak of the high context of the "grey market economy." They speak of "striking a deal" (doling out the "tomato juice," tearing out tones of scrap from an old Victoria site). They reveal an extraordinary competence in evoking an entire, intricate world of meanings in a single moment on the basis of the sudden awakening of this "internalized knowledge"—a practical and semiotic universe of this "excluded economy" (Wyka) or "amoral familizm" (Banfield 1958; Tarkowska and Tarkowski 1994), a certain "poetics of survival."

The result is an alternative plane of using the law, whereby it is established in impromptu fashion and, as it were, according to custom, becomes an unwritten code where everything is contextual, situational, open to adjustment, and yet hidden (implicit). This is something resembling a verbal "legal reasoning," as described by Jack Goody with regard to presenting a manner of creating and using the law in East Africa (1986: 140–142). Verbal and shorn of inscribed rules/precedents, legal reasoning is dynamic and negotiated knowledge, its rules known to practically everybody, though it has no professional lawyers or "thinkers-about-law" (ibid.: 141). The result is a certain "soft" (from our perspective) or "dissolved" legal order, where laws/customs are always being reconfirmed, and where there is an all-important possibility to negotiate events (facts) every time, and to "negotiate" the law (cf. Geertz 1985). As Walter Ong demonstrates, this improvised confirmation is very commonplace in circumstances of nonwritten practice; as he writes, eyewitnesses are *prima facie* more trustworthy than texts (written, formalized statements, documents signed by a notary) in pretextual practices, as one cannot directly interrogate a text. In a live context, texts simply "fall silent" (2002: 135).

What occurs is quite significant. This is visible in the whole strategy of dodges and methods of proceeding in dealing with the city patrol and the police and, moreover, in the attempts to cross over to informality. The result is a peculiar dissolution of the law, where "everyone knows how and what," or the conversations with guards, police officers, or coal clients, in which there is little to be said, because the gestures say everything. I believe there exists a hidden legal sphere, a *jus commune*, which holds an element of this special intimacy, familiarity, and also, in a certain way, a cultural intimacy, to use Michael Herzfeld's expression (see 2005: ix–xi, 1–4). Social transactions performed in this way mean that the potential to negotiate everything that is (and was) will always be there in reserve, whether, for instance, the extracted coal is cause for writing up a bureaucratic report, or for a gesture of dismissal. Then the other, extraordinarily close and intimate image of law/reality steps forward with great intensity; this is a law that practically everybody knows and is able to manipulate with great skill. It then becomes pliable to their actions (albeit in an imagined fashion).

Elżbieta Tarkowska and Jacek Tarkowski describe the formation of such family/neighbor informal groups when confronted by institutional agendas, work systems, and the economic crisis of the 1980s. However, they clarify that these are marked by a particular group individualism and egotism, or are "swollen" or "extra-individual," to use Adam Podgórecki's terminology (Tarkowska and Tarkowski 1994: 266–267). In Wałbrzych and in post-mining Boguszów, my impression is that this created "world of informal ties" (ibid.: 264; see also Sikorska 1999: 117–118, 137–138) also (and perhaps primarily) takes place in a certain *absence* of structure, in the absence of its internalized existence. The system and work underground create an institutionalized "world." When it disappeared, it was replaced by a "resourcefulness" within the society, taking place only in the current context, with the public law still being executed. For example, the prohibition of destruction or theft was replaced by digging in the bootleg mines or illegal scrap gathering. This situation might be explained through the social practice of mutually beneficial wheeling and dealing that began in communist times (Podgórecki, quoted in Tarkowska and Tarkowski 1994: 271). This was an entirely new field of social experience. Yet, these acts might be explained and understood as reinforcing rituals of "presence" or "existence," as a mutual form of reassurance that "one does what one can to get by," that "there's a way around everything" and that "everyone knows what we're up to here." Actions that provide a momentary sense of advantage over reality can create an imagined "community of resourcefulness" (cf. Sikorska 1999: 137–138), and thus a real community of permanent uncertainty, incomprehension, daily uncertainty about labor, and the poverty that each new day brings.

This is an essential world-building dimension of the "excluded economy."

The "Internal Circulation" and the Fragmentation of Transactions

In Wałbrzych and its environs a circulation of nonlegalized, verbal, and informal goods and transactions has emerged. Nearly all of my interlocutors know the prices of scrap and their various values (there had been a "scrap rush" in the years 1996–2005). They all know the semiformal and informal sources of various other goods (such as wood, pine cones, coal, antiques, berries, and wild mushrooms); they also know the prices in the depots, so that all these goods can later be cashed in (TR/WB/11, among others). And yet an extremely essential issue is, to my mind, the fact that all the prices and equivalences of the services and goods are constantly fluctuating, and none are recorded, established, or controlled from above in any way. City transport might serve as an example: to a large extent, the city lines have been replaced by private minibuses that offer various tariffs, use various tickets, etc. As I have observed, the interiors of these minibuses are independently designed, probably in small, semiformal workshops (city transport in Wałbrzych and its environs has been regulated, with local transport companies coming into existence). The Żuks and coal-transporting buses are reworked (reinforcing and stiffening the shocks) in similar workshops/scrapyards, so that they do not give under a load, and thus do not reveal the coal they carry. Therefore, in a sense, this delegalization and informality of the post-transformation Wałbrzych economy is all-encompassing, taking place both on a technical level (the reworked cars are nonformalized, nonindustrial) and an economic one (as unregulated, unofficial transactions).

Here we ought to point out one more very important thing. A relativization of the values of the circulating materials has been taking place. Coal is often sold through the numerous coal agents, their Żuk vehicles typical sights in many streets of Boguszów. From the fuel depot, their Żuks cart the coal in parcels of one hundred kilograms, and they sell it to those who cannot afford to buy their fuel all in one go—i.e., to unemployed families and pensioners. It is significant that Boguszów's residents often complain that the coal salesmen cheat them in their measurements, for example, selling them twenty kilograms too little, though there is no way to determine precisely how much their coal purchases weigh. Because of price fluctuations, there are similar problems in purchasing coal extracted from bootleg mines. It increases or decreases depending upon who is buying (e.g., a close family member). It is hard to establish its real weight, and thus the value of the coal as well (fine coal, *groszek,* ruddy-stale, etc.); the concept of the "Wałbrzych tone" is, after all, in currency, and this means somewhat less than a tone. The prices and values (real values) are thus changeable and uncertain, so one often feels cheated to some degree. We are therefore dealing with a particular signification of transactions, i.e., social negotiations to which prices of foodstuffs (e.g., with the traveling shops), coal, and transportation are all subject. At around thirty zloty for a tank of fuel, transporting people by minibus can cost anywhere from a few dozen to a few hundred zloty, depending on the negotiation and the quantity of combustible oil pumped into the diesel-engine vehicle. Meanwhile, I should point out that this creates an open field for socially functioning bargains that are impromptu, momentary, and signified, and that the world of economic relations then becomes semifluid and constantly open to modification.

Here we find one more astonishing post-mining practice. I have noticed that the diggers are capable of endlessly recounting the sacks of coal they extract, the sacks with fine coal or *groszek,* and they generally do this during their break time. They determine how much they have left to dig, for whom they have to dig, and how many sacks are already filled and how many are left "to go." This counting is quite vital and elicits constant comment. "I tell you—when I go out there's twenty-five sacks, so I go out and look: 'How many,' I ask myself. 'How many? Twenty-one.' Oh, I think, there must have been more than that. ... That's the way I am, I count down to the last bag, you understand? Right down to the last bag. I might be off by one sack, maybe two, but no more. 'How many have you got there, six sacks?' 'No, four.' 'Good, they want forty—let's do ten more'" (TR/WB/25). This counting sometimes fills the whole of their breaks, though it also resembles everyday, phatic chit-chat that does not entirely oblige anyone to take part, a way of filling up a break, as the figures never seem to add up.[32] And so, they are counted and recounted, in a fairly free manner, and they say: "If we come at three we still have an hour and a half here, that'll make forty sacks an hour and a half. It'll be an hour. Hold on, it's ten past two, an hour and a half, count, count, here's an hour and a half, one throws, the other carries, you got it? So how many have you got?" (TR/WB/23). I have the impression that this is a kind of play on words. There is an overriding principle of uncountability, for in these conversations the diggers are unable to establish the quantity of sacks. In fact, the numbers never seem to add up. In a sense, this is less a matter of counting than one of *collecting* numbers, i.e., assembling what is and what could be, and creating an imagined depository/storehouse. "Learning to count," writes Manfred Sommer in his dissertation on collecting and enumeration, "is enlivened and supported by the ability to collect. Counting is a form of collecting that which is scattered, it is a kind of assembly" (2003: 383). This continual recounting is a manner of reaching what is new—though then the "old" may slip out of sight (ibid.: 386). In counting their sacks and in the time taken collecting them, the diggers are constantly re-working one and the same calculation, a certain "fluctuating state"; and a figure that has been established is constantly being broken down, so as to begin counting anew. "'We can do 30 here as well as some fine coal?' 'How much?' '20?' 'Who knows if that much will come out.' 'I see it different, tomorrow's Saturday, we'll do a tone—22 sacks and 13 will be fine coal.' '13?' 'There'll be 35.' 'I don't know. ...' 'We'll have to pack 30. ...' 'If we'd done 20 of fine coal, we'd be home by now.' 'We won't get 30 out of this place'" (TR/WB/23). The sacks, used as seats when work is finished and the diggers are waiting to load up the vehicle, again become beings in transition; their numbers vacillate when they are counted, becoming uncertain and requiring collection, recounting. Their contents are estimated, even if there are only a few: "We'll just do some building and dig out maybe 5 more sacks, then we'll have 10 or 12—that'll make an even ... 6 sacks ... in half an hour ..." (TR/WB/23). "Can counting be collecting even if what is being counted is already collected, evenly 'lined up' in a row?" Manfred Sommer wonders at one point (2003: 388). He responds: "Perhaps. ... If what is laid in a row is to be collected, you have to divide it, spread it out, scatter it once more." Collecting (counting) coal, bags, work hours, etc., is thus a constant process of collecting and scattering, building an ever-new relationship to what exists. We might say it is a reply to the question, "How much do I possess?" but with no capacity for a clear response. It is, I believe, a certain fear of countability.

Among the coal diggers in Wałbrzych and its environs, the status of various things, of goods and their values and numbers (uncountabil-ity), is not constant. The coal that lies beneath the surface of meadows gains value when extracted, poured into sacks, "counted," and sent by uncertain transport. The scrap lying there in the earth becomes valu-able through extraction, evaluation, successful dismantling, and finally through the whole exploration process. These goods are always given their value, and this process is again based on a social (mis)understand-ing, i.e., negotiating or "counting" an object's value while simultane-ously knowing its true worth. In short, there is a discrepancy between their statuses, and this precisely is the source of the movement of goods. Furthermore, at a certain point these goods undergo change, become equiv-alent, translating, for example, into a concrete sum of money—i.e., they become commodities (Appadurai 1986a: 14–15). The very social act of assigning things value is important here, as are the conditions by which these acts are carried out, which were frequently nonmaterial or invisible. Among the inhabitants of Boguszów, the ex-miners and their families, an evident transformation, a *release* from the frozen circulation of social "value regimes" occurs in these nonmaterial conditions of "knowledge of values." Arjun Appadurai writes less of the standards of goods' values than of particular "value regimes" that allow for the existence, however temporary, of standards functioning according to changeable social circumstances (ibid.). At one time, back when the mines were operative, goods were mainly received in large quantities, including, for example, coal allowances, which often exceeded a family's needs (TR/WB/12). Moreover, there was an official circulation of goods both in the ordinary shops and in those exclusively for miners, with the value of these goods defined from above. This circulation presently no longer exists, and the official sources of supplies in the majority of cases remain beyond the reach of unemployed families. We might therefore conclude that the circulation of goods in the official, mass, industrialized sphere has been transferred to the semiprivate, invisible, unofficial sphere, into a place we often call the black market.

This is where the field opened wide for constant bargaining, negotiations, etc. Here is where we find a mechanism of great importance, namely, the fragmentation mechanism, that accompanied this shift in Wałbrzych's value regime. The fragmentation of transactions is a kind of bargaining management or initiation of economic microsources. Briefly, it is the initiation of an energy that exudes from the circulation itself. It is what I would call the "flow" of economic material, its movement. Some of the families interviewed greatly appreciate this fragmentation of goods, as it ensures a minimal circulation. For them it is utterly essential, more important in itself than in any real economic benefit that it might bring. They speak incessantly about how it provides them with the opportunity to purchase coal in smaller quantities, and also how it allows diggers selling coal by the sack, coal dealers selling it in allotments of one hundred kilograms, and other "fragmentation" middlemen to make a living. They also speak of how large quantities of groceries purchased in the supermarkets (Tesco, Szczawno-Zdrój) are divvied among a few families, generally neighbors. I witnessed this practice in the blocks of flats, as a chicken was divided among various families. There was a lot of bragging about how low the price had been (the chicken had been purchased at a budget shop), but there was also talk of how this strategy of fragmentation and dividing of goods gave the various families "purchasing power." In turn, residents of a block of flats in Boguszów bought milk in large quantities from the neighboring villages and then exchanged it for eggs from a woman who came around especially for this purpose; they then swapped assurances about the profitability of this "business." The characteristic effect of the accessibility of goods, achieved more through their distribution and redistribution than by their actual presence, then emerges. The result is an increased economic effectiveness for both the buyers (purchasing power) and the salespeople (demand creation), though, from an economic point of view, this effectiveness is largely illusory.

This fragmentation that facilitated survival is also reflected in the diggers' manner of earning money in the bootleg mines and in the scavenging of the scrap collectors. A "payment" is almost always for a single day, and both the diggers and the collectors generally speak highly of this means of earning money. Economic fragmentation is compulsory here, if only because the amounts they make in collecting scrap or other refuse are always small, and only for a single day. Sometimes I would hear the diggers say that they would happily go back to set monthly wages, because then they could "plan" or "do" something, which should seem obvious. Yet, I also noticed that many appreciate their daily payout, and depend on the daily inflow of a small amount of cash: "I prefer to do things slow but sure, so that there's always those twenty or thirty zloty." "It's no problem earning a hundred zloty in the pits. ... But today you get the money, and tomorrow it all collapses. ... That's why you have to go *bit by bit,* and I prefer to earn thirty zloty a day, but be sure that things will somehow carry on from one day till the next, and I'll have my thirty zloty. ... Because I have to know where I stand. ... That's very important—you earn something every day, and not just all at once" (TR/WB/35). "You can always afford five or six sacks [of coal], but you'll never afford a tone" (TR/WB/12). I would like to emphasize that this fragmentation ensures an imagined efficacy of actions. Some teams organize money collections that last several weeks. A zloty or two are thrown into a jar for organizing a "Barbórka" celebration or for purchasing sacks or tools. Were it not for the collections, I was told, they would never have been able to afford such things. In these circumstances, fragmentation is a universal method of moving things forward. This is constant motion, much like the collecting of numbers; it is circulation of the most diverse goods and supplies, though in the final analysis, very little actually changes (it recalls the above-described manual labor, always performed "a bit at a time," which makes it remarkably "effective"). The result is an economy that is always extended over time, in small segments, an economy capable of great changeability and always impromptu, allowing people to survive in a minimal, but very energetic and provident circulation.

Home-Oikos: *Internal Circulation*

This informal and fragmented economic circulation is also visible in a remarkable fashion in how post-mining households and blocks of flats function. The significance of all sorts of services has increased, from welding and installation to "electrical work," and many who once worked in the mines have gone on to provide these services. Most jobs inside the home are now arranged informally, without consulting the administration (ADM), and often involve the installation of illegal electricity or heating equipment (TR/WB/12, 13, 35). Heating tile ovens are installed or reworked to improve their cost-efficiency, as are electrical installations, and central heating is provisionally installed. This is a clear effect of the process of the liquidation of the mines and their patronage; and the centrally administered households that have appeared have clearly begun to be autonomous. Initially, the mines were responsible for renovations, repairs, and installations, as they ensured coal deliveries for the winter. Now everything, the whole burden of maintaining the crumbling buildings, has fallen on the shoulders of the residents, many of whom are months or years behind in their rent payments: "No one pays rent here! Who could afford the rent! One hundred and seventy-six zloty" (TR/WB/35). All of this has caused the creation or reinforcement of a sphere that is new in terms of its scope, i.e., a sphere of informal attention to everyday household affairs. It is on this plane of the household (the *oikos*) that a certain, internal circulation of household materials has begun to take place.

The necessity for an efficient, internal reworking of materials in the household sphere thus translates into an extremely conservative approach to economizing resources. This is an ability to make use of an ultimately minimal quantity of goods. "I call this 'dribbling,'" one of the diggers' wives told me. "They're surprised that we're able to live off of seventy zloty a week ... to buy ... dish soap, washing powder, so that I've got enough, and I don't run short. ... I have to have flour. ... It has to be warm" (TR/WB/35). My hosts, a coke man and his unemployed wife, often showed me the stove they installed in their flat and told me how efficiently it worked; burning coal in the oven was a kind of daily ritual. Diggers' families also told me similar things about private heating installations (everyone was constantly speaking of the necessity of heating). In the cold periods, when there was not enough to burn, they were reminded of the worst of times, full of powerlessness and suffering: "Now what's most important is that there's enough for supper, there's bread on the table, and it's warm inside the house. And that's the most important thing, because when it was cold, we warmed ourselves by the gas oven ... our potatoes froze over there in the corner, the pipes would sometimes freeze, there was nothing to burn. ... We heated the pipes so that the water would run" (TR/WB/35).[33]

The home-*oikos* is thus a space aiming for an imagined "condensation" of powers to rework, in which the marrow must be sucked from every item of energy (warmth, fuel, and sustenance). Many households apply an autarkic, closed economy, using various goods to the full, e.g., brewing multiple cups of tea from the same bag and using all kinds of scraps, shreds, and remains. Moreover, there is a principle of shared goods, which automatically initiates a mechanism of increased efficiency. I often heard: "Everybody knows that when it's a shared pot, then things are always different, you can get down to doing things" (TR/WB/35). This economizing, this family/community "efficient reconstruction," has its genealogical tradition. Of course, on the one hand, it is a repetition of the autarkic economy of a poverty-stricken village (Kocik 2000: 75–76; 2001: 56–58; Laskowska-Otwinowska 1998: 24–25, 36–37). On the other, it is a typical strategy of impoverished families, with insufficient funds from outside resources (Elam, Ritchie, and Hulusi 2000; see also Sikorska 1999: 126–127; Tarkowska 2003: 9–12), though this internal, autarkic economy corresponds, in a way, to models of "inhabitancy" compulsory in a typical miner's family household. This is shown by Wanda Mrozek (1987: 30) through an analysis of miners' household budgets in the 1960s and 1970s (money was chiefly spent on groceries, clothing, and fuel for fire, and was practically never spent on services). Moreover, in the time I spent living with digger families in Boguszów, I often noticed this peculiar autarky on a spatial level. Living space is perceived in an entirely different manner, quite the reverse of what we might assume after the experience of the permanent insufficiency of living space in Poland's communist period. Cramped quarters are approved as ensuring autarky and a certain mindset of "effective reconstruction," through, for example, the efficiency of the heating installation. I heard several times from the people I lived with that they had the opportunity to acquire a larger flat, but had refused it, because, as they said, "who would have heated it?" My students' hosts had a similar mindset, saying that they would happily exchange their old German two-room flat for a smaller one, because their present flat was impossible to heat (TR/WB/40).

The home-*oikos* reaches beyond the single-family home, however, spreading along with its reconstructive power, radiating upon the neighboring flats and buildings. It is characteristic that in this environment of autarky, in these constant reconstructions and "wild" montages, the families cooperate in a neighborly/social fashion. This translates into acquaintance/service ties typical in working-class *famuły* (blocks of flats for workers' families.), i.e., internal relationships, as opposed to acquaintance/ceremonial ties found in more formal relationships (Gogolewska 1984). Descriptions of the old residential districts in Upper Silesia (Wódz 1989: 35, 67–71; Świątkiewicz 1983) note the creation of this sort of community, whose borders are marked by three environments: work, domicile, and extended family (ibid.: 69). Within these a unique "inner-district social order" is created (ibid.: 43). However, this structure among the residential buildings of Boguszów-Gorce, Kuźnice Świdnickie, and old Sobięcin has undergone a marked narrowing. Whereas at one time a network of friends (daily meetings) stretched far and wide, to other miners and their families, now it has become more limited, and generally based on ties through work or business (bootleg mines, scrap, minibuses, workshops, etc.) or family. As such, this more current circle of "acquaintances" also stretched beyond the place of residence. It is created by entirely different, more casual, and sometimes defined ties, such as "lending" ties; the miners generally have their steady loan-givers, generally a pensioner from next door who was once a miner himself. Often, however, my interlocutors (and hosts) from Boguszów complain of the loss of their once wide circle of social acquaintances: "Everyone sits at home"; meeting during the evenings for good times had long come to an end, and the only group party was the bootleg mine Barbórka (in a local bar), the proceeds for which were collected several months in advance. One observes a certain distaste toward the neighbors in the buildings next door, who are venomously described as "Germans," "Frenchmen," or "Ukrainians" (Zubelewicz 2005: 10).

The bonds inside the closest neighbor/family groups working together have undergone an evident concentration. This is a certain continuation of the forms of social life of small, informal family/acquaintance groups in communist Poland, closed off in "their own lives" from the wider social structures and institutions, though, of course, this also takes place in different, post-transformation conditions (cf. Tarkowska and Tarkowski 1994: 266–269). This concentration has taken place in tandem with the encroachment of a more confined living space of both home and district, of the home-*oikos,* which they practically represented. Due to nonpayment of bills, the power of a poorer family in a Boguszów block of flats was shut off (TR/WB/13). After some time their next-door neighbors found a way to bring them electricity (by running a wire under the ceiling). After this, both families pitched in to pay a single bill, until the first family was able to pay their dues to the electric company (which took about a year). In such situations, close circles of cooperation are forged. The families of the diggers inhabiting a block of flats in Boguszów with whom I had closest contact divvied up their food in times of harshest poverty and shared various household appliances, including washing machines, clothing irons, kettles, and radios. Almost every evening after work in the bootleg mines, the diggers from the building and their wives would get together to drink coffee and discuss the day's events. They signaled to one another by banging on the water pipes at night, and during the day this was an almost ritual signal of invitation to come for an after-dinner coffee. These families knew almost everything about each other. The building (the space and the substance) and its group of user/inhabitants thus created their internal ties, a certain ecological unit, which was also a unit of the survived world (cf. Karpińska 2000).

This unit, the home-*oikos,* thus enclosed the circulating materials and everyday affairs, and sometimes the most painful, interpersonal matters. I was forever under the impression that this facilitated the creation of practically watertight capsules, in which everything flowed in an efficient manner, "quietly," "bit by bit," ensuring the most from their meager goods and an internal sense of circulation, i.e., the ability to "survive."

Freedom in the Mines
"Do-It-Yourself" Equipment

In the communist period the mines in Wałbrzych created a modernized or industrialized space for daily life. A shift-work system was organized, whereby work was done "round the clock," as they said, and, most crucially, things "were done" under supervision, according to overriding safety regulations, an external system and organization of work. The miners were supplied with oxygen tanks, and were bound by rules on movement in the mines. Miners had special signal boards, where the safety level was reported at marked intervals; they reported on the state of their team and on the danger levels of carbon dioxide and methane gases. The miners' tools and their uses were also regulated from above, as were the safety measures and the miners' gear, i.e., their helmets, glasses, lamps, and oxygen tanks. The miners worked strictly according to the foreman's (or head foreman's) orders; the foreman led the team in and out of the mine, and, in fact, a miner was not allowed to move about the mine on his own. "Nothing got decided on your own" (Plińska 2005: 5–6). Even the site they worked was established from above, a fact to which the miners simply had to grow accustomed. "A man working on a sloping wall where everything poured downwards would get used to this after some time," one of the ex-mine directors told me, "but a man who was working on a vertical wall would come to enjoy this as well. He would say that he had it good, because he was able to work standing up" (TR/WB/37). This organization, which was external, and involved control from above over people's actions and the objects they used, was thus very deeply ingrained. As we know, the industrial organization also affected the way people spent their time after work, organizing life outside the mine and family life ("clean living"). "The wife would gather up the children," the ex-miners recalled, "and in the summer, a guy could just go and sit in the concert bowl" (WAŁB 22). The mine also established and defined the kind of objects the miners used, the everyday objects, i.e., clothing, furniture, and equipment. In the "type-G" stores (exclusively for miners—trans.) they bought washing machines, refrigerators, radios, and clothing prepared especially for them. "You worked on Saturday and then you went out and bought yourself a refrigerator" (WAŁB 22).

The ex-miners (later diggers in bootleg mines, gatherers, and scrap collectors) are no longer part of this finely tuned mine machine. They have devised their own ways of salvaging for scrap or remains, and independently plan how to extract coal and how to build their own reinforcement structures, simultaneously acting as geologists, foremen, and engineers. This situation in the post-mining, post-employment environment is entirely new. A completely new relationship has been forged between man and reality, whereby man has begun creating and "molding" his state of affairs—though, of course, a sort of non-system, bottom-up action has also been created, along with a special culture of material resourcefulness (see, among others, Marody 1991b: 236–237). One might say that the technology and organization of the Wałbrzych mines has risen to the surface with the birth of bootleg mines, scrap collecting, gathering, and all the other improvised forms of earning a living. The once hermetically sealed sphere of mine work also has risen from underground, emerging from out of the social and symbolic threshold that was the shower room and the mine gates (despite what I have said, the miners collected themselves before and after crossing the gates to the mine). Through the bootleg mines, mining work became generally visible and accessible, witnessed by those all around: by neighbors, passersby, motorists, and, ultimately, journalists (cf. the massive quantity of articles and "exotic" photographs of bootleg miners at work, black from coal dust).

Thus, certain social and cultural competencies that are at once deeply symbolic signatures, are carried from the mines up to the surface, into the rest of the post-mining world. However, perhaps what chiefly emerges is the mine's practical/applied sphere, the technological knowledge, its work organization. The meadows and forests outside of Wałbrzych have become a "liberated" or "open-air" mine. The mine and the industrial factory technology have ceased to oblige. In the bootleg mines and the scrap-collecting practices, new techniques of extraction, processing, and producing have been created, remains are used for recycled materials and coal extraction, and scrap, cast iron, nonferrous metal, and wood collection are "planned." The ex-employees of the industrial basin are forced to construct their own work sites and tools.

Extraordinary occurrences come about. As I have already described, these technical solutions, tools, and the whole "do-it-yourself" micro-infrastructure fascinate the diggers and the collectors. This departure from the technical regulations imposed from above has forced them to take a fresh look at materials, to be inventive, to see things for their capacity to be reworked. All sorts of homemade equipment and reworked machines, both simple and complex, have begun appearing in the bootleg mines. These include homemade pickaxes and hammers, reworked saws, hanging coal carts, stands, and sieves for sifting coal. Among the more complicated tools are provisional lighting systems, provisional extractors made of moped wheels, machines for carting coal (from a three-wheeler cart off an old German motorbike and Polish parts), and other things. Every tool is a source of pride. The diggers told me how they had made these items and how well they worked (the ergonomics of a pickaxe with a metal grip). However, as I described in the previous chapter, they also discuss among one another the phenomenal properties and extraordinary efficiency of these objects; in fact, the diggers constantly speak of how they work: of the constructions, the *taczaki,* the props, the seams, and the clay interlayers. They carefully analyze every new part of their equipment (such as the fastening of the sieve for sifting coal). How all these elements, springs, and movable fastening surfaces function is of the utmost importance (TR/WB/43), as are all the inventions that make the coal practically sift itself, so that the sieve is "semi-automatic" (WAŁB 2). "These sifters and sieves are there so we can relax a bit" (TR/WB/23). "Oh, I thought I'd also make a guide in here" (TR/WB/43). The diggers are proud of the contraptions they build and invent, such as the electric lighting inside the bootleg mines or the cradle car system pulled on steel cables wrapped around trommels. To my mind, however, this is more than a psychological concentration on objects or "practical" things; it is an entirely new way of apprehending materials, their capabilities, and their potential applications. Many things become *possible* upon reflection, much can be done to make things work better, more efficiently.

Furthermore, many diggers told me that certain items were their original ideas and that "they came up with everything." Even more, there is a clear fascination for the technical solutions, tools, and constructions they themselves invent, which they make on their own. "What you're looking at is a wheel from a moped [a pulley on a tripod placed over the shaft that served to extract the takings, which set up differently every time, for every shaft]. ... It's my own construction ... there's no pulleys, you can't buy them anywhere. ... But just a *little bit of thought*, and there you go, *it runs smooth ... I came up with all this* [emphasis mine]... I put the sieve like that, so it would be easier on the women ... I even had the idea that I could bring in a potato machine from a local village and then it turns downwards and they would do the sifting. I wanted to bring it over here ... but then I thought it would be too heavy to cart around, and I forgot about it" (TR/WB/14). "We thought up this whole rig, we built it all ourselves ... how to build it, secure it, get it to pull ... when the pressure goes ... the car glides pretty smoothly and you load on the baskets and then it goes ... and you're set" (TR/WB/10).

The Wałbrzych scrap collectors speak with similar pride about their tools: their sheet metal clippers, the cart they just welded that can cart a whole tone, the rail construction and methods of prying the rails loose with their iron-rod jacks (TR/LUB/4). They speak of the most various kinds of carts, reworked from baby prams, shopping carts, or industrial carts. One scrap collector spontaneously began telling me: "Here's my cart, look, I added on a wheel, I did it so that it supports everything perfectly, it balances on it and I don't even have to hold the thing—it goes by itself" (TR/WB/9). They also spoke of their various hoes, crowbars, *brechy*, and knives for cutting cables: "Oh, here's a good rod," one scrap collector told me, "oh, here's my knife, it cuts through everything" (TR/WB/28). In these statements what astonishes the listener is the disproportion between the tools and the massive quantities of materials, soil, scrap, rocks, or bricks that the tools can rework, unfetter, transport, or shape. The diggers once told me with visible pride how with a single tool (a wire-cutter) they had bored through a two-meter wall of hard rock to a vein of coal, digging "bit by bit," as they put it, until they finally "broke through" (TR/WB/12). In a similar vein, I was constantly being told of a scrap vehicle, a homemade three-wheeler adapted to carting coal in one mine shaft, that could "pull anything." It could "carry a tone" or "haul the most terrible weights" as long as the collector "pulled it one step at a time" (TR/WB/100). In turn, the electric lighting in the bootleg mines drew power from an old car battery, and made things "just like in the mine." These objects, tools, or whole constructions are all used differently, almost "more effectively" than they were in the mines. This demands a special kind of attention, concentrating on objects, and their functions and how they "work."

Working and Efficiency in Manual Labor: Resources and Deposits

Thus was born a new, socially created sphere of material beings. Both the surface coal and the scrap lying about were recently perceived as worthless, i.e., they were invisible as resources of concrete, economic value. Then came a sudden realization of the properties and worth of goods. Over the course of a few months or years, the ex-miners and scrap collectors discovered that the deposits all around could be used, exchanged, and turned into money. This manual activity, from the body to the tools, led to the sudden colonization of the deposits of coal, scrap, and other objects—to their appearance in the collective consciousness as potential "resources." "Who would have guessed there was so much coal under the earth?" (TR/WB/35) "Who used to really care whether there was scrap lying about?" others said (TR/WB/32). These resources, the coal and the scrap, were discovered in places where, until just recently, there "was none"; they turned out to be "in arm's reach," revealing their presence in an astonishing fashion, coming to the surface "with the blink of an eye." "No one knew, there was no time, and now they're starting to search and dig ... they didn't even know that there was coal near the surface, someone must have seen it somewhere, and now you have it—coal on top of coal.... We all live off of it" (TR/WB/35). "There's so much iron, from those motors, other things, cables, you just walk around and pick them up" (TR/WB/25). We might say that becoming aware of these resources was a sudden offshoot of a social practice, something that was increasingly explored, analyzed, and sought out. New techniques and new methods of searching for deposits of coal or scrap were developed through this multifaceted exploration of all objects all around; they became present, i.e., what the environment "offers" (Gibson quoted in Ingold 1992: 42). These were tools for increasing efficiency (Ingold 1992: 46), causing the very environment and surroundings to be imperceptibly changed; and through their "activities," the scrap collectors began to perceive "resources that [the environment] had to offer" (ibid.). In Wałbrzych, Boguszów, and particularly in Lubsko, it became clear from various conversations with scrap and brick collectors how the nature of the environment was being changed. Resources were appearing all around. "They gather old and dilapidated props for firewood.... They take the rafters from the roofs.... They collect bricks till the evening, and scrap till four o'clock; there was scrap, bricks and whole walls from the brick clinker ... a three-floor hall, all on metal beams" (TR/LUB/6). "There's a piece of steel that holds it all up

... it's fastened with screws. ... You take a wrench and unscrew it, then slide it off, get the jack, and we pull off all those parts [flat iron bars: the man is referring to unscrewing railroad tracks] and so on for twenty meters. And with the screws that's four hundred kilograms already. ... But when the brick collectors work, they take an axe, working in pairs ... They're good German bricks ... the steam engines are there around the corner. ... Maybe we'll unscrew something else there, but you've got to press down and work it a bit ... tones of rubble ... but they dig through everything ... beams, rails, it's all pulled up—and there you've got four or five hundred kilograms of scrap" (TR/WB/4). "If there's scrap, you load it up ... metals and semiprecious ones ... and copper. ... These places are abandoned ... you can always find wires there, wires and cables ... you can pull them out of the sewage pipes, old German sewer pipes ... you take your hammer, or a swingle ... you always end up pulling something out" (TR/LUB/4).

The perception of the material world also changed. The infrastructure, buildings, and railroad tracks now became great storehouses of resources: bricks, roofing tiles, rafters, props, rails, shelves, copper cables, flat iron bars, and so on, infinitely. Ingold has developed one of Gibson's notions to demonstrate that an environment is primarily an offshoot of an active subject: "Affordances are properties of the real environment as directly perceived by an agent in a context of practical action" (Ingold 1992: 46).

All the while this "emergence of goods" arose from manual labor, i.e., the manner of using tools, combined with new body and tool techniques, which paved the way to finding new uses for coal, scrap, and bricks. Through a combination of manual practices, external body projections, and an active perception of the world, these subterranean "deposits" (of coal and scrap) suddenly seemed to appear all around. The unexpected availability of these goods, this "sudden breakthrough," this abrupt shift in relationship between man and his surroundings, resources, and tools is also significant. "Look, here's some cable, I've got some cable here. ... Just watch, I've got to unscrew it" (TR/WB/7). "This is surface coal ... that's how it is—you dig it up, and it's there ... and look here ... that's stone-coal ... a bunch of nonsense that it's supposed to be a thousand meters underground ... here it is ... great ... right on the surface, up top" (TR/WB/13). "Here's a cable just popping right out, something must have torn off ... and I said: 'Dig up whatever's there.' ... We scorched it a bit, and there you are. ... Patted it off, scorched it, then onto the bike and off to the depot" (TR/WB/25). "Wild mushrooms popped up around here," a coal digger told me, "there didn't use to be mushrooms ... now it's covered in ceps ... red ones, brown ones ..., but once there were no mushrooms, I'm telling you, I carried off the trees ... I brought my saw, and bit by bit ... I carted them away" (TR/WB/25). "This is where we dug up a whole septic tank ... used to be in the gas works ... and suddenly there's this whole septic tank" (TR/WB/25). This man/resources relationship is thus sudden and abrupt; it means that, in the blink of an eye, a difficulty in searching turns into a discovery, often when the work is just beginning. Things are then perceived less for their practical properties than for their capacity for new applications, their new properties. This releases the above-described changeable and dynamic way of being in an environment, of being among things (cf. Merleau-Ponty 2002: 323–324). Tim Ingold cites Jakob von Uexküll and James Gibson (Ingold 1992: 41–42) to demonstrate, as we have already found, that, in the world of humans (or animals), ownership of an object is less a physical attribute of the object than a relationship between the object and the body, the being who gazes upon the object, touches it, picks it up, and senses it. The possession of an object is thus, in fact, a relationship between it and the body perceiving it, building a new and subjective disposition toward things, a certain spontaneously created "subjective universe" (*Umwelt*). From this point of view, a crab shell can be a "shelter" for a crab, while for an angry man it can be an "object to throw" (ibid.). As such, man is always somehow prepositioned vis-à-vis objects, furnished with a disposition, i.e., he *expects* something from things. From this statement we find a certain attention that the body pays to its surroundings. This is because the body is, at every moment, in a relationship of sorts with its surroundings, and the environment thus becomes an extension of the body itself, while things, as Merleau-Ponty will have it, are "encrusted" in acts of perception and manipulation. The "structure of my body" dynamically "imprints itself" in every segment of the outside reality. As Ingold concludes, "far from fitting into a given corner of the world (a niche), it is the organism that fits the world to itself, by ascribing functions to the objects it encounters and thereby integrating them into a coherent system of its own. Hence its environment (its *Umwelt*) is the projection or 'mapping out' of its internal organization onto the outside world" (Ingold 1992: 42). A "corner of the world" is thus adapted to the organisms (to the digging and scrap-collecting bodies); this accounts for the enormous significance of efficiency that emerged in using manual "homemade" tools, which create strata of goods and resources. I have already described my interlocutors' fascination for the manual efficiency of their work, the efficacy of their body/tools, the stress placed, for example, on the "effectiveness" of a coal cart that can "haul a tone." For these people, these elements marking their environment are, we might say, collapsed acts (G. H. Mead), i.e., they acquire their attributes only in conjunction with the actions carried out (ibid.: 50).

This statement allows us to look afresh at these practices of digging "pits," gathering, dismantling factories and halls for scrap and bricks and reclaiming wooden beams. The actions imposed through these new professions (bootleg mining, scrap collecting, and gathering) cause things and environments to be suddenly perceived in a whole new light, that is, through their capacity to be reworked, and through their capability to be made active. All the things that were theretofore ordinary (the familiar environment, ruins, old halls, the surfaces of the meadows and the forests on the outskirts of town) changed their socially generated properties and became entirely different from what they once were. They became correlates or "adapted environments" of the exploring body of the scrap collector. Sometimes they became less ruins than sources of materials, of metal and steel parts, of copper cables and wooden beams; the earth, meadows, forests, and squares became, in turn, deposits of materials to be mined: coal, scrap, copper. The diggers and scrap collectors emphasized that, in the times of the mines' prosperity, no one was interested in these deposits of coal and iron. Only since a few years previous had the diggers and scrap collectors paid any considerable attention to them, analyzing every detail of the steel rafters, of the course of coal veins visible on the surface of ridges or of the rusting infrastructure of the mine factory. As Merleau-Ponty has written (2002: 35), the knowledge that catches our attention "gives rise to the 'knowledge-bringing event,' which is to transform it, only by means of the still ambiguous meaning which it requires that event to clarify."

The result of this was a social space of increased transmutability of material beings. A sphere was created in which things revealed their practical and significative potentials, displaying something that always "remains to be defined." Objects were seen through potential innovations, which could be executed upon them, through their possibility of being reworked or adapted to serve entirely different functions. Breadbaskets served as coal sieves, a car battery became a power source for bootleg mine illumination, and a moped wheel turned into a pulley for extracting coal. At this moment there was an explosion of the transitory space of objects, and the digger and scrap collector became like the *bricoleur* who, as Lévi-Strauss notes (1994: 18–19), "interrogates all the heterogeneous objects … to discover what each of them could 'signify.' … A particular cube of oak could be a wedge to make up for the inadequate length of a plank of pine or it could be a pedestal—which would allow the grain and polish of the old wood to show to advantage." Objects changed their status. Suddenly waste became tools (a bootleg mine's winter fireplace from an old barrel), waste became raw materials (scrap metal from an abandoned washing machine), tools became raw materials (scrap from a gear transmission by the railroad tracks), or raw materials became tools (a breaking/digging implement from a reinforcement rod). All of these examples could be multiplied. Reworking need not be technical, there is also reworking in "seeing" things. A man who is reworking something must, according to Lévi-Strauss, "turn back to an already existent set made up of tools and materials, to consider or reconsider what it contains" (ibid.: 18). Old chairs, armchairs, tables, winter fireplaces made of barrels, and various tools often sit at the mouth of a bootleg mine. Similarly, every digger has his post. There are seats made of crates, tools, digging implements, and small magnets for checking the materials and initially sorting through the waste—metals, papers, food, clothing, rags, and so forth. These objects sometimes end up in the hands of diggers and collectors; and in their hands they become materials once more, thus compelling them to foresighted productivity, to build things. In this way they create whole "cabinets" of tools and useful things, which lend character to the surroundings and build internal households—an ecological "world" of sorts.

Demolition—Collecting—Objects

The diggers and collectors who once worked underground thus "surfaced" along with the bootleg mines and the scrap "deposits." To gain access to the goods they require, they comb the surface of the land, the surface of the cities. A great deal hinges on their skill, on their planning (in searching for coal veins and scrap "deposits")—on the whole economy of their search. They search the surface layers of coal and soil, and trace the courses of coal veins and inactive gas pipelines. In one bootleg mine field (near Sztygarska Street) the diggers often find granite marking posts, boundary stones with German inscriptions that once indicated coal allotments; they also find other old German objects, such as boards with technical inscriptions and parts of old mines. The poles have enormous value for these diggers, who claim that the Germans are willing to pay great sums for them. Furthermore, instead of selling these posts, the diggers often preferred to keep them at home or to hide them in the forest, as a kind of security deposit "for a rainy day." "When there's no other place to get a hold of some money, then I'll always have that to sell" (TR/WB/8, 13). "It's very valuable ... we've got one, but we're saving it for a rainy day. All we have to do is dig it up, you just have to prise it up" (TR/WB/35). "Look, there were some old signboards there in German," I heard in another conversation, "some old vaulting, it's written in German, there was an inscription, I guess the name of the

owner and the sign number, the year. ... On the Thorez Mine there was
a signboard, with the year 1876; there are still more signs like that. I've
got that stored away, because for just one sign like that I've got eighty
euros in my pocket, and I get as much for one stone ... in euros ...
here's the number of the sign, you can see everything ... I even have
one that's dated 1806." I also heard: "I know where those posts are.
Actually, they're all around here, they stick out of the ground. ... I know
where they are and I don't touch them. ... Because only I know, and no
one else is going to find them" (TR/WB/25). The functions of these
stones and signboards thus become altered, come to contain an excess
of significance. They are shifted in time, becoming a resource of goods
set aside for later. It is impossible to say, after all, if these stones will ever
really be bought by anyone, or if, in fact, they should be sold at once.
These families clearly ought to cash in every object of value, as they
are always short of money. And yet one continually hears talk of these
peculiar resources, of a stone hidden somewhere in the undergrowth,
of a valuable picture frame someone has come across, of unearthed
"antiques" that will doubtless "gain in value over time" (TR/WB/24).
They become treasures of sorts, in Aron Guriewicz's sense of the word
(1976: 223), i.e., that they must not be cashed in, they must remain
hidden somewhere, somehow "sealed," precisely in order for them to
become treasures, much like Renu's treasure in the Nibelung,[34] sunken
in mud. The diggers remove various odd objects from the top layers of
the coal. An old glass with a Gothic German inscription was unearthed,
and thereafter stood on display (!) in one of the diggers' hutches in Boguszów. "Everyone 'round here collects antiques. My son dug up a big
German glass, and now I've got it here in the apartment; it's inscribed
'36,' which is the date" (TR/WB/17). The diggers have found methanometers (of Soviet and Polish manufacture), a signal horn presumed
to have once belonged to the foreman (though of this they were uncertain), and some old porcelain (TR/WB/8, 17, 24). Similarly, the scrap
collectors in Lubsko find old German objects, "old" construction parts,
and mysterious "clay bottles left behind by the Germans," for which the
Germans "supposedly pay through the nose" (TR/LUB/4).

My impression is, however, that objects have in general become an
extraordinarily vital manner of perceiving and experiencing the world
after the liquidation. This is, of course, a paradox—why this fascination
for objects procured during the widespread demolition of the mining
and industrial cities, built over the course of a century? Moreover, I
should like to stress that this experience is new, to some extent, one to
which no one would have paid heed earlier, before the transformation of
the 1990s. The miners and laborers work in shifts, and, as I have men-

tioned, their whole outside world was organized by the mines, coking plants, and factories. On Saturday and Sunday, miners' bands arrived, and the miners and laborers laid down "boards" (dance platforms) and danced till the morning (TR/WB/12). Now, time is entirely "theirs." "Now you can do as you like," as they themselves put it. "Twenty or thirty years ago, no one was interested in the treasures all around here," said one digger from Boguszów, "people were afraid, and anyway, they didn't have any time to spare" (TR/WB/35). For the last dozen or so years, the diggers and the collectors began displaying these objects in their homes. Often they use the pretense of keeping the items in order to sell them at a later date ("I know where they are and I don't lay a finger on them ... because I know, and no one's going to find them"; "I've got that tucked away, because for just one of those signboards I can get eighty euros"). One worker at a Wałbrzych scrap depot collects various objects that he thinks highly valuable, claiming "I could sell, but I'm not going to" (WAŁB 11). These objects are perceived as mysterious and special, though in hard times, of course, they are sold to collectors and middlemen; one digger's family long regretted selling an old stoneware eagle of German origin (TR/WB/24).

It is particularly astonishing that, for all those decades of the People's Republic, when the mines were going full steam, no one was interested in these objects, or "treasures," as the diggers call them. "In the communist period there wasn't any time, no one knew anything, you weren't even allowed to know anything" (TR/WB/35). This mysterious and valuable past rose to the surface only then, after the liquidation of the industrial, communist regulation of life and work. At present, in the majority of unemployed Wałbrzych households, we find old items of German origin, as well as German postcards with German-language names of places where Polish people have been living for three or four generations. This phenomenon of rediscovery and reacquisition of ex-German lands is widespread in the Polish experience. These same postcards are used, for instance, to supplement memory records, or the childhood palimpsests described in Stefan Chwin's *Brief Course in the Archaeology of Memory.* Wałbrzych's ex-miners also fill their collections with such postcards, simultaneously collecting every possible kind of souvenir, photograph or object: mining maps, boundary stones, tools, methanometers, and lamps with German inscriptions. "My name is Aleksander Mucha. I'm a mining engineer. I used to work in a coal mine." This is one example of an inscription a collector (indeed, once a mining engineer) wrote under his private showcase (with the title "Souvenirs of the Wałbrzych Coal Mining Industry"). As he wrote, "This showcase simply and accessibly presents some of the many pieces and objects *that are found almost everywhere* [emphasis mine] in the former mining city of Wałbrzych, but which one seldom takes time to notice." As I have indicated already, this shows an astonishing repetition of the experiences of postwar history—the demolition and plundering of the Recovered Territories (i.e., today's western Poland—trans.). The assimilation of the German legacy repeatedly commenced with the destruction and devastation of things, homes, and infrastructures. Only later did the inhabitants' attention shift to things, to fragments of objects, to the German inscriptions that had been unquestioningly destroyed and wiped out.

At present, half a century later, the unemployed residents of Wałbrzych and Lubsko are demolishing and devastating buildings, retracing the old layouts of the German tunnels, the skeletons of constructions and the technical signage. In tearing up scrap and steel rails they have to trace the old fastenings, the old constructions; they "rediscover" the old plumbing systems, pipes, wells, sewers, old equipment in the mines, instrument panels, and safety valves left by the Germans. We might say that they are once again "discovering," half a century later, that everything they are "tearing up" and "lugging around," what is there "underneath," this whole infrastructure is a part of history, belonging to the epoch when these were German lands. In this way the diggers, the former miners, digging in search of coal veins, break through into old adits and tunnels once used by the Germans. Following where these lead, they come across coal deposits and the edges of onetime divisions. The past—and the German past in particular—has thus become the most available and fundamental "map." Some diggers claim that there are German underground areas not far from the coal fields, on the grounds of the demolished gas works. "Hard to say what exactly's down there," I was told in one conversation. "Apparently there are storehouses of machines and other things, going two levels downwards, all the way over to the Victoria Mines—that's where somebody saw some stairs going down, but the entrance had caved in" (TR/WB/23). The groups working nearby told me, "There's treasures all over the place, somewhere here is the Amber Chamber, and somewhere around here a train went under a bridge and never drove back out again" (TR/WB/17); and "Somewhere not far from the old director's office a train filled with bars of gold apparently drove into a tunnel and got trapped in a cave-in … some tried to break through to it, but there was gas, and so they had to leave it where it was" (TR/WB/23). Here the German past takes on its most extraordinary form. According to the ex-miners, the German coal fields, tunnels with Gothic vaulting, stretch almost everywhere underground. Some diggers have even purchased old geological maps, once used by the Germans, to identify the surface deposits, to know where to dig: "We've got some old German maps and this is where we're working. ... All the deposits are laid out clear as can be" (TR/WB/9). The German maps make the coal deposits a source of meaning and mystery for the ex-miners. They showed me the Germans' old adits plunging into the depths of the mountain and said: "They dug up this whole mountain, the whole place is criss-crossed with tunnels. ... One's thing's for sure, they didn't do anything by accident, there had to be something in there. ... We haven't got a chance of digging in there now. ... Anyway, the boys once dug into a German tunnel, but there was gas running through it, so they quickly walled it right back up" (TR/WB/23). Another Wałbrzych digger told me: "A German came round here with his son, and they had an old, yellowed map. They stood there, and the father explained that this had been his field ... that he'd worked there ... and he said it'd all been covered with concrete. ... He cried ... and he told his son to buy that land ... he only had to hang onto the map ... something must be there" (WAŁB 14). These remarkable underground areas are newly revived in the consciousness of the residents of the Recovered Territories. "Do you know where we live?" one young digger asked. "This is God's Mountain, God's Mountain, you understand? [the name 'Boguszów' comes from the German 'Gottesberg']. You can find anything in these mountains. The Amber Chamber is supposed to be buried here, but they were afraid to look for it, because it's God's Mountain. ... All sorts of things are buried under here, there's tunnels going through all the mountains" (TR/WB/33).

Thus, the diggers and the scrap collectors have brought the underground networks, the old infrastructures, up "into the daylight." Not unlike their childhood explorations of old adits and tunnels, a typical activity of children in other locations (e.g., Karpińska 2000), as adults the diggers and collectors make their own discoveries through acts of demolition and devastation. As in the postwar years, while dismantling and demolishing old German constructions, and plundering factories and underground storerooms, there have reemerged legends of the Amber Chamber, of trains filled with gold hidden somewhere near Szczecin and of underground tunnels and highways to Berlin (Kowalewski 2004). "There's still tones of stuff here ... you've got to dig your way down to it. ... My neighbor has a metal detector, and he just lives off of the scrap and aluminum. ... He's found all kinds of things, he's brought in sabers, coins, medals ... but he hasn't shown them to anybody yet" (TR/WB/34).

This exploration of the surface and destroyed buildings, this *demolition* of the city is simultaneously a kind of *collecting*—at any rate, it is a very short road from demolition to collection. In Lubsko, every brick that is dismantled and cleaned off by the unemployed is (and must be) carefully studied and admired. Dismantling operations afford the necessity and the opportunity to trace the entire construction of an old engine house, for example, or the construction and layout of the old technical conduits that join the mines (they also explained how those old, "fantastic" German conduits and underground connections run). And yet, how might one qualify these practices and objects—these dismantled buildings, acquired things, extracted metal bars and fixtures, these old, "valuable" German objects? I consider this issue extraordinarily problematic—for how are we to name this transition from demolition and liquidation to collection and setting up a museum? Marcin Kula (2002: 68–69) has written of the highly problematic nature of these transitional spheres, demonstrating this through the category of the monument. Examples would be the piles of rubble in postwar Warsaw that were given plaques that read "national monument," or the outdated factories of the first half of the twentieth century, whose status as monuments is up in the air. Similarly, in her book *Historic Preservation: Collective Memory and Historical Identity,* Diane Barthel (1996: 55–77) has demonstrated that the notion of protecting industrial heritage sometimes concerns factories that until recently employed workers and saw production. Much like Marcin Kula, she shows how delicate the line is between one and the other—the closed and devastated industrial factory and the museum. Here we encounter a certain paradox, for the museum would not have come to exist without the devastation and demolition. Regardless, it is neither the twilight of the textile manufacturing industry of which we are speaking, nor of the dismantling and transport of sarcophagi of Egyptian kings to Europe. In Wałbrzych and in Lubsko this picture is remarkably clear. A mining museum (the Museum of Industry and Technology), with the equipment that had not yet been "plundered" or sold, was established in the old Thorez Mine.[35] The museum's curator was the former mine director, and the employees were ex-miners or mine rescue workers. However, Wałbrzych's residents continue their scrap collecting, entering the museum territory through underground tunnels and dismantling all the "valuables" remaining there, collecting whatever has any sort of value, either as raw materials, scrap, or as objects in themselves. This makes the museum a bizarre one, to say the least; it is as though it has yet to acquire full museum status.

This begs a question: Where is the line between refuse and treasure, between monument and ruin, between liquidation and museum? It is in this "in-between space," between treasure and refuse, that something has begun to happen in the Recovered Territories. In *Oswajanie niemieckiego dziedzictwa kulturowego* (Assimilating German Cultural Heri-

tage), Andrzej Brencz (1997) notes that the people in the vicinity of
Gorzów Wielkopolski have developed a new manner of apprehending
and treating unearthed German objects. "At one time, [those objects
were] generally removed or destroyed, owing to a lack of knowledge
about how they functioned, or because of their origins; at present they
have become furnishing elements that are put on display like pictures,
mirrors or clocks ... the classic coffee mills, the ceramic containers with
German inscriptions or the table-setting pieces" (ibid.: 206). He also
writes of a collector from Santok who had been collecting various objects for several years—various small antiques, mostly German. This is
an entirely new field of research, which is only now coming into view. As
I have already mentioned, through this phenomenon we saw a paradoxical repetition of history. Initially, as a means to eradicate the foreignness
of the land where Polish settlers were compelled to stay, German objects,
photographs, "Tyrolean figurines," porcelain objects, and even water-
pipe blueprints were utterly destroyed, only to now acquire incredible
new value (cf. Kolbuszewski 1988: 78). This activity is spontaneous,
remaining beyond the criterion of rational practicality, heritage protection, and so forth. A collective transformation has occurred in the way
of life, and even in the collective consciousness. Many people spend
every day collecting the most valuable things, sometimes of surprising
derivation. These objects are examined, dusted off, admired, and sold
to antique shops, or they appear in antique markets. Some are kept for
special reasons: as treasures, mysterious antiques, as fantastic relics. This
is an astonishing extension/consequence of the general demolition, of
the widespread dismantling of the material heritage of the deindustrialized Recovered Territories.

Things

As demonstrated by Arjun Appadurai and Igor Kopytoff (1986), the
social circulation of goods and objects is drawn between two extremes:
between total commodification and standardization on the one hand
(Marx's commodity theory), and the uniqueness and individuality of
things on the other (Mauss's "Gifts"). The former situation presumes
the attribution of certain standardized values to various things, which
become "equivalent," and thus directly exchangeable and "commodified."
They therefore concern societies in which values of goods are standardized to some extent, and where exchange involves merchandise and
money, and is equivalency based. In the latter situation, we are dealing
with the uniqueness and individuality of things, and with non-equivalent
exchange—an economy of gifts and counter-gifts, services and counter-
services, operating on a principle of mutuality found in "archaic cul-

tures" (Mauss). What we have here, therefore, are two poles: on the one hand, culturally accepted commodities, and on the other, unique, one-of-a-kind items, often resembling semiophores (to borrow Krzysztof Pomian's term), stripped of their applied function in favor of their significance and status as "valuables." Between these two extremes there are, however, in-between zones. Objects can depart from this external code of values, from the "regime of values" (as Appadurai has called it), though this "regime" already holds a certain susceptibility to shifts in significance and value (see 1986: 14–15). The object then becomes undefined and weighed with a potential of sorts, shifting from being more or less interchangeable, its interchangeability deriving from social significance and consensus. Moreover, things can be said to have "roads," "paths," or "biographies" (ibid.), in which the various phases of these processes come about: the phase of "being a commodity," of "being refuse," of "being garbage," or of "being a valuable item or a piece of history." During its trajectory (path), a thing can turn off the road, perform a diversion, and create intermediate stages, ties of object-centered social codes (ibid.: 18)—transitory objects.

In Wałbrzych and its environs, in Lubsko, and probably in other deindustrialized cities, trajectories and significations are subject to these processes of "liberation" and the ongoing creation of transitory states for things. The circulation of objects creates an entirely new quality, an object goes through consecutive stages that are only several moments or periods in their social existence, and the spheres of their exchange create entirely new configurations. Things that are theretofore almost imperceptible acquire a whole new value. Their "biographies" grow longer and assemble into entirely new patterns, crossing well beyond the production-monetary exchange-consumption/use formula, and increasingly begin to adhere to an undefined, transitional sphere. In this fashion, a thing shifts between one and their signified world, and the link between the thing and the signified world undergoes a loosening of definition—objects, buildings, and parts of the infrastructure lose their permanent, socially generated aspect. An example might be the history of an instrument panel with German technical codes. The scrap collectors stole this from the Museum of Industry and Technology (to which they had gained access through old German underground tunnels). In essence, this museum was an intermediary place, something between an (official) museum and an (unofficial) scrap reservoir, a hovel (many scrap collectors joked about the notion of creating a museum in a liquidated mine, of all places). This panel ultimately ended up in a scrap depot. It had gone from the status of rubble to being an exhibit, to raw material, scrap, though that was not necessarily its final destination, because "wondrous things" were found in the depots, the bootleg mines and the rubbish tips. This panel, as one such wondrous thing, could once more become an exhibition, whether in secret, as a display-treasure, or in the scrap depot—after which it could once more end up, albeit in parts, at the weekly market of German antiques and old postcards in nearby Świdnica. In this manner it became an undefined object, one that was changeable, and therefore, full of potential (possessing the ever-renewable possibility of becoming "something more"). This was an extremely characteristic attribute of Wałbrzych's post-mining objects.

Further links of potential social significance attributed to other things were created in Wałbrzych. I have already mentioned the unearthed and stored boundary stones, "which might someday be sold"; the German glassware/relics ("impossible to say whom they once belonged to" and "whose writing is impossible to read"); and the German antique picture frames, once ignored, but at present "must be valuable," and "worth a lot." "But there are such things here. … I have an old German methanometer … they dug it up … it's a real treasure, any German would want it … they collect them" (TR/WB/4). I would like to point out once more that their potentiality derives in each case from a social practice, albeit strengthened by the trade of German antiques, the digging of pipes and bootleg mines and the reworking of tools. The transmutability of things and their socially established significance is thus constantly present in common experience, and concerns everyday objects, the industrial infrastructure and whole buildings. As one curator informed me: "They (the unemployed and the scrap collectors) take one look at our museum and think, 'Look at all the scrap they've got!' … They think it's a museum of scrap" (TR/WB/37). The transmutability of refuse and junk into valuables and back again is possible in this socially mobilized and liberated sphere of material beings.

In Wałbrzych and in Boguszów-Gorce the diggers and scrap collectors are energetically uncovering a subterranean and dynamic relationship between people and things. In her work *Wild Things: The Material Culture of Everyday Life,* Judy Attfield (2000) demonstrates that a contemporary method of engaging with everyday objects is generally created in a standardized (or modernized) fashion. Through a lifestyle produced in an externally modeled manner, designs for the aesthetics and the practical application of objects (designs for being amid objects) are established in workers' communities. The design that a person places upon things and the manner in which she or he creates it cross significantly beyond the mere act of standardized production. After all, objects are also created in the very act of their being used; after their phase of production and design, there are numerous transitional phases in which objects adopt other kinds of significance. Attfield calls them "things with attitude" (2000: 11–12). In Wałbrzych and its environs this whole invisible sphere has become omnipresent. After decades of a uniform culture of objects and mining equipment, of People's Republic design, there has occurred a kind of "liberation" of material beings/testimonies, something like a spontaneous and imperceptible slippage from the prior standardized connections between people and objects. Things have formed ever-new and unexpected relations with their social significance (ibid.: 15–16), alternately annulling and reinforcing it, and have begun to spin in new orbits, to *mean* something entirely different. At this point they can be adapted at will to fit the surrounding world. The diggers dismantle and collect everything from the Victoria Mine buildings that can possibly come in handy: "My brother took the door frame because ours at home was old and warped—he swapped it." Over one bootleg mine I found signboards with inscriptions saying "conference hall," and a door taken from the same building serves as a platform for carting off coal (Plińska 2005: 5). In another bootleg mine field, the hoods from broken-down, dismembered automobiles (Żuks, Fiats, Maluchs) have been adapted for use as coal carriers. Another thing has occurred after this widespread experience of demolition and gathering. This daily and spontaneous exit from or abandonment of the cultural pattern/design of things causes objects to acquire their own vitality; they began to "reflect" certain content and significance. As Judy Attfield, quoting Peter Pels (1998: 93), phrases it, objects can "talk back" (2000: 33).

These "talking objects" include, among other things, the unearthed and dismantled German "treasures" and "marvels" of old. When these objects diverge from the standardized, externally designed paths, from the modernized worker's style of inhabitancy, these "curiosities" then find their way into the collections of private owners, or into their imaginary collections. These found objects primarily have a fantastical (or perhaps sentimental) dimension, and only afterward a historical one. These "wild things" present, as Attfield claims, in every daily experience, are a disorderly, wild world of things—in short, everyday reality (ibid.: 50). Their collections (in a mental/imaginary sense) are thus most often something like a collection of "historical" curiosities. The collection or "cabinet of curiosities" is, in turn, a form of historical and museum narrative (Pomian 1990; Clifford 1988c: 218–220), except that, from our point of view, this narrative is bereft of a sober, cause-and-effect type plan. After all, in a cabinet of curiosities, collections are created that are entirely accidental and senseless from a historical perspective. One Copenhagen Kunstkammer, for instance, contained miniature slippers made of cherry pits, a model of a skeleton made of ivory, and the "helm of Bishop Absalon," which was in reality a Hungarian helmet from the sixteenth century (Wieczorkiewicz 1996: 37). And yet, does this collecting follow any rules? This question remains open. We might indicate a particular dimension of time and history in the collections that were formed. My impression was that this was history experienced with particular intensity, but above all, experienced in the present tense, in the here and now. Whole epochs were concentrated within it, as these collections would alternately contain German cups and methanometers, as well as communist-era Polish miners' lamps and coils of copper cables—and each of these objects was, in its own way, a kind of treasure or trophy.

Memory

What kind of narrative was it, then, that appeared in the ex-mining de-industrialized town of Wałbrzych? Firstly, to my mind, it was a self-recreating course of collective memory tied to the emerging situation, to the history of the liquidation of the mines and the socioeconomic catastrophe that followed. Memory underwent local mythologization, concentrating whole epochs. The period in which the mines functioned took on an entirely new emotional dimension, one that defied a linear and continuous sense of history. Time was generally split in two parts: before and after the liquidation. The narrative was forever ruled by the principle of division between "how things used to be" (when the mines were running and worked "nonstop," when "there was everything," "boards" were laid down for dance floors, concerts were organized) and the "today" of this writing (when, as they said, "there is nothing"). As I have already demonstrated, these are pat phrases that characterize the narratives of groups excluded and marginalized in the flow of the transformation of the Polish economy; they come to resemble ritual-ized complaints, collective laments, and condolences. We might say that this is a certain condensation of the structure of recollection, one that simplifies time divisions (Sulima 2003; Tarkowska 1993a); some elements of the past develop and strengthen, becoming elements of the present, while others immediately fade and are excluded from the social communication. We might also call this a collective "structural amne-sia" of the time of the actual liquidation, when time contracts between the present (unemployment, liquidation) and the past (the operating mines). There is no interval. It seems that such a memory structure sharpens or even "explodes" in circumstances when modern/industrial history is suspended, i.e., the state structure for regulating workers' lives, imposing order on everyday life, creating a reality measured in shifts, output, yield, etc.

Secondly, the memory and structure of recollection in my interlocutors, the Wałbrzych diggers and scrap collectors, has shifted to the
above-described level of "liberated objects," material things. There, however, the collected things and underground networks to which so much
time is devoted, the remnants of the "underground city," are generally
arranged in an entirely random fashion. In the private Wałbrzych show-
cases, for instance, communist-era methanometers and mining lamps
are displayed alongside old German equipment and other finds, as well
as old German postcards depicting Wałbrzych, Lubsko, and Świdnica.
This memory does not follow a straight line, nor does it pertain to events
in a linear fashion to create a sense of continuity. This is a peculiar,
bottom-up Wałbrzych archaeology: the digger and the collector involuntarily extracts and creates objects of memory, formed by their animate
imagination and their present activities. "The neighbor downstairs has
a metal detector," said Andrzej Pietrzyk, "he made it with his brother
in the mine, and they were always searching for the [Amber] Chamber
that used to be here, and they began looking for silver, semiprecious
metals and also scrap" (TR/WB/34). The result, as I have demonstrated,
is a series of things of indefinite status, suspended somewhere between
refuse, treasure, and useful object. The Wałbrzych narrative of the diggers, scrap collectors, antique collectors, and ex-miners creeps into this
stratification, into this place of the fluctuating and transitional status
of various material testimonies/correlates of memory, forming an ac-
companiment of sorts to the liberated objects. In a sense one might
speak of a breakdown of the frameworks of objects and of memories, to
borrow a concept from Maurice Halbwachs (1992). Only then do the
German remnants seem to "rise to the surface," and, as I have shown,
through entirely new acts of remembering, of fantasizing, things acquire
new functions and new meanings. To paraphrase the term *Les lieux de
mémoire*, Pierre Nora's places where memory is condensed (1989), they
become memory things, i.e., the correlates of memory practices. These
are the "memory sites" that explode in a space marked by history and
the everyday life produced in the People's Poland (in which, as they said,
"no one was interested").

The history spoken of here thus lacks cohesion and appears chaotic,
collapsing the linear course of events in a peculiar way. The German
heritage of these lands and "Germany" as a pre-epoch of sorts appears
almost everywhere, coming out onto the surface and "spreading"; in
Wałbrzych, in Boguszów, its presence is seen wherever one cares to look.
"This [coal] was excavated, it was already excavated, the Germans once
worked here, and they dug it all out.... There are old German tunnels everywhere here" (TR/WB/21). "This was all done when the Ger-

mans were around. ... It's all German doing, from the bottom up" (TR/WB/23). This knowledge of the German remnants has, furthermore, a "functional" quality, that we might call a kind of tool for dealing with reality in a practical way. Here is a fragment from a conversation between diggers: "We'll go past the stand, and we'll take it from there." "Fine, then we'll see." "There won't be any Germans there?" "What?" "Look, I guess they drove a wedge in there. ... Yeah, look, that's the way they dug" (TR/WB/8). What we find is a sort of "mapping" of the bootleg mine fields, a mapping of the Wałbrzych underground full of German mysteries and goods, which becomes a mutually communicated local knowledge, both practical and imaginary, one that is constantly evoked with every new bootleg mine. The "Germans" are thus continually evoked and mutually communicated trails by diggers and scrap collectors alike. "You've got to have the German maps. They've got everything. The coal veins are in black. The water veins in blue. And they have posts marked out. With those posts you can find everything" (TR/WB/35). Another team, in an adjacent bootleg mine field, told me that they had come from another place, Biały Kamień, because they had managed to steal some old German maps from a museum, and since then they had been unerringly finding coal veins. This memory was revived with every new find. There are endless variants on imaginary tales about the end of the war, and about hidden riches: silver, gold, weapons, trucks, and tones of steel. As one digger told me: "Because all that there is piled high with stones. And nobody knows how many stones there are, and they're afraid to move them, because they might come tumbling down. If we had a torch we could go right in there this minute and I could show you, because it's not so far from here, but without a light it's no good. But in that tunnel everything's leveled out, the walls are smooth, the ceiling's high. It must have been done that way so that trucks could drive in there" (WAŁB 20). This speculation resulted in the idea of an imaginary treasure hidden somewhere in the vicinity.

Remembering is thus a way of transferring a fragile, unstable, and extemporaneous knowledge of the past. Things appear from one day to the next in an unintentional fashion, in what might be called the memory of inertia (Olick and Robbins 1998: 129–130; Connerton 1989: 76), which is associated with acquiring a routine, performing repeated actions, searches, and body movements. The memory of inertia searches for details (an unearthed German shot glass) to provide an immediate structure for its activities around it. This experience—a sort of precivilizational collecting, "hole" digging, etc.—collapses, to some degree, all history and factography, prompting many flights of fancy. This is a world where, in spite of the clear presence of history in the gathered objects (for instance, the German "treasures"), everything has been around for only a brief, recent time. The history so clearly visible in the collected objects vanishes; the structure of time, along with the conventional narrative of past and present, snuffs itself. Through the practice of collecting, the whole of the past changes into objects and begins to recall a palimpsest—the present is inscribed on the German layers, restoring these signs of the past and lending them a fascination of sorts. As a scrap collector from Lubsko told me: "Sometimes you can dig up things the Germans left behind. ... You can find old clay bottles, you can dig up ... some real marvels" (TR/LUB/4). The diggers plowing up the layers of earth and the collectors dismantling the old buildings thus return to the historical roots, becoming "self-made archaeologists," trembling with excitement, digging and dismantling in much the same way as the British once did in Egypt.

The history of the liquidation of the Wałbrzych basin is therefore a history of people who suddenly shifted from legal, regulated work based on principles of security (regulated by order, document, or writing) to gathering or "pre-Neolithic" work. Simultaneously, the former reality, the official (bureaucratic) reality based on documents, has ceased to exist. The imposing buildings of the onetime Victoria and Belweder Mines are scattered with vast quantities of documents: work safety–standard sheets, regulations for shift work, and workers' medical documentation, carefully written out by doctors. All of these papers, deliberating the possibility of a stay in a health spa or qualifications for medical benefits, for example, lie there utterly irrelevant and ignored by one and all. Moreover, all the fixtures, window frames, and installations have disappeared; in one room I spotted a gigantic plaster statue of a white eagle (with one wing broken off) from the communist era. The collectors I came across said that no one was interested in those scattered archives, but that perhaps "one day they would be valuable" (WAŁB 10). The ex-miners are therefore, in a sense, contemporary versions of Hegel's "people without a history" (1991: 372–377; see also Wolf 1982)—their "history" is, after all, in the piles of useless reports and forms in those directors' buildings. And when, during this time of deindustrialization and parallel demodernization, this written and constructed history of the Wałbrzych basin collapsed, the freed methods of social recollection I described began to appear.

Facing Reality after the Mines (2)

What surprises us is the evident correlation between the experience of destroying and dismantling the city and plundering its "stores" on the one hand, and the imagination of its mysterious, underground past on the other. The flip side of this experience of liquidation and destruction is, after all, the collecting, the social focus on detail, on the goods that are invisible to the eye. In Wałbrzych and Boguszów tales of the collapse of the city and the undermining of its foundations are often also tales of hidden goods, of secret passages and underground tunnels. "Boguszów will collapse any minute now," a digger told me, "there are too many holes underground. It's a catastrophe. All of Kuźnice [a village neighboring Boguszów] is about to fall ... everything's hanging by a thread." A moment later he added, "There are still so many surprises here, you can find so many things under the ground! I know of one hidden place in Ratusz, underground, the door's closed all the time, and there's got to be something in there, there's got to be. There's probably an entrance to a tunnel.... Yeah, all the foundations here are destroyed" (TR/WB/35). I heard many statements about countless resources, countless layers of coal and endless "deposits" of scrap. Many indicate the areas around the closed Victoria Mines as a place where the ground conceals heaps of installations, scrap, and precious metals. One digger, an ex–rescue miner, explained that "everything" was still under the ground in Wałbrzych, that "everything was waiting to be dug up—machines, whole corridors full of gear, railway cars, installations, steel lines and copper cables" (WAŁB 3). They began to see all these riches (!) when they broke through into some old German mine shafts. These underground goods, by some accounts, are intact, "miraculously preserved." These riches or the access to these riches appeared in tandem with the search for coal and scrap, with demolition and collecting. This was visible on many levels of conversation—and this fascination (or hope) in particular gave me pause. One digger indicated the fields around the Victoria and told me, "Everything's here, you'll find everything.... There's still so much scrap! People dig for copper, aluminum, pipes.... Everything's here, somewhere" (TR/WB/34). "There's so much of these things ... in communist times no one knew, there was no time. And now people have begun searching and digging, finding things.... They didn't even know there was coal up at the surface ... nobody knew it, and here you've got coal and more coal; we all live off it now. The mines have shut down, they said there was no coal, but here's your coal—the walls go for four to five meters!" (TR/WB/35)

Similar fantasies inspired by the old found or discarded objects emerge, the finders convinced of their extraordinary value. Many people who find old German objects see them as remarkably valuable; for example, some are made of silver. An old German object "always might be made of silver." This could correspond with the legends told in several bootleg mines concerning the hidden Prussian silver in the nearby mountains (WAŁB 3). Many people turn up at scrap and nonferrous metal depots with the metal objects they find, asking if they aren't by chance made of silver (WAŁB 11). What is the significance of all these imaginings? What is happening with the memory, with the imaginations of these diggers and scrap collectors? My impression is that, above all, a major role is played by the problem-free access to these imagined and over-signified goods/riches. We might therefore say that we are dealing with an abrupt drop in the tension created by a merciless reality, the reality of the widespread post-mining unemployment. "There's still so much coal here, so much coal.... There are probably millions, even probably billions of tones of coal. ... There's more coal here than in all of Jastrząb"; "We're still going to dig as much as we can. ... There are still deposits everywhere. ... Oh, here's one, and there's another. ... You can dig here ... think how much coal there must be still, there still has to be coal here" (TR/WB/25). Almost every digger repeats every so often that this is the best and purest coal, extraordinarily filled with calories, "pure anthracite." "There's no coal like it in all of Poland"—this is a kind of refrain repeated in the bootleg mines.

Here I must return to the profound sense of loss that emerges in the collective narrative. During my stay in the Wałbrzych dumping ground in Sobięcin, I had a long conversation with a collector of nonferrous metals who lived in a tumbledown block of flats. He had a magnet for checking the things he found, using it to root out the nonferrous pieces, leaving the iron behind for others. He had worked this way for years. His statements revealed a view of reality that began to take on new and more incredible shapes over the course of our conversation. "It's not just any old junk I've been searching for," the collector told me, "here everyone is very alert, they wouldn't spare anything. People are very alert to all these things. There are all kinds of antiques here, the people take them to the antique dealers, sell them; sometimes they come across some real marvels. I found some old German books here, beautifully written, I've found some beautiful hand-written sheet music. ... Those were original scores by Haydn, Beethoven and Mozart. I don't know exactly what year they were from, but maybe it was eighteen-sixty-something, something like that. ... The Haydn scores were definitely authentic. ... But I tucked them away somewhere, put them someplace, maybe sold some of them. ... Now I regret it" (TR/WB/6). The aim of these statements is, to my mind, quite analogous to mental "work"—and also to the processes described in the opening section. This is a moment where the subject tries to ask him or herself: What is the reality around me like? These statements reverse the experiences of demolition and liquidation, and change them into a sense of "everything being there." During this liquidation, demolition, and scrap collection, the sudden result is that there are still many goods lying all around, though they are invisible. Characteristically enough, access to these things is sudden, almost immediate: "You can find everything here. … There's still so much scrap! They dig for copper, aluminum and pipes. There's everything here, somewhere." "There's everything here, all those things that the Germans wanted to cart away. … You only have to have the money and the power to search, to dig. … It only takes money" (TR/WB/35). This kind of work—collecting and imagining—creates a potential world, irrespective of the external circumstances, "softening" them and giving them a different shape. This phantasizing of the diggers and collectors pays no heed to the hard and fast rules of objective reality, what we might call the Freudian "principles of Reality" (Bielik-Robson 2004: 154–157). "With the introduction of the reality principle one mode of thought-activity was split off; it was kept free from reality-testing and remained subordinated to the pleasure principle alone. This activity is *phantasizing*" (Freud quoted in Segal 1991: 12).

The above-described imagining and wishing for an abundance of goods are thus a kind of defense reaction, which involve a perception of the liquidation and degradation underway, less through destruction than through its mirror image, the act of phantasying. "The very fact of phantasying," writes Hanna Segal, "is a defense against painful realities" (1991: 16). In this case phantasy is, moreover, a correlate of practical everyday activities, and of "historical" recollection; it is also a new way of perceiving objects, their new "mental usage." Ultimately, this is a kind of message that creates a certain circulation, a sort of experience that liberates it from the individual actors, from the individual statements, and thus becomes a separate being. What does this social imaginary truly entail? I shall return once more to the practice of phantasying. In her famous work "The Function and Nature of Phantasy," Susan Isaacs (1948, quoted in Bielik-Robson 2004: 155) demonstrates that the very act of phantasying is inscribed in what Melanie Klein has called the subject's relationship with the object—with what lies outside. Between the subjects of the statements I have collected and the outside reality there is a chasm of misunderstanding, filled with primal anxieties, and it is precisely in this space, in this newly created area, that attempts to negotiate or to "phantasy" reality are made. According to Melanie Klein, this is one of the most primal actions. "In Klein's view," writes Hanna Segal, "from the beginning of life there is sufficient ego to experience anxiety, to form some object relationships in reality and phantasy, and to use primitive defenses" (1991: 15; see also Bielik-Robson 2004: 153–159).

Our precise aim here is not to separate phantasy from reality. The mechanisms of phantasy, defense, and projection are, in this case, far more problematic. They serve rather to engender a sense of "contact with reality," or, in general, a sense of contact with the outside world. And this began the whole game, when reality became fragile. To my mind, this constant act of setting aside findings "for later" strives to arrive at in-between existence—real at some point, unreal at another.

Yet another aspect of post-mining behavior might hold a similar sort of significance, i.e., the "way of being." I repeatedly observed that, at the end of the workday, the ex-miners would hide their tools in the forest undergrowth ("throw them in the bushes"). Further off, fifty meters or so from the shaft, they would hide their more valuable items, mining helmets and batteries, while at a distance of ten meters they would stash their protectors and pickaxes, all of which they would then retrieve on the next workday. Hiding these objects frees the ex-miners from having to carry them home—sometimes a distance of several kilometers (TR/WB/12). It is astonishing, however, how "easily" and "immediately" they find and retrieve these things. The collectors behave similarly: often they hide what they happen to find. "Leave that scrap here, just hide it," I was told on one occasion, "and then come collect it tomorrow. ... Tomorrow it'll be yours." Another time a digger found a good pair of trousers, threw them in the bushes, and told me, "Oh, I'll get those tomorrow. ... Tomorrow I'll pick them up" (TR/WB/12). The result was something resembling treasure depositories, where items were now accessible and other times not, now easy to retrieve and other times slowly and end-lessly sought. In a situation like this, one had an object in hand, while a moment later it might not be there at all. I got the impression that the collectors saw owning things as a game, "playing" with the existence of their resources. "Look, here I've got five wires. Should I take it all for scrap? I'll toss them into the bushes. ... I won't collect them today, I'm not ready to be collecting scrap. ... I'll throw them in the bushes and if they keep ... then they keep. ... If they don't keep, well, they'll be some-one else's" (WAŁB 1). We might state once more that this is a creation of reality that forever remains "incomplete"—its guidelines keep changing.

On the one hand, therefore, this is a certain practice of ownership, and on the other it is a way of taming a hostile environment. Agata Bielik-Robson has written about the intermediary reality of this sort of "survived world." As the philosopher claims, "Its character is entirely different from the external/objective world, though the problem is that there is no way to deny its status as the most real sort of existence. These fragile and fantastical shapes of the world [here the author quotes Laplanche and Pontalis, authors of the *Dictionary of Psychoanalysis*] thus imperceptibly take on the *force of reality*" (2004: 152). The "riches" the diggers find and later store thus become a surplus value, like the silver and gold sunk in the Rhine, which later set the stage for the mythological treasures of the Nibelungen. The procrastinated cashing in of these goods facilitates what I would call this "sudden shift": all the blessings, the rich deposits of coal, and the stores of scrap are found just a step away, "all you have to do is look, but there's no money to do it." "I've been digging so long already. I'd go back to the 'Germans' and there I'd dig blindly, because there are so many things there.... The earth here is so rich.... There are tunnels, and corridors. You just have to dare to go in there, and there's definitely still some money, some kind of ... valuables" (TR/WB/24). The diggers say that by Chełmiec Mountain there are secure bootleg mines "for a rainy day" (WAŁB 27). That is also where the best coal deposits are hidden, and according to one version, there is something called the "mountain of coke," where over a dozen tons of coke were put aside "for later." If you know how to get there, they say, you can heat your apartment in times of hardship. Coke is a symbolic condensation of what is best, i.e., coal; in the bootleg mines they sometimes dig for three days through clay and earth to get to a black vein of pure, multiply-condensed coal in great quantities, hence the "mountain of coke." What my interlocutors told me was thus a kind of social confirmation of reality, i.e., a testing, a kind of intimacy with the daily practice of digging shafts and digging up old pipes, prying things up, an attempt to survive in a period of unemployment. And at precisely this time when "nothing is for certain," this "mountain of coke" makes the world seem less foreign, makes it become somehow "open to the senses"; there appears a *general* sense of the real and (consequently) a *general* subjecthood. "This is [no longer] merely *phantasy*," writes Agata Bielik-Robson, "[i.e.] a conscious formula of their weakness toward what truly exists; it is a phantasy which, in its primal weakness in the face of the *Realitätsprinzip* contains a different source of strength: in it is planted and from it sprouts "mental reality," which differs from the reality of the world" (2004: 153). Therefore, to use this key metaphor of Bielik-Robson's, this was a kind of graft, a "grafting/defensive" strategy. As she writes, "That which is originally weak, defensive, helpless phantasying confronted with the all-powerful might of the real world now becomes a paradoxical source ... of provocation" (ibid.: 153).

The above-described action and imaginings of the bootleg mine diggers, scrap collectors, and ex-miners thus stand as a sort of challenge set before the dramatic and helpless situation in which they find themselves. Their phantasies and legends are *quasi*-historical recollections, they are a second life for objects—not in reality, but as correlates and daily investigations—and they mark an entirely new experience. This gives a new impetus to their investigations, inspires them to speak with a sense of involvement about the things of the present, and provides the opportunity to be forever building a new world, and a new *situation* for themselves. There is an in-between road running from the statement "there's nothing" to "everything's still here," a road that, like it or not, they will have to travel.

Notes

1. This does not, of course, take into account hidden unemployment, which means that actual unemployment could reach even as high as 50 percent or more. Since 1991 this has constantly been a massive group of people: 9,201 people were registered at the Regional Employment Board in 1991, in 1994 there were 19,500 people, and in 1999 there were 14,700 (*Eksploatacja ...* 2000: 378). According to data from 6 June 2002, in Wałbrzych alone 14,723 people were registered (based on a document by the Wałbrzych City Council of September 2002, entitled *Wałbrzych w latach 1994—I półrocze 2002. Najważniejsze wydarzenie* [Wałbrzych from 1994—to the first half of 2002. Major events]). In December 2004 the number of unemployed registered in Wałbrzych was 13,716, while in Boguszów-Gorce alone it reached 2,144 people (figures from Signal Information on the Job Market Situation, Regional Employment Board in Wałbrzych).

2. The tradition of bootleg mines in Upper Silesia reaches back to the 1930s (see, among others, Hajduk-Nijakowska 1988: 153; Morcinek 1981).

3. There are no precise data on the number of people, of course; the local press cites the estimates of the City Patrol, the Police, the City Council, and the estimates of Wałbrzych journalists. A collection of several hundred press cuttings dealing with the bootleg mines (File VI 4b) can be found in the Social Life Documentation Division of the Regional Library in Wałbrzych.

4. Nonetheless, these payments did become a major social event. Most of the bureaucrats and job holders or mine pensioners I spoke with mentioned in almost their first words, and with great regularity, that much of the money flowing into these families was spent recklessly, for example on automobiles, toys, and alcoholic drinks, or simply on "the good life." Another group was the mineworkers, who received mine holidays and held off until their mining pension began, which then gave them a steady source of income.

5. This refers to the changes in the legislation made in 1997, when the definition of those qualifying for pension was changed. Job-performance capability (after retraining, for example) became important, and was linked to the state of health, which had formerly been the sole criterion (see the Order of the Ministry of Labor and Social Policy, of 8 August 1997, on rulings of inability to work for receiving pension). Previously, poor health did, indeed, sentence many former miners to unemployment and poverty.

6. These trajectories were, however, quite diversified within particular groups. There were various reasons for ex-miners to become scrap collectors or rubbish gatherers at the city tip. The majority, however, were former factory workers, workers on the

mine surface or in industrial security, unsuccessful traders from the border and unemployed youth with little job experience; some worked in minibus transport, but also, some in the bootleg mines. It sometimes occurred as well that bootleg miners had had no previous mining experience.

7. Some tenement houses, for instance, had no staircase railings, and had functional but dilapidated bathrooms on the staircase landings heated with old, sometimes poorly functioning coal heaters, leaky roofs, and crumbling attics.

8. The development of German mining in Wałbrzych in the nineteenth and early twentieth centuries began to clearly collapse, and by the 1930s there was already talk of local unemployment and "Wałbrzych poverty" (Michalkiewicz 1993: 146).

9. According to information received from the former manager of the Wałbrzych Bituminous Coal Mine, around ten lethal accidents (1 in 1,000 workers) were noted on a yearly basis in the mines of Wałbrzych. This number could be significantly higher, in fact, as, according to miners and middle-rung workers, some of the victims died after having been registered in the hospital ("died in the hospital from wounds incurred"), which reduced the number of recorded deaths at the place of the event itself. During our conversations during my research, former miners stressed the disproportion between the real numbers of victims and the figures that were officially provided, especially in the 1960s and 1970s. The collection of press cuttings entitled *Mining Catastrophes,* located at the Regional Collection Workshops of the District Library in Wałbrzych, should be acknowledged as a supplementary source of data. The average number of fatal incidents in Polish mines in general in the 1960s and 1970s affected 0.4 in 1,000 workers (cf. *Wałbrzych* ... 1970: 102; Zacharzewski 1996: 20).

10. At the beginning of the 1980s the mines and coke plants employed over 45 percent of industrial workers (Skiba 1997b: 18).

11. The blue-collar population of Wałbrzych was a true ethnic and cultural melting pot: apart from the Polish settlers, there were groups of Polish re-emigrants from France and minorities from Belgium and Westphalia. Moreover, Ukrainians resettled from the Oil Basins of the Boryslav/Drohobycz area came to Wałbrzych, as did settlers of Greek or Jewish ethnicity (Markiewicz 1960; Skiba 1979: 70–88; Czajka 1985: 28–29; Bełdzikowski 1998: 17–35).

12. The housing districts of Piaskowa Góra and Podzamcze, built in the 1970s in Wałbrzych, were principally inhabited by workers of the newly built offices and institutions associated with the creation of the Wałbrzych Voivodeship (Kłopot 1997: 74).

13. These abandoned quarters of the old buildings swiftly succumbed to degradation, particularly after additional tenants were introduced; these flats were of low standard with no comforts and with faulty, broken-down infrastructures (plumbing, heating, etc.). The socially marginalized tenants lived in poverty, which caused the increase of petty crime (on the basis of tenement houses in Łódź, see, among others, Warzywoda-Kruszyńska 1998; on the basis of old buildings in the cities of Upper Silesia, see Wódz 1983; 1989: 54–55).

14. Joanna Wawrzyniak (2006: 1–2) writes on this topic in her article, "The Recovered Territories," in *The Ideology of Polish Communism: Symbols and Everyday Life on the Basis of Military Settlers.* In a school text from the postwar years, a mother tells her children about the Recovered Territories (Lower Silesia) by saying that this is ancient Polish land, "full of riches, and most of all, coal."

15. Some of the dismantled and demolished local sites acquired symbolic significance, as for example the demolition and scrapping of the Barbara Shaft and the demolition and filling of the modern Kopernik Shaft, built in the last years of the People's

Republic period. For many the latter was a construction that signified mine expansion, development, and, consequently, more work, and from which not a single coal transport left.

16. Such dangers do, indeed, exist in various parts of Wałbrzych (though not on such a scale); thus far, however, there have been no substantial catastrophes. It ought to be mentioned that there is a certain realistic fear of the accumulation of mining damage (for which no one may now be held responsible, since the mines have all been closed), or the danger arising from the systematic flooding of the inactive mines. Be this as it may, people frequently forecast future calamities (*Doświadczenia ...* 1999).

17. People spoke of accidents and dangers in active mines before their liquidation, and of the deaths and risks involved, in a fashion entirely different from the dangers in the bootleg mines. At the time, images of destruction and death were in no way presented in the foreground of events. However this may sound, in the days of mining prosperity, even the death of work mates in mining accidents was treated as a phenomenon that was natural and subsumed within the society (in the official/bureaucratic sense as well). As the diggers phrased it, "a state death was something totally different, you knew that it was how things had to be."

18. Somewhere around ten people died on a yearly basis in the Wałbrzych mines. On average, one person dies every year working in the Wałbrzych bootleg mines (six lethal incidents). The number of people working in the bootleg mines is more or less one-third (or sometimes one-half) that of the Wałbrzych miners who worked "down below" in the 1980s. Our conclusion is, therefore, that the risk of lethal accident was *higher* in the legally functioning mines than in the bootleg mines. My interlocutors said "that was a 'state' death. You couldn't do anything or find anything out. ... There was an accident, and that was that' (TR/WB/25, also 31).

19. Moreover, the diggers themselves had no sense of extraordinary or even unusual danger—as they put it, their pits were "one hundred percent safe." "If I build it myself, I know there's no way that something bad could happen." "This is our hole, and it's a safe hole." Accidents occurring during demolition are also clearly overrepresented in the statements I gathered.

20. Such an analysis of the unemployment experience was presented in the 1930s by the authors of *The Unemployed of Marienthal* (Jahoda, Lazarsfeld, and Zeisl 1933; see Sułek 2005), and by authors of Polish equivalents of such research, conducted in the time of the Great Crisis of the 1930s (Zawadzki and Lazarsfeld 1993). They described typical psychophysical consequences, such as a sense of degradation and of futility, an oversensitivity to the environment, a somatization of emotions (ibid.; cf. Sułek 2005: 5) and recurring acts of aggression ("aggressive fixation"; "and a vengefulness boiled in me, I didn't know towards whom, but I did know it was terrible"; "I was struck by such fury that I couldn't stand anyone around me"; Zawadzki and Lazarsfeld 1993: 114–116) and autoaggression ("sometimes I thought: throw your whole body into the display, sink your teeth into that intricate pile of chocolates and devour, devour, gobble up whole chunks at a time ... and then they can hang me if they like"; ibid.: 106, 113–114).

21. Aggression toward functionaries sometimes even took on an active aspect, and it seemed that during some confiscations of coal, the police cars' tires would be punctured with pickaxes. I often heard such declarations as: "Again we have to take to the city hall with our pickaxes—their days are numbered now!" This response is described in the research of Zawadzki and Lazarsfeld (1993: 115), and also in the diaries of the unemployed from the late 1990s kept by Anna Zawadzka: "I'm not going to steal, because I don't know how," reads one of the fragments. "Should I go

ask one of those directors again if they'd be so good as to do something for me? I won't go! The best way out would be to bash myself in the skull. That'd be the easiest thing. But first I'd like to go … shoot them all, one by one" (2005: 41).

22. To the statements of the Wałbrzych unemployed we might add the complaints and the cries of the street salespeople, the representatives of "bootleg entrepreneurship," "oppressed" by the city patrols, quoted by Sulima: "Let us earn a living, we only want bread!"; "Soon I'm going to have to start stealing, because you've got to live somehow!"; "I don't know how to steal, and I can't sell things!" (2003: 3–4).

23. An analogous example is the motifs of village funeral laments described by Sulima, in which there is a dialogue with the "empty hereafter" (1980).

24. We are not dealing, therefore, with the direct, clinical, and psychopathological dimensions of depressive/destructive disorders, with the clinical notions of melancholy or mourning. "At a first glance," writes Paweł Dybel, opening his essay on the Freudian concept of melancholia, "this strictly clinical concept [melancholia] is identified with powerful states of depression, with a kind of spiritual disempowerment and crisis, which can even lead to suicide in extreme cases. … When, however, we take a closer look at this interpretation [of melancholia], it becomes clear that it indicates the complex psychological nature of this phenomenon, which would be hard to find in even the most exhaustive clinical descriptions of melancholia. … It grows to the rank of the central figure of human self-knowledge" (Dybel 2000: 149). As such, this is a particular way of considering people and their collective experiences found in their cultural expression—we are dealing with a psychosocial crisis situation, with deformation and shock occurring simultaneously within their private and their collective narratives.

25. This phenomenon was described by Sigmund Freud in his analyzes of mourning/ melancholia (2005).

26. However, this does not prevent them from being able to learn at least the basic principles of bootleg mine construction in a few months. At the beginning of the history of the bootleg mine fields, experienced miners taught others—often for payment—how to construct a bootleg mine in over one hundred "holes" around the Barbara Shaft.

27. Mutual solicitude was also visible in the miners' residential districts; there was a certain standard of mutual assistance amongst miners' families, which, as Jacek Wódz suggests (1989: 58), was tied to a shared experience of permanent and unforeseeable threat to men's health and lives.

28. I once went into the bootleg mine of a team I had befriended and said that I had perhaps seen three city patrol officers headed their way; no one paid this any mind, however. Suddenly from above we heard some unfamiliar voices. Two of the diggers stopped what they were doing, and said: "Aw, no, it's impossible, what are they doing up there—sleeping?" He was referring to the "sifters" working outside of the shaft who also served as lookouts, who joked, a few minutes later, about the three other diggers who had arrived, whom I had thought to be patrol officers. The diggers down below were basically angry that the men on lookout might have missed somebody, might not have seen them in due time, though they, themselves, had not believed there was any danger, since from above there had been no signal. The whole affair ended with a round of laughter, because there had been no actual danger. I believe this was a continuation of the mining system of warning one another, or, perhaps, of the mining community's work ethic. Simultaneously, it was also its discontinuation, since it applied to work that was temporary, unstable (but not short-lived—I often heard: "my grandchildren will still be digging [in the bootleg mines]," and "the boot-

leg mines are going to be made legal soon"), and illegal, the external organizational norms no longer applying (allowing breaks, "liquor" consumption, etc., at will).

29. In Upper Silesia there was a religious ritual to God and to Saint Barbara, regarding the miner leaving his home. On the one hand, it was extraordinarily spare in words and gestures, while on the other it was an act of extraordinary gravity. Children were awakened to say goodbye to their fathers as they left home to work the night shift (Gerlich 1989: 127). There were also stories circulating in Silesia that certain fatal accidents had occurred because a wife had failed to bid her husband goodbye (ibid.: 129), had failed to entrust him to Saint Barbara, had failed to sigh (for the significance of "sigh" in mining culture, see, in particular, ibid.: 129–130). Before descending into the mines, the foreman would wish the miners God's solicitude, and there was a common prayer for protection from the dangers of the job, such as stealing.

30. In particularly difficult moments in a conversation, such as when he had lost his day's earnings through the collapse of a shaft wall, one digger felt somehow obliged (toward himself? toward me?) to react with a joke of some kind, punctuated with short bursts of laughter. In similar fashion, whether while digging or during conversations at home, in the morning or at night, though extremely tired, or in the evening sitting down for a coffee after a full day's digging, there were a few other diggers who interrupted nearly all of their conversations with peals of laughter. Though they might have been speaking to me about things that were in no way humorous, such as the problems they had keeping the flat heated, or of getting free of debt, the laughter was mandatory, creating a frame for the various series of conversations.

31. The former miners had been without free dental coverage for six or seven years. Every miner had a medical card filled with only one inscription: "dental cleaning." My students found these cards, rendered utterly insignificant, lying about in "Belweder" among abandoned documents in the director's office of the Victoria Mine, where they became part of the characteristic "history of written documents" after the mine's collapse. The liquidation of the mines thus translated into a meaningless keeping of dental documents, and as a result, the former miners had untreated cavities and missing teeth.

32. They were also reluctant to assess the value of their day's taking, as their monthly earnings were variously approximated, and outsiders had difficulty estimating. In the case of the diggers I knew best, I do not suppose this resulted from distrust toward me. According to my estimates, the diggers were probably able to earn from eight hundred to one thousand złoty a month.

33. Wanda Mrozek (1987) has described one such internalized ecology of mining families, revealed in the process of modernizing transformations—moving to new buildings of large-module blocks of flats. The author cites typical statements by the young mining families, who saw the old, cramped flats of their parents as better and roomier (!): "My parents' flat was much better. It was only a room with a kitchen, but you could put a bed in that kitchen!" "My parents had a room with a kitchen, but the flat was big, not like ours, *you used to live in the kitchen* [emphasis mine]" (ibid.: 45). This space was thus understood in terms of activity, and not geometry. The miner's kitchen "had space for everything." At night it was a bedroom (blankets were spread out for the children), and during the day it was a kitchen and a dayroom/dining room, serving whatever function was required. This may explain the mining families' custom of keeping a kitchen floor clean enough to eat dinner off it.

34. Guriewicz's statement here, of course, concerns the medieval cultural category, but Arjun Appadurai (1986) and Igor Kopytoff (1986) have presented this aspect of the

function of objects from a wider perspective. These objects, as Appadurai claims, become "incarnated signs" through their individualization and "decommoditization." To paraphrase the text, such an object "has no price" (Appadurai 1986: 19) and remains beyond the sphere of equivalential exchange (Kopytoff 1986; cf. Appadurai 1986: 24). When it escapes from this culturally created regime of values, it is easily lifted to the rank of "treasure" or "luxury item" ("transvaluation," "decommoditization"; ibid.: 23), something that cannot be "spent" or exchanged; it becomes of particular preciousness, and acquires added value (ibid.: 25).

35. The authors of a British-Polish publication on the management of postindustrial heritage write of a similar state of suspension between an old ramshackle factory and a museum of technology filled with "valuable exhibitions," and of the ways of giving them new significance and new functions, on the basis of Polish (Lower Silesia) and British (central England, the Birmingham vicinity) deindustrialized areas (Mende 1997: 143–153; Watson 1997: 353–361).

Figure 1. A mining museum

Figure 2. Mines

Figure 3. Bootleg mining fields

Figure 4. Work/A Break

Figure 5. A "do-it-yourself" hoist

Figure 6. "Belweder", deserted director's office of the Victoria Mine

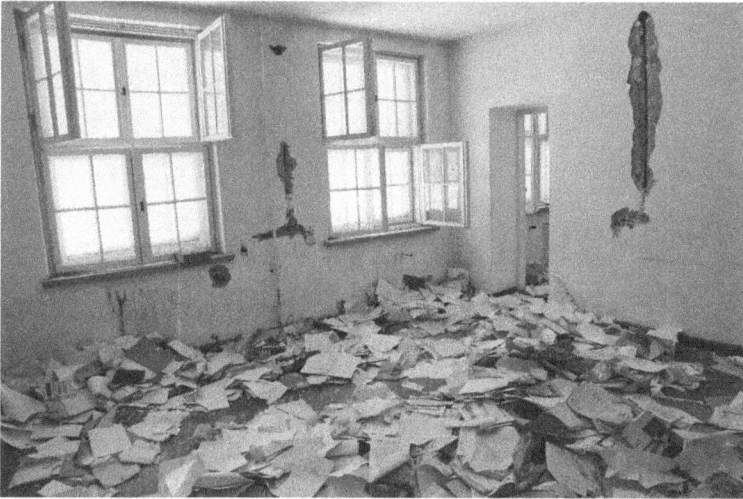

Figure 7. Written documents of the mine

Figure 8. Sacks of coal—after counting

Chapter 3

The Bełchatów Brown Coal Mine—The Shadowlands of the Exposed Mine

The Mine/Power Station

The Perfect Balance, an Abrupt Modernization

The sandy lands of the Bełchatów environs in the 1970s was a region with no industry and poor agriculture. The villages were mainly composed of hundred-year-old collapsing wooden huts, while postwar Bełchatów was a dreary backwater, counting just barely over ten thousand inhabitants (Wieruszewska-Adamczyk 1971; Zawilski 1967). This area offered no prospects for development. Its residents traveled all about the country, chiefly toward the mines of Silesia and the factories of Łódź, taking pick-up jobs or longer employment wherever they went. However, when vast deposits of brown coal were discovered and documented under Bełchatów in the 1970s, the construction on an enormous exposed mine began, the Bełchatów Brown Coal Mine. Layers upon layers of earth and coal disappeared into the mouths of the gigantic machines; single farmsteads and whole villages were bought out and resettled. There also began the process of settling new arrivals who had come from all around the country to work, and constructing blocks of flats and concrete buildings to accommodate them. The explosion in industry and modernization swiftly encompassed the neighboring vicinities; construction began on the mine's twin sister, a huge power station, the largest conventional (brown coal–fueled) power plant in Central Europe. Rapid social and economic advancement took place, particularly for those building the plant, and for the employees of the dozens of side-service companies, while the rest of the country's industrial centers

slowly became mired in stagnation, suffering the beginnings of the profound crisis of the 1980s. This led to a concentrated social experience
of transformation, development, and modernization, creating a closed
acreage, an anthropological laboratory.

On various layers of social significance, the experience of abrupt
modernization that took place over the last thirty years has etched itself
in the memories of the inhabitants of the villages and the colonies, of
the areas surrounding the exposed mine. Put simply, new meanings,
statements, and images in certain local discourses circulated in local
systems/receptacles of knowledge of the world. In its present usage, a
discourse is an ethnographic field of communicating knowledge and
thus a space for creating local ideas, pictures/representations, and local meanings (Grzymała-Kazłowska 2004: 18–22; Malewska-Szałygin
2004), which results in a circulation of social meanings; and in their
wider context, a certain experience of modernization is inscribed "in-
between them." At a first glance, the areas around the exposed mines
portray a local industrial/energy ideology, I would even say a form of industrial propaganda. This forms a textual and visual background for the
circulation of discourse, which extends very far. It embraces all the local
propaganda and prospectus undertakings, such as the mine newspaper
bulletins and folders distributed to workers, power plant brochures and
boards, and office posters and billboards in the vicinity of Bełchatów
displaying modernization projects (e.g., depictions of enormous steam
plants reflected in an artificial lake, with the catchphrase "The pure
power of the 21st century"). However, to the same extent as the ideology of necessary and immediate industrial/social development appeared
in the 1970s and 1980s alongside the mine (Monografia KWB 2000),
the current situation is dominated by the notion of balanced curbing/
retrieving of natural resources (a local take on sustainable development).
In the above-mentioned monograph (ibid.), published on the occasion
of the twenty-five-year anniversary of the company,[1] the industrial zone
is portrayed as a perfect organism: the series of charts included in the
"Kopalnia Węgla Brunatnego Bełchatów" book (which look much the
same in all the other folders of the mine, such as "The Bełchatów Mine"
or "Environmental Protection at the Bełchatów KWB" of 2002) present the splendid internal "metabolism" of the company, a state of ideal
balance. On the one hand, we have the fuel/raw material, i.e., the coal
deposits that are digested and burned in the power plant, and on the
other, the refuse, the excreta: the pumped water, the soil and the cinder
tips. In the KWB promotion/information pamphlets, these excreta return to economic circulation via the principle of the minimal use of materials. The water that is pumped from the ground powers several water

and drink manufacturers neighboring the mine; the soil is enriched and packaged, then sold in gardening shops or used in recultivation projects; while the recultivated soil banks serve as exclusive hunting grounds. The Kleszczów region and its populations are presented in like fashion, as a perfectly functioning organism. The image of the mine thus corresponds to the promoted image of the Kleszczów region (whose terrain holds the majority of the areas used by the KWB), creating the typical rhetoric of contemporary success—i.e., a utopia. The various pages of the region's bulletin/periodical arrange the parts of the local social organism: children's education, occupational training, the numerous civic bodies, emergency services, the new refinery, the new bakery, the new sewage system. This range of transformations all together create the (regional/ mining) "landscape" of the ideal society—an autonomous, self-sufficient, harmonious whole. The photographs and the folders contain images of flowers in bloom, swaying over a network of water pipes and sewers.

This prospective/promotional image of the great industry thus has strains of the contemporary myth of the renaturalization of the modernized world. What follows is a rearrangement of the natural order and the social (artificial) order typically found in contemporary mythology, i.e., the mechanism described by Roland Barthes (2000), whereby the orders of nature and culture are rearranged. This is also commonly found in the propaganda and mythology of Socialist Realism (Tomasik 1999). The mine, as an artificial environment, is presented here as nature, which is also why the massive digger/stacker unit shown in numerous brochures and prospectuses rears up from "colorful" local grain fields or green meadows, emphasizing the abundance and "purity" of the environment. This process reveals something even more essential, for here we find a reversal of the order of things. The vast structure of the mines of the region emerges as a "natural" being meant to create a perfect, self-sufficient organism (a perpetual motion machine), which simultaneously remains external, alien, unpredictable, and irreversible. This is not merely about an "imitation of nature." (At any rate, how could this be maintained in a landscape as lunar as Bełchatów's?) It is also about a portrayal of the outcome of technological activities that seems, in a sense, to be a true, ideal state of nature. This propaganda image of the mine district as a second nature and, furthermore, as a perfect, natural environment forms an essential backdrop to the above-described social experiences.

The internal context of this promotional image is a long-standing local discourse, a way in which the area's inhabitants tell and speak of large-scale industry and the infrastructure behind it. During our conversations, both the residents of Bełchatów (generally tied to the mine and the power plant) and those of the villages surrounding the excavation initially spoke fairly approvingly, and to some extent automatically, about the changes that were taking place all around. The majority more or less recited the same microhistory of the construction of the power plant. At first, their statements rendered an image of technological/ civilizational advancement, as well as progress in their "lifestyle." They spoke of the roads, waterworks, and electrification, the blocks of flats and the power station combines: "They made access roads, people got their own flats, they expanded the whole town" (BEŁCH 14). After some time, however, these initial statements changed into more vivid tales, depicting the external, all-encompassing transformation reaching places where "no one would have suspected" or "would have predicted." "The asphalt roads are everywhere! Even the field roads ... I can even say the field roads are paved, because I know them well. ... Even those field roads are paved with asphalt" (BEŁCH 4). At the same time, we see once more the typical image of the newly created world of the mining district as a perfect, modern, economic, and ecological organism. This image is supplemented by the neighboring districts' perception of the mine environs as somehow exceptional, and the Kleszczów district in particular, where the greater part of the KWB is located, depicted as a place of inexhaustible resources and civilizational/technological success. As the residents of a neighboring district said: "They live on those roads, on that gas, on those pavements ... on that structure. ... Over there, there's a pavement on every road" (BEŁCH 4). There are various takes on this industrialized paradise. Depending on the conversation, one can hear that the district ensures its inhabitants free electricity, and on other occasions, free telephones, and finally, supplies of inexpensive/cost-free plumbing, gas, fuel for the stove, and discounts on nearly everything. In many areas, such as neighboring Kleszczów, one encounters the profound conviction that "the municipality pays for all the telephone bills," "the municipality pays for the gas," "it's the richest municipality in Europe. ... They have money coming out of their ears, people there have water and light practically for free, all the pavements are done" (TR/BŁ/10). "The whole municipality has [natural] gas" (BEŁCH 4). We ought to note that this very image is a sort of local mythology in itself. For in Kleszczów, of course, there are no free telephone services, free gas, free fuel shipments, etc. (however, the water drawn from the depths of the pit is indeed made available for free, and the mine pays the farmers "meadow payments," a small compensation for drying out their meadows).

The Experience of Alienation and Control over the Environment
At a second glance, these statements do reveal a characteristic attribute of the perception we are sketching out, a state of the perfect modern-

ization of the surrounding lands. In the statements of the people employed in the Bełchatów industry, as well as among miners and workers
of factories near the mine, we constantly find a mechanical inertia of
the mining labor, and above all, a facility with which the technological
extraction process takes place. "Do you know someone who works at
the mine? How's the work, hard or easy?" "I'd say it's easy, what they
say around here is that it's not too rough" (BEŁCH 8). "Now we've got
the 'eserki' and 'eerki' [type of machine]," say the miners and inhabitants of Łękawa. "Everything just *goes by itself,* it just goes straight down
the conveyor belt and there you are.... Off to be sold" (BEŁCH 10).
The ease in succession of the technological, and simultaneously modernizing, process could be even better defined as a sense of the minimal
resistance posed by the material reality. One might say that "everything
goes by itself," and requires almost no manual exertion, engaging neither man's body, muscles nor mind. As one of the miners phrased it: "I
know a guy that works on the conveyor belt, and all he has to do is make
sure it keeps running smoothly.... Even if some big stone falls on the
belt, then that stretch shuts off automatically, and a group of specialists comes in to remove the boulders.... Well, and there's his work for
you, he *just stares* at the belt moving" (BEŁCH 6). In these initial
images we can see another extraordinary attribute, i.e., a perfect self-
sufficiency of the organism, working on the basis of a *perpetuum mobile,*
a self-propelling machine. In these statements the mine/power station
(and also the mine/municipality) recalls a structure that is continually
turning and operating, creating new spoil tips, creating and dismantling
conveyor belts, the massive digger/stacker rhythmically swaying about,
and all this taking place before the eyes of the inhabitants. At the very
beginning of these statements we find a standard form marking someone's activity, the words always in the third-person plural: "They made
a road," "they made a path," "they set up some lamps for us," "they've
brought in the stacker," and "they've resettled everyone by now." From
the internal perspective of my interlocutors, the experience of indus-
trialization/modernization is constantly described as an outside force
that in no way relies upon them. On all sides large and small trucks
drive by, new roads and pavements are built, new spoil tips, new ru-
mors are spreading of the mine's progress toward Western models and
of new plans "from above" for managing the degraded terrain (the spoil
tips and the dried-out fields). I would call this experience a thoroughly
industrial one, for, on the one hand, it is an experience of superiority
over the reality of the natural creature, whose "remaking and reworking," to quote Daniel Bell, enhances "man's powers" and a certain collective "sense of power" (1996: 148–149). On the other hand, it is a total

alienation from the essence of the process taking place (Watson 1987: 105–107; Blauner 1964: 15–16). At the very least, this alienation arose from the essentially sensory resistance in raising the earth. If, however, the inhabitants of the areas surrounding the pit share a clearly collective experience of the presence of the mine/power plant, then this precisely is the experience of the inertia of industrial labor. In the statements and the conversations around the exposed mine, verb phrases are forever cropping up that show a lack of influence on the changes taking place all around, and the absolutely "external" position of the mine. "They went and built some roads. ... Now there's trucks that drive by here" (Rogo- wiec village). "They set up some street lamps and now it's all bright ... now you can see everything clear as a bell even when it's dark ... to hell with them" (Wacław Okoński). "They once set up an orchard here. ... First there was nothing, then suddenly this orchard. ... They laid cables, pumped in water, sprayed the whole thing. ... Now the mine's moved on ... and they've left it there" (TR/BŁ/17). One impoverished farmer, living with his brother in a dilapidated hundred-year-old hut alongside both a vast digging site and the grounds of the power plant, told me: "And so ... we've got cabbages here, a few potatoes. ... When the wind picks up then the dust flies in. ... All you see are those lights, and we can hear the noise and rumble of the machines at night" (TR/BŁ/4). In the interviews and the conversations around the exposed mine, the unpre- dictability of the changes taking place all around are a recurring refrain. For example, one impoverished farmer from Rogowiec whose flock of sheep still grazed outside the power plant said, "What can really happen here? There's ash-filled water apparently running under here through pipes, they force through the ash, they mix it and mix it all up with sulphur, and force it all on us" (TR/BŁ/5). The network of big industry, governed by completely different and unfamiliar laws, thus lies overtop of the network of small farmsteads and their remnants of crops, live- stock, and recycling of household goods; these phenomena come from the outside and create an entirely new environment, a "second nature."

I would say that the mine/power plant creates a social experience of a modern, extra-individual, and, to some extent, natural control of the environment, setting a precedent for modernization that embraces the neighboring settlements and the people residing there. The process of modernizing and industrializing the local sandy farmlands is taking place almost everywhere, and there is evidence of the construction un- derway, the movement of the vast shovel stackers and the growing pit all around. Moreover, the work performed around the exposed mine is generally perceived as mechanical activity, a kind of inertia. This has ruptured the ties between one's immediate actions and their disproportionately powerful effect. As Daniel Bell writes about the experience of modernity: "Energy has replaced raw muscle and provides the basis for … large *leaps in productivity* [emphasis mine]" (1996: 147). My impression is that these were processes and experiences that appear as part and parcel of the above-described modernization process, allowing for the exercise of power over reality, its reduction to "a simple, maximally homogenous play of substances and powers" (Bielik-Robson 2004: 107).

The experience of socially mediated control over nature (the living environment) is absolutely essential here. For there has come about an intermediated universe that is technologically calculated, technologically evident and inevitable, an enterprise that is the pride of many local residents, the local authorities, and the Kleszczów authorities. The walls of their offices are hung with images of the environment transformed by the mining, generally of the marvelous lake and the recreation complex. All this is accompanied by the society's conviction that these modernized surroundings have been created "with no manual effort." We might say that this mine/machine organism functioning on all sides has become as natural and, at the same time, as inert/inevitable as the fact that the sun rises. This experience calls to mind the attempts to conceptualize the experience of modernity and modernization taken up in the twentieth century by its theorists and critics (Adorno and Horkheimer 1997; Benjamin 1996; Berman 1983; Jedlicki 2000; Ortega y Gasset 1994; Weber 1993 and 1978). Jose Ortega y Gasset (1994), and shortly thereafter, Walter Benjamin (1996), write of this specifically modern perceptual and existential role reversal of nature and industry. In Ortega y Gasset's *The Revolt of the Masses* this is chiefly the figure of the mass human, the consumer, who regards social technological constructs less as "organization than as aspects of the natural world." A recurring motif in Benjamin is the socially assimilated "shocking experience": the abrupt strike of a match, connection of a telephone, or click of a camera shutter (Rejniak 2002: 23). Like the flame on a match, a conversation or a photograph "releases itself," all the comforts of civilization, from electricity to plumbing, are assimilated (on a perceptual level) in European culture, automatically creating the "natural" environment. Moreover, this ubiquitous artificiality, naturalizing all phenomena of the "cultural poetics," is accompanied by an existential and behavioral distance from the activity being performed and the process underway. From the perspective of the worker or the neighbor of the gigantic power plant station, this is a phenomenon akin to the Marxist concept of the experience of "alienation" (see Blauner 1964: 15–16; Marx 1992 [1907]). In his sketches of the 1930s, Benjamin describes, after Marx's *Capital* (1992 [1907]), the perceptual/existential structure of this experience—the industrial experience—as alienation. According to Benjamin (who is paraphrasing Marx), the laborer or industrial worker undergoes a "breaking in" process, working in time morseled into little pieces, in unconnected, monotonous, and endless movements of the machines and of his hands; "in working with machines, workers learn to coordinate 'their own movements with the uniformly constant movements of an automaton'" (2003 [1940]: 328). This is an experience encompassing the whole of "being in the world," an experience of alienation from the "matter of the action" that is transpiring. My impression is that, to some extent, this "industrial experience" of organizational alienation (Blauner 1964: 15–16; Watson 1987: 82–86; see also Beyon 1975) concerns those neighboring the new environment being revisioned by the KWB, the immediate neighbors of the enterprise and its actors (workers), for whom the road, installation, and extraction work always have a semi-automated quality, coming, as it were, "from the outside."

Nonetheless, I believe that the inertia of the mine existence has a major role to play here. We might say that it creates the environment independently of humans. It is particularly all-encompassing and overpowering for people from the impoverished, excluded farmsteads surrounding the exposed mine. It is their profound experience of inferiority toward the outside reality and, to all intents and purposes, their *powerlessness* (after all, they were forced to be neighbors of the KWB, and shunted aside, if only in terms of their knowledge, from the course of these powerful processes). Robert Blauner (1964: 15–16) has written on the isolation of modern workers from the overall sense of the industrial process, the resulting powerlessness, as well as the sense of the meaninglessness of their actions, their ignorance of the process as a whole and of their isolation and professional inertia. He has, in fact, shown this to be a characteristic position for the industrial worker in general, citing those working chiefly in factories or branches of the chemical and pharmaceuticals industries (where the sense of causation is fairly high) as the exception, since, in his opinion, this kind of work demands a certain technological awareness from all the workers (see Blauner 1964; Watson 1987: 106–107). This is, therefore, a more general characteristic of the experience of modern industrialization. As researchers have shown, this is the experience of an unclear structure that is inert and mediated through various institutions, from which it is hard to say precisely "where" the authority comes (Blauner 1964: 15–22; Watson 1987: 64–68; cf. Giddens 1991: 38, 184–185).

At the Margins of the Great Industry: Marginalization and Exclusion

A peculiar game, described in the media as *Buying out Faustynów, or: A State of Suspension* (Torański 2000), has begun between the vast mine/

power plant and the section for the inhabitants of Bełchatów. This is another background of vital importance for the above-described anthropological laboratory of transformations. The mine has paid relatively large
sums of money for the land it takes from the farmers, and such buyouts
have become a way for the farmers to get wealthy overnight. There were
many families just waiting to be bought out, waiting until "they [the
KWB authorities] came along to buy them out," proposing a substantial
sum of money or, as sometimes happens, a home in Bełchatów. Some
of the residents inflate their property value and its potential price by
planting fruit trees, installing nonfunctional heating systems (etc.) in
the hopes that the mine will pay them more for their land. This practice
is so familiar to the local inhabitants that "buyout" has become a general
catchphrase, and the place the mine happens to be developing at a given
time has become the subject of a hidden, though widely known game,
or competition. Those who "wait it out" the longest, as I was told, who
"plant a fake orchard, bushes or trees from one day to the next, so that
they grow knee-high" (Kamień), gains a fortune, often expressed in abstract quantities. In his article, Błażej Torański (ibid.) shows that many
local farmers wait years for their land to be bought out. They negotiate
the price, inquire into the KWB's further construction plans, complain
about the terrible environmental damage, write up protests, and use
various forms of blackmail, concluding with correspondence exchanges
and trials that can last several years. Above all, however, my impression
is that this process reveals the local significance and peculiar circulation
of the catchphrases "buyout" and "dispossession"—extremely emotional
matters that change entire living strategies. Every parcel of land is or
could be (at least potentially) subject to the possibility of a "buyout,"
and the whole area lives for only one thing, for the moment when "they
come and buy them out." On the one hand, this leads to a whole range
of calculated moves and decisions (the installation of sham central heating, the planting of decorative trees to raise land value, etc.), creating
this "state of suspension." On the other hand, a certain *modus operandi*
of the mine/power plant has appeared in the local consciousness that
took the character of a random force, a "coincidence." Simultaneously,
the great power of this reality (Kamień, Zarzecze, Łękińsko, Szamów,
Trząs, from the majority of statements; see among others TR/BŁ/3), a
buyout, means sudden wealth and "social advancement" for a household. A "buyout" is thus an event the residents hotly anticipate, though
it is also unpredictable and external—in a word, random.

However, over the last decade or so, this dispossession has bypassed
many of the residents of the villages surrounding the exposed mine. As
development changes direction, the mine decides not to purchase some

land. These homeowners are then left with infertile farms dried out by the mines, right alongside the speeding industry, the conveyor belt machines running twenty-four hours a day (Szamów, my research, TR/BŁ/14). This study is, therefore, the story of these many families who for many years, until just recently, lived in hopes of being dispossessed. As one resident of Szamów and an ex-farmer told me: "There used to be a village here, a dairy, there were depots.... Now they've taken away the depots and the dairy, and so what am I supposed to do with my milk? There's no more earnings ... there used to be a village here—and now almost the whole village has been dispossessed, and whoever wanted to, bought himself a flat, because he got money for his land.... But us they didn't buy out, and we have to sit here in this accursed wasteland, in this poverty.... Not a drop of rain" (TR/BŁ/21). Remaining on land that has not been bought out is an experience shared by many families, and the farmsteads on the unpurchased land function more or less as they had previously, before the history of the land buyouts and the construction of the factory. Their residents continue to work the dry earth (in the case of farmers), or in the vicinity of the industrial plants (if they have a job), while simultaneously trying to tend to their small patch of soil. Some have not, however, found employment in the environs of the exposed mine. Some take advantage of social welfare and unemployment insurance, while others take odd jobs in the public work organized by the municipality. During my research, unemployment in the Bełchatów region fluctuated between 13 and 17 percent, while in the Kleszczów municipality, the range was from 10 to 13 percent, with a particularly large number of unemployed women (statistics taken from Regional Work Bureau in Bełchatów).

At present, over a dozen villages are scattered around the exposed mine; some are entirely populated, while some are already half resettled. The houses in these areas, built chiefly in the 1970s and 1980s (with the occasional home from the 1990s), have typical, simple, cube-shaped constructions, though one finds the odd wooden thatched hut, stuck with roofing paper or sometimes a tin roof, heated with a coal oven or wood-burning stove. Some of the residents of villages like Trząs, Kurnos, Janów, Kamień, Rogowiec, Faustynów, Żłobnica, Łękińsko, and Szamów have modernized, "tidy" courtyards, though between them are yards filled with all varieties of building materials, wood, tools, and reworked parts of fences and gates. In the small community of Szamów, at the very edge of the exposed mine, right next door to the gigantic, overgrown spoil tip, this contrast sketches itself out most vividly. This is a small village, a colony that remains after the greater part of the village was bought out and resettled (my research). Between the modernized roads and the few new buildings (private homes, public buildings), there is a scattering of impoverished, collapsing, and sometimes neglected houses, village farmsteads with numerous extensions and courtyards filled with various materials: garbage, waste, old tools, junk, and rusted machine parts. Both those who somehow function in the local economic circulation and people on the margins of the local job market (generally impoverished farmers and jobless ex-employees of the KWB complex) are living there. The majority find no work in the area, either because of their low qualifications, their lack of skills in dealing with employers, or for other reasons, of which we will speak later. At the same time, it is essential for them to take part in the construction of the enormous KWB enterprises, and they sometimes work in them for many years.

They generally live in poverty, and many indexes (including the ministerial index) show that they take advantage of social welfare, either on a regular basis or periodically. Moreover, within the municipality these households are clearly marginalized socially, economically, politically, and in many other respects, even if only with regard to the wealthy surroundings modernized in "model" fashion. This marginalization has a concrete dimension, in that it pertains to a certain topography, i.e., settlements of people who are either unemployed, or living off poorly paid or odd jobs, the "working poor" (see, among others, Stanaszek 2004), those found along the edge of the Bełchatów mine. This means that geography, or real location, translates immediately into topography, and that the hubs and ties of the large enterprises rub shoulders with the homes of the unemployed and the poverty-stricken farmers. From this perspective, the situation is that the sprawling terrain of the mine/ power plant and employing establishments, which have settled here to take advantage of the tax benefits and the rich infrastructure) create a "special economic zone" and become an industrial network, surrounding the villages and colonies. The inhabitants of these settlements thus neighbor (in a spatial, socioeconomic, and, I would say, existential sense of the word) an enormous power plant and mighty financial concerns.

By marginalization, I mainly have in mind a dynamic process of diversifying roles or social positions that is a characteristic in every society, one which brings about a state of marginality of certain social groups and/or individuals (Kowalak 1998: 20). Fred Mahler (1993: 193) defines this state as a calculation. He contrasts elements of a dynamic state of marginality, such as deprival of power and of access to decision making, possession of fewer rights and choices, a poorer financial situation, fewer opportunities to education or professional training, etc., exposure to social pressure and to crises, and finally, discrimination in the legal system (definition summarized by Kowalak 1998: 25). I believe that this conception of marginality through processes (of marginalization) allows us to demonstrate the intricacies of the phenomena of poverty, social inequality, impairment, deprivation, and disqualification in a more relative and dynamic fashion. It allows us to grasp these phenomena in a way more reflective of a relationship with the outside world of society, the relationship between a group pushed onto the "social periphery" and one in the "social center." This marginalization also takes place amid excluded subjects, groups, individuals, within their social self-definition. This is, for example, according to Gino Germani (1980), a "lack of participation in spheres of life where, in accordance with defined criteria, an *expectation* [emphasis mine], a mutual expectation that individuals and groups should participate in them is justified" (cf. Kowalak 1998: 23). The deprivation of goods, privileges, and power or the chance to participate in a mandatory lifestyle is thus simultaneously experienced and socially constructed, imaginary, tied to the relativity (the relative deprivation) that W. G. Runciman (cf. Hagenaars 1991: 137; Kowalak 1998: 17) has used to define such a state. It also means a desired state of ownership, of managing properties, as well as one's own life, and not only of being "deprived."

Marginalization and deprivation of the chance to satisfy social needs, a sense of imagined degradation, is thus relative in this case, i.e., oriented toward the "living environment" in a wealthy, industrialized municipality, and pertain to selected, though basic spheres of life. Mainly this pertains to exclusion from the circulation of employment, a poor financial state, and a lack of access to local economic decisions, or more accurately, a lack of access to *knowledge* about these decisions. To clarify, it is, at the same time, an example of marginalization in which deprivation of rights, privileges, or goods touches various and sometimes disassociated spheres of life (cf. Frieske 1999; Kowalak 1998; Washington, Paylor, and Harris 2000). In the Kleszczów municipality, to a large extent, securing and satisfying certain needs, such as education (including, for example, learning foreign languages) and access to social services or care are ensured (my research, interview—municipal center of social welfare). Moreover, there is good public transport to and from the center of town and a range of other conveniences, such as access to the infrastructure—plumbing, sanitation services, etc. Social marginalization has thus become more of a situation in which the sense of exclusion is linked to experience, and simultaneously, to imagined mechanisms of exclusion. More precisely, it is linked to their mirror image, the mechanism of the social usurpation of rights, knowledge, and privileges (cf. Frieske 1999: 24), and to their appropriation by the figure of local authority, i.e., the KWB authorities or the mine/municipality. Usurpation, the flip side of exclusion, would thus be the experience of "various interest groups demanding increased participation in the benefits, as a result of past services, special qualifications, etc." (ibid.). In the present case, the "imbalance of services" and qualifications chiefly concerns the local impoverished farmers, the ex-workers neighboring the economic "success" of the region, waiting years for their land to be bought out, working the "leftover" land, grasping at poorly paid odd jobs. To my mind, this is the innermost mechanism of the social creation of the economic divide, the creation of boundaries, of self-reinforcing images of inequality—the experience of imagined marginality.

Encompassing the greater part of the mine terrain and some of the above-mentioned villages, including Szamów and Łękińsko, the Kleszczów municipality is among the wealthiest and best organized municipalities in Poland. The houses and huts have long been powered by electricity, supplied with water, plumbing, and pavement, equipped with telephone cables, and the main roads covered with asphalt. For the last few years, the nearby settlements/farmsteads showing dilapidation and disorder have, perhaps, become more visible, if only in contrast to the regulated and modernized networks of roads, homes, and transit stops. Between the cracks of the network of the industrial complex, the bodies of the impoverished, age-worn huts and yards have been created, or rather, revealed, and they looked very run down. In Szamów, a village on the margins of the mine (in both a spatial and a social sense), several of the sometimes solid homes are decorated with objects from the nearby industrial tip, and the basic fuel is carefully selected ribbons of rubber belts abandoned inside the mine. The modern, red brick bicycle path stretches for kilometers through places where bicycles are often used to cart off scrap, rubber, and all manner of waste.

The Mine: *Orbis Exterior*

In Szamów, Łękińsko, Trząs, and Kamień, and in the marginalized and degraded houses in particular, the inhabitants of the farmsteads situated on the edge of the exposed mine see the premises and expansion of the mines in an entirely different light. I have noted that the inhabitants of these areas often stress that the mine has introduced certain anomalies in the places immediately surrounding it. This all generally began with observations of meteorological phenomena, or phenomena in the "nature" surrounding the mine. According to my interlocutors, rain, clouds, and storms do not come near their houses, and "cannot come near." "They all pass us by," say the Trząs farmers, "the rains pass right on by, nothing gets through here. ... The mine gathers up all the clouds" (TR/BŁ/10). "When a storm comes round, everyone knows that as soon as it flies over the pit, it scatters off. … No storm comes round here" (TR/BŁ/4). "When the storms come round here," I heard in Łękińsko, "soon as they pass over the pit … they scatter left and right … they stop in their tracks … and scatter" (TR/BŁ/18). Or, as a man in Szamów said, "No rain, not even a drop came down yesterday, the waste-heap stopped it; and there was nothing, no rainfall, just like there was nothing the day before. … There's the pit, there's the waste-heap, and there's nothing else" (TR/BŁ/21). "The mine and the power plant suck everything up, all the rains … and nothing falls down" (BEŁCH 7). The earth is presented as "dry" and "crumbling," and is simultaneously described with the storm clouds. The villagers also perceive other signs of the extraordinary contamination of the region, something that all the locals call "the sulphur." By this they mean the yellow deposits (sometimes also a green or multicolored layer) that appear on puddles, roads, trails, and on the leaves of trees and bushes (one unemployed resident of Szamów showed me places on the road where there were shiny, rainbow-colored traces of "sulphur"). As they say: "There's sulphur round here, we've got sulphur around. … They burn coal, suck energy, the sulphur falls on the grass, on the bushes and the grain" (TR/BŁ/22). "When it rains, you can see it goes green … but in the morning, there's grey smoke. … That's when they release it, you can see" (TR/BŁ/17). "The sulphur's all around here … it falls down from the sky … then things turn yellow. … We suck it all up. … Things are tragic here; there's no way to live. … You can't see it right now, but keep watching those puddles, watch after rain falls. … Have a look at the trees … at the leaves" (TR/BŁ/18). The result is a landscape contaminated and stripped of all regulations. Unstoppable changes, things that people cannot "turn a blind eye to," are taking place in this environment as a result of the vast industry that is developing right alongside. This results in images/imaginings of the violent climate change, sulphur precipitation, and drought that appear along with the mine. One constantly hears that the whole area is drying out, gradually turning into a desert; whereas the enormous excavation pit, the creation of the spoil tip, and the drying out of the local ground is mentioned as an unexpected and catastrophic transformation coming from the outside. As one farmer from Łękińsko told me: "I'm no geologist, but I know what's going to happen here. … I know what's going to happen here, and that's that. … Everything's getting pushed aside by the excavation pit. … The summers are totally dry … there was just a little rain in spring … as they said—*this is going to be desert*" (TR/BŁ/18). In Szamów they said: "The clouds—if they get here at all—they're cirrus-cumulus … they cause flooding. … Just wait till those waste-heaps start to shift, and then *we'll all be drowned in mud* … the others round

here don't realize" (BEŁCH 2). One might say that these statements
about the creation and the activities of the mine, the local mythologies that circulate, are continually shifting from tales of civilizational
progress toward an unassimilated topography (*orbis exterior*), revealing a
sense of a latent catastrophe or disaster descending from above.

The result is a landscape of the world of the mine as a place in which
remarkable and terrifying things take place, things that are mysterious
and fantastical, observed by nearly everyone, and frequently the subject of remark in everyday chance conversations between neighbors. A
premonition of the destruction that comes from the work in the mine
gives an entirely new significance to the transformations taking place
all around. My interlocutors' statements continually demonstrated the
inevitability of the mine, and simultaneously, the irreversibility of the
changes that were taking place; there was the recurring use of phrases
such as "they forecast," "they said," "that's how it'll be from now on,"
"and where's the water going to come back from? ... Where? ... If
they've gone and dried it all out, the water's gone for good" (TR/BŁ/13).
Even where the mine had ceased all activity and the water springs had
begun to return, they still spoke of a "drought," a "crater," or a "desert,"
of an essentially irreversible and latent change that one might call a "rural catastrophe" (Kędziorek 1996; Kocik 2001; cf. Tokarska-Bakir 2000:
101–102). Then the mine became an alternate natural world, appearing
right next door, near the farmsteads, powered by some force from above
and changing and regulating the whole environment for years on end;
after all, none of its neighbors—my interlocutors—had any way of affecting its spatial progress.

In one of his transcultural interpretations, Jacek Olędzki (1999:
183–186) states that one's attitudes and emotional responses toward
the external world and its uncontrollable phenomena, such as storms
and lightning (over which he or she is powerless), can, in a way, be
derived from a local sensitivity, a certain local manner of "cultivating"
the outside world. Olędzki contrasts the European peasant population's
limitless terror of thunder and storm clouds, often marked by religious
ritual (prayers to St. Agatha, burning blessed candles), with the absolute
trust and happiness of the Maasai, who performed gestures of delight
and thanksgiving during storm periods (ibid.). Thus, a sprawling cultural middle ground, filled with a dynamic play of meanings both profound and obvious, from expressions of delight to the heavens (Kenya),
through terror (Europe), to expressions of cultural falsehood, evolve between humans and their surroundings. In each case, we are dealing with
an initially invisible reality of constant and intensive management of
the uncontrollable world of physical phenomena. What does this mean?

This relationship with the world is a field in which the local manner of perceiving the environment and functioning within it is severed, along with the local/native way of life and its internal nature/culture dialectic (cf. Descola 1996; Ingold 1992). This is a space where the fragment of the world that is closest at hand is assimilated, a space of "cultural nature" (e.g., the landscape). To some extent, the residents neighboring the exposed mine demonstrate this peculiar local relationship with the world in their descriptions of the motionless, "blocked" storms or the "sulphur" whirling in the air. The surroundings of the power plant/mine thus become this alternate natural world in its most basic definition. It is something external, experienced on a daily basis, and also something upon which the state of the surroundings as a whole depended.

In these places there emerges a special example of the local landscape, an image of a world that had been emotionalized and profoundly socially internalized. Aspects of such a landscape are outlined by Ludwik Stomma (1986) in creating a model for the peasant "isolation of awareness" (*izolacja świadomościowa*), as it pertains to the Polish peasant society of the nineteenth century, finding its causes in its multifaceted separation (spatial, economic, social, etc.). We also ought to stress that experiences of everyday existence are translated into that socially created internal image. Here I have in mind the experiences of profound dependency on the outside world, the manor, the state, the rulers, and their various hypostases, and finally, on the natural world and atmospheric and biological phenomena, i.e., on the world from which catastrophic events came forth for centuries. Such an internal and socially generated counterpart (cf. Berger and Luckmann 1967) of the image of the world thus comes about at a given historical moment/economic situation, the image described by Stomma. Such an "internal landscape," I feel, has also come about under different circumstances in the environs of the Belchatów exposed mine. There has also emerged a group of impoverished farmers and workers, who are, in their own way, isolated—from the inert mechanism of the municipality/mine and the local economic/industrial circulation, all of which is external to them. These people, perhaps, create a local landscape of "isolation of awareness" that is very similar to the old peasant societies, a whole cosmos, including a familiar and orderly sphere, the home, the farmstead, the village—in a word, the assimilated *orbis interior*. They have also created a sphere of the unknown, an external and imposed being, the mine, which broke off from the internal order, an unassimilated zone, the *orbis exterior*. From an external research perspective, the mine (as an external and inert structure) thus became the field for the operation of the world of the unknown. In the minds of the "isolated" Polish peasants, it became a world filled with fantastic shapes and, simultaneously, of a wild, unassimilated, and incomprehensible topography, the position generally occupied by far-away lands, mountains, and seas, or nearer things like swamps, forests, and wild animals (Stomma 1986), and later machines. All of these land-scapes and things are chiefly of no use, or at least do not fit into the categories of things designated for use; they are all that is "different" and, in practice, is prevailing, oppressive in their simultaneous incomprehensibility and impracticality. Following the above-described logic, almost anything could appear in such a foreign world, in this *orbis exterior*: towers of diamonds, four-leaf clovers, and buried treasures. In the vicinity of the Bełchatów Mine these are the above-mentioned scattering storms, motionless clouds, the contamination taking place, and the sulphur dust falling from the sky.

I would like to stress, however, that this does not necessarily invalidate the observations of the farmers from the fields lying fallow near the exposed mine. Some of their observations are quite accurate, after all, and are actually taking place, such as the phenomena involved with the "drought," for indeed, the mine is drying out the terrain and creating a massive depression in the earth (Monografia KWB 2000). This may have an impact on the rainfall, though this particular area has never enjoyed a great deal of precipitation, accumulating very little over the course of a year. On the other hand, "sulphur ash" precipitation is staunchly denied by the specialists (impossible from a chemical point of view, according to consultations with the KWB environmental protection department). And yet, the perception of these events and phenomena is clearly undergoing a gentle shift. These statements do not refer "directly" to changes that are truly taking place, but are, to borrow a term from Stomma (1986: 138), more of a *reductio ad essentiam*, i.e., an overemphasis of the significance of events that are truly happening. This myth-making mechanism functions in similar fashion to the folk recollection of historical fact, where things that truly take place are supplemented by fantastical events, thereby emphasizing their spontaneously fabricated significance (Tomicki 1973: 50). Natural meteorological phenomena in the fields outside Bełchatów are supplemented with fantastical phenomena, which naturally take on unsettling and alarming attributes. The "sulphur" dropping from the sky and the columns of clouds "stopping" over the exposed mine are phenomena that may or may not have occurred. They are observations of nature and of the sky, made by people who have absolutely no way of affecting the mine, its presence, and the contamination and changes it has brought with it.

The mine/power plant coexists with the village/colonies scattered about its edges. For the inhabitants, it has become the cultural environment, natural world, one upon which they are entirely dependent, but which is, in the peasant world, also dependent on humans, making for a dialectic dependency (Tomicka and Tomicki 1975: 148). The world stretching all around creates this interstice, this sphere of experience and imagination upon which so much depends, and toward which people are forever turning, making observations and creating images. These neighbors to omnipresent modernization, these former farmers and workers (those in the town of Kamień, for example [TR/BŁ/3]), wait in crumbling huts for their land to be bought out and for sudden wealth to arrive. In a manner like that of nineteenth-century Polish villagers who observed sprouting grain and nearing hail clouds, they observed, it seems, the unsettling "stopping" clouds. My interlocutors thus apprehend the outside world as opposed to them and to the environment in which they live and upon which they, in fact, depend. After some time, these external beings become oddly tactile, vehicles for the incomprehension and lack of control they have on their surroundings, on the mine and its "top-down," structured movements, transforming whole environments. "Will they or won't they buy us out?" they wondered for years in Szamów, as I was told. "Will the pit swerve to one side or run right through us?" The clouds over Bełchatów seem to "stop" right over the exposed mine, creating "enormous pyramids" and "spinning all about," much as in (eighteenth- to nineteenth-century) folk wood carvings depicting the peasants fighting yearly storms, where a plump wind demon hunches in the clouds, and the eyes of a mischievous *płanetnik* (a Slavic weather demon—trans.) glimmer from somewhere down below.

From the researcher's point of view, the extent to which the mine area is a source for people's imagination is astonishing; for its residents, the farmers and marginalized workers, this is rather an untamed and uncontrollable place. We could call it a farmed wasteland that still holds the power of external, impersonal obligation, a significant power that changes the environment in a radical fashion (changing living and economic conditions and means of surviving along the way). There is one more very essential and paradoxical attribute of the mine wasteland, the local *orbis exterior*. The mine region is a place one neighbors, and yet from which one remains in conscious separation—it is isolated. As the impoverished farmers of Trząs said: "All you see are the lights, and all you hear is the hum of those machines at night, that's how it is." Jacek Olędzki (1971: 185–186) is supported by Stomma in stating that in the life knowledge and practices of the village populations, useless animals, plants, areas, and objects are not only terrifying and fantastical, but are also, in a way, uninteresting, insignificant, almost indifferent. "It's vile, what they call 'mosquitoes,' it's a waste of breath. ... That's how it is, and that's all there is to it. I don't want to think about it any more." Stomma introduces a certain chain of dependencies (1986: 134), where the cultivated world, a safe and tamed space, is connected to all that is familiar and pretty (*orbis interior*—beautiful—assimilated/useful—familiar), while the outside and uncontrolled world is a foreign, terrifying "indifferent" space, that is also "ugly" (*orbis exterior*—ugly—wild—useless—foreign). The outside zone is thus frightening, fantastical, and yet simultaneously *insignificant*, remote, and bland—in fact, "ugly." It is something that truly is unworthy of consideration, detached and isolated from what is known and what is the daily subject of attention. "I was walking through the forest with a neighbor," said one unemployed inhabitant of the eastern edge of the exposed mine, a social welfare recipient who farmed a small piece of land, "and suddenly the air went strange, smelled awful as if something had died. ... The further I went, the worse it got. ... And so I thought, What's going on? ... They must've poured out some substance ... over there ... on the spoil heap. ... I happened to have been up there before [a distance of around two hundred kilometers] and I saw it. ... They were making a lift [they had recently made a ski lift on the spoil tip], they'd created lighting, and the machines were standing there. ... And I thought: If we hadn't gone up there, *a person wouldn't even know* the things that were going on up there. ... We wouldn't have had a clue" (TR/BŁ/17). Indeed, this is splendidly recalled by statements of Olędzki's interlocutors (1971: 183–184, Okoński) concerning the wilderness, the wild animals that are not bred or used for gain, to which no one pays attention and which are, to some extent, invalidated. "About birds I know nothing at all ... maybe just the sparrows and crows that happen to pass right by my face." "I haven't seen any wild animals at all, so I can't tell you which ones I like." Bronisław Malinowski's "natives" speak in similar fashion about their local wastelands and animals of no practical use—they are little more than an insignificant backdrop for the cultivated world. "That's just the bush," they say. "That's just some flying animal" or "Those are just some plants" (see Ong 2002: 81; see also Lévi-Strauss 1994). The whole problem in understanding these statements is that certain extraordinary phenomena of the outside or isolated world are accompanied by the conviction that they are obvious and nondescript, or useless. The mine wastelands are thus invalidated—they are simply what was found "right next door."[2]

Violence, Guilt, and the Building Sacrifice

In these statements we also see the building of a wider context, a special memory of the beginnings of the KWB. It is present in stories about the past, and its traces are legible in the events that are still unfolding. The stories of the origins of the KWB emphasize the total transformation: the plowing bulldozers, the felled trees, the towering smokestacks, and flowing concrete are freely exchanged for destroyed forests, rivers, ponds, and whole landscapes, ending with certain destruction. One former builder, currently a pensioner, told me: "So much work went on here, day and night, we worked ourselves to the bone, because they had their deadlines, and everything had to keep moving. ... *So many people died back then* [emphasis mine], that was very dangerous work. ... Because everything was chop-chop ... and so there were accidents, people gave it their all. ... But now, who gives a damn ... it's all done and built ... nobody remembers any more" (TR/BŁ/29). A statement from an unemployed man in Trząs is astonishingly similar, as it concerns the vast wastage accompanying the construction and simultaneous death in the building: "There was so much work, and how were we supposed to get there—through the swamps. ... Not a month went by without a fatal accident! *Someone was always dying* [emphasis mine] ... everything was all slapdash, all of Poland came to work: from Pomerania, Poznań, one guy would break something and then another guy would fix it ... , somebody would forget, because he was fresh at work, and the way they wandered about. ... I get goose pimples. ... Nobody paid attention to the quality ... a spoil tip of wire ... they would dig a hole, then fill it all back in ... *it poured into the ground* [emphasis mine]... the oil barrels got holes in them, it ran out—you think somebody gave a damn!? They poured it into the ground, it all ran out." And further: "It all got wasted. ... They cut everything, plundered it, cut down a hundred-year-old pine." "Why did they cut down those forests? Why did they cut them all down? They could have left them where they were! They didn't have to cut them down—but they did" (the mother of my interlocutor, an ex-farmer [TR/BŁ/10]). Following the logic of "the peasant economy" (my interlocutor was the son of impoverished farmers who had worked at building the mine), wastage is a disharmony, something that sets things off balance. This shaking of the natural order in later statements concerns, to my mind, a past violence, occurring alongside the fierce development of labor. The construction of the mine has brought terrible consequences, as one of the inhabitants of Szamów repeatedly informed me: "Anyone who came here to work didn't last long. ... By now he's bit the dust ... they all died off. ... *As soon as those smokestacks started to burn it started happening right away. ... The boys just dropped off one by one* [emphasis mine]" (TR/BŁ/9). He further claimed that those who survived were made infertile for the rest of their lives. Such imagined social crippling was constantly recurring during my conversations with the impoverished farmers and the ruined workers: "People here got sick from the mine and from the power plant ... those sicknesses ... their eyes got sick. ... Nobody knows here if the ash is radioactive or not. ... One month or two, and a woman can't see anything. ... Is anybody researching that? Nobody" (TR/BŁ/10). "There were some shake-ups. ... And all that sulphur. ... Now they've put on those sulphur filters ... but even still, I'm sure we're still breathing the stuff in" (BEŁCH 1). These conversations reveal very characteristic catastrophic visions filled with future suffering, destruction, or at the very least, enormous wastage—such are the stories of building the structures and digging the exposed mine.

This shift in "social power"—the creation of these buildings—thus illuminates the accompanying experience of the external, inert forces that have their effect on the whole environment. Many other building rituals also contain this sort of social experience of sacrifice. For example, when huts were erected in Slavic lands or yurts were built in Mongolia, ceremonies were held that, in a practical and symbolic way, accented this moment of "chaos," and asked the simplest of questions: Would it succeed or not? Slavic building rituals—*zakładziny*—of animal sacrifices emerged, as did (in an imagined sense) human sacrifices (Bajburin 1990; Dalewski 1990). This was a "feasting with the gods," with the sacrificial "first-fruits" of the gods, as Roger Caillois phrases it (2001: 30–31), the equivalent of a different, compulsory death. The people circled the newly built house, sprinkled it with the blood of a slain animal, and the builders cursed any "accidental strangers," causing their magical death, lest they themselves were to die (Bajburin 1990: 63; cf. Dalewski 1990). In antiquity, things were much the same with the sacrifices to the patron of the Phoenician cities, the Phoenician god, Moloch, to whom children were sacrificed and many other building rituals were performed. For example, in numerous legends builders were buried alive and blood was required to make an adhesive/mortar. In this fashion, a sacrifice became a building payment (ibid.). The old custom of drinking alcohol at a *zakładziny* perhaps shares the same origins: alcohol must flow, just as blood once did (there is a simultaneous analogy to blood and to sowing).[3]

Building a new construction—a new order—is thus accompanied by a certain consciousness of making an offering, or more broadly speaking, a memory of some obscure violence. As a gigantic construction in the local experience, particularly among people living on the margins of transformation and development, the mine fits this universal sacrificial model in many respects. It is, above all, an inert structure of enormous strength, with the power to transform reality. It is also accompanied by a mythology of artificial perfection acclimatized as a second natural world (somewhere in the background) and as a terrifying, almost cosmic catastrophe. Its origins are described in the same way: drops of blood, accidents, death, and incomprehensible sterility. In the languages of both mythologized and modern experiences, these bear testimony to an anxiety of the price—the "building sacrifice"—extracted in exchange for abrupt societal advancement and the development of the sandy earth of the Bełchatów area.

* * *

The experience I have just described, of the building/modernization of the KWB, also delves, one might say, down into the roots of the processes of modernity, or, as Giddens would have it, of "late modernity." It includes certain aspects of anxiety, of terror descending from an environment that has been technologically and systematically transformed. A change in the very manner of apprehending the technological process underway is essential here (cf. Adorno and Horkheimer 1997; Bell 1996; Bielik-Robson 2004; Giddens 1990; 1991; Weber 1993). If treated as a relationship with the world, as well as a plane for creating frameworks of subjectivity, a modern "I" formed around what lies "outside" begins to loosen the ties of the natural world and (at the same time) the premodern, preindustrial existence, of a Marxist "idiocy of village life" (Bielik-Robson 2004: 59–60). As we know, Max Weber and many other critics of modernity have pointed out that the panorama of technological development is an extraordinarily mentally ambivalent and terrifying process (these anxieties have been described by Marshall Berman, Agata Bielik-Robson, Anthony Giddens, and Jerzy Jedlicki, among others). Anthony Giddens (1990; 1991), in turn, has shown that this same modernity conceals fascinations and anxieties that are unique to it, manifesting themselves, for instance, in an obsessive need for "risk assessment." As he writes, these are practically two sides of the same process, which are extremely characteristic of the condition of modern society. The processing of reality, which is the main idea of modernization/modernity, in itself contains elements of anxiety and of obscure violence. This is what Marshall Berman calls the "tragedy of modernization" (1983).[4] Social perceptions of the destructive powers of modernity, of its unintended consequences, thus generally find articulation and—at the same time—confirmation in imagined future catastrophes, as images of humans' destruction through phantasmagorical social mechanisms, creating whole eco-calyptic cataclysm scenarios (Weiner

1999; see also Giddens 1990): the depletion of energy resources, the greenhouse effect, freshwater shortage. Moreover, such anxieties are accompanied by a need for a cosmic order, or perhaps a nomic one.

The Consequences of "Excess": Metaphors of Exploitation

In these circumstances we see the creation of a peculiar narrative of the experience of modernizing transformations and the development of the environs. An internal language of survival emerges as does a perception of the transformations surrounding people as a catastrophe against which they are powerless. This narrative transcends simple phenomena and builds internal relationships—those of my interlocutors with the outside phenomena, with the mine as an inevitable environment of daily existence. In this way the marginality of the impoverished farmer or ex-worker vis-à-vis the KWB, with its clear advantage and inertia—i.e., its neighboring presence—become experiences communicated both internally and socially; the whole story is contained, as it were, in the locally circulating conversations. These speak of the above-mentioned sense of powerlessness, while the organism of the mine/municipality has clearly negative, even diabolical attributes (also in terms of imagined social relationships and power relations). It recalls the figure of the gloomy, all-powerful Leviathan. Using "they," the standard figure for rhetorical power (e.g., see Hoggart 2009 [1957]) in reference to the mine/municipality, a farmer from Łękińsko once told me, if "they" wanted to, they "could do anything to us, they don't watch out for anything … they've got their own damned business to take care of here." In stark opposition to the image of the social harmony of the mine/municipality, here is a ruthless world of violence and conflicting interests (*homo homini lupus*). I repeat, in these statements the mine or the municipality appear to use their inert influence to crush. This is an imagined social violence, a power of most evidently diabolical origin. "The ones who worked on it got what was coming to them," I heard many times when one of my interlocutors, Wacław Okoński, indulged his fantasies, "because there were cameras here…. Cobalt bomb gauges … they're the ones to blame…. My son-in-law and I took down the last one from a machine six months ago … they know everything that goes on in the mine, they've got whole archives … but you don't know, and you won't find out … those are carefully guarded files" (TR/BŁ/9). The clear dichotomization of the social world into "us," the ruled, and "them," the rulers, generally creates the first fruits of an informal language of social resistance, a certain "hidden transcript," to borrow James C. Scott's formulation (1990). This dichotomy creates a very negative image of the rulers and of those who belong to them, "against whom you can't win." The officials, who are signified through phrases like "they said," "they made," and "they resettled," and who accompany these diabolical events, are always potentially responsible for every bad twist of fate (Hoggart 2009 [1957]).

Łukasz Józefowicz has written of these socioeconomic roots of metaphors of power in the following fashion: "Anyone who has seen at least one film about Count Dracula is struck by the clear division of the world presented ... the village/castle opposition saturates the entire structure." He further writes, this castle's owner "is not a farmer ... and moreover, does not work at all. He willingly and contentedly condemns himself to 'sin and eternal damnation'" (2004: 14–15). This division assigns a series of work-related signifiers. The village on the one hand is insufficiency, while on the other is the work-free excess of the castle. We thus have a connection between this "excess of goods" and an "excess of backbreaking labor," and a metaphor emerges that links demonic authority with a defiance of the principle of reciprocity, or of the principles that go into creating the "spiritual body of the society" (Mauss 2000). The metaphor of economic exploitation therefore joins aspects of social dependency with physical, somatizing images—images of an aristocrat who is also a vampire (on the complex links between these metaphors, see Janion 2002b), as this privileged social stratum, so often put, "sucked people's blood" during the day. "They didn't die, they rotted. Those bloodsuckers inhabited not the cemeteries, but gorgeous palaces," wrote Voltaire (quoted in Józefowicz 2004: 15; see also Janion 2002b: 48). Insofar, therefore, as the KWB is ascribed an excess of goods, so too do there appear images of unjustified development, unjustified profit, and human sacrifice, while the destruction of humans or the environment is always present.

The mine towers over the Bełchatów landscape, practically creating an image of a "Count's castle," and the line between the company and the excluded farmers and ex-workers creates a typical socioeconomic dependency structure. In essence, therefore, this is an economic image—one of economic disproportion, of an extraordinarily effective structure that disrupts the balance. Of course, it also disrupts the above-described and deeply internalized social principle (economic image) among peasants of "limited good," a category formulated by George Foster in his work "Peasant Society and the Image of Limited Good" (1965; on the same concept, see also Tarkowski and Tarkowska 1994: 272–273). According to this premise, goods in the world are always ready-made and distributed, and with each new transaction, their total number remains unchanged; they are somehow limited, closed, unable to increase. An excess in one place, in "the hands of one person," must necessarily equal a shortage elsewhere, combined with the experience of poverty and exploitation, or an image of "profligacy." Such a picture of the KWB, based on an image of "limited good" and "mouldering excess," makes it appear to be an automatic, self-sufficient mechanism, and at the same time an enterprise destined to bring about catastrophe, destruction, and exploitation. "It's all desert here. I won't get anything. ... There's only small potatoes in this field, it's dug shallow. ... What kind of potatoes are those? The mine's taken them away, dried everything up—taken them away for good! I sure don't know how it'll all end" (TR/BŁ/14).

Once again we find ourselves confronted with a picture of the mine as both supernatural and unjust—the "injustice" of its rule and its economic clout. In conversations I had in Szamów I often heard convictions of an evil slumbering in the mine authorities—both in the contamination buried in the earth and in the suspect undertaking done under the cover of KWB activities. As one interlocutor told me, "Over there right now on the spoil tips, in a place I know like the back of my hand, in a hunters' lodge, something rotten's going on. ... Lights turn on, but where are they getting the electricity ... something's up with the keys and locks. ... But what's all that money there for ... what are they doing? ... and why?" (TR/BŁ/9). These are images that build a picture of excess and well-being: "Who would've thought there'd be two banks in a village like Kleszczów. Have you ever heard the likes of it?" (BEŁCH 9). This recalled pictures/images deeply rooted in European culture, those of the (im)balance of the world and its goods (cf. Mauss 2000), and the associated images of possessing an "excess/shortage" of goods: "They're collecting chalk from the spoil tip at the moment, you can't imagine how much there is ... the cars drive in day and night ... they take so much of it, and keep taking ... they must be profiting off it somehow" (TR/BŁ/25). "They bought themselves a flat and some land—the mine gave it to them. ... They just liquidated it—they paid for sterile land!" (TR/BŁ/13) "Where's the water supposed to come from now? They've dried it all out and it's never coming back ... and when they're finished, what's going to be left? That's none of their concern" (TR/BŁ/14). Furthermore, this "excess" of economic goods was in no way limited—the tie was cut between work and profit, and in these images this transition took place "all by itself"—this "excess" produced itself. Following this stream of logic, when these surpluses were squandered in the social imagination, they caused goods to "rot." More than once, I heard: "If it's not yours, if it belongs to them, then don't touch it ... let it *rot* ... let it go to waste." An unemployed ex-farmer from Szamów raged about the refuse, rubber, and copper wires discarded by the mine (see TR/BŁ/22), which prohibited collection of these materials and punished all those who disobeyed with a hefty fine.

This imagined "privileged" (as compared to the other local groups—in this case, the inhabitants of the edges of the exposed mine) stratum that possessed economic surplus thus creates an image of economic "decay," of squandered "goods." In a characteristic fashion, not working, or a technological ease in working, is associated with the disproportionate and unnaturally high profit that is gained, with over-effectiveness.

The Mine: *Orbis Interior*

The Players, Their Families, and Their Means of Sustenance

As I have mentioned, my chief field of research was the village/colony of Szamów, a small place situated at the southeast edge of the exposed mine, right in the shadow of the massive spoil tip of ash and sand. The majority of the inhabitants of Szamów whom I encountered had many years previous lost their jobs in the mine or in other industries around it. In the main, they were also impoverished, downtrodden farmers. They are presently vegetating in fields the mine has dried out, picking up the odd public intervention job. Like other inhabitants of the environs of the mine, they once lived with the hope, with practically the certainty, that the mine would purchase their land for enormous sums of money, which would allow them to live in comfort in a Bełchatów block of flats. Then later, when the purchasing bypassed them by a span of literally a few meters, they were cut off from the mine for various reasons, and thus from the company (and the Kleszczów "economic zone"), which is the principal employer and privilege-provider in the region. The majority of these villagers have never received employment in this company (either because they lack the qualifications, or because of their work around their farmstead); or else after a few weeks in the KWB factories (or those surrounding them), they lost their work, generally through internal downsizing and layoffs. Moreover, in the 1990s, probably over a dozen Szamów residents took part in the "copper affair." For several years they had collected and melted down electric cables that the mine had discarded practically in their front yards, and thus, they obtained pure copper. A number of people were sent to court for salvaging and selling copper—for "stealing" it. Each of these people remained stamped by this incident, which made them reluctant to participate in long ethnographic interviews. I confess, I was unable to overcome their mistrust for practically the entire research period, in spite of the fact that I lived in one of these households and spent a great deal of time there.

Some Szamów homes are in a terrible state of mess and disintegration. The yards look like dumping grounds for every conceivable sort of junk. From the outside, all these residences, virtual "museums" of junk, make a similar impression, with their collections of refuse inside and around them. These collections are found in part in the homes, in part in the yards, and the vast quantities of industrial waste strikes the visitor at once. From the external appearances of the farmsteads, the contents of the collections, the gathered, repaired, and painted objects, one can, to some extent, extrapolate what the inhabitants do with their time. They find the most peculiar things, such as dismantled industrial transformers, reworked and modified kitchen stoves and parts for their repair, dishes, industrial tools, ceramic pipes, weights, and coils of steel cords. They also build small sheds, where bags, springs, and dishes are placed and arranged in rows. By the entrance to one home is a shelf that somewhat resembles an altar. Upon it sat a mirror, bits of a broken vase, and a few rusted machine parts, all of which made for a provisional bathroom for a few months. I noticed that later the arrangement of the rubble was changed to match the colors of the packaging of the cosmetics that sat alongside. Everywhere one sees an overabundance of objects, as though the inhabitants are incapable of fending them off, wanting to store them up as provisions, and perhaps, through them, to survive (Palska and Sikorska 2000: 254). In Szamów this community was made up of eight or nine farming/laborer households, all situated very near to the exposed mine and to the spoil tip of earth and ash (one hundred to five hundred meters away). Of these, the most distinctive are the farmsteads of two families, the Okońskis and the Białases, neighbors located in the center of the village. In full consciousness of my "marginal position" and the constant presence of my interlocutors' affection for the "accepted ignoramus," combined with their mistrust of the "suspicious expert" (I was for interviewees both a stranger and a well-known, assimilated acquaintance), I spent the majority of my time conducting many conversations with these families, and ultimately befriending them.

The former family, the Okońskis, consists of a couple named Wacław and Bożena, their daughter, Joasia, and Bożena's mother (Wacław's mother-in-law). Their adult sons, Rafał, Krzysztof, and Jan, also sporadically appear in their house. Wacław is a scrap (industrial waste) collector, and a former employee of the KWB and of various other companies. He has worked in many places, and has been a driver and a security guard in Koło Łowieckie, where, as he himself put it, he was a "jack of all trades." He had apparently had a hand in the "copper affair," for which he spent a few months in jail. His wife, who does not work outside the home (though she did work taking meteorological measurements for a few months), took care of their ailing and disabled daughter. Her mother was once a farmer, and the mine purchased a small portion of her land. The family's regular income is about six hundred zloty a month, a sum that includes family benefits, social welfare, and nursing benefits (for their daughter), as well as Bożena's mother's small retirement pension. Their monthly expenses (around one hundred and fifty zloty) are electricity and bottled gas. They have no plumbing, and they use the well outside the building. It is chiefly Wacław who provides for them, earning money for food, fuel, and clothing by selling industrial scrap and waste (which he also uses to make many useful things around the house).

The second family, the Białases, have a house right next door to the Okońskis. This is an old, partly wooden two-room house, with a stone barn that the younger family members are remodeling into living quarters. The family consists of a married couple, Józef and Zdzisława (the sister of Bożena's mother), their daughter, Elżbieta, her husband, Zygmunt, and their children (a three-year-old boy and a one-year-old girl). Zdzisława is an unemployed farmer, trying to get welfare from KRUS (the Farmer's Social Aid Fund), but there have been legal complications; she has had to sign her land over to her daughter, who has a legal education but is unemployed. Her husband, Zygmunt, who has an elementary education, worked at packaging cosmetics for a few months, was a security guard for some time, and has recently worked at a job organized by the municipality. The family's regular income includes Elżbieta's nursing benefits, social and family welfare (for the children), her husband's pension (around six hundred zloty a month), and the money from whatever the father can scrape together and sell. The farming products are entirely consumed by the household (as animal fodder and for feeding the family). Józef Białas has been unemployed for eight or nine years. He once worked for the KWB, but was fired (apparently for drinking on the job); along with other inhabitants of the village, he was accused of stealing waste materials (the "copper affair"). He is an introverted and quiet man who gives the impression of one who is resigned. For over a dozen years he has been supporting himself and his family by collecting industrial scrap and waste, and by growing crops on his single hectare of land.

In front of the other homes mentioned are pieces of the most various kinds of scrap, parts of cars and old farming machines, tires, tarpaulins, canvas sheets, and industrial plastic materials/waste. Another family, the Kocots, living in the dilapidated yard closest to the pit, was very suspicious of me, and not once did I manage to converse with any of the family members. However, I also visited the Małek family (who was situated further from the pit, and whose life was relatively in order), as well as other neighbors in the village, where I also found great quantities of industrial waste, and car and tractor parts. Among these others is the Grąd family (three brothers and their elderly mother), farther on is the large Sianowski house, and beyond them, the crumbling house of an unemployed woman (mainly supporting herself on social welfare) who lives with her adolescent son. On the other side of the village, right near the mine's spoil tip, lives the Karcz family, a married couple about forty years of age, and their two elementary school daughters. Their front yard is filled with all manner of materials and rubble, but it makes a tidy impression. Things inside the home are spruced, and the walls are freshly painted (though evidently damp). Jan Karcz works odd jobs, and sometimes he also collects waste. He was looking for work during the course of my research, and ultimately found some in a cement factory; his wife is unemployed, and at times they are compelled to turn to social welfare. Apart from them, there are also the two Gacan brothers, who were fairly suspicious of me; they collect scrap and waste, and sometimes land intervention jobs in the municipality.

Self-Sufficiency, Subsistence: Gathering and Processing Goods

The objects, waste, tools, and industrial-part processed materials gathered in these farmsteads played a major role in my research. Their all-encompassing presence was well in evidence from my very first visit with the Okońskis. Some of the fitted carpeting in the house was made from fragments of semi-industrial fabrics, while the heater, with its corrugated inner surface, was a homemade contraption made from the metal steps of shovel stackers. "It's really good, solid steel," said Wacław, "those are reinforced steps, with a hardness of ST 20" (TR/BŁ/15). "This elbow for the chimney pipe," he explained, "is dislodged, the duct has a wider circumference, and that lets you heat industrial waste, mainly rubber" (TR/BŁ/9). All of this goes to equip a solid brick house built in the 1960s, with the typical wall shelving unit, television, and glass-topped coffee table. The abundance of junk and rubble is also visible around back and, to a large degree, in the wooden shed, where there are a few windowpanes and a few metal rails. In the shed (which also serves as a living space in the spring and summer, a private retreat) beside his house, Wacław collects all his objects. Inside there are all kinds of useful things, such as a welding torch retrieved from the mine garbage bin, a heating tray/kettle (found at the dump), and a homemade bicycle pump devised from a discarded washing machine motor. There is a coal stove on which he cooks, dries mushrooms, and heats rubber, a "power" switch for single-phase electricity, and a whole collection of tools, saws, scissors, and pliers. There is a homemade soldering iron and welding torch, countless washers, cables, and oil and paint cans, and finally, a hoist dangling under the eaves (for hanging and curing wild boar meat).

The Białas family has a similar relationship to objects and materials, which are collected all around. Józef Białas's workshop is a large court-yard with two sheds, a dugout, an old barn, and countless homemade appliances. In the middle of the courtyard is a water intake—a straw-in-sulated pump. Nearby, in a corner, there is a provisional shed with a coal stove (used year-round to cook for the family and sometimes for the animals) and a few shelves. Everywhere one sees enormous tires that are sliced up and being used as duck and goose feeders. In the middle is an old cooker spread with a net, used for sifting grain, alongside a packed dugout for potatoes. In the shed and all around there are many porcelain electric insulators, parts of power generators, and then all kinds of pipes, nuts, metal nets, switches, old sparkplugs, steel cables of various widths, tubes, and rubber straps. The shed is also filled with numerous window frames brought from the "marketplace" (a dump inside the mine) and hung up like pictures, and then machinist squares, an old oil tank in need of repainting, and a range of paint and solvent cans (TR/BŁ/14). Józef Białas also has a homemade tractor (not suitable for plowing) with an engine from a threshing machine that he uses to bring home scrap, and sometimes to work the soil.

The picture of these homes confirms the above-described tendency to collect goods, objects, and waste, and the matching tendency to use (process) them on a daily basis. I would also say that this is a firmly anchored sort of managing or even assimilating the environment, of cre-ating a home/household mechanism for circulating numerous materials and goods. It is a way of cultivating a world that is closed to outsiders, an act based in both perception and usage. This is, therefore, a method of inhabiting and maintaining a home, and in a wider sense, it is a daily practice of creating meaning and significance. I consider this practice to fit Max Weber's statement: "The definition of economic action must be as general as possible and must bring out the fact that all 'economic' processes and objects are characterized as such entirely by the *meaning* they have for human action in such roles as ends, means, obstacles and by-products" (1978: 64). This is, therefore, a certain attribute of "hu-man action" that is particularly visible in poor village households, where the "anything might come in handy" principle dictates how the house and yard are run, where the impression of self-sufficiency grants a feeling of security. This collecting of goods in the village was, as I have already mentioned, a certain reflex tied to a sense of danger, to recurrent periods of shortage, poverty, hunger, or war. These reflexes were also reinforced during the postwar period, in the social-realist economy (Tarkowska and Tarkowski 1994), in a period of widespread incapacity and existence in circumstances of constant scarcity (Marody 1991b: 236–237; Sikorska 1999: 117–118, 120, 143). This rural survival strategy also had its place in experiences across Poland. It was particularly visible in the cities, in the newly created housing estates and factory settlements, where, for some time, people would cling to whatever they happened to find, from food to machinist squares and the most varied prefabricated parts, which "might always come in handy." As Jacek Wasilewski has phrased it, in these conditions, "the habit of collecting goods, which evolved from rural hardship and the fickleness of fate … , has set in and endured" (1986: 52; cf. Tymiński 2002: 126; cf. Sulima 2000).

I would merely add at this point that in circumstances of postwar modernization and migration from the villages to the cities, from agriculture to industry, and from the huts to the blocks of flats and tenement houses, these patterns of household economizing manifested themselves with increasing visibility. The factory settlements already had numerous pigsty/storage areas, generally in the backs of the tenement houses, where just about everyone kept livestock—hens, rabbits, piglets, and even coypus (Boguszów). This was highly visible in the old mining districts (Wódz 1989: 50; cf. Gerlich 1988), but also in many other industrial settlements (in Żyrardów, for example). Things looked much the same wherever sudden changes took place in living conditions, in the PGRs (State Agricultural Farms), where pigsties and gardens adjacent to houses helped to maintain existence, in both an economic and a non-economic sense. Similar conclusions might be drawn from the research of Maria Węgrzynowska (2006) on life in rural block-housing areas, such as Bondary in the Podlaskie Voivodeship, the villages created after resettlement near Siemianówka Lake. The new inhabitants of those blocks of flats were "entitled to" pigsties and gardens, where they gathered and assembled a wealth of different useful items. The significance of these things was not mainly economical. Rather, these "entitled" areas served to create a "farming ritual," providing the inhabitants "their own" space to operate. "These plots of land are only tiny ones," they said, "but they give you something to do, at least." "I'm used to walking around and working a bit." "Everyone here would like to have his piece of land to do as he pleases" (see Węgrzynowska 2006). As I have also demonstrated in previous chapters, these statements reveal a hidden significance in the very act of farming.

Farming in strange and unfamiliar circumstances (having moved to blocks of flats) thus creates a strategy of "ensuring existence," a certain reflex response, providing the opportunity to recreate a pattern of ritualized rural agency ("minding the world"). This might well be why the villagers migrating to the blocks of flats in the city were called "backward" and "uncivilized." They were said to keep piglets and hens on their balconies, in their bathrooms, or in their bathtubs, to use their toilet bowl to wash their potatoes, to take their livestock "out for a walk," etc. These images appeared in gossip, tales, jokes, and mockery. This behavior was undoubtedly exaggerated in these tales, and did not bear testimony to being uncivilized, but rather expressed certain deeply rooted cultural reflexes (cf. Bąk 2006; Kamińska 2006; Węgrzynowska 2006).

The collection of all manner of objects in the farmsteads I researched is therefore, I believe, a repetition or recreation of a self-reliant peasant strategy of survival that has surfaced in a new reality, in new circumstances. It draws, perhaps, from the rural identity of the "good housekeeper"; and the goods collected are confirmation of the worth and resourcefulness of these people, who follow the principle that it is not profit, but the quantity and quality of goods accumulated that is the measure of labor, of a "job well done" (Pieniążek 1995: 28–30; Kocik 2000: 58–59, 71–73; 2001: 46–47). Once again, this reinforces the model of the autarkic peasant farm, of the creation of an internal circulation that processes everything. As Lucjan Kocik (2000: 75) writes in his ecological study of the countryside: "The autarky of the traditional local societies is based on using *all* [emphasis mine] available materials." Thus, "all available" materials should indeed be found there, and every missed opportunity to use them is a wastage of goods. Such an economy, particularly pronounced in periods of crisis and challenge to basic livelihood, is a form of ensuring survival. This is, therefore, a certain existential, or perhaps more accurately, *subsistential* internal reflex. To quote Kocik once more: "A broken window served to patch a stable window, some rubber or a bit of leather could go to patch footwear, while hole-ridden pots and pails were used as chicken feed containers, which, when plugged with straw or a rag, could serve for spreading ashes" (2002: 84). One morning, Józef Białas brought in two sheets of corrugated sheet metal; and, as I noticed on another day, on his way home from work his son found some old wooden slats that had been discarded in Kleszczów, which he tied in a bundle and took along with him. In the Szamów families I have described, this internal circulation of everyday things had precisely this aspect, the families motivated by the need to survive and to be secure. They said of slaughtered and devoured hens and ducks: "They breed for us like rabbits" (TR/BŁ/6). "The ducks hatch themselves for us—soon as I kill one, another one's born" (TR/BŁ/21). The grain that falls on the dry ground serves only as feed; they also plant their own potatoes, and then keep them in dugouts.

Their clothing (usually work clothes) and many other goods come from the mine rubbish tip; and meat from wild boars caught on the spoil tip is later stored in an old communal freezer. This circulation of goods and resources for survival is the primary method of managing and running a house, a minimal interior economic "transformation of material" made as effective as possible (cf. previous chapters). I would say that all these actions have an axiological dimension—there is a certain imperative to make use of what is provided, to assimilate and cultivate the goods "lying all around." The residents of the outskirts of the Białowieża Forest, for example, have a similar attitude: taking good care of the forest paradoxically entails using it, as opposed to the "ecological protection" projects (see Bąk 2006; Kamińska 2006).

This economizing is thus an especially vague concept, difficult to define. It simultaneously finds itself beyond all outside control, and evades all measurements of household budgets (cf. Podgórski 1996) and every kind of quantitative measure of economic status, poverty line, ministry indicators, absolute indicators like minimum living standards, and their social combinations (Golinowska 1997; Szulc 1996). In practice, household-level, domestic consumption (sometimes called "prosumption"; Sikorska 1999: 126–127), and cashless circulation defy all precise equivalencies or external calculations. It is, therefore, a "natural economy," with an internal form of calculation and a practice involving more *rationing*, as a "modest beginning of calculation," to quote Max Weber (1978: 105), than counting and calculating. Unpredictable processes of economizing, cultivating, and assimilating these external and internal extra-monetary sources to supplement their low and insufficient incomes thus take place.

This is, therefore, a continuation of the hidden, covert economy based on quantitative equivalencies that takes place beyond the reach of economic measurements. It is a window to unpredictable, internal processes and methods of economizing (and by the same token, it bestows significance upon various actions). Among these are all the other "non-countable" (economically, quantitatively) domestic practices adopted in Szamów—collecting scrap and waste, burning/heating with waste, theft, poaching, mutual aid/neighbor exchanges, village self-reliance (Kocik 2000; 2001), and the use of all variety of raw materials. These are autarkic acts that have in no way been formalized. Another attempt to describe these impoverished families' informal sources of additional income can be found in the report of British researchers, "Eking Out an Income: Low Income Households and Their Use of Supplementary Resources" (Elam, Ritchie, and Hulusi 2000). As demonstrated, this sphere of impoverished family life remains "in hiding," and is, to a large extent, incalculable, though sometimes it does play a very significant role (Sikorska 1999: 117–118, 120, 143); many now classic research studies on poverty, such as the pioneering research of Seebohm Rowntree and Maud Frances Davies (Elam, Ritchie, and Hulusi 2000: 222), and then the research of Peter Townsend (ibid.: 223), have mentioned it. As Townsend (see 1979: 46–54, 186–247) wrote, the problem concerns its translation into objective and quantifiable measurements: the transformation of these household-level uses of vegetables, household constructions, livestock breeding, acquiring of raw building materials and prefabricated products and other "goods." In turn, Polish research on this issue has been tackled by Agnieszka Golczyńska-Grondas (2004), who describes the informal, unofficial domestic practices in Łódź enclaves of poverty, generally entailing the collection of raw materials from the workplace or construction sites to be used at home (ibid.: 75–76), and the reworking of living quarters, such as the independent introduction of plumbing or the installation of heating systems (ibid.: 130–131). Elsewhere, Elżbieta Tarkowska has shown that this nonmonetary "circulation of materials" is generally oriented around women, who manage the budgets of impoverished households, and are thus forced to employ a great deal of skill in "supplementing," or "making ends meet" (eking out a living). As Tarkowska writes, it is here that we find the majority of "prosumptive (natural consumption) actions, i.e., production for private needs" (2003: 11; Marody 1991b: 136–237; cf. Sikorska 1999: 126–127). In Szamów this hidden economy is the center of all domestic and "existential" activity. Around it circulates everyday life and everyday images, as well as anthropological research. Around it grows the unique space of these people's experiences, as it develops on the edges of the mine, and becomes included in the circulation of these practices. Consequently, this is a certain concentrated experience of managing and bestowing significance upon their actions, upon their surroundings and their world, which is reworked and processed and yet always remains dependent on the mine. It is a path to a certain existential dimension of self-sufficient economic production (subsistence) in the face of their own marginalization.

Hunting and Gathering

A clear aspect of these households / junk collections is the way they are spread out physically, as all imaginable things and equipment are brought outside—junk, tools, and dishes eventually overran almost entire yards, and sometimes extended even farther. Everyday activities are consequently performed outside the home. For example, the water source is found outside, though collecting the water is not a problem, as the Białases' kitchen is also found outside, in one corner of the yard. Similarly, the Okoński family often cooks on an old stove in their shed, though there is also a stove in their home. In these families equipment and household appliances are often scattered about outside the home, in the yard. The freezer used for deer and wild boar meat stands in an old stable, the refrigerator in the shed, and in the Białases' home, the "Frania" washing machine is located in the attic of the kitchen shed. The Białas family's spring/summer bathroom is composed of a water pump and a shelf, upon which the selection of objects changes over various periods of time. Next to the large mirror, the pieces of broken vase, the soap, shampoo, etc., were electric coils and a few electric switches. After a few months, these were replaced with plastic chemical packages of various sizes, but generally of the same sandy color (perhaps Zygmunt Białas's job at a cosmetics packaging factory might explain their presence). The adults bathe themselves out-of-doors, and also do all their cooking in the yard. However, in Szamów, the borders between yards are very much comprised of a series of shifting commodities. The gathered rubble, old machines, and tools spread beyond the perimeter of their farmsteads, beyond its boundaries, "spilling out past the fences" and onto the shared road. The public land thus becomes part of the household space, while not entirely part of the home, and the household "spreads itself out."

As we have already seen, these households use as much (and as great a variety) of the raw materials and scrap from the mine, of the material components of the world exterior to them, as possible. They use everything they can, including the lands around the village—the mine grounds—which were previously seen as wastelands. These materials and objects chiefly come to the farmsteads from the surroundings and from inside the mine, and in particular from the rubbish tip, as well as from the spoil tips alongside the drainage canals, from the dried fields. This is a consequence of the aforementioned autarkic subsistential way of getting by that recycles all its internal substances, an often feature of rural skills and experiences. This is once more an ecology of sorts, in which the outside world is treated, as far as possible, as one's home, one's farmstead. In this farmstead nothing goes unused, wasted, or left to "just sit there"; at the same time, we ought to recall that in their consciousness there is a constant threat of catastrophe (cf. chapter 1) and instability to one's existence (Wasilewski 1986; Kocik 2001: 31–32). The nearest environment to these farmsteads is thus the *oikos,* the profoundly internalized world that requires constant reworking, minding, management, lest things "end for the worst." To quote Wiesław Myśliwski (Jackowski, Myśliwski, and Sulima 1994) once again, "the peasant would just as soon domesticate every animal." The Szamów farmsteads thus "spread" into neighboring terrain in a natural (or, in fact, cultural) manner, in particular the neighboring mine area, the "treasure trove" of all sorts of goods, and the dried meadows, absorbing everything that can in any way be assimilated. The autarky of the village farmstead and its outstretching *oikos* are therefore ruled by an ingrained "imperative to use." "If something's just lying there," an ex-farmer from Szamów told me, speaking of the copper cables discarded by the KWB, "you can't take it. It belongs to the state ... and if it's the state's, you walk around it, don't touch it. ... Just let it lie there, let it *rot!*" (TR/BŁ/22).

The place or environment worth "using" is, in this case (in Szamów and its environs), the mine territory, particularly its internal rubbish tips, a place where one can find used cables, gaskets, workers' clothing, expired food, scrap, or anything that has ceased to be of use. Among the Szamów families this is known as the "marketplace" (*giełda*). All these gathered objects found in sheds, in homes, cluttering up the yards, are thus originally pieces of the world external to the village, of the all-encompassing mine. This creates a certain relationship of necessity, a space of activity between the people inhabiting the edge of the pit and the spoil tip and what is happening all around them—the finding of raw materials, the operating mine, its grounds and its whole mysterious economy of success. It has also changed the manner of apprehending the outer world, i.e., the environment that, for the main subjects in my research, is the dominant external structure of the mine/power plant, the external "nature." Once more, they are managing the area that has changed around them, into a postindustrial world of dried fields, a spoil tip, human-made mountains of sand and ash, the pit, and hundreds of conveyors, machines, pieces of equipment, and conveyor belts. The everyday activities of Wacław Okoński, Józef Białas, and the other Szamów gatherers are thus divided between the mine and their homes. Every item they find becomes extremely vital, handy, exceptional (a tool for bending wires, a large-capacity hoist, an electric pump), and is seen as highly significant. Wacław Okoński, for instance, is forever stressing that the well-pumped tires (filled with his homemade electric pump) on his homemade cart (made of machinist squares welded together) easily enable him to haul home up to half a ton of scrap and other rubble from inside the mine. Paint and varnish tins, obviously taken from the mine, line the shelves of his shed/storage space. He is very proud of these (and offered me a particularly "good" one). With these he paints the window frames, his carts, and the walls of his home. In this way the home stretches into the mine, and the home/mine line becomes the axis around which all activities took place.

In the households I have described, situated around the edge of the Bełchatów exposed mine, the inhabitants thus collect scrap and other postindustrial rubble. However, they are also quick to gather wild mushrooms and berries; and they even hunt (or rather, poach) animals—the wild boars and deer that inhabit the spoil tip, where, *nota bene,* exclusive hunting grounds have been created for the local establishment. This made their hunting another informal or illegal practice (bordering on the social definition of a criminal act). Faced with this great industrial structure, they remain on the level of "hunters and gatherers," of people "living off the land," or, in this case, off everything that might come in handy from the mine/nature (cf. on this sort of hunter/gatherer strategy, Laskowska-Otwinowska 2002: 228–229; on gatherers of "shell scrap" and its "defusing" and reworking at home, see Piotrowski 2004). This is generally postindustrial rubble, old cans of oil paint, washing machine motors, rubber, synthetic materials, and power generators, generally from the mine and its "marketplace," all of which end up in the habitats of my interlocutors. This is also precisely how the wild boars, deer, mushrooms from the damp spoil tips and ash, berries, evening primrose (a medicinal herb), willow wood,[5] field potatoes, and fish from the reservoir (which, as Wacław Okoński enthusiastically claimed, "the foreman just stocked with fish") all come to be in their homes as well. In this way, hunting and gathering also serves to blur the boundary between an industrial, technical (human-made) product and an organic (natural) one. As Wacław once told me, indicating the spoil tip spiked with machines: "Look—these are my hunting grounds" (TR/BŁ/25). He repeatedly took me to see the best mushroom-gathering fields on the grounds of the mine. He was also adept at tracking wild boars and deer, following their tracks "in the earth," in precisely the same way as he perceived "deposits" of discarded scrap, "courses" of underground electric cables (rubble), and "stockpiles" of combustible rubber. In Szamów, the domestic areas of the homes, or the domestic activity of their inhabitants extend far outwards, the house/lumber yards come spreading out onto the mine's "wastelands," conquering new space and ignoring the boundaries of the mine. These activities generally reach beyond the closed sphere of the "home" and out toward the "outside world," encompassing regions beyond the home, creating and reworking the world on the premise of the unceasing assimilation of more and more materials. As such, it is a husbandry that has not been domesticated; yet at the same time, it intensively domesticates everything it encounters all around.

The home, the farmstead, the *oikos,* as a closed space of domestic activity, is not, therefore, a closed and irretractable structure in the current (and in any) case. This brings about a certain shift in the home/

outside world relationship, the *domi/foris* opposition, between what lies inside and what lies outside the home, the building and its door, or more precisely, what lies beyond that door, "outside" (Spieralska 2004: 33–35). The Greek word *dómos* and its significance as a place "where one belongs," or "at home" (ibid.) in a familiar, constructed space, is not radically opposed to what is found outside, in the same way as it has become in the Indo-European languages. The same applies to the Greek *oikos,* marking the home/cultivated area, an area with a few buildings, fences, farmsteads, or a village (ibid.). The home/outside world relationship can, however, only be recognized when an enclosed image of the home, of a "domesticated" and appropriated area, splits off, when, in short, the notion of the permanent address or the "settled" lifestyle is isolated. In order to illuminate the further significance of the home/ *oikos,* I shall outline the complexity of the very category of domestication. By the received definition (Childe 1947; cf. 1957; Harrison 1996: 442–442), domestication took place during the Neolithic Revolution, circa 10,000–4,000 years BCE. It was then, we are told, that a distinct sphere of home, plants, and domesticated animals gradually appeared, a sphere of the *oikos,* and it was only in opposition to this that the sphere of otherness, the "outside" world "beyond the front door," came to be (Harrison 1996: 437–438). And yet, the very beginning of the division into predomestic, pre-Neolithic hunter/gatherers as "undomesticated" and "domesticated" plant cultivators and animal breeders is fluid, to say the least, and our general notion of it has often been criticized in anthropology circles as excessively rigid (Chase 1989; cf. Harrison 1996: 442). It has been demonstrated, for example, that the domestication of the hunter/gatherer lifestyle took a rather indirect course, and that there were often situations where the home seemed to stray outwards, overlapping onto the rest of the world. This often took the form of an interplay between humans and nature. For example, the reindeer shepherds milked their animals "outside" the settlement, though the animals would sometimes enter people's homes for salt—the microelement that they always needed. Thus was formed an image of partial domestication (Chase 1989), leaving the environment "on the borderline" between home and nature. Furthermore, in various contemporary undomesticated hunter/gatherer cultures, this sphere is often quite vague, imprecisely defined, dependent on the context or activity of the group at a given moment. By way of example, Roy Ellen has shown that for the Nuaulu, the rain forest, the environment in which they live "outside the home," can be alternately treated as a foreign region and as an assimilated one (1996: 110; cf. Descola and Pallson 1996: 10). Other research has called attention to the varied, situational status of the tropical forest

for hunters and gatherers (Ingold 1996a: 151). The environment, moreover, may come to include other distinctions. With the Mbuti Pigmies
(of the Ibuti forests), it is simultaneously home and an external space
of experiences and anthropomorphism, where inanimate beings (such
as rain and earth) coexist with plants, animals, and people, forming
numerous mutual relationships (Ingold 1996a: 122–129; Bird-David
1992; 1999, cf. Buchowski 1993: 41–44).

This Szamów practice/activity or management strategy that draws
the home/*oikos* out into the nearby terrain epitomizes, to some extent,
one of the conditions of the pre-Neolithic hunter/gatherer reality of
being-in-the-environment, of seeing the environment outside the established home (humans), and the surroundings (the outside world)
as opposition (see Ingold 1996a). This is an ecological, domesticating
form of actively producing reality (and simultaneously depending on it
entirely), or, to borrow a phrase from Tim Ingold (1996a: 121), it is a
special form of living-in-the-world, which has a direct reference point
in the field of philosophy. Here I have in mind Martin Heidegger and
his concept of *In-der Welt-Sein* (see 2008: 52–62). Ingold (1992; 2000)
writes in like fashion on the perception of the environment in hunter/
gatherer cultures, as an experience in a very primitive sense, and to some
degree, as an attribute of the human species. He writes of the experience
of creating a model for nature as an "intentional" manipulation of the
world (1996a: 18), and also as a psychophysiological act of adaptation
(1992: 42–46; cf. 1996a: 117–121). Moreover, in showing the multifaceted and relative connections between wild and domestic, Ingold (ibid.)
claims that they are often more derived from Western cultural assumptions and ways of thinking (the constant oppositions of local/foreign,
culture/nature) than from any kind of testimony of the reality of an
ethnographic being, group, or individual with its own, quite primordial
(foreign, incomprehensible) ecology.

This figure of the hunter/gatherer reveals another, less comprehensible relationship between humans and the surrounding world. This manner of perceiving the environment (functioning in the environment)
collapses the boundary between civilization and nature, between the industrial and the natural. This relationship surfaces in many astonishing
places, generally at the crossroads of various stages of technical practices. In Warsaw's vegetable allotments, Roch Sulima (2000) has observed similar practices that break down the nature/culture division and
reveal primordial "hunter/gatherer" activity. For example, the allotment
owners "plant" prefabricated figures, children's furniture, and whimsical
fountains made of "salvaged" or "collected" postindustrial rubble in-
between their mallows, sunflowers, and rows of vegetables, thus building

a new kind of "nature." To my mind, this practice recalls the behavior of the Mbuti Pygmies. According to Colin Turnbull (1987), the Mbuti Pygmies' holy "molimo" trumpet, carved from the inner bark of a special tree, releases the voice of the "spirit" of the forest; but it was happily exchanged for a more practical metal drainage pipe pulled from a broken installation. A whole gamut of hunter/gatherer methods of using objects in post-Soviet conditions has also been shown by Zuzanna Grębecka (2006: 3–4), who writes about farmers setting up a hen house in a pressure chamber, and of Old Believer women who made decorations for their iconostases[6] from plastic bottles. They all show participation in an environment that, from our point of view, serves to "disintegrate" it; they delve into this participation with their living practices and allow them to be processed, absorbing everything that was "within arm's reach," everything that could "come in handy."

The construct of Indigenous, hunter/gatherer knowledge of reality as partially known and simultaneously exceptionally incomprehensible, often reduced to the idea of gathering whatever lies around, or is "within arm's reach," is of course the point of departure for Claude Lévi-Strauss's essay on the "science of the concrete" (1994). Essentially, this refers to, I would say, an intimate relationship with one's surroundings, in which external divisions into, for example, "natural" (a tree) and "artificial" (a plumbing pipe) cease to be taken for granted. This relationship is marked by focused and continual contact with the world/environment, filled with "questions" and "responses." It was this active and exploratory relationship with the living environment that so fascinated Lévi-Strauss in his analyses of native hunting/gathering natural science (ibid.). In Lévi-Strauss's view, Indigenous people usually possess a remarkable facility for recognizing the fragments of the natural world that interest them, and are aware of the morphological and tactile differences between animal and plant species. While Europeans make use of a few familiar cultivated plants, such as sugar cane, the native inhabitants of Hawaii know of hundreds and thousands of plants and their uses (ibid.: 2). Such cognitive activity, Lévi-Strauss writes, is "to take care that nothing be overlooked" (ibid.: 9), and further: "it seems to be the case that man began by applying himself to the most difficult tasks, that of systematizing what is immediately presented to the senses" (ibid.: 11). This initiated the exploration of the "science of the concrete." Lévi-Strauss was fascinated by the abilities of the botanists in various Indigenous societies. As he quotes from A. H. Smith: "Even a child can frequently identify the kind of tree from which a tiny wood fragment has come … by observing the appearance of its wood and bark, its smell, its hardness, and similar characteristics" (ibid.: 5).

This aspect of Indigenous knowledge chiefly comes about as a result of a physical, sensual knowledge of the world, and at the same time, is combined with linguistic exploration. Lévi-Strauss writes of the splendid differentiation and classification of various species of trees, lianas, and herbs. He evokes an image of an Indigenous person wandering through the jungle, every other moment turning his/her attention to a natural resource: a bark that protects the tree from leeches, an orchid that wards off parasitical insects, shoots that are delicious to chew, much like sugar cane, and many other things, thus "completing the body" (ibid.: 7). In Indigenous cultures, the body and its requirements are "reflected" in natural science. Moreover, this multifaceted application is reflected in the linguistic practice, as there are several dozen variants of the names of things that are most essential in a given environment (on Indigenous systems of natural science, see a more contemporary work: Ellen, Parkes, and Bicker 2000). As such, this is a renewed gathering of knowledge about the outer reality, which testifies to the necessity of having previously adopted an active stance toward the environment; furthermore, this perception is continually "remade," reworked, essentially becoming a cognitive activity. Maurice Merleau-Ponty's concept of "attention" (2002: 30–59) might serve us well here, in analyzing this constant "reworking" of the undivided material of the world known through cognition and the senses (i.e., essentially, through extensions of the body). To his way of thinking, this "attention" (as opposed to "judgment") is an active and dynamic act in which relationships are created between human/body and the external world/stimulus, i.e., through touch, or an individual's sight. As such, it is always linked to an event. As Merleau-Ponty writes (2002: 34), attention does not exist "as a general and formal activity." By setting in motion a series of reactions and images occurring "inside the body," attention and perception allow one to expand one's range of perceptual exploration in a way not encountered or possible otherwise. From this point of view, the world of "undomesticated thought" is further enriched by a prereflexive structure (in operating and orienting itself toward external objects), one that Lévi-Strauss, to some extent, had taken from it (cf. Cichowicz 1999). What is the nature of this broadening of the horizon?

Much as the Pygmies can endlessly divide and classify tree bark, for instance, with regard to its application, taste, appearance, and smell, so too can Wacław Okoński and Józef Białas divide waste rubber. They classify which is firmer or more malleable, which smokes more when burned, and which is more useful according to its function, i.e., for building or for fuel. In showing me their trash, hardly a second passes without them exhibiting some kind of material, such a rubber gasket, enumerating its dozens of uses, all of which are new to me, demonstrating its pliability, its smell, how it is cut or "torn off," etc. (TR/BŁ/9, among others). In Szamów, these kinds of "natural science" activities (though collections of postindustrial materials stood in for nature, here) are highly developed, and they astonished me in much the same way as the jungle dwellers had once astonished Claude Lévi-Strauss. The families of Wacław and Józef, the hunter/gatherers, also know a great deal about the resources in their nearest surroundings, that postindustrial "nature," and what they "offer" (see Ingold 1992: 42). This is also derived from their daily practice, from their constant focusing of attention, discussing and exchanging information, evaluations, and estimations of their collections. Collecting rubble, scrap, and raw materials for fuel (as well as wild mushrooms) is a daily routine in the households of Szamów. They gather great quantities of rubber (worn-out pieces of conveyor belts), which they call "raw stuff" (*surówki*) and which they use to heat their homes. Moreover, they collect tiles of human-made material (for cleaning the conveyor belts), which they call "tablets" (*tabletki*). These are divided into the better black ones (soft rubber that burns almost entirely) and the more inferior yellow ones (hard rubber that exudes a semifluid substance when burned, which needs to be removed). "Concrete" (*beton*) is the word for rubber tiles well-suited for patching walls of buildings, sheds, hen houses, and for spreading over parts of the yard (TR/BŁ/15, among others). I was shown an incredible taxonomy and knowledge of the materials culled from the mine, and of their material specifics, while my ignorance concerning varieties of rubber was even a source of mirth. The rubber used for fuel[7] is a particular focus of the family's attention: they talk about it, rate it, and estimate how much there is. The knife for cutting the rubber lies at a prominent place on the Okoński family's table, testifying to the significance of this activity, and its recognition as a natural thing. At that time I was shown which kinds of rubber were worth using, why and how, the varieties demonstrated with the knife. "Look, this one gives smoke, it's no good, and this one only sweats a bit, you just have to cut it up and it'll burn like petrol, you won't even be able to put it out" (TR/BŁ/9).

During one night that I spent with the Okoński family, an exchange of hunter/gatherer information took place at around four o'clock in the morning:

Joasia (the daughter): "Has Father come back yet?"

Bożena: "He's asleep. ... Are you getting up? I'm going to make breakfast, anyway. ... Father was at the 'marketplace.' ..."

Joasia: "And?"

Bożena: "He brought home some *tabletki* … the black ones … good thing, too, because those yellow ones are good for nothing. …

Wacław: Białas went to get his bike—Zygmunt, that is. …"

Bożena: "And?"

Wacław: "There's some more *surówki* there. Heniek (Grąd) went out in the morning, there's no mushrooms, he says there aren't any, but maybe by the canal. …"

Bożena: "Maybe at the dykes?"

Wacław: "There was steam coming off the dykes. … There might be new mushrooms, maybe agarics. … There's smoke coming up and good weather … it's crawling along the ground. … I saw Fredzio going out with the cows, maybe he's going down to the canal. …" (TR/BŁ/16)

Gathering these "goods" is thus a subject that crops up in this family's "marketplace information." On every occasion we find this characteristic interchangeability or equality of scrap, raw materials (rubber), industrial artifacts, and mushrooms, for example, of natural undergrowth—the scrap collectors "come across" all this as "natural goods," as goods to be hunted down and gathered. We might say that in the industrial, techno-cratic (also much logocentric) perspective on "effectiveness," embedded in European languages, this is a world in which a "reduction to acces-sibility" took place, in which an isolated "collection" of goods remains quite apart from processes of technology and production, apart from knowledge of causes. Wacław Okoński often showed me the various useful things, the "raw materials" and "goods" he would bring home from the inner rubbish tip of the mine, the "marketplace," indicating their plenitude, and his ease in acquiring them: "The sofa-beds from the 'marketplace,' so's that armchair … look, it's marvelous. … I didn't need to buy anything you see here … it's all from the 'marketplace'"; or as he told his wife, "I'll go to the 'marketplace' in the morning, before it gets light out. Then I'll bring home better rubber" (TR/BŁ/15). He also found his shoes at the "marketplace" (he had a few pairs), and, as he endlessly repeats, they were very comfortable. He said that he had once purchased a pair of shoes, but was unable to wear them, because they were uncomfortable, and it was only there, at the "marketplace," that he had found a good pair, as if the ease in acquiring these things had somehow increased their value. This special form of ecology, of being in the environment, of acquiring and collecting materials of all sorts, is thus, at the same time, a practical and cognitive *activity*, and a hunting/gathering skill in managing postindustrial, ready-made resources, like those found in nature.

Wacław Okoński—*The Stalker,* Orbis Interior

This domestication of the world of the mine by the Bełchatów hunters/gatherers is the source of a certain incomprehensibility/untranslatability inside the cultural structures of my research language. This is an experience and an internal processing of the presence of the outside world, which reveals itself in a very unclear fashion. It occupies the space of their lives spent dealing with the "resources" of the mine, its "goods" and that daily practice of searching for scrap, mushrooms, clothing, tins of varnish, and wild boars, which they catch in snares (nets). The mine, the rubbish tip, and the postindustrial marshes are, it seems to me, mentally colonized by the Szamów gatherers, who know these places through-and-through. Wacław Okoński and Józef Białas know all the spoil tips, upcasts, thresholds, and canals extremely well; they know the fields where the mushrooms grow, the places where the mine discards its scrap and other extraneous things, and the areas where the deer and wild boar roam. They constantly discuss the topography of the spoil tip. Wandering about the spoil tips with Wacław and his wife, we often came across Józef Białas scanning the ground. On one such occasion, an exchange of information took place between the collectors.

> Wacław: "There's a depression here, because there used to be a conveyor belt."
> Bożena: "What, a conveyor belt? It's the fifth ledge. ...."
> Wacław: "What do you mean, the fifth? It's just the third. ... Look where you are."
> Józef Białas: "I'm on my way, there's mushrooms, I saw them at Adamówek just off the path. ... I'll see if they're over there, I'll go up onto the first ledge."
> Wacław: "I'll go there too. ... Maybe there'll be honey fungus. They've got to grow up there, onto the dump. ... Give 'em two days and they'll grow, there'll be mushrooms on Monday. ... I've already had a look around. There's nothing here ... we've come here for nothing." (TR/BŁ/16)

This is how they perform a survey of the hunting and gathering field, the terrain of their work, always creating their own map of the mine area that brings them such a variety of goods.

Wacław generally considers himself to be a privileged collector who has settled into the mine area, treating the mine in very intimate terms, almost on a personal level. It is his very familiar (in many senses) "hunting" ground, practically his "home away from home," in the sense of a cultivated space (domiculture; cf. Chase 1989). As he often said, "When

I come here to the dump, it's like coming home, all my anxieties go away" (TR/BŁ/23). Or, on another occasion: "Now we'll walk around my hunting grounds" (TR/BŁ/27); or, "Look here ... this is where I set traps. ... I know about everything that goes on in this place" (TR/BŁ/27). The place where Wacław feels "at home" is a hunting lodge (belonging to the hunters' club) on the spoil tip. He is forever monitoring its equipment and its functioning, and the hunting news. "This is the hut I told you about. I ran the place [he claims to keep watch over it]; over here, look, there's a small wood house, here a cable runs under the ground. They shot exactly ninety-six wild boars this year, there's poplars growing here, they've done some work, built some walls" (TR/BŁ/14). When a car of mine workers passes through the spoil tip, the hunters greet them with a wave. Repeating constantly that he was once a guard there, and therefore, knows how the place used to be, Wacław goes to the hunter's club a few times a week (he also claims to have worked repairing airport mechanisms and tanking up the aeroplanes at the mine's own airport).

Furthermore, Wacław is creating a whole map of places inside the mine and in the surrounding spoil tips where, he claims, he is working, which gives him a direct sense of functioning as an accomplice. He showed me machines (cranes, conveyor-belt scaffolding, and gigantic stackers) inside the mine, and described the work that went on there: "Here, you see, everything is new, you see ... new ... the rusted ones they leave behind. ... And that stack, I helped build right from the beginning, right here in this square. ... Three years ago it underwent total renovation ... you see that crane ... I made it from the ground up, a total renovation" (TR/BŁ/27). Wacław claimed that he had taken pick-up conservation and renovation jobs, often working with foreign-speaking workers: "I worked at the Electroinstallation ... we worked on the desulphurization of the combustion gas ... the Swedes and the Danes oversaw the whole thing" (TR/BŁ/14). He also claimed that the Danes, Swedes, and Germans considered him to be a great professional (a real "handyman"). There, in this personal map, his past emerges, a time filled with a sense of his own indispensability, and the much-fabricated story of his employment at the KWB, where he sees himself as a necessary, irreplaceable builder and conservationist. Knowledge of building the mine machines allows him to continue to feel like the master of this terrain, to feel as though he were a familiar figure, known to the security guards and the tractor/stacker workers. He monitors and follows what they do, and several times he took me at night to survey the machines and the people at work, explaining the details of the technology and the organization. He still feels his untapped potential and skills; and, as he

himself likes to say, he knows "the ins and outs" and "how to do everything." In this behavior of his there is a clear sense of regret, a feeling
that he is "overskilled," of unaccomplished actions, and of work, i.e.,
"steady" work, not of the "hunter/gatherer" sort. With a note of resignation, Wacław Okoński once told me about the kind of work that went
on in the mine workshops:

> They do everything *slowly* there. They don't hustle about.... I once
> worked with one of them ... the screws started to strip, and I said, "come
> on, we'll heat up the screws and get them in," and he said, "get off it" ...
> he worked slowly. Things are real clean there, you never find any dirt or
> oil just lying around ... and the workshops make you want to just get
> down to work. And he just took some hydraulic wrenches and worked
> slowly, waiting till it was after three. And you know why? Because he's
> got a *steady* job there—and that's a completely different sort of work. He
> goes over to the lift, checks it out, fixes it up a bit. And I would have done
> it right off, heated up those screws, fitted them in there, and everything
> would've been set, it would've worked, just look." (TR/BŁ/8)

For Wacław Okoński the grounds of the KWB are both mysterious
and mythologized—he believed that only he (and Józef Białas) would
have been able to take me about them; only he knew the paths and the
"secret passageways" to get inside. "We'll take this road, you see ... it's
nothing, they won't even notice us ... and if they do, well then, everybody there knows me, you see.... A bit further.... Just a bit further
and we'll get inside ... that's water ... we've got to cross here.... I got
some scrap here, took it apart, there was a rail here [rusted ties for a
concrete path] ... *and no one's got the right to go here apart from me*" (TR/
BŁ/27). He once showed me engineering/geological plans that had been
discarded onto the spoil tip: "Here's the plans—the conveyor belts go
this way, yeah, you can see everything here, there's a map of the driving
roads.... There's the coal excavation ... that's where the pit runs....
Here's the raised levels, the bore-holes, the barriers and the wells that are
always collecting water" (TR/BŁ/14). Wacław was forever and exhaust-
ingly recreating his "internal map," showing me places of hidden significance, known only to him. The map of the technician/conservationist's
knowledge then imperceptibly transfigured into the map of the collector: "There's a whole pile of pipes here.... The set weighed some two
hundred eighty kilos.... I carted them all off in a single night ... but
you've got to know where these places are ... only I know this place";
and furthermore, "Here's a stash, just behind this bush.... There's fifteen kilos of copper here, you see.... And over there, further on, there's
twice as much.... These are my storehouses" (TR/BŁ/27). "*It's all just*

waiting there" he liked to repeat. Wacław personifies this hunter/gatherer relationship with the reality surrounding him, with his living environment, and ultimately, with his own history. This picture, this intimate, personal map of the mine, is created by his points of orientation and involves all manner of storage places. This is a memory map of his activities. Simultaneously, in fact, it is also a map of memory "in action," both in the past tense ("you can see the counterbalance here [a small, inactive, half-dismantled industrial crane]—there are four here, there used to be eight ... they weigh eight hundred kilos apiece ... I hauled them off in my cart ... that's strength for you" [TR/BŁ/27]), and in the future tense ("Have a look ... that's my stash. ... I'm all set for that rainy day to come. ... If something goes wrong, I'm all set, here on this hill. ... I forgot ... oh, here it is. ... This is worth five hundred zloty. ... I just go up the hill and I've got it" [TR/BŁ/27]). The experience of being in the mine thus naturally transforms into an experience of remembering oneself, creating a narrative for a certain modus of being in the mine, or perhaps even his "being-in-the-world" (see Rosner 2002: 12).

Another aspect of Wacław Okoński's activities, and another subplot in this tale of self-reliance, is the "hunting" (poaching) itself. He speaks of himself as the lord of the lands, of the slopes of the newly forested spoil tips, where the wild boars (bred by the hunting club, founded by the KWB Board) forage for food on the site of the aforementioned hunting cabin. Wacław told me that he grabs the boars by the "eye," then either finishes them off with his knife, or sometimes shoots them; later the boars are gutted. There is often enough to feed his whole family, and even to share some with his neighbors. "If I shoot or catch one, then there's enough for my sons, and I'm still left with fifty kilos" (TR/BŁ/27). "If I catch one, it gets me through the winter—there's a hundred and twenty kilos, and we eat boar all winter" (TR/BŁ/15). The remainder is stored in a huge freezer. Once again we find he gained a sense of agency and of his ability. He has recently made an old-style firearm out of a gas pipe and an oak board, acquiring the lock "in Łódź," and buying Czech shotgun slugs for it as well; he proudly explained its unique construction. On the occasion of his fiftieth birthday he and his wife explained how the wild boar meat gave their children a "healthy" upbringing: "It was the game meat that cured them of every wound, of every broken bone. If one of them broke something, like that one broke his hand, and Joasia had troubles with her spine, well, a little bit of boar and they were right as rain ... every little bone grew right back" (TR/BŁ/15). I could see clearly his sense of satisfaction, his pride in the goods he had gathered from the KWB and consumed, including those boars, whose meat helped his family to survive. Nonetheless, this sense of agency and of ability are combined with an evident dependency on the "hunting grounds," with subjection to the mine's ecosystem. He and his family observe all the species of wild boar that appeared on the spoil tips. On one of my trips he told me, "They've released a kind of boar that has lean meat and doesn't smell at all gamey" (TR/BŁ/15). He keeps an eye on the animals—the changing species of boar, the number of deer and hares—in much the same fashion as he observes the other signs of the mine's activity: the traveling machines, the growing spoil tips. Much like the mine's landscape, the boars take on fantastical shapes. Wacław claims that these boars, having begun to forage on the "radioactive ash" from far inside the KWB compound, are growing to massive proportions.

In this way, Wacław depicts the mine environment as his own, tracking its movements, and forever drawing from its resources. He once told me: "I'm the kind of guy that senses everything.... *I know what's going on.* Look, there's some stashes there, and a few meters on, next to that bush, there's loads of copper" (TR/BŁ/27). For him the mine is an *orbis interior* that he feels he knows better than all others, on which he tries to advise. This mine affords him access to provisions, scrap, and rubble. It allows him to steal and to dismantle old machines. Finally, it serves as his hunting grounds, a place to poach (as he said, "Let's have a walk round my hunting turf—I know where all the trails go"). He is equally involved in his gathering and speaks constantly of the traces of postindustrial installations ("A cable ran underground here, under this road ... about a hundred meters of the stuff is left ... but you've got to know it's there ... that this was there, and that"). Of his hunting/ poaching, and his ability to track an animal by its footprints ("Oh, deer left tracks here," "Oh, boars have been by this way"), he speaks with equal enthusiasm. The space of the mine has penetrated into his inner experience, he bears it within him, and when he is there, at the dump, he feels "right at home."

Once I went with him (in July 2004) for an all-night "stalk" inside the KWB compound. Upon entering inside the industrial guard line, he imparted some of his wisdom, explaining how and when the guards' cars would pass and how to pass the canals filled with water pumped from deep below. He knew where the best places were to hide (over a dozen in turn, e.g., behind remnants of machinery and minicranes, in large bushes or tall-grown meadows of shoulder-high grass) and at what time of day. "If I get all *riled up* [emphasis mine], " he told me on that occasion, "if there's no money at home, Bożena's all mad about something, the kids are starving, that's when I head for the dump ... and only then I start to breathe freely ... I start to feel all that.... There's something here that really makes me feel alive" (TR/BŁ/25). That night, after we had fished for some carp that "the foreman had stocked" in the reservoir, we found ourselves on almost the very summit of the spoil tips. And then, already somewhat tipsy (he had a flask of liquor in his haversack), he began telling me again, in a mumble, "There's something about this place that makes me feel ... I don't know, but who could possibly understand it.... Who could understand? Who could understand it? When the fog rolls in, the air is clear ... all you can see are the smokestacks and the sun coming up. Who knows what I get out of it." Two hours later we were lost amid the canals; and, having spotted us in our hiding place, the KWB guards had lit up the grassy fields with their spotlights. When finally I had asked him in vain if we might return home, he told me: "I could return from here *even if it was black out*" (TR/BŁ/27).

Goods and Trophies: The Hunting/Gathering Existence on the Edge of the Mine

The mine area, as we have seen, is the gatherers' source of daily goods. Wacław Okoński stresses that almost everything his family owns—clothing, rubber for fuel, machines for reworking, and boar meat—comes from the mine, from the "marketplace." He also says that he keeps his stores of goods, scrap, rubber, and copper—his stores of "pure cash"—on the mine grounds. In this way, the mine is a life-giving force for him and his family. As a hunting/gathering space, it is the flip side of the mine, conceived as a modern, extremely lucrative, and progressive company, providing employment and a certain standard of living in the local area. Here we can see with even greater clarity that these "storehouses of goods" that appeared in "a single moment" (they could surprise you like a "jack-in-the-box") are easily accessible; one merely has "to know," as Wacław said, or know how "to look." These uncovered "treasures" and "trophies"—a piece of good galvanized metal hidden under coal dust, a dozen "almost brand new" telephones with coils of cables, or Energomontaż-brand work clothes—appear easily and all at once (on the mine rubbish tip or on the way home). They pop up almost all on their own, with no effort, no laborious searching, hunting, or collecting, "nature" offering itself up to them. The memory of following the trails of the mine is thus the memory of this benevolent universe.

I would say that this leads to a local narrative about gathering, an internal image of a universe strung between them (the gatherers) and the mine that surrounds them. The collected objects, accumulated in homes and in yards, are material condensations of their special ties or relationships that they thus form with the KWB. We might even say that these goods are evidently magical, in the sense that they testify to an indirect power over the grounds of the mine. The gatherers take these objects into their possession on terms of practically magical contact (the sudden appearance of these "goods" as objects that are always "stumbled across," or "appear all on their own" is in itself characteristic). These objects, gathered treasures, and hunting trophies (there is a whole drawer filled with boar tusks and goat antlers) possess special properties, being at once trophies, practical items, and mysterious emblems of the mine. I would say that they mark an imagined participation in the mine's activities. It is for this cause that Wacław Okoński collects them as valuable records of his unique knowledge of the corporation, as well as his knowledge of the world as such (of meteorology, of the pit, and of mine engineering). He is in possession of knowledge about which others "haven't the slightest clue" (TR/BŁ/9). These collections in their yards, sheds, and houses not only provide an effective circulation of materials, but also a material testimony of the villagers' existence in the mines. These objects thus create a private tale of journeys made to the mines, of sneaking past the patrol line, and of stories of great "discoveries" and "treasure troves." As such, Wacław collects and amasses his activities, and his collection is, as it were, an "extended self" (Pearce 1995: 175–177). The boar tusks, the secret maps of the spoil tips, the "apparatuses" and "cobalt bombs" (TR/BŁ/9) collected in his home and his shed are extensions of the mine, which is conquered a bit more with each passing day. His words—"I've got everything I need here, and it all comes from the 'marketplace'"—become, as it were, an echo of the statement "I'm the kind of guy that senses everything ... I know what's going on. Look, there's some stashes there, and a few meters on, next to that bush, there's loads of copper, worth a hundred zloty ... who knows about this stuff? Only me" (TR/BŁ/27). I would even say that these objects are metonyms of his possession of the mine or of his participation in its activities. After all, he is forever repeating that he is a "hunter," a "stalker," that he knows "everything there, every blade of grass." "They [the guards, the police] look in all the wrong places, they know what's going on [that 'I'm on the prowl'], but they don't say a thing" (TR/BŁ/27). They serve as magical objects, filling the collector's home and yard, making the mine closer at hand, existing as traces of his participation in the mine or his power over its grounds, yet all the while present in his yard. In collecting things, he applies something resembling magic, creating a metaphorical/metonymic passageway (Pearce 1995: 172–173) to the outside reality—to the terrain, to the history underway, as well as to his own, private history.

Through acquiring goods, through amassing and collecting them, Wacław owns part of the mine, as it were, and this is a contact and participation with it. The objects gathered in his yard create a metonymy of the mine, a passageway to it. They are magical symbols of being in the mine. Here, the word *magical* is not used to signify magical practices, treated and recognized as magical. This concept is closer to what Michał Buchowski has called "primary magic" (1993: 38), i.e., one that is a certain "hunter/gatherer" presence in the environment, a presence that grants an animized and dynamic significance to all performed activities, to all practices of using and being in the environment. These are acts of being in the environment that transpire through humans and enter into personal relationships with objects, substances, all forms of nonhuman beings and through their intensive participation in the world, as if—as a European would say—they were human beings (Bird-David 1999; In-gold 1996a; Pedersen 2001). These objects, things, and even the goods and resources found by the gatherers are laden with a special dynamism in this primeval, magical world; all these resources have appeared sud-denly, on their own, much like those unearthed telephones from the KWB and, moreover, they generally lead to a mystery. These objects, whether radioactive "cobalt bombs" (TR/BŁ/9), tusks from radioactive wild boars, meters and medicines (tested on the employed collectors of Szamów), or significant, animated places, such as the hills, forests, and streams in India (Bird-David 1999: 73) or Northern Asia (Pedersen 2001), are highly significant. In a certain sense, the gatherer "converses" with nature, the living and active universe in which the gatherer, the *bri-coleur*, "does not confine himself to accomplishment and execution: he 'speaks' not only with things, as we have already seen, but also through the medium of things" (Lévi-Strauss 1994: 21). Through the medium of his hidden troves of copper, our gatherer Wacław speaks with himself. Józef Białas speaks through the medium of the fields of scrap he seeks and discovers, and on other occasions, with the fields of mushrooms; he speaks with rubble he accumulates and later reworks in his yard.

This particular practice of inhabiting the environment—of being in the environment—is, as I have said, primordial and, on some level, hardly comprehensible. It involves no distinct magical practices, unlike the magical attempts to assert control over the weather, such as those which James Frazer has described (1993: 60–82; cf. Kisielewska 1970), as ways of functioning in the environment. Rather this is "magical be-ing" in which the very manner of perceiving the environment (as in In-gold's use of the phrase) allows us to call something magical. This is not the same magic we use to describe the practice of a wizard or of a small group and its relatively set, structured elements and social contexts (cf. Buchowski 1993: 55). This "magical" way of being in an environment and its manner of treating things or endowing them with significance of these tales. At one point these tales wrench free and begin to live their own lives, creating a framework of transferred knowledge, in which, as Pyotr Bagotiryev and Roman Jakobson have written on the creation of folklore, a certain collectivity was "both producer and recipient" (1982 [1929]). These stories are forever being repeated. To what do they refer? To what do they bear testimony? We are dealing with a particular sort of game that transforms meaning and designs a new and improvised sort of social relationship. These jokes and quips are, on the one hand, meant to prove access to authority and its representatives, and on the other, to emphasize the diggers' sense of distance from these acts of trickery, rearranging, and derision. This repetitive and scoffing formula, a kind of improvised folklore, creates an entirely unanticipated framework for post-mining communication. They speak laughingly of a "Wałbrzych tone," for everyone knows that this describes a weight much below an actual tone. What are these stories truly about? I would like to return at this point to that undefined space, the empty place in social relations and transactions, the vacuum that requires filling. I believe that this empty space in the post-mining world keeps the ex-miners in the bootleg mines from asking themselves and others the basic questions: Who are they? How could they have responded to this? Are they honest working men, or do they steal coal on a daily basis? Many of them dig by night so that they won't be seen, carting off the coal in their Żuk vehicles in the morning, and they live in constant fear of being called to court, of having their equipment confiscated. Many of them have been through city court and are on probation. And yet they are digging coal as ex-miners, in a professional manner, minding their work as best they can, working hard and honestly and, upon returning home, giving their earnings to their wives. Almost everyone, including the police or the forestry workers, understands and respects this situation, or takes it into account. Thus I repeat: What is the nature of their situation?

The diggers are incapable of giving a clear response to this situation. However, they are forced to make daily efforts to understand their actions (digging holes for over five years), essentially, to explain their actions to themselves. Life goes on its daily course and poses daily questions, and jokes are a form of response. Through scoffing anecdotes, they invent momentary responses that topple the norms of honesty, the hierarchies of power and social relations. These go from imaginary and almost carnivalesque play at swindling, to spectacles of sorts and bursts of laughter (much like at carnival or mid-Lent), scoffing at others who are swindled in a mocking and absurd fashion. If we may permit ourselves such an expression, then, this is an *interior* spectacle; the actors/ diggers easily succumb to jokes and laughter during their unstable work,

Epistemology" (1999). Against a backdrop of theories proposed to date, including those by Ingold (1992; 1996a) and the ecological psychology of Gibson, she describes a certain relational aspect (in the cognitive sense) of animism, drawing from her own research conducted among the Nayaka hunting/gathering tribes of southern India. Bird-David argues that they are entangled in a network of needs/goods/need fulfillment dependencies—in a train of succeeding activities oriented toward nature, as well as imaginative/psychophysiological states. The Nayaka incarnate their relationships with their surroundings. A forest, a rock, or the water in a stream act as spirits/presences called *devaru*, something that might be provisionally compared to a being that has "agency" (not precisely a deity or spirit) that destroys humans while bestowing them with gifts (this is only one element of its multiple relationships with the world). In this case a coherent being in the environment is scattered into many survived events and experiences flowing from the outside and the inside, which later accumulate, are "cast" out, and, as single stories affecting the collectors, turn back toward them, taking on being (agency). Herein we have the opportunity to understand this universe more deeply. This is a world of interplay between humans and their surroundings, a world that simultaneously includes all elements, both animate and inanimate, human and nonhuman, "artificial" or "natural," and which are thus equally significant, animized, polyvalent (cf. Ingold 1996a; Bird-David 1992; 1999; Descola 1996: 87). This is, however, a constant attempt to break out of a modernist, European-centric ontology, which is why we forever encounter difficulties in capturing the described reality in words. We might speak of a practiced "intersubjectivity" in the human/world relationship here, which would, of course, be a certain exaggeration. It would be better to join Ingold (1996a: 129) in speaking of an "interagency," that is, of a multiplicity of natural and supernatural subjects that the outside world "produces" and with which it "operates." As such, this is the field of a primordial game between humans (and their bodies) and their needs and experiences, their necessity for survival and for natural resources, which facilitate this survival. In this space the bodies/persons of hunter/gatherers remain closely tied to nonhumans (trees, animals, etc.) and inanimate items/objects; this is a form of Indigenous ontology (cf. Bird-David 1992; 1999; Ingold 1996a; Pedersen 2001).

In a similar fashion, this "relation of being" buried in animistic ontologies creates, to my mind, a certain framework that organizes the innermost narrative of Wacław Okoński, this hunter/gatherer from Szamów, and, to some extent, the remaining gatherers. His manner of relating to the grounds of the mine, his observations on its various areas, and his dependency on both its fascinating and abundant wealth of mysteries and its destructive effects lend a certain reality to this "experience of the environment." The internal maps of their wanderings, so "cluttered" or "stuffed" with gathered materials because they have to contain all these relationships, the whole internal topography, the whole secret "knowledge" of the mine, contains all these relations. As Jan B., getting ready for another bicycle expedition past the line of security, put it: "I've got the transformers ... I took everything. I took those broken transformers, those porcelain balls.... Now I'm going to untwist them" (TR/BŁ/13). "There's meant to be a chalk spoil tip here," said Wacław. "They add foil here, I'm sure of it.... This is where they add it.... I've got friends here, there's some hunters I know there" (TR/BŁ/14). "You can gather a ton and a half of scrap here in a single night.... Oh, here's the place ... you've got to know where it is.... Only I know" (TR/BŁ/27). Their daily gathering is, of course, known in the area. Almost all the mine guards know of the scrap collectors from Szamów and—as far as I could tell—they treat the collectors quite forbearingly. And yet, the scavengers collect refuse that the company means to protect; and, in rooting out the refuse there, they open themselves up to any eventuality, including arrest (depending on the mine, its security guards, and the municipal functionaries). Meanwhile, this mine simultaneously "offers up" its resources to the collectors, who are forever noting what is transpiring in the vicinity, i.e., where the machines are wandering, what boars have been "released" by the KWB hunting club, where the mushrooms are growing, and where the foreman has "stocked" the reservoir. As Józef Białas said, indicating toward the marshlands by the rubbish heaps: "They could make an overflow here—they could really stock this place.... The fish there'd be! You could really ... make a lake here" (TR/BŁ/13). This being in the mine (or the mine environment) reinforces the ubiquitous impact of the corporation on their daily lives. They live, after all, in daily contact with the KWB, with its work, its refuse, its topography, and its environment. It constitutes the daily backdrop for their imagined hunter/gatherer activities.

Records

Cabinets of Curiosities, Collectors' Museums

The objects collected by the Szamów gatherers are both functional and prestigious. It is quite essential that the rubbish tip from which they acquire their objects belongs to the mine. Helped by a bit of luck, the collectors have been carting off steel rails, rubber washers, nuts, cables, and copper wires for over ten years. It therefore seems as though this practice serves at least a few separate functions. First of all, it provides a livelihood for the gatherers, enabling them to participate in the "internal economy," providing the opportunity to function in an informal "grey" market. They salvage rubber and other fuel sources, parts they need to build vital machines, clothing, and scrap, and hunt for (wild boar) meat. Secondly, in a spontaneous fashion, these items are used to create unique "private museums"—or perhaps cabinets of practical curiosities. Thirdly, as stated above, this is simultaneously a magical attempt to participate in a world that has been closed to the collectors, and yet is so close by that it is impossible to ignore.

I would say that this is a certain manner of assimilating and representing reality, assembling a space and objects, giving the latter functions, significance, and interpretation. All behavior toward the external space—the KWB—is, as such, condensed into the material sphere. To describe these collections, I would, moreover, use the term *museum,* i.e., a place of objects/exhibitions and bearers of significance. I apply the term cautiously, however, as there are none of the tools and objects that once were practical, but have since ceased to serve their function, becoming mere "semiophores," or bearers of significance (Pomian 1990: 44–45), as in the average modern museum collection. These objects have found themselves midway between exhibition and practical item, shifting first to one side, then to the other. Nonetheless, I do intend to make use of the notion of the "museum," as, from an anthropological perspective, it contains the meaning of a unique record of a survived world, a space that reflects the structure of the world and the manner of its reception (Wieczorkiewicz 1996: 37–38). It is an institution that gathers objects and shuts them up. After all, the word *museum* derives from the idea of things "devoted to the Muses" (see Pomian 1990: 22–23), but it also gives them significance through the simple fact of having chosen them for collection. Therefore, I shall treat these gathered objects as a record of the world of the Szamów collectors.

As James Clifford has written (1988c), however, for any museum to be created, the collected world represented must have been made remote. This clear spatiotemporal distancing of things is my central motivation for applying this category. The basic rhetoric of the museum is, after all, a spatiotemporal "retraction," making an exhibition a journey through time and space. Generally, it legitimizes itself through little plates informing the visitor about the time when an object was made and the place in which it served a function (or its belonging to a particular cultural sphere). In the houses around Bełchatów this distance is spatial but also temporal, as the collected objects possess an evident distance from both the social and the economic. By "social distance" I am referring to a material distance, to an inability to participate in the institutions and companies that organize the local world. The owners of these collections are, after all, deprived of various forms of privilege, employment, and means of subsistence, at least in a relative sense—in comparison to the lifestyle in the wealthy Kleszczów municipality (the local yardstick of social exclusion).

Collectors Wacław Okoński and Józef Białas, as I have mentioned above, are forever stressing the ease and randomness with which they come across things; and by their testimony, finding objects is never the result of carefully planned searching. They stress that the rubbish tip has everything they need: wardrobes, armchairs, a good pair of shoes, and enamel pots. As I have mentioned, it is particularly the most interesting items, the mysterious ones, of whose existence they said only the mine authorities knew, that appear by accident, by a fortunate coincidence. And so, taking a shortcut on his way home, Wacław found a radiation meter lying beyond the rubbish tip; this was also how he found a steel cord with clamps protruding from under the rubble, as well as two coils of fuel rubber and sheets of good metal under a layer of coal dust. "It was all lying there and going to waste," he said, "they throw it all away. To solve your problems around here sometimes all you have to do is look down, and everything's there for you, everything comes out and shows itself" (TR/BŁ/9). Then the abandoned riches of the mine fall right into his hands, as Wacław said. Like his neighbors, Wacław and his wife wear work clothes stamped with the logos of the mine and its subsidiaries in the mine compound. The collectors also seek to possess more mysterious objects—"radiation meters," ordinary transformers, unidentified med-icines, and radioactive materials. As previously mentioned, this gives them (not without an accompanying pride) knowledge and power inac-cessible to others, i.e., the ordinary working population of the munici-pality (various "crimes" and "dark secrets" of the mine came to light on the rubbish tip). In their tales, and in Wacław's in particular, a myth of wampire-entrepreneur then appears. The medicines they find have been tested on the employees; their municipality is, in fact, a field for experi-ments where human immunity to contamination is being researched—though "no one knows all this is going on." They claim that this is why they come across various meters and pieces of equipment: "What's going on here is a secret experiment on a European scale," Wacław said while we searched through one of the internal rubbish tips (TR/BŁ/9). This creates an emotionalized image of the mine as an unnatural, diabolical economy of "excess," a corporation that flies in the face of all common sense. This message is therefore unusual, multiplied, and moreover, inaccessible to others. The things spirited away from the rubbish tip become trophies in the fullest sense of the word, sometimes occupying places of honor in homes. The tusks of a radioactive wild boar (that allegedly lived and foraged within the mine area) are kept behind the television set, allegedly "top secret" papers are stuck behind the calendar, and something meant to be a Geiger counter prototype (I was unable to ascertain precisely what this device was) stands propped against a shed wall. This brings us to the original meaning of collecting: it is collecting, museum, and hunting activities all rolled into one. "Look, these are my hunting grounds," said Wacław Okoński, indicating the spoil tip spiked with various machines. A moment later he told me where the scrap (a copper coil worth a fortune, and silver links embezzled and wasted by the mine, which he intended to go after in a few days) was buried underground. When setting out for a hunt, Wacław digs into the deepest history of the company, into a truth that still remains hidden. His trophies from these expeditions—the rubble he collects—end up in his home, as do the tusks of the boars that he actually hunts, and with which he feeds his family.

These objects—the junk and the trophies—make the inaccessible world of the mine present, though they do this in a special fashion, i.e., in the form of a museum. Here the history of gathering junk near Bełchatów runs parallel with the history of the modern museum. The history of the museum as an institution that satisfies certain needs began with a particular sort of collection: the cabinet of curiosities. These were private exhibitions that brought together all that was alien, unassimilated, and incomprehensible. It was only with the advent of the modern museum that space was designed for the objects and exhibitions to be placed into the sphere of a clear concept, presenting various forms of tools, variants on costumes, consecutive links in the chain of evolution, simultaneously constructing a linear, cause-and-effect narrative. This manner of presentation is tied to a typically European tradition going back to Plato, in which the removal of the representation from the object-in-itself functions as a negative value, or an obstacle. How, then, to walk this road from things to reality? This was the basic question for both the philosopher and the modern museum curator. From the seventeenth century onward, this question plagued European collections of art, artisan handcrafts, and oddities from overseas. At the same time, it seems remarkable that, precisely in the sixteenth and seventeenth centuries, when the New World, alongside other *terrae incognitae*—the Antilles, the Great Plains—appeared on the map, European salons of curiosities exploded everywhere. Collections and museums came about, gathering peculiar specimens of tropical flora and fauna and mysterious Indigenous fetishes (Clifford 1988c: 222, 226–229). Framed in the context of an exhibition and representation, it might seem that the world these things came from became a little less foreign and unsettling, and became one facet of a private, domesticated landscape. And yet, we know all too well that these "savage" objects lost none of their foreignness. In much the same way, the objects "hauled" home from the mine lose none of their foreignness, none of their link with the truth that Wacław is discovering. As such, the fundamental practice of the Bełchatów collection is not unlike that of the sixteenth- or seventeenth-century collections from the New World—a practice of assimilation, of incorporating an unincorporable foreignness.

The underlying structure of museums are characterized by multiple forms of distance. These include: the economic distance of those excluded from the formal, market economy; the historical distance of those excluded from history, or the distance of colonizers from a foreign culture. There are, therefore, moments in which the Bełchatów collectors discover that they are collecting histories and mysteries that have, in all likelihood, always existed. Even more, they discover that they are collectors of facts about which no one will ever ask them or show any interest. They are creating a language for the incomprehensible world of the mine and its affairs, which has shut its doors to them. In this sense, this is an amateur occupation.

While showing me around his collection, Wacław Okoński pointed out the radioactive tree stump that he had once brought into his garden, the husk of a "cobalt bomb" and the coils of electric cables. "My secret passion is actually archaeology," he once confessed (TR/BŁ/9). This makes him an amateur archaeologist. The mine and all its mysteries and privileges literally take their places in his home—on the walls, in the garden, in the shed outside. And yet, this collection signifies something entirely opposite. The flip side of this sudden transition, of this sudden access, is precisely his daily absence from the mine in Bełchatów, which he last visited over a year ago, from the municipality and its ideology of economic success, for over a period of a dozen years. The mine and all its mysteries and riches—again, we are speaking of the gathered junk, treasures, and trophies—is virtually present, within arm's reach, which means that it is utterly inaccessible.

* * *

In accumulating things around himself, Wacław also accumulates knowledge of the world, of the mine—in other words, he gathers in one place everything that allows him to become present, and which also allows him to *rule*. As I have attempted to show, there is, as such, a certain magical connection at work here; in possessing the "parts" (knowledge of "cobalt bombs"), Wacław tries to grasp the "whole" of knowledge about the mine. This whole/parts relationship allows him to exert a certain imagined control over it. In fact, he sees the mine as a source of great interest. Whenever I walked with him, he wanted to observe the latest changes, the new activities of the mine. He identified the new machines, the new workers; and judging by the discarded rubber, he was able to determine what protection they were using on the stackers. In short, Wacław constructs something resembling an "internal museum" of his knowledge of the mine with the objects he collects in his shed, his home, or his yard. In showing me, for example, used varnish and paint tins he had gathered from the KWB, he spoke of their virtues and their applications—alternately in the mine, and at home, around his farmstead. The result was a cabinet of curiosities, and he himself became an enthusiast and amateur of these oddities.

In describing European collectors of the sixteenth and seventeenth centuries, Krzysztof Pomian (1990) demonstrates that these were by and large amateur collectors whose collections were meant to satisfy their desire to materialize the world around them, and in particular, the world that was remote and not accessible in a direct way. Every cabinet was a "microcosm" of sorts, a "reduction of the universe" (ibid.: 67, 73); it contained all its oddities and curiosities, thus apparently exhausting the hermetic principle of diversity (ibid.: 64–70); in the cabinet of Master Borel one could find such things, for instance, as a "coconut shell tray, a Chinese porcelain cup and a very artistically designed … thermometer. Also many various musical instruments and … lovage powder." According to Pomian, this was a passion, an insatiable, cognitive desire—these collectors were people who "longed to know and to encounter everything" and thus, in the full sense of the word, they were amateurs, i.e., those who cherish learning, who adore knowledge even more than scholars (ibid.: 74–76).

This particular manner of "cherishing" and acquiring knowledge (through collecting objects) is thus an undeniable internal reflex. It is a state of desire, of yearning for a knowledge of the rules governing the world that is unknown to all others. In collecting, Pomian writes,

> instead of being content with knowledge of the ordinary and correct, one longs to gain knowledge of curiosities, searching out … rare, extraordinary and unusual objects that develop a privileged relationship with the whole, as they bring in additional information, without which a knowledge of the world as a whole, or its parts, would be no more than fragmentary. These objects are called *curieux,* as are those who are interested in them. The same applies to attempts to acquire knowledge

of things not only apparent and generally accessible, but also of those things that, for the majority, remain obscure ... as one attempts to claim the mysteries from others. ... This is also why these concealed affairs are called *curieuses,* and he who seeks to delve into them, a *curieux.* (ibid.: 76)

In delving into the spoil tips and the regions of the mine, Wacław Okoński behaved precisely like a *curieux,* searching for his bizarre objects and radiation meters, observing the clouds and the storms. He longed to know and to grasp the mine, to fit it into his head, into his yard, his shed, and his house.

Pomian shows us that this is the fundamental difference between the modern explorer/researcher and the collector, with his passion for knowledge—the former is in search of the regular and recurring, while the latter searches for the bizarre, the exceptional, the fantastic. This second approach is precisely a form of desire, a "blind curiosity," as it yearns for a sudden knowledge of the world's principles—sudden in that it comes from discovered objects. The predictable world manifests itself through typical, everyday things, while the mysterious world, the collector's world of curiosities, is filled with untamed forces and appears—as it must—through things that are secret and fantastical (ibid.: 66). The Szamów collectors gather everything that the mine discards, and it is from these objects that they gain their knowledge about it. They collect these things to use or to sell, and yet, with the passage of time, they begin to be accompanied by curiosity. Józef Białas is curious about what he will find, and proud of his findings—proud of his abilities and his resourcefulness. Wacław Okoński is fueled by an unquenchable curiosity, collecting all his peculiar objects and then later observing and analyzing them, building and reinforcing his imaginings. His collector neighbors, the impoverished farmers, behave in much the same fashion, constantly collecting objects and periodically rearranging them, finding various applications for them, and putting aside the odd find as particularly valuable. Okoński collects his "treasures" and "trophies," is forever planning and predicting the finds to come, and going where "something just might turn up" or "be found." "He who is swept up by curiosity," wrote Bernard Lamy in the seventeenth century, "that is, who madly desires knowledge, is incapable of conducting normal research. *He* [only] *constantly desires knowledge* [emphasis mine]" (Lamy quoted in ibid.).

The Work of Memory: Reconstructions, Objects, Collections

I shall return once more to the habit of collecting objects. The Szamów farmsteads bear testimony to a remarkable inventiveness. The yard of the Białas family is laid with rubber tiles from the mine, the same ones that Józef Białas uses to plaster his shed. With my own eyes I witnessed a grain sieve being made from a barrel and pieces of a transformer. The entire yards of the Białas and Okoński families are built from old objects and waste materials whose functions have been adapted. The objects my interlocutors possess are first and foremost designated for sale as raw materials (I witnessed the selling of copper, valves, pieces of sanitary equipment, and steel scrap), but there are also many that serve for labor, repairs, and reworking. With the use of a pump he made and designed himself from a washing machine motor, Wacław's cart could haul a ton, a fact he was fond of repeating. He claimed that with this cart he could easily and adeptly bring home large quantities of scrap, that the cart gave him the wherewithal to carry scrap home from the mine. This work as a tinker/repairman engenders a sense of the power to create. Wacław Okoński, Józef Białas, and the other collectors—the Grąds, the Gacans, and the Małkas—all rework parts of the mine, ascribing them new shapes and new applications. This building of machines vis-à-vis the great machines, stackers, cranes, diggers, and conveyor belts is a repetition of the mine's activities. Wacław's heater was, after all, built from the landing of a stacker ("st20" density, as he claimed); and his welder and "vacuum machine," and Józef Białas's collection of switches, his "spit/ umbrella" contraption, and his tractor are all inventions they themselves built. For this reason they become somewhat similar to builders. As Roch Sulima has written in his research on garden allotments, people shunted to the peripheries of great industrial structures sometimes crave to reproduce them, to replicate them on a microscale, and through this reproduction, they momentarily become artists (2000: 26). On a farmstead where this circulation of all conceivable materials takes place, an autonomous world could be created precisely through self-reliant creativity—which also occurred through the acts of "acquiring" and "reworking" objects. The world at the edge of the mine—a microcosm of the KWB, a cabinet of "all things"—has thus been reconstructed and recreated; it is an "internal museum" declaring the magical intention to "shrink the world" (Pomian 1990: 67, 73). These are more aptly called "museums of powerlessness" than "museums of power."

We would therefore say that this constant attempt to forge a comparison to a great structure (through miniaturization and reconstruction) is a way of constantly seeing oneself "in relation to." Wacław works as though he is forever grappling and wrestling with the existence of the mine's machinery and resources, as if wanting to function in its place, comparing himself, in whatever limited capacity, to its gigantic reconstructions. As he has said, "You see those counterweights, you see ... there used to be more of those ... they weigh eight hundred and twenty kilos, I brought it all home on my bicycle. … A bike with a trailer—now there's power for you! In one night I carted home a ton and a half, in a single night I was capable of carting home one and a half tones. … But this is my place" (TR/BŁ/27). With his bicycle and his cart he does indeed carry home enormous quantities of materials, whole tons of scrap, as the mine does hundreds and thousands of tons with its machines.

This use of waste on the edge of the Bełchatów exposed mine has another, less evident meaning. The practice of reworking objects and granting them new functions is, generally speaking, rather weakly represented in theoretical language, which prefers to make do with "set" notions. Here I have in mind the very changeability of the raw materials and objects brought home from the mine, or the "marketplace" (the word *marketplace* suggesting that the collectors gain things, knowledge, and a certain control over what transpires). This is visible in the yards: in Józef Białas's workshop/collection, for instance, all the objects are in a fetal, unfinished state. "I've got a welding iron," he said, giving me a tour, "and another welder over here … this thing [an industrial oil receptacle] used to be empty but I welded it up; over here I'm making a new workshop… Here, what's this, some cement rubber … I'll burn some of that. Over here I've got copper …, this stuff's raw.… That rubber doesn't stretch, but that one stretches, because it's been pressed, and then you've really got rubber … they use it to keep their brakes from flying apart.… I brought back, oh, now this … this is an 'S' motor … the strap used to pull a threshing machine … it pulled like the devil. Here's the angle iron, here's the bridge, it's been welded.… Anyone could do it … you can do it yourself" (TR/BŁ/13). Wacław speaks in similar fashion of his collections and homemade machines. The very act of reworking and reconstructing things acquires enormous importance here; analogously, the peasant farmsteads were continuously reprocessing materials, until they could no more (Sulima 2000: 47–48). This multifunctionality (Kocik 2000: 84–85), this application of an object in an entirely new and different manner, takes us to the very core of creating and using objects.

Zuzanna Grębecka (2006: 54-59) has written on such reconstruction of objects, and their adoption of the most astonishing functions. Among the pieces she presents are a pressure chamber used as a hen house in a Kolkhoz village farmstead, plastic bottles (PET) used to build a greenhouse or to decorate an iconostasis, and old refrigerators to mark boundaries or to fortify arable plots on steep land in Cyprus. According to Grębecka, these are testimonials to an inventiveness and to the multifunctionality of products in cultures "with high oral coefficients," cultures normally labeled "traditional" or "folk," held up in opposition to modern cultures. We might say, however, that this is a certain kind

of "being with objects" that goes beyond the industrialized, standardized network of people's coexistence with things (cf. Appadurai 1986a;
1986b; Sulima 2000: 29), beyond their specialized specifications, i.e.,
they have to be used in many different ways. Lévi-Strauss quotes a researcher who studied Hawaiian peoples as saying that the "utilization
of their natural assets was well-nigh complete—infinitely more so than
that of the present commercial era which ruthlessly exploits the few
things that are financially profitable for the time being" (1994: 3). Then,
too, new forms of being are shaped for objects—through their shifts as
signifiers/actions, they create an excess of potential space that must then
be filled. Lévi-Strauss (1994: 34) has written that the *bricoleur* (collector) is forever "interrogating objects," "picking out" their new forms and
applications. These interrogations are, to some degree, effective, though
the effectiveness of this practice of reworking and eternally recombin-
ing is not comparable with "technological" effectiveness. Nonetheless,
through their shifting and changing position, surroundings or context
(cf. Appadurai 1986), these objects begin to create new states of being—new forms of significance for their being and their relationship
with the user.

This manner of being with objects and things is a special productivity grounded in an unusual human/object (or human/handmade-thing)
relationship. This is a very intimate form of contact with things. Jacek
Olędzki (1991) has written that, much as he observed petrol barrels in
Africa that had been sliced with a machete and used to repair homes,
he encountered in a home on the Vistula River, in Murzynów, an even
more reconstructed object. "It involved laboriously joining a few dozen
pieces of scrap metal of various sizes with a welding iron. This so-called
barrel was meant to serve as something both unattainable and indispens-
able in the farmstead—a cooker" (ibid.: 254). In the yard of the Białas
family, there was precisely such an African cooker, welded together from
pieces of sheet metal Józef Białas had spirited home from the "marketplace," and secured at the top with a wire screen. Practically everything
in this yard became a potential material to work with—it could become
anything, and "everything could come in handy," as Lévi-Strauss said
of the *bricoleurs* (1994: 16–17). As Lucjan Kocik wrote in his book on
villagers' "ecology" (2000: 84), "everything was a *precious material* to be
used in a closed circulation, even before the notion of recycling came
about." In this type of culture the whole of the outside world is constantly being reworked into assimilated material, into a human element,
and every material is potentially of value; every object carries potential.
In a place of existence or subsistence, it is not just a profound strategy
for survival, it is also an unassimilated, almost precultural relationship

between humans and the world in which they live—with their own bodies, and with the object that is created or used. This may explain why the practices I have observed involve continually adapting scraps of the environment to human needs, going from industrial waste to useful objects and back again (often passing through the stage of momentary raw material).

These objects then acquire their potential fluidity, building ever-new relations with their surroundings, with the outside world, and a whole network of meanings and their active relationships shift along with them. They create successive transformational states, not necessarily in a physical sense, but primarily in a categorical sense, becoming waste/materials, waste/treasures, waste/rubbish, waste/elements-of-industrial-"nature"; and as such, they become "holes" in the network of cultural signifiers, of the cultural specifications of things. These are new, potential locations for objects, which, as Sulima has written (2000a: 29), require completion, play, or reconstruction. As he writes about objects in garden allotments, "objects search out their own location" (ibid.). And yet, what from the outside might appear to be "holes" in the network of cultural specifications for objects also constitutes, to my mind, a more intimate relationship between objects and the world. This is more like "regard[ing] my body ... as one of the objects of that world," to use Merleau-Ponty's phraseology, that is, remaining in contact with objects (constantly in potential activity) that contain all their possible applications (2002: 79–81). In the experience of collecting and then of constant reworking, objects then come to have a kind of dynamic relationship with the surroundings, a state of being vis-à-vis the environment—a "subjective universe." In this way objects internally remain open to new meanings and new uses, new applications, and "through this opening, the substantiality of the object slips away," as Merleau-Ponty (2002: 80) explains further (while their "natural uses," in accordance with typical function, become "overwhelmed by a foreign existence"; ibid.). A fixation thus occurs with objects in their "usual" natural functions, while under their unassuming exteriors they are "wild things" (cf. Attfield 2000) capable of constant transformation. This is being amid "transactional objects," to some degree a reiteration of Donald Winnicott's thesis on the manipulations of early childhood (1971; on "flourishes," see also Barthes 1965), an attempt to "speak" with the world and oneself not through words, but through wordless "squiggles." These are unique collectors' narratives. Here we reach a point where we find a nearly intangible, extralinguistic form of communication between collectors and their objects, the world, and consequently, with their own selves. These objects, their collection, and their reworking in the likeness of the mine, are the first fruits of recording oneself in the world—as I have already stated, it is an internal and spontaneous ecology. This occurs through the very fact of their accumulation, their collection according to various categories, their division, sorting, reworking, and spontaneous "extraction" from their previous contexts and applications. As Sulima phrased it: "objects are constantly speaking, and particularly when in new locations" (2000: 28). Collectors carry and show (themselves) the contents of their bags (i.e., their objects/goods), and by the same token, what has happened or what is happening. This makes for the appearance of a new transition, the creation of a fluctuating, actively signifying and, we might say, "speaking" combination. Then kitsch, fetishes, rarities, and miniatures take on the attributes of "internal condensations" of events in moments of transition, and also in the unstable time of memory/recollection (see Spyer 1998; also Stewart 1993; Sulima 2000). Each of these objects is also an "item" of mine memory and of its imagined future activities. Collectively, they create something that resembles a material record of the past, and also of the time yet to come.

As such, there is constant motion and fluctuation in these frameworks of objects and transactions between them; it is like a cabinet of the unconscious that combines the collecting of mine souvenirs/fetishes and their reworking, the reconstruction of these objects. In a sense, this is a way of recording memory. And yet, how are we to understand it? These hunting/gathering objects that have been sorted and reworked (i.e., they are multifunctional) are, as I have already stated, open-ended, bearing testimony to traveling consciousness. In a sense they are, therefore, tied to motion, creating the unguided, internal, "silent narrative" (Cardinal 2001: 25) of the collectors; the objects "respond in turn" (Pels 1998: 154), and are a kind of "ecstatic auto-ethnography" (Fabian quoted in Shelton 2001: 18). This movable cabinet—the workshop of Józef Białas, or the secret collections of Wacław Okoński—is, therefore, a certain material correlate of being in *one's own* world, a method of recalling various movements and references to reality.

Though Józef Białas is generally reticent and quiet, as he guided me around his collections he suddenly changed, becoming more loquacious and acting more freely. His every statement concerned what he was doing, what he had done, or what he had yet to do; not just the statement, but also the activity, the imagined act of reconstruction (giving objects new meanings) was also set in motion. In similar fashion, Wacław Okoński told me most of his stories of his mine expeditions while showing me materials and waste, the "secret objects." In this way the objects become a compendium of knowledge about oneself and the world, creating a sphere in which the "symbolic" (worldview/communication) and the "practical/applied" orders of material beings have not yet come apart, in which objects and meaning are one and the same "agency," though this is a state that is extraordinarily difficult to conceive (cf. Buchowski 1993: 38; Kmita 1985: 29; Pałubicka 1990: 133–140). This is therefore a collector's "memory of himself being externalized," as Susan Stewart has phrased it (quoted in Cardinal 2001: 23), or a collector's "extension of himself" (see Pearce 1995: 175–176). It provides a constant basis for a personal sense of capability, of creative power and of self-sufficiency, albeit—as we have seen—only in "miniature."

"The Science of the Concrete": Inscriptions, Journals, Enumeration

We might metaphorically say that these people are endlessly collecting the world, gathering it up into their hands, creating an internal cabinet of curiosities—a "shrunken universe." Such internal cabinets of "knowledge about the world," cabinets of memory, are sometimes created through writing, often accompanied by a collection of objects. One example of this is the chronicle writing and object collecting of Michał Więcko, the chronicler of Pomygacze (Sulima 1992b). Throughout his life, Więcko scrupulously noted down whatever he deemed crucial, noting the important and less important events, keeping a nonchronological chronicle and journal wrapped into one ("because I know how to write, I record everything"), pasting in photographs and newspaper articles and creating a personal collection. In much the same way, in the villages of Jałówka, Kaniuki, and Pasynki in the northern Podlaskie Voivodeship, there are still a few collectors who create their private "records of reality" (Kot 2006). They systematically record the state of the weather, the clouds, the atmosphere, wind, temperature, rainfall, and appearance of the sun, pasting photographs from family events, postcards, bits of gossip, and homemade figurines into the collection as well (one of these men, an older fellow from Jałówka, paints on everything he can find, including PVC tiles, bits of glass, and packing paper). In these practices we witness a certain yearning for materials and information, a need to make use of every type of material available, and to describe everything. We might add that this is typical for a certain kind of diary writing (Rodak 2004: 5–9; Sulima 1997; cf. also Zięba 2004)—some who keep journals write on whatever material is within reach: on packaging, labels, scrap paper, packing paper, and books. These collected materials, doubling as inscribed word/objects (information/objects concerning the weather, the quantity of purchased materials, local, and world events), are memory strategies and, as Sulima has written (1992b: 57), a particular way of grasping the world, albeit through magical metonymization, enumeration, and reduction. I would say, nonetheless, that this is less objectified and externalized writing than note taking, as an agency that follows memory and is a mnemonic technique that facilitates "being near objects," near the notes themselves, and finally, being near oneself. We might join Walter Ong (2002: 65) in calling these material centers of the act of "running out" toward objects and back again, reorganizing one's knowledge of their existence, a somatic component of memory, recalling events by repeating them in words and in counting off prayer beads, weaving string, threads ("text" derives from *textus,* i.e., "weave")— in the "activity of the hand." But how do these records proceed?

To present this in full, I must turn to one of Jacek Olędzki's (1991) field discoveries in writing about the old huts in the vicinity of Murzynów. He was particularly interested in the ribbing of the inner surfaces of the walls, which were covered with a clay coat. What astonished him was the "extraordinary precision with which the slats were affixed to the beams and the layout of stones or bits of brick, with the even regularity of decorative ornaments." Olędzki continues: "Naturally, given that this ribbing was to be covered with clay, they could have allowed themselves quite a bit of freedom or sloppiness in doing this work, which was, of course, ultimately invisible" (1991: 249). This is a very apt depiction of the attention given to objects, the way they serve as a framework for "memorable acts"—it shows both a manner of using things, and a way of remembering them (see also Sulima's remarks on children's garden allotment stencil ornaments, 2000: 31–32). My feeling is that this runs through daily activities, preventive management, collecting, reworking, and even through a certain *intimacy* with objects (to borrow a term from Piotr Szacki; cf. 2003: 175). This intimacy is also found when people write journals, which they often address as "Dear Diary" or "Dear Note-book" (Rodak 2004: 5–9), as these objects—the journals become in a sense practical, almost applied objects (ibid.)—serve to keep a unique memory. Such "memory objects" revealing a "knowledge of the world" might also include all kinds of practical household calendars, such as the peasant ideographic calendar from late nineteenth-century Cieszyn Silesia (Gładysz 1971), made of wooden boards with symbols recording knowledge of the weather and the passing of the seasons (the phases of the moon, seed time, etc.). I should also like to recall a similar find, whose origins went back to the Paleolithic era. Here I have in mind the stone calendar/notations with numerous "geometrical ornaments" described by a team of archaeologists that includes Alexander Marshack. These "ornaments" or "geometric engravings" were most probably, Olędzki writes (1999: 351–354), mnemonic markings, signs of maturity, initiation, the seasons, quantities, and animal behavior. As Olędzki demonstrates, here we see a special kind of relationship between humans and the things "within arm's reach," through miniaturization, through the fact that a thing fits in the palm of the hand, that it is equal parts geared toward the outside receiver and oneself, and is therefore very close and intimate: "In the small, even the tiny objects of which I speak," Olędzki writes, "we find the most deeply rooted ... creative inspiration ... , they are manifestations of profound internal needs that remain somewhat obscure—a memory of something or a signification of the presence of something, someone, or oneself" (ibid.: 353).

To my mind, the Szamów collectors' yards and sheds also fill the obscure function of "things in reach." They are, ultimately, a fairly intimate collection that serves to record and to create private significance, imaginings, a private knowledge. I could say that Józef Białas, for one, is a collector full of such hidden, silent passion for his objects and his capabilities; he collects an enormous quantity of refuse, searching the mine grounds, the "marketplace," and its outskirts on a daily basis. He claims that "they don't see me any more at the mine," "I've no more reason to go back to work there," and simultaneously: "Oh the scrap I can take home from there, shoes if I can find them, coats sometimes, I've also found oil paints" (TR/BŁ/13). In his sheds and under his provisional umbrella roofs he is forever taking apart junk, insulators, unscrewing discarded subcomponents, then setting them in a row, alongside one another on shelves; he remembers the story behind practically every one of them, including where he found it and what he is planning to do with it. At the time, my impression was that these gathered objects were a substitute for speech, a way of viewing the mine, and a way of seeing himself—that indeed, this was a form of "mute narrative." "Here's where I keep the transformers," he said, more to himself than to me, "they were there at the marketplace, just left to go to waste. They were lying there because nobody needed them.... But for me they come in handy" (TR/BŁ/13).

Wacław Okoński's yard, his shed in which he builds his tools, burns his rubber fuel, and dries his mushrooms, in which he invents his home-made devices and equipment and examines everything he brings home from the "marketplace," is also a collection that is always in reach; more-over, to some degree it is also his inner diary, a day planner/notebook, a place to vent his concerns. Wacław is constantly making surveys of the junk in his shed, constantly reworking it; one might say he is always rewriting it. I got the impression that there was an ever-closer relation-ship between collection and making memory "records," that these were message/objects kept, as it were, "in readiness"—as Roch Sulima (1997: 190) wrote of both peasant collections of objects and their written texts—or that the materialized "fragments," extracts, photographs, and objects "bore the memory of their most recent (previous) use" (ibid.:

196). This changeability of the material quality of the collection and its potential to record meaning are, at any rate, characteristics of keeping a journal, a day planner, a calendar, or a log book, as Paweł Rodak has shown; writing then takes on its own extraverbal, material dimension, it is "a kind of non-verbal communication" with the world and with oneself through the accumulated material (2004: 5–9); these are object letters to oneself (collecting and accumulating the inscribed pieces of paper, letters, photographs, and objects).

The result is an absorption of reality through objects, a replacement of "symbol objects" for whole "fields of reality" (Sulima 1997: 198). An instance of such a collection, where gathering things is simultaneously the gathering of a written journal, are these peasant journal/collections, log books, and diaries that double as collections of keepsakes, such as the collection of Tomasz Skorupka analyzed by Sulima. Here we find the strategy of collecting and materializing information, knowledge, objects, and keepsakes, as apart from the notebooks and the farmstead log books there are also family keepsakes, photographs, letters, etc. All these "items," "facts," and farmstead acquisitions are recorded there or "cataloged" in some fashion. As Skorupka himself notes, "It is good to make such juxtapositions" (ibid.: 176). This collecting "knowledge of the world" (cf. Frydryczak 2002) or "absorbing the world" (Zięba 2004) is also a recollection (it is the sphere of "private memory")—we might call it "memory inscription," while noting that it is inserted in writing and in the collection of objects at the same time.

Wacław Okoński puts his finds in even rows and segregates them—much like his neighbor, Józef Białas. At one point, thinking of his collections as records of his "knowledge" (or "memory"), I asked him directly, on his fiftieth birthday (over a bit of vodka with the family), if he wrote down what he did and collected; it turned out that he did. "All he does is write everything down," his wife said on that occasion, "he notes down everything we've got in the attic, Lord only knows what for, he keeps his notes in the shed somewhere, they've been mislaid somewhere, he used to write in the kids' notebooks when they'd finished going to school" (TR/BŁ/15). As it later turned out, he had been writing down almost everything that went on around him, and increasingly so, creating his own journal of entries, in all kinds of calendars, day planners, and in his children's schoolbooks. Wacław has been writing for many years, even back when serving in the army (letters and poems to his wife), and then later, when he served two several-month terms in prison, he became the "legal authority," and was known as the "writer," when he copied out articles of the penal code and also wrote out letters for the other prisoners—this may have been a very important piece of background for his "writing activities" (I know this part of his history only partially, based on his spontaneous recollections). The "diary" I received he began writing when he worked at the airport, and on the rubbish tip, where he was "boss." "I was a boss," he said, "and head of the airport. At that time I got a notebook and a day planner [inscribed with the Aviaeco Airline Company insignia] from the owner. And I began to write. Day after day, hour after hour" (TR/BŁ/15). Thereafter, he wrote "on everything"; he wrote when he lost one of his jobs, when he was taken on and then fired by the KWB, and he wrote on every day of his unemployment. He recorded everything by the date and the time, according to the rubric of the day planner, though later there were breaks, and his notes became less precise.

To my mind, Wacław's journals create another "art of memory." In broadest terms, they create his inner space for responding to the world; a temporary space, and in some mysterious fashion, a pragmatic one. They are one element of an ongoing need to grasp what is taking place around him, and then an attempt to capture it in letters, in digits, in records—as Jack Goody would have it; it is a primary attempt to de-contextualize (Goody 1984: 80–89; Ong 2002: 162–166). At present (2004–2005), these journals have somewhat slipped his mind; some of them got lost (the children's notebooks), and the ones that remain, which we looked at together several years after their writing, he had not opened for quite some time. "In the forest, struck and cut the rails," I read, and elsewhere: "A walk with Z. about the rubbish tips," "non and raw," "earned 25 zloty [on scrap]," "an animal came round in the morning," "for a kuroń [unemployment benefit—trans.]." Each time he searched his mind, trying to find the context and the significance of the event, explaining his entries, his brief jottings, the hours of work or the hours of drunkenness, or the quantity of wine consumed, the tally of bottles, his debts to be paid, and descriptions of work rendered and objects found.

In his day planner/diary he wrote the following (following the rubric):

9:00—"Non," 10:00—"Tidying the garden," 2:00—"Wine". On subsequent days: 10:30—"Z.—to the bailiff," 11:30—"Got my work certificate in the post," 4:00—"Bored," 8:00—"To Bełchatów for a kuroń.—took 197.20"; 9:00—"2 beers + 3 wines with Heniek + 1 wine at H's," 8:00—"At the marketplace—brought tiles," 3:30—"Out for a walk," 4:30—"Kilo non [nonferrous metal scrap]," 5:00—"Bugs [a captured hare]"; 7:00—"Bored," 4:30—"Kilo scara [scrap]; for a kuroń—was there [added later]," 11:00—"Paid what I owed at the shop."

The result of all this was an internal map of recurring everyday activities. We sometimes find descriptions of astonishing events, or of entire days. Sometimes they form chains of events:

> 9:00—"In the dump," 10:00—"With Joasia and Z.," 11:30—"Chej the yellow [pill?]," 3:00—"Borrowed 4 zloty off Barbara," 7:00—"A walk along the tracks. Kilo scara"; [the following day] 7:00—"Cooked break- fast with Zynta," 11:00—"With Zynta to the cow"; [the following day] 9:00—"7x Bugs."

Sometimes there was even a show of pride: "K. [Wacław's son] collected 82 kg. today," "At the marketplace with the sons. Boards and tiles." These last inscriptions are written more clearly than the others.

These notebooks are therefore a peculiar sort of "diary"—we see them more or less observe a kind of structure. We might hazard the state- ment that in jotting down his notes, he creates a provisional order, and through writing (its interiorization) he tries to structure the "scattered acts of existence," as Jean Hébrard has phrased it (1999: 20; quoted in Rodak 2004: 14); in other words, he tries to create a framework for (or the possibility of) "managing his knowledge," or indeed, for "managing his life" (ibid.).

And yet my impression was that precisely the reverse was happening. Like the collecting of objects/goods ("interagentive" parts of the mine) this record taking is not (only) a structure, or a way of creating rational "lists," "agendas," or "records." These entries are more of an attempt to rein in what is taking place all around, though not in a strictly writerly manner—in much the same way as the collecting, which draws all that is fantastical and peculiar (or irregular) from the world, and not what is typical and average. As such, Wacław's entries are not, I believe, a structured record, though this is how they might look at first. As Beate Frydryczak writes (citing Walter Benjamin), a collection is not a group of objects selected and put in order according to some pre-established plan—it is rather an amassment of what "speaks through objects" (Fry- dryczak 2002: 160; Zięba 2004: 59), a way of "speaking about one- self through objects" (Sulima 1997: 198). As such, Wacław records less the things that occur than what he collects and enumerates—what is "spoken" through these "things," or these inscriptions. It is therefore a matter of constantly noting, counting and recounting: "To Bełchatów (kilo scara). Brought 3 books and a few nuts [later inscription, with a different pen]—7 total," "2 wines with Zynta and Białas 7 wines be- tween us on the pond. 1 wine alone. 4 wines on my tab." The result is an accumulation, a summing-up of things and events, "passing" from dispersion to accumulation and back again (cf. Sommer 2003: 388). By this description, an inscription is more essentially chaotic—it is a redundant gesture that rebounds toward itself, and is only seemingly orderly (cf. Rodak's comments on the oral dimension of diary writing and its material nature, on record taking, 2004: 11); I would call it an accumulation and not a summary in terms of a syllogism, i.e., an equation, from the Greek *syllogismos,* and the verb *syllegein*—"reading together" (Sommer 2003: 402–403).

We might approach these inscriptions as hunter/gatherer "objects" with all of their internal "interagency" or "ontology," and we might follow Joanna Tokarska-Bakir's lead in speaking of a certain oral, "ontological" dimension; inscriptions are, after all, autographs in a sense, they are a real activity (1999a: 32–33). Tokarska-Bakir has written (ibid.: 30) about such redundant accumulated inscriptions—as concerns the pilgrims to Kalwaria Pacławska who count (inscribe) how many times they walk the paths of calvary, how many times they decide to make a trip there,[8] how many cups of tea they drink, in much the same spirit as Wacław's collections and notebooks—more of an accumulation of numbers than an actual counting: "I made 400 trips for a cup of tea, for a hunk of bread. The cook gives no hand-outs," "I did the P. pilgrimage 437 times, the Pacławska Kalwaria 4,000 times, I've got a certificate from Guardian Sroka 30 times, and they gave me a new Guardian.… I signed up 7 times.… I spent 4 days on the Assumption and now that I've been to the Assumption it makes 437 times." We must also make mention of other notes, similar in spite of their "secular" nature—the records kept by a young farmer from Opatów, a diary of sorts (a "Farming Journal") analyzed by Barbara Fatyga and Jadwiga Siemaszko (1989). This is another kind of ongoing "spontaneous calculation" of objects, an "enumeration" of events, as it were. The researchers claim that these notes are marked by a "book-keeping" quality—that they are a "roll call" of daily events (ibid.: 177, 181), "4 November, Wednesday … Daddy starting to plough by the beets. In the shop, bread—60.00, breakfast paper—3.20, notebook—4.50, toilet paper—3.50, altogether—71.20." "In the afternoon the *sołtys* [village administrator—trans.] started going to bring aid to flood victims in the Płock Voivodeship. Jan and I went by horse. We were given 35 kg wheat and 200 zl cash, then we downed 0.5 liter of vodka and we went to Lisów, drank 4 wine at Rumieński's." "Daddy and the rascal are going to Opatów for some sausage, Mum and I ploughed about half the soil by the beets. Daddy bought 0.5 kg of sausage—200 zl., 0.5 kg of blood sausage—100 zl., błony—250 zl. and a side of bacon—100 zl.—all together 650 zl." As in Wacław's notes, there was constant "book keeping" of quantities of alcohol consumed and a "record taking" of expenditures and goods exchanged or acquired—as materializations of "recalled activities": "In the evening we make a swap ... 15 packs of Popularnys for 33 eggs. Jurek buys 5 wines and that's how the evening goes by ... we drink 3." "The four of us went, they took 32 bottles from us. 30 wine bought, 20 drunk up." "The oats were pounded, the wreaths all finished, 5 wine drunk. In the evening a few beer with Sławek, then 4 beer in the bar" (Fatyga and Siemaszko 1989: 179).

Citing the research of Jack Goody, Walter Ong writes that lists, and the ability to create them, facilitate a certain liberation of content from the situational context, and consequently provide the opportunity to grasp reality in another, decontextualized manner (Ong 2002: 125–126; Goody 1984: 74–89). Jack Goody, in turn, demonstrates that this is basically when abstract categories are expressed, and the limits of logic become visible (ibid.: 81)—a framework of logocentric communication is created. Wacław Okoński, however, does something entirely different in his notes/collections. His journals and notebooks are, after all, collections created in a dispersed fashion, marked by a spontaneity. "He writes everything down," as his wife said, and indeed, he wrote down how much "raw" or "non" he had collected, how many "bugs" he had caught; he inscribed ("counted") expenses, "kuroniówkas," and his "lists-of events" were little more than an intermediate form of collection and were not a record that was regularly checked. I repeat, it was the very act of writing that was essential here, as well as that hunting/gathering, preliterate and preverbal "interagency" of material being (Ingold 1996a: 129), and its ontologization (Tokarska-Bakir 1997: 30).

This situation is the diametrical opposite of the birth of lists and writing, a process described by Goody (1984). As a result of a "civilization of writing"—represented through the rubric notebooks (day planners, records, journals), creating a whole internal cosmology of linearity and chronology (consecutiveness, "accountancy")—something entirely different emerged. Through the holes in this network of thinking in writing ("transfigured consciousness"), this mysterious communication full of spontaneous movement emerges in full clarity, created by lists of everyday life. In the place where he lives and "hunts," he creates another internal "science of the concrete," "transferable" knowledge (or "transferable texts"; Sulima 1997: 194–195) written on sheets of paper.

Hunters and Gatherers—Practitioners of Powerlessness

To portray how Szamów's unemployed citizens—Wacław Okoński and Józef Białas, their families, and to some extent, their neighbors both near and far (with whom they are constantly exchanging observations and skills)—function in the face of the mine, I must draw once more from the metaphor of the hunting/gathering, premagical/animistic existence. Nurit Bird-David (1999) presents the "way of being" and the "epistemology" of the Nayaka people of southern India as a typical hunter/gatherer existence, and as such, as an animistic, "lively" existence. She demonstrates that this is a certain practice of being in the world, in which the "I" is built from a network of relationships with other beings, which less leads to a mistaken drawing of conclusions, the creation of a "bastard sister of science," as Frazer once phrased it, than to a human existence in the world that plays itself out according to humans "being-in," i.e., their always remaining in a relationship with the "not-I," with what is on the outside. Bird-David, after Marylin Strathern (1988), introduces a special concept here, that of the "dividual," the individual in relation to other things, a being essentially oriented toward other beings—in contrast to the self-conscious, always-distinct "individual." The world for such a "being-in" is thus always created in relation to an event, in relation to the "not-I," and thus "enlivens itself" or "is enlivened." The Nayak gatherers see the world through their future and possible actions, through their involvement in the world; the trees, objects, land, the places they work and upon which they depend become, in my research language, cooperative and sympathetic. They create a network of relationships with the outside world, which the hunter/gatherers are perpetually recreating.

How Wacław Okoński and his household exist at the edge of the exposed mine is precisely, as I have suggested, such a permanent relationship with the KWB company, his "natural world." The places where he finds scrap and copper cables, where he waits out the company patrol guards in hiding, are a way of animating and mobilizing his relationship with the KWB, which is guarded from and closed to him; these resources are marked by the fantastical strategies of the mine, after all, and allow him to "rule" the terrain—he changes his observations and records into a substitute for action. His stores of goods and the mysterious objects located in a sudden fashion, later gathered in his shed, are fragments of his reign over the mine; as George Herbert Mead would phrase it, its "shaded actions" (a paraphrase of Mead's concept; see Ingold 1992: 50), or as Manfred Sommer would have it, a "purse with memories of actions and occurrences" (2003: 342).

This practice—both that of a hunter/gatherer and a collector—has a special and primordial bond with the "outer world," or in this case, with the inert and isolated universe of the KWB, with the environment transformed by the mine, full of spoil tips, canals, and equipment, the whole industrial "natural world." This is also a certain relationship with the foreignness and inaccessibility of the world of the mine and its riches, with the severance from the "human resources" of and labor in the mine, all of which is constant and, one might say, *felt* on a daily basis. It is also the Szamów collectors' relationship with everything that the above-described experience of industrialization has brought in its wake, i.e., the enormous changes, and at the same time, the causative alienation from the process of modernization and the isolation and exclusion that they, the unemployed and impoverished farmers and laborers, are left to experience on their low-yield farmland. "The forests are gone, along with the villages," I once heard from Wacław's wife, Bożena, "think how many villages there once were! All those heaps used to villages. Whoever had the chance sold his land … *and we're left behind, and we sit here in this poverty* [emphasis mine]." (TR/BŁ/14). We might also claim precisely the reverse: the "environment" in which these marginalized and impoverished farmers and ex-workers from Szamów function—with all the clouds and retreating storms, the sulphurous yellow rains, and the hidden destructive influences on their health and life—is nothing more than a testimony to the gatherers' subordination to the KWB ("shaded actions"). The destructive impact of the mine is, in this way, a conversion of the changes, both actually experienced and imagined, that have occurred since the creation of the mine, the changes in the nature, and at the same time, a rift in their sense of having a causative impact on the environment. As such, we might say that it is a conversion of their powerlessness in the face of the events, decisions, and plans adopted through the municipality or the mine, their real/imagined impotence: "What do they care about that sand!" Józef Białas once said about the heads of the mine/municipality. "What do they care about that sand?! Or all those heaps they've made! Now they've got work at the mine, what do they care about the sand?! Or the sulphur … they've got their own. … They bought themselves some new homes, garden allotments—courtesy of the mine … had their homes leveled to the ground, and the mine paid for barren earth!" (TR/BŁ/13). The land dried out by the mine is only a testimony to these influences—it is only a consequence of its existence, and this testimony "spills over" into many other possible sectors of experience, detaching itself from the physical reality visible in the perishing land, in the sulphurous ash. The result is a confirmation of the extant state of things—the mine/power plant working right next door.

This double manner of being and management—of actively taking from the mine and of being fully subordinate to it—creates the dynamic, enlivened (animated) character of this way of being in the world. People speak of the mine almost like a living creature, constantly using the pronoun *they* in their portrayals of the vampiric (in the sense of a social metaphor) organization that works to harm them and feeds on their injury. Postindustrial nature thus becomes an active subject, and the fetishized surroundings (of the primeval magic sort) characteristically transform into a "cognitive extrapolation," as Buchowski writes, "of imagined factors into real factors" (1993: 42). I should like to stress that these are not isolated imaginings, pantheons of "spirits" or "souls"—these are rather recalled social relationships with the outside world, the world it is their lot to inhabit. One example of such an unbroken relationship between people and the world is the Mbuti Pygmies, who treat the forest as someone/thing like an impersonal parent, a creature that bestows gifts and brings life (Bird-David 1992; cf. Ingold 1996a: 122–129). Nevertheless, further research and reflection on the hunter/gatherer method of "being in the environment" has indicated that this primarily recalls Ingold's interagency—the forest changes its appearance and significance depending on the context and the "recalled activity" (see also Ichikawa 1992; cf. Ingold 1996a: 151). Like the forest of the Mbuti or the Nayaka, the mine has become an animized sphere for the gatherers, the scrap collectors, and the poachers; the inhabitants of Szamów (and other villages) have given it a whole range of "beings" ("agencies"), sometimes friendly and subordinate, at other times hostile, adopting different kinds of significance. It "functions as" an incarnation of power whose goods can be assimilated, "collected," "hunted," and "mapped," or as a destructive universe that is purportedly ravaging the local population, changing "everything" all around; "everything collapsed into nothing," "they have their own cursed interests, so they don't watch anything they're doing," and "these are secret ['human'] experiments on a European scale."

In this way, Wacław "drags home" the very memory of having been in the mine along with the scrap he collects. All of his secret stores, all the places where he stalked the radioactive wild boars and where there once were "cobalt bombs" find their extension in the junk that fills his home, summer shed, and yard. As I have demonstrated, he treats the pieces he acquired as trophies. "The boundary between collection and fetishism," as Susan Stewart has written (1984: 163), "is mediated by classification and display in tension with *accumulation and secrecy* [emphasis mine]." Thus, he hauls home the collected rubble and the mysterious objects, and recreates the closed world of the mine, creating a sense of participation. "You see that crane," he said, "I made it myself. ... I renovated it entirely, I know it like the back of my hand" (TR/BŁ/27). On another occasion, he said, "With my professional knowledge I'm on the mine list ... they could hire me at any moment, but only on call. ... The diggers and stackers are my thing ... the work I do. I've been marked down there, in the mine, permanently, that I can get in there, I've always got the right to go in. ... And for another thing, I know almost all the watchmen" (BEŁCH 2). The objects—like shaded "influences" and "actions"—frame the collectors' narrative, less representing the mine than allowing it to finally function in the lives of the collectors, and allowing them to function in it. Objects in unstable spaces, objects that "cross boundaries," thus undergo a special animation, creating something like "border fetishisms": they became hybrid, composite entities comprising heterogeneous elements, contexts, and meanings, and thus bring us to a denial of "proper distinctions" that the things are to establish (Spyer 1998: 7–8). In this sense Wacław was forever reading them, time and again, and was constantly reacquainting himself with their hybrid, unstable meaning, more creating or recreating their mine existence than drawing its image from them. In this way, these objects, fetishes, and curiosities take on a significance that is not precisely theirs, but is more an active and functioning significance *within* the object (see Pels 1998: 94–95, 107), the memory of action, as it were (collecting refuse within the KWB). We might join collection philosopher Manfred Sommer in concluding that Wacław "takes in, understands, "grasps" what he sees and hears, but also what he feels and does. He stores it somewhere and carries it with him. At home he shows his loved ones what he has brought; the edible contents of his bag, or the narrative contents of his memory" (Sommer 2003: 335; Ingold also comments on experience and "physiological stimuli" collected "in reverse"; 1996a: 128).

Wacław keeps his secret objects in hiding, in his home, and above all in his hidden stashes/storage places. As he said, "I've got all the most important things there. ... I don't keep my real treasures here, as you know. ... I just go there and I've got everything I need ..., I've got everything within arm's reach" (TR/BŁ/25). In this (magical) manner Wacław exerts a certain power over the KWB, and by the same token, over his own life: "When I haven't got a penny to my name ... I've got nothing to eat ... then I know where to go. ... I go there and I've got as much as I want ... three, four hundred kilos. ... I've got those places, and so then there's money" (TR/BŁ/25). In this way, he changes his everyday problems, his constant debts, his lack of money, his quarrels about unpaid bills ("At the moment I've got maybe eight hundred zloty in debts ... for bread alone. For bread alone I'm eight hundred zloty in the hole. My son paid the electricity bill yesterday. ... He was saving that money for something else, as well" [TR/BŁ/23]) into the stores of goods that are awaiting for him, which can ensure him "a couple hundred zloty cash" at any moment and sort out his ever-present debts ("This is my stash, you can't see it from here. ... I'm all set for hard times. ... I could earn five hundred zloty ... if something should happen. ... I just have to go up that hill" [TR/BŁ/27]). Living among his hunting/gathering sites, objects, trophies, and curiosities, Wacław exercises power over the mine and over his own situation as well; in this way he creates an animized universe and affects it, recalling every one of his actions, uncovering and mastering the mine's arcana; he is, as it were, a depositor of its mysteries. As a collector, Wacław affects the mine in much the same way as it affects him. In a sense he faces the absolute reality of the internal states and external events that transpire. In this way, the mine covers a vast area in his private history, rooted in daily discoveries, in daily explorations, in recalling (or imagining) his mining/conservation abilities ("Back then I worked for a company. ... I worked as a professional, the mine called me specifically to come work for them ... but the mine only hired me from a company ... the mine paid twelve zloty an hour for me, and the company paid me 3.40" [BEŁCH 2]). In times of unemployment, of hunting wild boars and collecting scrap, Wacław exerts his power over his surroundings through his objects and his excursions—as he himself puts it, he is a "hunter." In this situation of evident marginalization he has created an agency subordinate to him—people (the authorities and their mysteries, the watchmen), places (the internal topography), objects (fetishes and trophies), and animals (wild boars)—and with all of them he struggles, seemingly trying to seize power, in the most magical sense of the word.

The mine therefore stays in the hands of the collector; it stays in his household, albeit in the form of a heater made from the platforms of stacker machines and radiation "meters." This leads to a specifically magical bond—to an internal relationship between a man and a neighboring company. Wacław has covered the mine with his fantasies to the utter limits; this is something like an imaginary omnipotence, or, in Freudian terms, the "omnipotence of thoughts" (2005: 88). Freud defines the omnipotence of thoughts as the state of one of his patients, a certain "highly intelligent" neurotic (ibid.: 88) named Daniel Schreber, whose thoughts were accompanied by curiously real correlates in the physical space; when he spoke of someone new, however, it seemed to him that his thoughts brought to life his own image, that he stood there alive in front of himself. For Freud, Schreber was thus not unlike the "savage," who "imagines he can change the outside world merely by thinking" (ibid.: 90). We might therefore state that the animism of the "savage" or the neurotic is, according to the psychoanalyst, a childish act, in which a person is incapable of fulfilling his desires (e.g., to stretch his hand out far), and thus gives orders or invents curses that are extraordinarily real, and are even somatic "imitations" of the fulfilled desires (ibid.: 87). Mapping out his hunting grounds and planning the dispersal of his resources, Wacław similarly creates oddly real replications of his desires. He is a "hunter"—as he put it, "I always have the right to come in here … everyone here knows me, I've got stamped papers" (BEŁCH 2). His thoughts are always filled with mysterious and secret knowledge, which is then confirmed on the outside, in all the discarded equipment.

"Magic" is, in its traditional understanding, a practice of unreal actions upon the outside world, an "overestimation of mental acts," as it was in Freud's writings (2011), or a casting of a spell on the outer reality—in Frazer's texts, these are attempts to extract rain and fertility through letting blood from the veins in the elbow, "piercing of the hut" and "ploughing the rain" (Frazer 1993: 64–66, 70), or young people wallowing in the furrows of dried earth (Niewiadomski 1999). I would say, however, that the exact reverse is the case—thoughts of the Szamów hunter/gatherer world are not, after all, omnipotent; their only necessary condition is their most internal experience, their constant dependency on the surroundings. This magic is thus the omnipotence of thoughts in the sense that the world *cannot* succumb to change; in this world, as in the child's, the subject's capabilities do not allow them to acquire the things he or she desires (and therefore they are replaced by a curiously real hallucination filled with emotional tension). Józef Białas's and Wacław Okoński's capabilities are unable to "reach" the mine authorities, i.e., its foremen and overseers. My conclusion is that these thoughts and magical objects are nothing less than a source and experience not of omnipotence, but of precisely the opposite—they are an experience of their powerlessness against the world surrounding them. In this sense we might say that the hunter/gatherer omnipotence is curiously real. In exploring the mysterious regions of the mine and speaking about the deposits of scrap in the spoil tips, Wacław knows "how the things of the world are, which is to say how he himself felt them to be" (Freud 2005: 93). Exploring the interior of the rubbish tip, the rubble of machines, and his own lumber room, he makes use of all of his knowledge about the world and himself; and outside himself he finds his own "internal processes."

In this internal hunting/gathering landscape humans have no omnipotent impact on their surroundings. This is essentially a practice of powerlessness, a constant state of living with no real causative power over the environment (which Wacław is forever extracting from himself). This practice defines the essence of this manner of being in the world. The Szamów collectors grasp at everything they find, gathering up the scrap, rubber, plastic moulds, boards, and scaffolding, and upon this they base their survival, they build their fantasies, discoveries, emotions, and all their experience of the life of gathering objects in postindustrial grounds. The Białas family lines their barn, right up to the rafters, with rubber tiles hauled home from the mine, and in this way they stay in permanent contact with it. My impression is that their world, much like the whole world of Wacław Okoński, takes on the most bizarre kinds of significance. The connections and dissolutions of his daily desires (to paraphrase Freud; cf. ibid.: 94) appear with a likeness to the neurotic Schreber's "divine rays." Wacław's collecting explorations are thus everywhere his curiosity and desire to know can reach, where he finds his "mysterious devices" and constructs his "extraordinarily useful tools." They are everywhere that he can follow the movements of the stackers and the conveyor belts; first he dreams them up, then unearths them, with the omniscience of the mine.

Notes

1. The mineworkers received this book, known in the mine offices simply as the "Monograph," as a sign of gratitude for their many years of work. Both the book and the miner's home wherein it resides in a special place of display are spoken of with enormous gravity.

2. We might say in summary that the wonders and oddities of the *orbis exterior* occur as part of the daily routine in folk/isolated consciousness cultures (Zając 2004: 26–27; cf. Tokarska-Bakir 2000). The power plant/mine was always depicted in such a double or "split" fashion: as a place that was entirely unintelligible, and therefore uninteresting, but also extraordinary, terrifying, or fantastical. Though it may be rather bizarre in our modern conditions, even that which was unassimilated and terrifying was part of an everyday, ordinary experience. This fantastical quality in the Belchatów stories of meteorological phenomena is more related to the distortions of the academic language. The researchers themselves named the "supernatural," but it is an element of everyday existence in the peasant preindustrial cultures, a sphere that both is and is not worthy of attention. On the supernatural in folk cultures, Paweł Zając writes, "Not only did this group of phenomena fail to appear as supernatural, but it ought to be supposed that, in the villagers' consciousness, it *was also deprived of the extraordinary* [emphasis mine]" (2004: 27). At the same time, those who spoke of the sulphur rain and the strange clouds over the exposed mine did not treat these phenomena as "fantastical inventions" or "freaks of nature." Some said that "the area's profited, and that's that," while others said that "there's sulphur flying everywhere from out of the sky"; and though this is sometimes the cause for quarrel, the issue of logical argumentation takes a back seat here. Quite crucially, these complaints about the sulphur falling everywhere are often accompanied by a kind of "jesting argument." It turns out that some of my interlocutors had differing opinions, and thought that the "sulphur" was no more than an effect of the pines' pollination (the yellow sediment being pollen gathering at the edges of the puddles). "Everyone talks about sulphur this, sulphur that … but they don't think, they don't understand, they're too busy shouting, and you have to stop and wonder. … Maybe it's just the pines pollinating in the spring? But they just want to have it their way … [the words of a candidate for the local office]." In similar fashion, Józef Białas ex-

plained to his daughter-in-law, who complained constantly about the yellow puddles and about how "we always have to breathe it all in," that it was the pines pollinating. In these conversations meteorological events were treated as odd phenomena about which people bickered and quarreled, yet this was a random narrative full of impromptu imaginings, since these statements paid no heed to objective or official indicators of environmental damage.

We must also concede that the spoil tips and waste heaps have indeed been planted with dwarf pines, which can pollinate in the spring. This phenomenon does, however, stand as a widespread argument of sorts, a kind of disputed knowledge that divides various social groups. The director of the Brown Coal Mine's Environmental Protection Division entertained no doubts as to the fictitiousness of the "sulphur," while at the Regional Starost Environmental Protection and Water Conservation Bureau, my question released a real hailstorm. After a few official statements and demonstrations of charts (which were illegible and did not measure such factors as pollution), a heated discussion ensued among the office workers, wherein half confirmed that the pines were pollinating, and the other half maintained that "sulphur was coming from the sky." I had the impression that, at times, the mine and the environment were indifferent subjects of local conversation, in the same way as one speaks of the weather. Yet at other times they became a sphere of "local knowledge" that was a part of daily discussion, a kind of communication game (TR/BŁ/2).

3. "One glass before we hit the scaffolding," they often said at People's Republic construction sites.

4. Goethe's *Faust* trilogy became a particularly inspiring model of the catastrophe of modernization ("the tragedy of development," to quote Berman 1983), as noted by Daniel Bell (1996), Marshall Berman (1983), and then Agata Bielik-Robson (2004). As Berman demonstrates (1983: 66–67), Faust is a figure of the constant builder and modernizer, working day and night without concern for the toll it will take; in the final part of the trilogy, he works to dry out the sea, digging deep canals in the earth. The sacrifice he makes concerns a pair of layabouts ("people in the way"—the aged Philemon and Baucis), who die as a result of Faust and his plans. Faust initially pays no mind to this, but after, he is quite unable to forgive himself. His belief in ongoing change transforms into an obsession combining with his guilt, with death, and with accidents, his faith turns into its reverse; the consequence, as Berman demonstrates, is a general image of the modern experience of the might of modernization.

5. The goods were "discovered" abruptly, all at once, with a sense of "sudden abundance": "I gathered the plants. I had them, and there was primrose! We gathered them up, they paid by the kilo; I could even … it was growing up over here … and behind the stable! I collected a hundred kilos, and that paid for the next four months" (TR/BŁ/9). "Willow gets you ten for a bundle. … And it grows the best right where I live" (TR/BŁ/19).

6. Iconostases are a sacred part of the Orthodox church / Old Belivers temple. It is a wall, separating the main nave from sanctuary, filled with icons and devotional paintings.

7. According to my interlocutors, all the villagers at some time heated their homes with rubber, though now, only a few "burn rubber," and the rest complain of the smoke it produces. The neighbors burn rubber, as do the residents of the "dale," though they claim that this is only sometimes, when they cannot get a good fire going (TR/BŁ/12). Social workers and some district functionaries (interview with caretaker) are also well-acquainted with this somewhat vanishing heating method. As one resident said, "There's less and less rubber around—it used to come out of the woodwork.

People even used it for binding livestock, they burned it, everything was fine." We can see clearly here the extent to which this practice was assimilated, or at least, the conviction that this fuel was nothing out of the ordinary.

8. Kalwaria Pacławska is a popular pilgrimage site with a big calvary and miraculous image of the Blessed Virgin Mary.

Figure 1. The Mine/Power Station—orbis exterior

Figure 2. "Reduction of the universe"

Figure 3. "Storehouses of goods"

Figure 4. Workshops, collections, curiosities

Figure 5. "Eking out"

Figure 6. Collection, transformation, transience

Figure 7. Machine/power

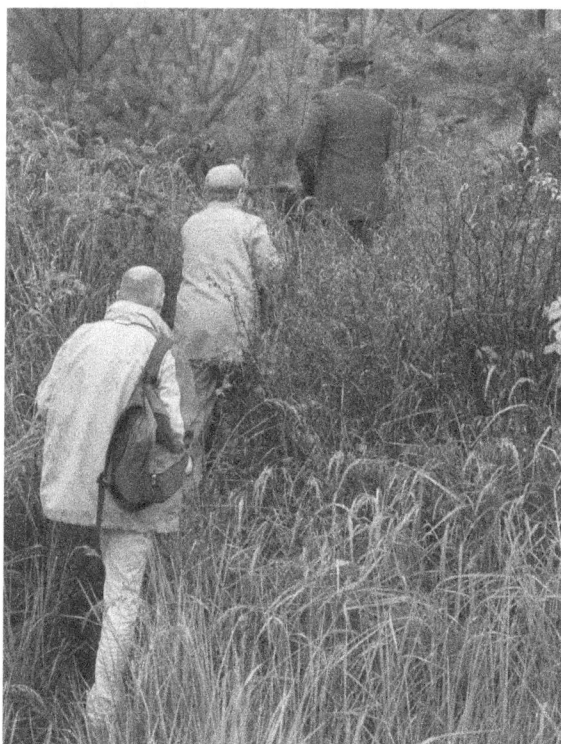

Figure 8. "Look here ... this is where I set traps ..."

Conclusion

The "Reality Testing"

What can really be written on the culture of the degraded, who have lived through the liquidation of their workplace and experienced the tragedy of unemployment, but who, like the people of Bełchatów, have also been neighbors to sudden progress? How to speak of them? As we have seen, the descriptions of the reality I encountered and the very processes of creating "paths of ethnography" lead down three different routes. At any rate, my "path" for discovering the invisible current of individual behavior, activities, impulses, and the collectively built narratives has run a different course. These three spheres demonstrate various methods of surviving events that occurred at practically the same time, i.e., stories of the liquidation of a previously assimilated reality, of an institutionalized or internalized space of work, and of everyday life and functioning in a reality marked by political and socioeconomic transformation.

In the villages of the Świętokrzyskie Foothills this situation led to the rebirth of a deeply rooted self-sufficient village economy. Further expressions of powerlessness and new methods of functioning arose from these bad changes, from the descent of very widespread unemployment and from the transparency of what was happening. "New ecologies" were created, which made their way into private households and the surroundings "within reach." The unemployed villages thus created a form of functioning by reflexively closing themselves within a "culture of survival." This involved a vague dependency on external events, but also required a certain omnipotent power—as a proper "state of the world."

Meanwhile, in Wałbrzych, Boguszów-Gorce, and Lubsko, in ex-German lands, the end of industrial labor and the sudden expendability of miners and industrial workers have been experienced differently. This situation has prompted a sense of aggression toward what was occurring all around. It is a silent attempt to respond to the question, "How have things become what they are?" The suspended sphere of practical being in the world has begun to be recreated—being "for oneself," outside the previous standardization of life in the industrial People's Republic town. A whole new sphere of activity has emerged, facilitating the creation of new "technologies," new competencies, and, at the same time, a new sphere of "freed" or "mobilized" material existences and their socially created forms. The dire experience of losing legal work and of long-term poverty has also had its effect on modes of coexistence among neighbors. New ways of thinking and imagining have also been born, turning the daily experience of degradation into images of hidden wonders, creating ever-new transformations of reality.

Other "methods of human life" have evolved on the edges of the Bełchatów exposed mine. This is tied to changes in the local labor market of the 1990s, but also, and above all, to the experience of abrupt modernization, which has excluded the society in question from the local development processes. For the farming/worker families described (the majority of whom had been unemployed for several years), their way of life and farming on the edge of the mine gives them a certain sense of influence. It also provides a kind of multiplied activity, i.e., of collecting and managing waste, and of an imagined "stalking" in the local environment (the mine area), to call their own. The result is a hidden internal circulation of content and perception of the mine, and of "making use of" or "recognizing" it.

These three descriptions are not, of course, "full" monographs of degraded societies, nor is this a "full" description of the social reality with all its strictures, or any kind of general outline. My research has revealed wider processes at work, such as the imagined suspension of the cost of living (perhaps associated with a "backlash" against the modernizing migration from villages to cities). However, in the majority of cases, I was dealing more with the anthropological significance located in human activities, in ways of speaking and in mutual and covert networks of cooperation. These anthropological studies, therefore, provide only an outline of some general cultural-economic phenomena, such as the enclosure of and focus upon the space of the household, or drawing upon and relying on the immediate *oikos*. Yet, more objective ("externalized") analyses only "shine through" from time to time. Where they are subordinate to a description of some kind, they are only an initial step, a diagnosis that requires further research.

Time and again, however, I have made an effort to proceed to another level of analysis, to another manner of "seeing." As I have said, this is an attempt to catch a glimpse of the "internal cultural world of human beings," a delicate world that takes place under the surface of the most ordinary activities, and as such, as Merleau-Ponty has written, a world that is "practically imperceptible." This is, therefore, more a question of "learning" to see, a kind of looking that is spread out over time, an ongoing attempt—backed by phenomenological methodology—to descend to the level of details, things, bodies, mundane statements, and so forth. This method's certain "instability" does not merely result from the research limitations themselves (time, cognitive capabilities), but also from the perspective for observing reality that we have adopted—learning meanings of cultural expressions that are very difficult to notice.

At this juncture, however, we ought to return to researching the human being experiencing degradation. Our research is an effort to face this reality as esstentially incomprehensible, which is why anthropology is, in this case, reduced to an "attempt to describe," a manner of cooperation. It is a path through the world of the degraded human being, with a growing ability to perceive and to render some kind of meaning—less to make certain processes comprehensible, than to adopt the aspect of a reality unto itself, a "private reality." The internal space of other people's behavior is not, after all, immediately accessible, or even directly isolable.

The present anthropological method is, to reiterate, an "attempt to describe"—it is an effort to render a certain cognitive process. By its "ethnographer's paths" it approaches some very dramatic forms of response to the transformation of the world, the loss of stable work, and established ways of socioeconomic functioning. After all, the experience of poverty encompasses even the least perceptible spheres of life, including emotions, behavior, and moods—as well as the subject's feelings toward him or herself. As such, this path is always wide open, filled with difficult and unfamiliar experiences that are often difficult to grasp, and which are often a cause of mutual misunderstandings—on the part of the anthropologist and of the research subjects. Again, this is only a sort of "visit," a temporary process that always retains a residuum of incomprehensibility. However, this is when a very real dimension of these people's activities is revealed: their "methods of using the body," their methods of reshaping matter and drawing new social significance from it. What follows is a shift to the more interior activities of the subjects—to something that remains largely unarticulated. My analyses and descriptions, following the model of a "patron of this ethnography," are grounded in the primeval almost physiological level of creating feelings, meanings, and ultimately, whole social imaginaries.

In this research this principally entailed the feeling of helplessness in the face of events taking place. This experience was also accompanied by a social "muteness," a refusal to communicate and a "silent" response to what was occurring all around (and around the subject as well). In a certain sense this is an analysis of the experience of social powerlessness, with considerable similarities to Robert Merton's findings in researching workers in circumstances where the "outside world"—and their own fates—were fully unpredictable (1996: 202–203). As Merton writes, with reference to E. Wight Bakke's *The Unemployed Man* (1934), the consequence is an incapability to understand the premises of social functioning, a loss of the "significance" of social events and a submission to fate, to the "tides of fortune." Additionally, there follow attempts to take at least temporary control over the world, i.e., something over which they possess no control (Merton mentions a proclivity for gambling and "counting games" under such circumstances, which is reminiscent of the constant "counting" I have analyzed).

Similarly, the experiences of the ex-miners, diggers, scrap collectors, the unemployed, and the impoverished farmers demonstrated that, in their case, there has been a loss of social knowledge of reality, of all the cultural "supports" (ontologies) and social sense of "what is real." Then, as I have attempted to show, the "internal increase" of the subjects became augmented. In terms of imagination, recollection, and even practical action, there was a peculiar recreation of knowledge of reality—we might say it was created anew. For many ex-miners, diggers in the bootleg mines, for the poverty-stricken farmers of the vicinity of the Bełchatów KWB, and for the unemployed peasant workers from the Szydłowiec area, this was, therefore, a moment in which questions were regularly asked in their silent language. As in mourning, this was a moment of intensive exploration of reality, a situation in which one and the same path was traveled, from imagined destruction and degradation to sudden "excess," "riches," and hunting/gathering "effectiveness" and "capability". On this level of constructing social knowledge about oneself, in this situation wherein the world is constantly being reconceived (with coexisting reflexes of weakness and powerlessness), there does appear a "critical moment." This is a moment in which it remains unclear what these people should think of themselves in this situation where the world is being constantly reconceived, and where what exists is forever open for negotiation.

I believe that this is also a key point in our thinking about these people's experience. Degraded individuals are forever negotiating with the things all around them, with "how things really are"; they function, communicate, and close themselves off inside their cultural reflexes, constantly exploring "what reality is like." In this sense these ex-miners, impoverished farmers from the Świętokrzyskie Foothills, and the "hunters and gatherers" from the edge of the KWB exposed mine are extraordinarily dynamic subjects. At the very moment when they lost their work, they swiftly fell into poverty. At the moment of their powerlessness in the face of what was happening, these ways of life and reflexes, this management, aggression, and auto-aggression, these delusions and imaginings, the "objects' second lives," all became of exceptional importance, the source of the most vital cultural expression. Then, too, this whole sphere took on enormous value, and became a worthy subject of examination, study, and anthropological description.

Outcome

This manner of presenting the world of the degraded gives social significance to all sorts of statements, evaluations, and complaints; they become fully fledged modes of expression. To my mind, however, the issue of discourse in socially marginalized societies that are excluded from economic development is also at stake here. As noted previously, this discourse contains a closed network of concepts (Dean and Taylor-Gooby 1992) by which these groups are defined—using terms such as "professional passivity," "resignation," and "learned helplessness"—as lacking the skills to exist in society, and to some degree, socially handicapped or "flawed." Through the imperative to rebuild "social competence," to "activate," and to "function," this perspective reveals the previous assumptions of the incapability of the described groups to perform their internal means of functioning and denies them their own cultural resources, their grassroots modernization mechanisms (see, among others, Hobart 1993: 1–12). These groups thus become "*residua* of the system."

Yet the problem remains that the people in these environments devote themselves to their surroundings. They view themselves as subjects of resourcefulness and of certain skills, of particular attention (though this transpires in a fashion that is not entirely visible and is, in many respects, contrary to social mainstream expectations). A popular educational slogan in Wałbrzych was "Bootleg mines are not a business." Typically, a social group qualifies to receive aid from social programs (such as the European Social Fund) if it demonstrates a degree of helplessness/passivity in its activities and a "flawed" approach to business. It must maintain minimal economic (and indeed, social and cultural) activity, break or loosen social ties, and retreat from life in society. The result is the widely known image of the exclusion of a social group that possesses insufficient sociocultural resources—or more accurately, an insufficient sociocultural life—combined with passivity in both life and profession;

this image makes use of black-and-white categories (cf. Buchowski 2003: 114–119). Social programs, e.g., ESF programs, are meant to address an economic, social, and cultural vacuum—a society that needs only to be "activated."

However, from my perspective (that of a cultural anthropologist), something entirely different is revealed. My research indicates that the world in which the unemployed, the gatherers, and the diggers of the bootleg mines functions is not filled with cognitive reluctance, with a "renounced universe" of sorts. Even more, it is in no way stripped of "culture," i.e., it was not an "unpatterned social existence." What takes place there almost always does so on the basis of an internal, practically reflexive cultural knowledge, which leads to the creation of new meanings, conversions, cultural transformations, and an intensive exploration of reality. The very reduction in the cost of living, the creation of an imagined self-sufficiency, becomes an "art" of sorts, providing a mutual sense of resourcefulness. Ways of reducing the cost of living are a central point of social interest, a main topic of conversation. The ex-miners in Wałbrzych call this dialogue "bootleg mine know-how" (knowledge passed on by word of mouth and mythologized). It consists of stories, mythologies, jokes, secret tricks of the trade, and so forth. They create a "hidden transcript" (Scott 1990), a "second social existence" full of resourcefulness targeted *against* the external circumstances, against the dominant structure. Meanwhile, it is precisely this sphere of social life that is entirely invisible in the standard discourse and assumptions concerning the assistance of degraded environments. With regard to current and "proper" social development, to the perspectives of "mainstream society," building business culture, and a "knowledge-based" society, etc., it is this internal sphere of "existing within a culture" that becomes entirely invisible, or imperceptible.

First of all, therefore, what is generally recognized as a sign of resignation or cultural "inertia" is often an important social act, the activity of people who are remote or different. Agnieszka Golczyńska-Grondas (2004: 177) writes—perhaps more from the perspective of "mainstream society" (though with a "dose of irony")—that degraded peoples and inhabitants of enclaves of poverty, to some extent "precursors of transformations, ... are pioneers of 'non-work' existences." And later: "The 'non-standard' aspect of the subjects' biographies draws our attention— these people have 'freed themselves' from the influence of most institutions." My research reveals something even more, however; something that I would call an element of "inner courage," particularly evident in my most intimate conversations in Boguszów-Gorce and in Szamów. This "courage" is in precisely that moment when, faced with their own degradation and their own poverty, stripped of all work and of all future institutionalization, they make the attempt with all their might to function in a world without a mine. Furthermore, they try to rein in this whole world of illusions, fears, and accusations, and the feeling of their own powerlessness, their own lack of greater purpose. This is an attempt to develop their "knowledge of the world" all over again, from scratch.

Therefore, we might say that this kind of anthropology is a particular brand of involvement. Being involved in the problems of these societies requires, to some extent, *relinquishing* action—as defined by the reigning spirit of values in our dominant culture—that would appear to assist the people, groups, and cultures being researched. For the most frequent responses to these "actions that assist" are an "internal" manifestation of shame, inadequacy, and a sense of personal incompetence. It is very easy to be persuaded as well that, from their (our interlocutors') point of view, this "second social existence," this stabilizing and neutralizing sense of the superfluity of the sphere of informal "resourcefulness," was negated or regarded as nonexistent, shameful, and improper from the very outset. At this point, the energy within them (we might even say a peculiar ethos, including the manual sense of the word, a multifunctionality of skills, invention, an "art of resistance") began to function silently, somewhere on the margins, awaiting a substantial outlet, which was, perhaps, precisely what occurred. Along with the great wave of emigration to the British Isles and the countries of the European Union, tens of thousands of the unemployed suddenly turned out to be inexplicably equipped with professional skills, necessary, full of forethought, a fact causing no little confusion in our local institutions.

Beyond Anthropology

In its simplest terms, I see the "anthropological inspection of poverty" as the study of the irrevocable presence of the impoverished and degraded human being. Lost jobs give rise to a swift increase in poverty, questions of self-worth, and a deep sense of powerlessness toward the reigning circumstances. "Ways of being," management, reflexes, aggression and auto-aggression, delusions, imaginings, and the "second life of objects" remain of the utmost importance and, such as they are, existing, or at least 'perceptible'. Then, too, this whole sphere acquires enormous value and thus becomes worth exploring and distinguishing.

This is not accompanied by a notion of "repairing" or "transforming" this reality, nor does it allow us to tackle this world through some formula, as though it were predictable or structured. This reality can be explored insofar as those being researched have a way of surviving their situation, as was the case with Wacław Okoński's creation of his "cabinet of curiosities" or the "hunters and gatherers". In much the same way, the erasure of the positive and socially desired meaning of culture in Wałbrzych and in Bogoszów have made the veil disappear, to be replaced with a new manner of cultural existence. This is a communal and mutually communicated attempt to communicate with "the outside," a confrontation that causes no little suffering. And so what is emerging, the things I have come across there, is in all events a "way of being," and, in accordance with a more primary notion of "culture," a way of "cultivating" what is all around. This is a sort of reflexive and very intimate action toward what lies "outside," a certain silent way of "speaking"—to oneself inclusive.

One may well ask, however: how might one come to know, or to perceive, this "way of being"? As I have suggested, this is not knowledge created parallel to the research process, with the process of doing fieldwork, of taking notes and writing. It would be hard to say with certainty if an ethnographic fiction is created in this way, or just as easily, a fiction of ethnography itself (see Clifford 1988b: 80). The problem is that this is precisely the case—it is merely a temporary inspection of misery and poverty in concrete surroundings, and a certain "closed" description that came about during this time. Yet the path I traveled did come to an end—and the lives of these people continue going their way.

Meaning is the first thing to be created in this manner, and then fictions (texts), sources of cultural knowledge of degraded societies, somewhere in the space between my interlocutors and myself. These initial "shifting of the fields," of being in the world (through the body, objects, behavior, language), provide the opportunity for proper observation and analyses, and for recreating contexts of events. However, these fictions, the creation of descriptions, "dressing up" others in my way of seeing, also facilitate *my own* way of seeing and hearing what is happening; they allow for temporality and impromptu randomness, for "time-economy" (Johaness Fabian) in my own research. As Clifford Geertz has written (2001: 37), "Fieldwork is an educational experience all around." The fieldwork I have attempted to perform is nonetheless marked by the partiality of the research process. Thus, the whole process of researching or "discovering" unknown cultures is, above all, one that takes place within a certain framework of time, related to a somewhat arbitrary research path and research activity. Consequently, this is also a process I am responsible for as an ethnographer, for indeed, this may just be the most sensible argument for the creation of ethnographic fiction and the fiction of ethnography. In an above-mentioned lecture ("Ethnography and Memory"), Johannes Fabian (2004) stressed that anthropologists take "full responsibility" upon themselves, not only for the materials collected during the course of the research, but also for their memory.

In this manner, ethnographic fiction becomes the result of having traveled a certain road—from assumptions and from the unexplored field of research to the knowledge that is acquired along the road. This is also, however, what I would call a "burdensome fiction," from which the ethnographer never fully escapes. I do believe, after all, that ethnography is a very serious art of interpretation, precisely because it does not leave a reality "untouched," "uninterpreted"; it takes up a challenge, and then, too, the whole weight of the responsibility for what emerges falls upon the writer.

* * *

This does not mean that "miracles"—i.e., research moments when there is no way to say anything—do not occur; and then, as Joanna Tokarska-Bakir puts it (1995: 17), reality triumphs over what comes from ethnographic depiction. During my research there were occasions when all the branches of meaning in what I saw dispersed like a fog, and then I forgot my own anthropological language. There was one occasion when Andrzej Pietrzyk, one of the kindlier diggers of Boguszów-Gorce, a splendid advisor and contributor to many steps of my research, invited me for a brief morning chat in his cramped, overcrowded flat. He had been digging all night, and in the morning, a part of the shaft had collapsed, which meant that he and the others had had to dig once more, at first through layers of snow. When he returned home, his spine hurt badly. When I came to see him, however, he was doing his best to be animated, witty, chuckling—as he had been on every other day of my research. At that time I realized anew that, while the ethnographer ultimately leaves his place of research, the reality carries on further, unabated; and here we have a very characteristic attribute of ethnographic fiction. There arrives a certain point when it is "closed." Meanwhile, in all the places where my research was conducted, things "keep carrying on."

The majority of the diggers who were my closest interlocutors resigned from working in the bootleg mines in 2006; in later months, only their sons remained to dig. Both they and their parents made unsuccessful attempts to emigrate to Germany, unsuccessful because, in their own words, they had too many problems with "the formalities." Similarly, Wacław Okoński's sons from the Bełchatów spoil tip began traveling to London to work. One of them sent his sister some lovely lily-white slippers, which she showed me with particular pride. In the villages near Szydłowiec, on the other hand, many more people began gathering herbs, though the earnings from this activity were constantly on the decrease. I heard more complaints on this count.

In July and August 2006 the overall job market situation began to change as well—unemployment finally began to drop dramatically. From over 20 percent (in the previous years), the unemployment rate began a swift dive, arriving at just over 15 percent. At present, it is still going down. This is largely due to the European market's absorption of the excess of job seekers, and in particular to an excess of employment opportunities created in Poland. "Unemployment Will Fall" (2006: 21) proclaimed a national newspaper, *Gazeta Wyborcza*, and then a few weeks later: "There's Work in Poland" (2006: 22).

* * *

In this way, history wrote its own epilogue, and one that few anticipated at the time. Over the course of only two years (2006–2007) the vast gulf created by unemployment to a large degree evaporated, becoming a distant memory. When I met with my closest interlocutors (guides) in 2007, I found that their situation and life in the nearby vicinity had changed almost beyond recognition. In the Wałbrzych area in 2007 one saw notices like, "Worker needed for immediate employment." Right next door in Kamienna Góra, hung on the wooden pallet factory, a giant sign read, "Now hiring on contract—good wages guaranteed"; and the ex-miners told me that there was "more than enough work around."

Andrzej Pietrzyk greeted me with an embrace, telling me that his rights to miner's pension for his injured spine had been reinstated. His son had received work in a coke plant. Andrzej was helping to renovate his neighbor's flat, and I could see that he was calmer and more self-assured.

When I managed to get to Wacław Okoński's farmstead a few months later, I realized after only a moment that the mine had hired him for regular work six months previous. Sitting in his hut by his homemade heater, I held an unbelievable thing in my hand—a mine employee ID badge with his name and photograph, which bore the inscription: "Front mining machines and equipment mechanic."

Appendix

Materials Used for This Research

TR/PŚ/1–47: Author's interviews and field notes, collected in the environs of Przysucha and Szydłowiec, from 2002–2006.

OST 1–12: Students' interviews and notes, acquired during the anthropological workshops guided by the author at the Warsaw University Polish Culture Institute in Ostałówek, near Szydłowiec, from 2005–2006.

TR/LB/1–10: Author's interviews and field notes, gathered from villages near Lublin, during an anthropological laboratory guided by Wojciech Pieniążek at the Warsaw University Institute of Ethnology and Cultural Anthropology, from 1995–1997.

TR/WB/1–43: Author's interviews and field notes, collected in Wałbrzych, Boguszów-Gorce, and their environs, from 2002–2005.

TR/LUB/1–6: Author's interviews and field notes from field research in Lubsko, conducted in September 2003.

WAŁB 1–27: Students' interviews and notes, acquired during the anthropological workshops guided by the author at the Warsaw University Polish Culture Institute in Wałbrzych and Boguszów-Gorce, from 2004–2005.

TR/BŁ/1–39: Author's interviews and field notes, gathered in the environs of the Bełchatów Brown Coal Mine, from 2002–2005.

BEŁCH 1–13: Students' interviews and notes, acquired during the anthropological laboratory guided by the author at the Warsaw University Institute of Ethnology and Cultural Anthropology in the environs of the Bełchatów Brown Coal Mine, from 2002–2004.

TR/Ż/1–5: Author's interviews and field notes from Żyrardów, September 2004.

TR/PR/1–5: Author's interviews and field notes from the Pruszków vicinity, May 2004.

TR/MN /1–6: Author's interviews and field notes from the Podlachia districts of Michałowo and Narew, 2003–2005.

The Szydłowiec and Przysucha Environs: Interviews, Field Notes

TR/PS/1: 32-year-old unemployed woman, gatherer of herbs and undergrowth fruit, Budki, July 2004.

TR/PS/2: 6 unemployed men, Ostałówek, August 2005.

TR/PS/3: 45-year-old woman supporting herself and four children through welfare, July 2004.

TR/PS/4: 60-something-year-old man, pensioner, Borki, May 2004.

TR/PS/5: 70-something-year-old man, retiree, Huta, May 2004.

TR/PS/6: Unemployed siblings in their 30s, picking up odd jobs, Zaława, May 2004.

TR/PS/7: Private fruit depot worker, around 45 years old, Ostałów, August 2004.

TR/PS/8: Social Aid Center worker, Szydłowiec environs, July 2004.

TR/PS/9: Mother, around 35 years old, supporting herself and nine children on welfare, gathering, and her husband's sporadic work, Gosań, May 2004.

TR/PS/10: Pensioners, two men, around 65 and 70 years old, Niekłań, May 2004.

TR/PS/11: Two unemployed men, around 30 and 34 years old, Niekłań, May 2004.

TR/PS/12: Herb gatherer, retired professional cook, around 65 years old, Zaława, July 2004.

TR/PS/13: Farmers, retirees, around 70 years old, Pawłów, August 2003.

TR/PS/14: Pensioner, farmer, around 70 years old, Skłoby, May 2004.

TR/PS/15: Retiree (early retirement), around 55 years old, Aleksandrów, July 2004.

TR/PS/16: Unemployed man, 48 years old, sporadically working, Ostałówek, July 2004.

TR/PS/17: Six unemployed men, Majdanki, July 2004.

TR/PS/18: Woman, 42 years old, Majdanki, August 2004.

TR/PS/19: Women, undergrowth berry gatherers, Borki, July 2004.

TR/PS/20: Farmer, professional driver, 40 years old, Ostałówek, October.

TR/PS/21: 38-year-old unemployed herb gatherer, two children, Cukrówka, October 2005.

TR/PS/22: Retiree, farmer, 62 years old, and a pensioner, 30 years old, Zaława.

TR/PS/23: Unemployed married couple, woman 40 years old, man 48 years old, Zaława, October 2005.

TR/PŚ/24: Farmer, professional driver, 40 years old, Ostałówek, October 2005.

TR/PŚ/25: Unemployed, herb gatherer, 30 years old, Cukrówka, October 2005.

TR/PŚ/26: Three men, two unemployed and a pensioner, Cukrówka, October 2005.

TR/PŚ/27: Herb gatherer, retired professional cook, around 65 years old, Zaława, October 2005.

TR/PŚ/28: Pensioner, farmer, around 70 years old, Zaława, October 2005.

TR/PŚ/29: Unemployed, social services client, two children, Mechlin, August 2005.

TR/PŚ/30: Retiree, around 70 years old, pine branch gatherer, July 2005.

TR/PŚ/31–32: Unemployed pine branch gatherers, 21, 40, and 56 years old, Stoczki, July 2005.

TR/PŚ/33: Retiree, farmer, 80 years old, Chlewiska/Zaława, October 2005.

TR/PŚ/34: Retirees, around 70 to 75 years old, Cukrówka, October 2005.

TR/PŚ/36: Retiree, farmer, around 70 years old, Smogorzów, September 2002.

TR/PŚ/37: Unemployed man, 48 years old, Lipno, September 2002.

TR/PŚ/38: Farmer, around 50 years old, Smogorzów, September 2002.

TR/PŚ/39: Retirees, farmers, 61 and 78 years old, Zawada, September 2002.

TR/PŚ/40: Bachelor, around 35 years old, working odd jobs, Ostałówek, August 2005.

TR/PŚ/44: Social Aid Center workers, Szydłowiec environs, July 2004.

TR/PŚ/47: Married couple, farmers, 35 to 40 years old, Mechlin, July 2005.

OST 1: Farmer, around 60 years old, Ostałówek, October 2005.

OST 2: Farmer, around 40 years old, Ostałówek, October 2005.

OST 3: Farmers, two men, Ostałówek, October 2005.

OST 4: Farmer, musician, 78 years old, Ostałówek, October 2005.

OST 5: Farmers, married couple, Ostałów, October 2005.

OST 6: Two retired farmers, Ostałówek, October 2005.

OST 7: Two inhabitants of Ostałów, April 2006.

OST 9–12: Several days of conversation with inhabitants of Ostałów, April 2006.

(speakers: W. Plińska, T. Pisarzewski, M. Laskowska, M. Mshlak, M. Wachowska)

Wałbrzych, Boguszów-Gorce, Lubsko: Interviews, Field Notes

TR/WB/1: Environment Protection Bureau employee, 40 years old, in Wałbrzych, June 2003.

TR/WB/2: Three diggers, former miners, 23, 35, 36 years old, bootleg mines, Wałbrzych, Sobięcin, June 2003.

TR/WB/3: Three diggers, former miners, 19, 43, 46 years old, bootleg mines, Sztygarska Street area, June 2003.

TR/WB/4: Four diggers, former miners, 23, 38, 39, 42 years old, bootleg mines, Sztygarska Street area, June 2003.

TR/WB/5: Three diggers, 18, 23, 30 years old, bootleg mines, Sztygarska Street area, June 2003.

TR/WB/6: Waste collector, 40 years old, communal rubbish tip, Wałbrzych, Sobięcin, June 2003.

TR/WB/7: Waste collectors, 45 and 50 years old, communal rubbish tip, June 2003.

TR/WB/8: Three diggers, former miners, 36, 43, 46 years old, bootleg mines, Sztygarska Street area, June 2003.

TR/WB/9: Scrap collector, pensioner, around 65 years old, Sztygarska Street area.

TR/WB/10: Three diggers, 24, 30, 40 years old, Sztygarska Street area, October 2003.

TR/WB/11: Scrap collector, 40 years old, Wałbrzych, Sobięcin, October 2003.

TR/WB/12: Conversation with three diggers, former miners, including Andrzej Pietrzyk, July 2004.

TR/WB/13: Large family (ten children), Boguszów, an unemployed scrap collector, July 2004.

TR/WB/14: Diggers (father, 50 years old, and sons, 20, 23, 24 years old), bootleg mines, Biały Kamień, February 2004.

TR/WB/15: Coal transporters ("Żuk"),former miners, around 50 years old, Sztygarska Street area, February 2004.

TR/WB/16: Five diggers (including three former miners), from 20 to 50 years old, bootleg mines, Sztygarska Street area.

TR/WB/17: Four diggers, around 20 to 25 years old, and one former miner (father of three diggers), around 55 years old, bootleg mines, Sztygarska Street area, February 2004.

TR/WB/18: Four diggers, from 30 to 40 years old, bootleg mines, July 2004.

TR/WB/19: Basket maker, former miner, 58 years old, Wałbrzych, Sobięcin, July 2004.

TR/WB/20: Scrap collectors, retirees, around 65 and 70 years old, Biały Kamień, July 2004.

TR/WB/21: 3 diggers, men, around 40 years old, bootleg mines, Biały Kamień, July 2004.

TR/WB/22: Father and son diggers, 60 and 28 years old, bootleg mines, Biały Kamień, July 2004.

TR/WB/23: All day conversations with diggers (including Andrzej Pietrzyk, bootleg mines, Boguszów-Gorce, July 2004.

TR/WB/24: Zbigniew Krycki, digger, former miner, and his wife, Krystyna, digger's flat in Boguszów-Gorce, December 2004.

TR/WB/25: All day conversations with diggers (including Andrzej Pietrzyk), bootleg mines, Boguszów-Gorce, July 2004.

TR/WB/27: Diggers (including Andrzej Pietrzyk), bootleg mines, Boguszów-Gorce, December 2004.

TR/WB/28: Scrap collector, former coke plant worker, around 40 years old, July 2004.

TR/WB/29: All day conversations with family of Bogdan Zawadzki, coke-maker, family flat in Boguszów.

TR/WB/30: Andrzej Pietrzyk, flat in a building, Boguszów, December 2005.

TR/WB/31: Diggers, including Andrzej Pietrzyk, bootleg mines, Sztygarska Street area, March 2005.

TR/WB/32: Unemployed digger, 28 years old, building, Boguszów, March 2005.

TR/WB/33: Zbigniew Krycki, social meeting, Boguszów, December 2004.

TR/WB/34: Andrzej Pietrzyk's family, building, Boguszów, March 2005.

TR/WB/35: Zbigniew Krycki, digger, former miner, and his wife, Krystyna, tenement flat, in Boguszów-Gorce, March 2005.

TR/WB/37: Conversation with the former directors of Wałbrzych's mines, July 2004.

TR/WB/40: Visit of a few hours with coke-maker Bogdan Zawadzki, the Victoria Coke Plant, December 2004.

TR/WB/42: Diggers, Andrzej Pietrzyk and Zbigniew Krycki's team, bootleg mines, March 2005.

TR/WB/43: Diggers, four former miners, from 40 to 60 years old, Wałbrzych, Sobięcin, February 2004.

TR/LUB/1: Retiree, Lubsko, September 2003.

TR/LUB/2: Brick collectors, men, around 40 years old, Lubsko, September 2003.

TR/LUB/3: Director, Social Aid Center, Lubsko, September 2003.

TR/LUB/4: Brick and scrap collectors, former Luwena Factory workers, around 40 years old, Lubsko, September 2003.

TR/LUB/5: Unemployed brick and scrap collectors, Lubsko, September 2003.

TR/LUB/6: Retired married couple, Lubsko, September 2003.

WAŁB 1: Scrap collector, Wałbrzych, Sobięcin, December 2004.

WAŁB 2: Diggers, bootleg mines, December 2004.

WAŁB 3–4: Diggers, bootleg mines, December 2004.

WAŁB 7: Second-hand shop, Wałbrzych, March 2005.

WAŁB 8: Scrap collectors, Victoria fields, December 2004.

WAŁB 10: Diggers, bootleg mines, December 2004.

WAŁB 11: Precious metals and scrap depot, Wałbrzych, December 2004.

WAŁB 12: Conversation with a collector, December 2004 (interviewers: M. Leszczyński, O. Wiśniewska).

WAŁB 6: Diggers, bootleg mines, Wałbrzych, Sobięcin, December 2004.

WAŁB 13: Bootleg mines, Wałbrzych, Sobięcin, December 2004.

WAŁB 16: Former miners, other inhabitants of Boguszów-Gorce, December 2006.

WAŁB 17: Former miners, Boguszów-Gorce, December 2004.

WAŁB 18: Youths, Boguszów-Gorce, December 2004.

WAŁB 19: Interview with a former miner, Boguszów-Gorce, December 2004 (interviewers: K. Mogilnicka, W. Plińska).

WAŁB 20: Diggers, bootleg mines, December 2004 (interviewer: Z. Zalewska).

WAŁB 22: Former miners, Wałbrzych, Sobięcin, December 2004.

WAŁB 23: Conversation with the former directors of Wałbrzych's mines, March 2005 (interviewers: P. Wrocławska, Z. Mioduszewska).

WAŁB 24: Conversations over several days with Zbigniew Krycki's family, digger's flat, Boguszów-Gorce, and interviews: city patrol, police, city hall, Boguszów-Gorce, December 2004.

WAŁB 25: Conversations over several days with Zbigniew Krycki's family, digger's flat, Boguszów-Gorce, March 2005 (interviewer: E. Zubelewicz).

WAŁB 26: Diggers, bootleg mines, December 2004, March 2005 (interviewer: A. Szanciło).

WAŁB 14: Diggers, bootleg mines, from field notes, December 2004.

WAŁB 15: Youths, Boguszów-Gorce, December 2004.

WAŁB 27: Diggers, bootleg mines, from field notes, December 2004.

Environs of the Bełchatów Brown Coal Mine:
Interviews, Field Notes

TR/BŁ/1: Conversation with an Environment Protection Division worker, Bełchatów Brown Coal Mine, April 2003.

TR/BŁ/2: Conversation with workers at the Regional Starost in Bełchatów.

TR/BŁ/3: Farmer, tinsmith, Kamień, April 2003.

TR/BŁ/4: Unemployed, 55 years old, Trząs/Janów, April 2003.

TR/BŁ/5: Unemployed, former farmer, around 40 years old, Rogowiec, April 2003.

TR/BŁ/6: Married couple, unemployed after moving from Bełchatów, Rogowiec, April 2003.

TR/BŁ/7: Białas family, Szamów, April 2003.

TR/BŁ/8: Conversation with Wacław Okoński, spoil tip, April 2003.

TR/BŁ/9: Conversation with Wacław Okoński, November 2003.

TR/BŁ/10: Retired former farmer, 65 years old; son, 45 years old, does the odd renovation job, Trząs, April 2003.

TR/BŁ/11: Unemployed married couple, large family (9 children), Janów, April 2003.

TR/BŁ/12: Unemployed married couple, two children, Szamów, May 2004.

TR/BŁ/13: Conversations with Józef Białas, October 2003.

TR/BŁ/14: Several-day conversations with Wacław Okoński, October 2003.

TR/BŁ/15: Several-day conversations with Wacław Okoński, March 2004.

TR/BŁ/16: Stay in Wacław Okoński's home, October 2004.

TR/BŁ//17: Unemployed former farmer, and her son, Szamów, October 2004.

TR/BŁ/18: Four farmers, men, around 40 to 50 years old, Łękińsko, August 2004.

TR/BŁ/19: Conversations with Wacław Okoński, October 2004.

TR/BŁ/20: Conversations with Rodziną Białasów, October 2004.

TR/BŁ/21: Unemployed retired son, Szamów, October 2004.

TR/BŁ/22: Farmer, 60 years old, Szamów, October 2004.

TR/BŁ/23: Conversations with Wacław Okoński, April 2004.

TR/BŁ/24: Conversations with the Białas family, April 2004.

TR/BŁ/25: Conversations with Wacław Okoński, April 2004.

TR/BŁ/26: Conversations with the Białas family, June 2004.

TR/BŁ/27: Conversations with Wacław Okoński, during a several-hour journey to the Bełchatów Brown Coal Mine, June 2004.

TR/BŁ/29: Pensioner, stoker at the Bełchatów Hospital, around 60 years old, May 2003.

TR/BŁ/39: Social Aid Center workers, Bełchatów area, June 2004.

BEŁCH 2: Conversation with Wacław Okoński, April 2003.

BEŁCH 4: Male farmer, 60 years old, Zarzecze, near Bełchatów, November 2002.

BEŁCH 5: 45-year-old resident of Bełchatów, November 2002 (interviewers: A. Dudzińska, K. Zawisza).

BEŁCH 6–8: Residents of Bełchatów, May 2003 (interviewer: J. Prus).

BEŁCH 9: Retired miner, Słok, November 2002.

BEŁCH 10: Miners, Łękawa, November 2002 (interviewer: M. Plichta).

BEŁCH 1: Unemployed married couple, Szamów, November 2002.

BEŁCH 3: Pensioner, former Bełchatów Brown Coal Mine worker, Kleszczów, November 2002.

BEŁCH 11: Inhabitant of Bełchatów, November 2002.

BEŁCH 12: Retired farmer, Szamów, November 2002.

BEŁCH 13: Resident of Bełchatów, November 2002 (interviewer: J. Wierzbicka).

In the majority of cases the names of my interlocutors have been changed. One of the place names has also been changed.

Bibliography

Adorno, Theodor, and Max Horkheimer. 1997. *Dialectic of Enlightenment*. New York: Continuum.

Alexander, Jeffrey C. 2004. "Toward a Theory of Cultural Trauma." In J. C. Alexander, Neil Smelser, and Piotr Sztompka (eds.), *Cultural Trauma and Collective Identity*. Berkeley, Los Angeles, and London: University of California Press.

Alexander, Jeffrey C., Neil Smelser, and Piotr Sztompka (eds.). 2004. *Cultural Trauma and Collective Identity*. Berkeley, Los Angeles, and London: University of California Press.

Aponte, Robert. 1990. "Definition of the Underclass. A Critical Analysis." In H. Gans (ed.), *Sociology in America*. Newbury Park, CA: Sage.

Appadurai, Arjun. 1986a. "Introduction: Commodities and the Politics of Value." In A. Appadurai (ed.), *The Social Life of Things: Commodities in Cultural Perspective*. Cambridge: Cambridge University Press.

——— (ed.). 1986b. *The Social Life of Things: Commodities in Cultural Perspective*. Cambridge: Cambridge University Press.

Aristotle. 2010. *Politics: A Treatise on Government*. Timeless Classics Books.

Arnold, Lois, and Gloria Babiker. 1997. *The Language of Injury: Comprehending Self-Mutilation*. Leicester: Wiley-Blackwell Press.

Attfield, Judy. 2000. *Wild Things: The Material Culture of Everyday Life*. Oxford and New York: Berg.

Babbie, Earl. 2009. *The Practice of Social Research*. Belmont, CA: Wadsworth Publishing.

Bajburin, A. K. 1990. "W sprawie opisu struktury słowiańskiego rytuału budowniczego," *Konteksty. Polska Sztuka Ludowa* 3.

Bąk, Natalia. 2006. "'Jak Indiańce w rezerwacie'. Ujawnianie się oikosu mieszkańców okolic Puszczy Białowieskiej na tle konfliktu o poszerzenie Parku Narodowego." Laboratory work prepared under my guidance, computer printout at the Warsaw University Institute of Ethnology and Cultural Anthropology.

Bąk, Natalia, and Monika Kamińska. 2005. "Las chroniony, las zamknięty," *Opcit* 3/4.

Bakke, Edward W. 1934. *The Unemployed Man: A Social Study*. New York: E. P. Dutton & Company.

Bakoś, Artur, and Igor Ryciak. 2004. "Powrót do epoki paleolitu," *Newsweek* 7.

Balcerowicz, Leszek. 1997. *Kapitalizm. Socjalizm. Transformacja. Szkice z przełomu epok.* Warsaw: PWN.

Banfield, Edward. 1958. *The Moral Basis of a Backward Society.* Chicago: The Free Press.

Baraniuk, Tadeusz. 2000. *Prześmiewanie świata. O przebierańcach zapustnych na północno-zachodnim Mazowszu.* Warszawa: Polskie Towarzystwo Ludoznawcze.

Barthel, Diane. 1996. "The Interpretation of Industrial Society." In D. Barthel, *Historic Preservation: Collective Memory and Historical Identity.* New Brunswick, NJ: Rutgers University Press.

Barthes, Roland. 1965. "Drame, Poeme, Roman," *Critique* 21 (218): 591–603.

———. 2000. *Mythologies.* London: Vintage.

Bednarek, Stefan (ed.). 1997. *Nim będzie zapomniana. Szkice o kulturze PRL-u.* Wrocław: Wydawnictwo Uniwersytetu Wrocławskiego.

———. 2000. "Współczesna refleksja nad dziedzictwem kultury PRL-u." In S. Bednarek and K. Łukasiewicz (eds.), *Wiedza o kulturze polskiej u progu XXI wieku.* Wrocław: Wydawnictwo Silesia.

Behar, Ruth. 1996. *The Vulnerable Observer: Anthropology That Breaks Your Heart.* Boston: Beacon Press.

Bełdzikowski, Ryszard. 1998. "Reemigranci ze Wschodu w Wałbrzyskiem," *Rocznik Województwa Wałbrzyskiego.*

Bell, Daniel. 1996. *The Cultural Contradictions of Capitalism.* New York: Basic Books.

Benedict, Ruth. 2006 [1934]. *Pattern of Culture.* Boston and New York: Mariner Books.

Benedyktowicz, Zbigniew. 1980. "O niektórych zastosowaniach metody fenomenologicznej w studiach nad religią, symbolem i kulturą," *Etnografia Polska,* vol. 24.

Benjamin, Walter. 2003[1940]. "On Some Motifs in Baudelaire." *Selected Writings,* vol. 4, 1938–1940. Cambridge, MA: Harvard University Press.

———. 1996. *Anioł historii: eseje, szkice, fragmenty.* Poznań: Wydawnictwo Poznańskie.

Berger, Peter, and Thomas Luckmann. 1967. *The Social Construction of Reality: A Treatise in the Sociology of Knowledge.* London: The Penguin Press.

Berman, Marshall. 1983. *All That Is Solid Melts into Air: The Experience of Modernity.* London: Verso.

Beskid, Lidia. 1992. *Warunki życia i kondycja Polaków na początku zmian systemowych.* Warsaw: IFiS PAN.

———. 1999. "Oblicze ubóstwa w Polsce." In L. Beskid (ed.), *Zmiany w życiu Polaków w gospodarce rynkowej.* Warsaw: IFiS PAN.

Beynon, Huw. 1975. *Working for Ford.* East Ardsley, Wakefield: EP Publishing Ltd.

Bielik-Robson, Agata. 2004. *Duch powierzchni: Rewizja romantyczna i filozofia.* Krakow: Universitas.

Biersack, Aletta. 1999. "From 'New Ecology' to the New Ecologies," *American Anthrolopologist* 101: 5–18 .

Bird-David, Nurit. 1988. "Hunters-gatherers and Other People: A Re-Examination." In T. Ingold, D. Riches, and J. Woodburn (eds.), *Hunters and Gatherers, Volume 1: History, Evolution and Social Change.* Oxford: Berg.

———. 1992. "Beyond 'The Original Affluent Society': A Culturalist Reformulation," *Current Anthropology* 33.

———. 1999. "'Animism' Revisited: Personhood, Environment, and Relational Epistemology," *Current Anthropology* 40, suppl.

Blauner, Robert. 1964. *Alienation and Freedom: The Factory Worker and His Industry.* Chicago: University of Chicago Press.

Bloch, Maurice. 1998. *How Do We Think They Think? Anthropological Approaches to Cognition, Memory, and Literacy.* Boulder: Westview Press.

Bogatiryev, Piotr, and Roman Jakobson. 1982 [1929]. "Folklore as a Special Form of Creativity." In P. Steiner (ed.). *The Prague School: Selected Writings. 1929–1946.* Austin: University of Texas Press, 32–46.

Braudel, Fernand. 1982. "History and the Social Sciences: The *Longue Durée.*" *On History.* Chicago: University of Chicago Press.

Brencz, Andrzej. 1997. "Oswajanie niemieckiego dziedzictwa kulturowego. Z badań etnologicznych na Środkowym Nadodrzu." In Z. Mazur (ed.), *Wokół niemieckiego dziedzictwa kulturowego na Ziemiach Zachodnich i Północnych.* Poznań: Instytut Zachodni.

Brocki, Marcin, and Dorota Wolska (eds.). 2003. *Clifford Geertz—lokalna lektura.* Kraków: Wydawnictwo UJ.

Bruczkowska, Amanda. 2003. "Codzienność etnograficznych badań terenowych: chłopskie narzekanie." MA thesis, Warsaw University Institute of Ethnology and Cultural Anthropology.

Brzozowska-Krajka, Anna. 1994. *Symbolika dobowego cyklu powszedniego w polskim folklorze tradycyjnym.* Lublin: UMCS.

Bubnicki, Rafał. 2004. "Dajcie nam pracę," *Rzeczpospolita* 59.

Buchowski, Michał. 1993. *Magia i rytuał.* Warsaw: Instytut Kultury.

———. 1996. *Klasa i kultura w okresie transformacji. Antropologiczne studium przypadku społeczności lokalnej w Wielkopolsce.* Berlin: Centre Marc Bloch.

———. 2003. "'The Other' in Orientalizing and Liberal Discourse." In L. Mróz and Z. Sokolewicz (eds.), *Between Tradition and Post-modernity: Polish Ethnography at the Turn of the Millennium.* Warsaw: Studia Ethnologica DiG.

Buchowski, Michał, and Marina Kempny. 1999. "Czy istnieje antropologia postmodernistyczna?" In M. Buchowski (ed.), *Amerykańska antropologia postmodernistyczna.* Warsaw: Instytut Kultury.

Bukraba-Rylska, Izabella, and Andrzej Rosner (eds.). 2001. *Wieś i rolnictwo na przełomie wieków.* Warsaw: IRWiR PAN.

Burszta, Wojciech. 1992. *Wymiary antropologicznego poznania kultury.* Poznań: Wydawnictwo Naukowe UAM.

———. 1993. "Czy istnieje dekonstrukcja antropologiczna?" In A. Jawłowska, M. Kempny, and E. Tarkowska (eds.), *Kulturowy wymiar przemian społecznych.* Warsaw: Wydawnictwo IFiS PAN.

———. 1998. *Antropologia kultury. Tematy, teorie, interpretacje*. Poznań: Wydawnictwo Zysk i S-ka.

Burszta, Wojciech, and Michał Buchowski. 1992. *O założeniach interpretacji antropologicznej*. Warsaw: PWN.

Bystroń, Jan S. 1947. *Kultura ludowa*. Warsaw: Wyd. Czytelnik.

Bytnar, Helena. 2003. "Legenda komunizmu." BA thesis, Warsaw University Institute of Ethnology and Cultural Anthropology.

Caillois, Roger. 2001. *Man, Play, and Games*. Illinois: University of Illinois Press.

Cardinal, Roger. 2001. "The Eloquence of Objects." In A. Shelton (ed.), *Collectors: Expressions of Self and Other*. London: The Horniman Museum and Gardens.

Chase, A. K. 1989. "Domestication and Domiculture in Northern Australia: A Social Perspective." In R. Harris and G. Hillman (eds.), *Foraging and Farming: The Evolution of Plant Exploitations*. London: Unwin Hyman.

Childe, Gordon V. 1947. *The Dawn of European Civilization*. London: Kegan Paul.

———. 1957. *Man Makes Himself: Man's Progress Through the Ages*. New York: New American Library.

Ciarka, Ryszard. 1994. "O sposobie zabijania," *Konteksty. Polska Sztuka Ludowa* 3, 4.

Cichowicz, Stanisław. 1999. "Poezja świata. Przedmowa." In M. Merleau-Ponty, *Poza świata. Eseje o mowie*. Warsaw: Czytelnik.

Clark, Terry N. 1975, "The Irish Ethics and the Spirit of Patronage," *Ethnicity*, 2.

Clifford, James. 1988a. "On Ethnographic Authority." *The Predicament of Culture: Twentieth-Century Ethnography, Literature, and Art*. Cambridge, MA: Harvard University Press.

———. 1988b. "Power and Dialogue in Ethnography: Marcel Griaule's Initiation." *The Predicament of Culture: Twentieth-Century Ethnography, Literature, and Art*. Cambridge, MA: Harvard University Press.

———. 1988c. "On Collecting Art and Culture." *The Predicament of Culture: Twentieth-Century Ethnography, Literature, and Art*. Cambridge, MA: Harvard University Press.

———. 1990. "Notes on (Field)Notes." In R. Sanjek (ed.), *Field Notes: The Makings of Anthropology*. Ithaca, NY, and London: Cornell University Press.

Clifford, James, and George Marcus (eds.). 1986. *Writing Culture: The Poetics and Politics of Ethnography*. Berkeley, Los Angeles, and London: University of California Press.

Coenen, Herman. 1979. "Leiblichkeit und Sozialität. Ein Grundproblem der phänomenologischen Soziologie," *Mens en maatschappij* 54: 34–61.

Connerton, Paul. 1989. *How Societies Remember*. Cambridge: Cambridge University Press.

Csordas, Thomas. 1990. "Embodiment as a Paradigm for Anthropology," *Ethos* 18.

————. 1999. "Embodiment and Cultural Phenomenology." In G. Weiss and H. F. Haber (eds.), *Perspectives on Embodiment: The Intersection of Nature and Culture*. London and New York: Routledge.

———— (ed.). 2001a [1994]. *Embodiment and Experience: The Existential Ground of Culture and Self*. Cambridge: Cambridge University Press.

————. 2001b. "Introduction: The Body as Representation and Being-in-the World." In T. Csordas (ed.), *Embodiment and Experience: The Existential Ground of Culture and Self*. Cambridge: Cambridge University Press.

Czaja, Dariusz (ed.). 2002. *Mitologie popularne*. Kraków: Wydawnictwo UJ.

Czaja, Mariusz. 2002. "'Z nieba upadną w morze gwiazdy.' Europejska wyobraźnia apokaliptyczna," *Barbarzyńca* 7, 8.

Czajka, Stanisław. 1985. *Przemiany Wałbrzycha*. Wałbrzych: Wałbrzyskie Towarzystwo Społeczno-Kulturalne.

Czechowski, Paweł, and Andrzej Stelmachowski. 1990. "Ewolucja pozycji właściciela indywidualnego gospodarstwa rolnego w PRL." In Z. Hemmerling (ed.), *Wieś polska 1944–1989. Wybrane problemy podmiotowości społecznej, życia politycznego, ekonomicznego, oświatowego, kulturalnego i religijnego*. Warsaw: Instytut Nauk Politycznych UW.

Czerwiński, Marcin. 1975. *Życie po miejsku*. Warsaw: PIW.

Dalewski, Zbigniew. 1990. "Zakładziny: obrzęd i mit. O słowiańskich zwyczajach i wierzeniach związanych z budową domu i zakładaniem miasta," *Konteksty. Polska Sztuka Ludowa* 3.

Danilewicz, Jerzy. 2006. "Wysypisko," *Newsweek* 2.

Dean, Hartley, and Peter Taylor-Gooby. 1992. *Dependency Culture: The Explosion of a Myth*. Hemel Hampstead: Harvester Wheatsheaf.

Descola, Philippe. 1996. "Constructing Natures: Symbolic Ecology and Social Practice." In P. Descola and G. Pallson (eds.), *Nature and Society: Anthropological Perspectives*. London: Routledge.

Descola, Philippe, and Gisli Pálsson. 1996. "Introduction." In P. Descola and G. Pallson (eds.), *Nature and Society: Anthropological Perspectives*. London: Routledge.

Dolińska, X. (ed.). 2000. *Chłop, rolnik, farmer? Przystąpienie Polski do Unii Europejskiej—nadzieje i obawy polskiej wsi*. Warsaw: ISP.

Domański, Henryk. 2002. "Ubóstwo w strukturze społecznej w Bułgarii, Polsce, Rosji, Rumunii, Słowacji i na Węgrzech," *Kultura i Społeczeństwo* 4.

Doświadczenia z likwidacji zakładów górniczych. 1999. Collective work. Książ Castle: Engineers' and Mining Technicians' Association.

Douglas, Mary. 2005. *Natural Symbols: Explorations in Cosmology*. London: Routledge.

Dunn, E. 2004. *Privatizing Poland: Baby Food, Big Business and the Remaking of Labour*. Ithaca, NY: Cornell University Press.

Dwornik, Bartłomiej. 2001. "Przekleństwo dawnych bogactw," *Słowo Polskie / Wałbrzych* 4.

Dwyer, Kevin. 1982. *Moroccan Dialogues: Anthropology in Question*. Baltimore, MD, and London: The Johns Hopkins University Press.

Dybel, Paweł. 2000. *Urwane ścieżki. Przybyszewski—Freud—Lacan.* Kraków: Universitas.

Dzięgiel, Leszek. 2001. "Miasta w filozofii władz PRL-u i społecznej praktyce. Wyzwanie dla badacza kultury." In Cz. Robotycki (ed.), *PRL z pamięci.* Zeszyty Naukowe UJ 'Prace Etnograficzne' 36.

Eckhardt, Annegret. 1994. *Im Krieg mit dem Körper. Autoaggression als Krankheit.* Rowohlt Taschenbuch Verlag.

Eco, Umberto. 1992. "Interpretation and History." *Interpretation and Overinterpretation.* Cambridge: Cambridge University Press.

Eksploatacja górnicza a ochrona powierzchni. Doświadczenia z wałbrzyskich kopalń. 2000. Collective work. Katowice: Główny Instytut Górnictwa.

Elam, Gillian, Jane Ritchie, and Alper Hulusi. 2000. "Eking Out an Income: Low Income Households and Their Use of Supplementary Resources." In J. Bradshaw and R. Sainsbury (eds.), *Experiencing Poverty.* Aldershot: Ashgate.

Elias, Norbert. 2000. *The Civilising Process.* Oxford: Blackwell Publishers.

Ellen, Roy F. 1996. "Individual strategy and cultural regulation in Nuaulu hunting." In R. Ellen and K. Fukui (eds.), *Redefining Nature: Ecology, Culture and Domestication.* Oxford: Berg.

Ellen, Roy, Peter Parkes, and Alan Bicker. 2000. *Indigenous Environmental Knowledge and Its Transformation: Anthropological and Critical Perspectives.* Kent: Harwood Academic Press.

Emigh, Rebecca J., and Iván Szelényi (eds.). 2001. *Poverty, Ethnicity, and Gender in Eastern Europe During the Market Transition.* Westport: Praeger.

Erikson, Erik. 1993. *Childhood and Society.* New York and London: W. W. Norton.

Fabian, Johannes. 1983. *Time and the Other: How Anthropology Makes Its Object.* New York: Columbia University Press.

———. 2004. "*Ethnography and Memory.*" Conference paper presented at the EASA meetings, *Vienna.*

Faliszek, Krystyna, Krzysztof Łącki, and Kazimiera Wódz. 2001. *Górnicy. Zbiorowości górnicze u progu zmian.* Katowice: Wydawnictwo Naukowe Śląsk.

Fatyga, Barbara, and Jadwiga Siemaszko. 1989. "Po co jechać na Triobriandy …," *Konteksty. Polska Sztuka Ludowa* 3.

Fedyszak-Radziejowska, Barbara. 2000. "Stosunek ludności wiejskiej do procesu zmian w polskim rolnictwie." In X. Dolińska and E. Wosik (eds.), *Chłop, rolnik, farmer? Przystąpienie Polski do Unii Europejskiej—nadzieje i obawy polskiej wsi.* Warsaw: ISP PAN.

Foster, George. 1965. "Peasant Society and the Image of Limited Good," *American Anthropologist* 67.

Frazer, James. 1993. *The Golden Bough.* London: Wordsworth Editions.

Frenkel, Irena. 2001. "Bezrobocie w rolnictwie indywidualnym." In Bukraba-Rylska and A. Rosner (eds.), *Wieś i rolnictwo na przełomie wieków.* Warsaw.

Freud, Sigmund. 2005. "Mourning and Melancholia." In S. Whiteside (ed.), *On Murder, Mourning, and Melancholy.* London: Penguin Classics.

————. 2011. *Totem and Taboo: Resemblances Between the Psychic Lives of Savages and Neurotics.* Ithaca, NY: Cornell University Press.

Frieske, Kazimierz. 1999. "Marginalność i marginalizacja społeczna." *Marginalność i procesy marginalizacji.* Warsaw: IpiSS.

Fromm, Erich. 1994. *Escape from Freedom.* New York: Holt Paperbacks.

Frydryczak, Beata. 2002. *Świat jako kolekcja. Próby analizy estetycznej natury nowoczesności.* Poznań: Wydawnictwo Fundacji Humaniora.

Gadamer, Hans Georg. 2004. *Truth and Method.* London, New York: Continuum.

Gans, Herbert. 1996. "From 'Underclass' to 'Undercaste': Some Observations about the Future of the Post-Industrial Economy and Its Major Victims." In E. Mingione (ed.), *Urban Poverty and the Underclass.* Oxford: Blackwell.

Geertz, Clifford. 1973. "Thick Description: Toward an Interpretive Theory of Culture." *The Interpretation of Cultures.* New York: Basic Books.

————. 1983. *Local Knowledge: Further Essays in Interpretive Anthropology.* New York: Basic Books.

————. 1988a. "Being There." *Works and Lives.* Stanford, CA: Stanford University Press.

————. 1988b. "I-Witnessing: Malinowski's Children." *Works and Lives.* Stanford, CA: Stanford University Press.

————. 2001. "Thinking as a Moral Act: Ethical Dimensions of Anthropological Fieldwork in the New States." *Available Light: Anthropological Reflections.* Princeton, NJ: Princeton University Press.

Geremek, Bronisław. 1989. *Litość i szubienica. Dzieje nędzy i miłosierdzia.* Warsaw: Czytelnik.

Gerlich, Hanna. 1994. "Obrazy świata minionego—oswajanie Ziem Zachodnich. Analiza jednego przypadku w świetle relacji autobiograficznych," *Etnografia Polska* 1, 2.

Gerlich, Marian. 1988. "Zawód górnika a tradycyjne wzory zachowań." In D. Simonides (ed.), *Górniczy stan w wierzeniach, obrzędach, humorze i pieśniach.* Katowice: Śląski Instytut Naukowy.

————. 1989. "Górnicza szychta a zwyczajowe wzory zachowań. Próba charakterystyki," *Łódzkie Studia Etnograficzne* 29.

Germani, Gino. 1980. *Marginality.* New Brunswick, NJ: Transaction Books.

Giddens, Anthony. 1990. *The Consequences of Modernity.* Cambridge: Polity Press.

————. 1991. *Modernity and Self-identity: Self and Society in the Late Modern Age.* Stanford, CA: Stanford University Press.

Gilejko, Leszek K. 2003. "Życie codzienne Polaków w drugiej dekadzie transformacji." In R. Sulima (ed.), *Życie codzienne Polaków na przełomie XX i XXI w.* Łomża: Oficyna Wydawnicza Stopka.

————. 2005. "Robotnicy w transformacji: ocena ich położenia i szans." In M. Jarosz (ed.), *Wygrani i przegrani polskiej transformacji.* Warsaw: PWN.

Girard, Réne. 1991. *The Scapegoat.* Baltimore, MD: The Johns Hopkins University Press.

Giza-Poleszczuk, Anna, Mirosława Marody, and Andrzej Rychard. 2000. *Strategie i system. Polacy w obliczu zmiany społecznej*. Warsaw: Wydawnictwo IFiS PAN.

Gładysz, Mieczysław. 1971. "Chłopski kalendarz ideograficzny," *Zeszyty Naukowe UJ*, vol. 3.

Godlewski, Grzegorz. 2005. "Potężne zbiorniki znaczeń—wywiad," *Opcit* 3, 4.

Goffman, Erving. 1959. *The Presentation of Self in Everyday Life*. New York: Doubleday.

Gogolewska, Hanna. 1984. "Obyczajowość sąsiedzka robotników zamieszkałych na Księżym Młynie w Łodzi w okresie międzywojennym," *Łódzkie Studia Etnograficzne* 24.

Golczyńska-Grondas, Agnieszka. 2004. *Mężczyźni z enklaw biedy. Rekonstrukcja ról społecznych*. Łódź: Wydawnictwo Uniwersytetu Łódzkiego.

Gołębiowska, Anna. 2002. "Po(d)kopane prawo. Nielegalne szyby stają się legalne," *Nowe Wiadomości Wałbrzyskie* 41.

Gołębiowski, Bronisław (ed.). 1973. *Pamiętniki górników*. Katowice: Wydawnictwo Śląsk.

Gołębiowski, Bronisław. 1990. "Kultura wsi i chłopów w Polsce. Procesy zmian." In Z. Hemmerling (ed.), *Wieś polska 1944–1989. Wybrane problemy podmiotowości społecznej, życia politycznego, ekonomicznego, oświatowego, kulturalnego i religijnego*. Warsaw: Instytut Nauk Politycznych UW.

Golinowska, Stanisława (ed.). 1997. *Polska bieda II. Kryteria. Ocena. Przeciwdziałanie*. Warsaw: IpiSS.

Goody, Jack. 1984. *The Domestication of the Savage Mind*. Cambridge: Cambridge University Press.

———. 1986. *The Logic of Writing and the Organization of Society*. Cambridge: Cambridge University Press.

Gorlach, Krzysztof, and Anna Pryć. 2000. *Węzłowe kwestie społeczne wsi polskiej u progu XXI wieku*. Krakow: Instytut Socjologii UJ.

Grębecka, Zuzanna. 2006. *Słowo magiczne poddane technologii. Magia ludowa w praktykach postsowieckiej kultury popularnej*. Kraków: Wydawnictwo 'Nomos'.

Grębowiec, Jacek. 2006. "Der Umbau de Breslauer Ikonosphäre nach dem Zweiten Weltkrieg vor dem Hintergrund der Ausbildung einer neuen regionalen Identität [The Rebuilding of the Iconosphere of Wrocław after World War II in Light of the Shaping of a New Regional Identity]." In P. Loew, C. Pletzing, and T. Serrier (eds.), *Wiedergewonne Geschichte. Zur Aneignung von Vergangenheit in den Zwischenräumen Mitteleuropas [History Retrieved: Assimilating the Past in Central European Regions of Mutual Interchange in the 19th and 20th Centuries]*. Wiesbaden: Harrasowitz Verlag.

Grossman, Gregory (ed.). 1987. *Studies in the Second Economy of Communist Countries*. Berkeley: University of California Press.

Grotowska-Leder, Joanna. 1998. "Łódzkie enklawy biedy." In W. Warzywoda-Kruszyńska (ed.) *Żyć i pracować w enklawach biedy*. Łódź: Instytut Socjologii UŁ.

Grzymała-Kazłowska, Aleksandra. 2004. "Socjologicznie zorientowana analiza dyskursu na tle współczesnych badań nad dyskursem," *Kultura i Społeczeństwo* 1.

Guriewicz, Aron. 1976. *Kategorie kultury średniowiecznej.* Warsaw: PIW.

Hagenaars, Aldi J. M. 1991. "The Definition and Measurement of Poverty." In L. Osberg (ed.) *Economic Inequality and Poverty: International Perspectives.* New York and London: M. E. Shaprp, Inc.: 134–155.

Hajduk-Nijakowska, Janina. 1988. "Opowieści górnicze." In D. Simonides (ed.), *Górniczy stan w wierzeniach, obrzędach, humorze i pieśniach.* Katowice: Śląski Instytut Naukowy.

Halamska, Maria, and Marie-Claude Maurel. 1997. "Rolnictwo polskie a kwestia integracji europejskiej," *Wieś i rolnictwo* 2.

Halbwachs, Maurice. 1992. *On Collective Memory.* Chicago: University of Chicago Press.

Hall, Edward T. 1976. *Beyond Culture.* New York: Anchor Books.

Hammersley, Martyn, and Paul Atkinson. 2007. *Ethnography: Principles in Practice.* London and New York: Routledge.

Hann, Chris (ed.). 1993. *Socialism: Ideals, Ideologies, and Local Practice.* London and New York: Routledge.

———— (ed.). 2002a. *Postsocialism: Ideals, Ideologies and Practices in Eurasia.* London: Routledge.

————. 2002b. "Introduction: Post-socialism as a Topic of Anthropological Investigation. Farewell to the Socialist 'Other.'" In C. Hann (ed.), *Postsocialism: Ideals, Ideologies and Practices in Eurasia.* London: Routledge.

Harrison, David R. 1996. "Domesticatory Relationships of People, Plants and Animals." In R. Ellen and K. Fukui (eds.), *Redefining Nature: Ecology, Culture and Domestication.* Oxford: Berg.

Hastrup, Kirsten. 1987. "Presenting the Past: Reflections on Myth and History," *Folk, Journal of the Danish Ethnographic Society* 29: 257–267.

————. 1995. "The Empirical Foundation: On the Grounding of Worlds." *A Passage to Anthropology: Between Experience and Theory.* London: Routledge.

Heald, Suzette, and Ariene Deluz (eds.). 1994. *Anthropology and Psychoanalysis: An Encounter Through Culture.* London and New York: Routledge.

Heald, Suzette, Ariene Deluz, and Pierre Jacopin. 1994. "Introduction." In S. Heald and A. Deluz (eds.), *Anthropology and Psychoanalysis: An Encounter Through Culture.* London and New York: Routledge.

Hébrard, Jean. 1999. "Tenir un journal. L'écriture personnelle et ses supports." In Ph. Lejeune (ed.), *Récits de vies et medias.* Centre de Recherches Interdisciplinaires sur les Textes Modernes, Université Paris X—Nanterre.

Hegel, Georg W. F. 1991. *Elements of the Philosphy of Right,* trans. by H. Nisbet. Cambridge: Cambridge University Press.

Heidegger, Martin. 1997. *Budować, mieszkać, myśleć. Eseje wybrane.* Warsaw: Czytelnik.

————. 2008. *Being and Time.* New York: Harper Modern Classics.

Hernas, Czesław. 1976. "Miejsce badań nad folklorem." In H. Markiewicz and J. Sławiński (eds.), *Problemy metodologiczne współczesnego literaturoznawstwa*. Kraków: Wydawnictwo Literackie.

Herzfeld, Michael. 2001. *Anthropology: Theoretical Practice in Culture and Society*. Malden: Blackwell Publishers.

———. 2005. *Cultural Intimacy: Social Poetics in the Nation-State*. New York: Routledge.

Himmelfarb, Gertrude. 1999. "Ubóstwo a dwa Oświecenia." In K. Michalski (ed.) *Oświecenie dzisiaj*. Kraków: Wydawnictwo Znak.

Hobart, Mark. 1993. "Introduction: The Growth of Ignorance?" In M. Hobart (ed.), *An Anthropological Critique of Development: The Growth of Ignorance*. London: Routledge.

Hobsbawm, Eric, and Terence Ranger (eds.). 1983. *The Invention of Tradition*. Cambridge: Cambridge University Press.

Hoggart, Richard. 2009 [1957]. *The Uses of Literacy*. London: Penguin Classics.

Hugo, Victor. 2003. *Les Miserables*, trans. by Norman Denny. London: Penguin Classics.

Humphrey, C. 2002. *The Unmaking of Soviet Life: Everyday Economies after Socialism*. London: Cornell University Press.

Ichikawa, Mitsuo. 1992. "Comment on Nurit Bird-David: Beyond 'The Original Affluent Society,'" *Current Anthropology* 33.

Ingold, Tim. 1992. "Culture and the Perception of the Environment." In E. Croll and D. Parkin (eds.), *Bush Base: Forest, Farm. Culture, Environment and Development*. London: Routledge.

———. 1996a. "Hunting and Gathering as a Way of Perceiving the Environment." In R. Ellen (ed.), *Redefining Nature: Ecology, Culture and Domestication*. Oxford: Berg.

———. 1996b. "The Optimal Forager and Economic Man." In P. Descola and G. Pallson (eds.), *Nature and Society: Anthropological Perspectives*. London: Routledge.

———. 2000. *The Perception of the Environment: Essays on Livelihood, Dwelling and Skill*. London: Routledge.

Jacyno, Małgorzata, and Alina Sulżycka. 1999. *Dzieciństwo: doświadczenie bez świata*. Warsaw: Oficyna Naukowa.

Janion, Maria. 2002a. "Trudna klasa w ciężkiej szkole," *Res Publica Nowa* 2.

———. 2002b. *Wampir. Biografia symboliczna*. Gdańsk: słowo/obraz terytoria.

Jarosz, Maria. 2004. *Władza. Przywileje. Korupcja*. Warsaw: PWN.

——— (ed.). 2005. *Wygrani przegrani polskiej transformacji*. Warsaw: ISP PAN.

Jedlicki, Jerzy. 2000. *Świat zwyrodniały. Lęki i wyroki krytyków nowoczesności*. Warsaw: Sic!

Józefowicz, Łukasz. 2004. "Kompleks arystokratyczny." Workshop piece, Warsaw University Institute of Polish Culture.

Kalbarczyk, Agnieszka. 2002. *O ważności pracy, zaspokajaniu potrzeb i wymianie społecznej. Garść refleksji na marginesie lektur na temat biedy i wykluczenia*. Computer printout, SNS PAN.

Kamińska, Monika. 2006. *Zewnętrzne pomysły, lokalny lęk. Zderzenie różnych sposobów myślenia w kontekście ochrony przyrody i kultury, przypadek Puszczy Białowieskiej i Krainy Otwartych Okiennic.* Laboratory work prepared under my guidance, Warsaw University Institute of Ethnology and Cultural Anthropology.

Kaniowska, Katarzyna. 1994. "Problem opisu w etnologii." In W. Burszta and J. Damrosz (eds.), *Pożegnanie paradygmatu?* Warsaw: Instytut Kultury.

———. 1999. "Opis. Klucz do rozumienia kultury," *Łódzkie Studia Etnograficzne* 39.

Karpińska, Grażyna Ewa. 2000. *Miejsce wyodrębnione ze świata. Przykład łódzkich kamienic czynszowych.* Łódź: PTL.

Karpińska, Grażyna Ewa, Barbara Kopczyńska-Jaworska, and Anna Woźniak. 1992. *Pracować, żeby żyć, żyć, żeby pracować.* Warsaw: PWN.

Katz, Michael. 1999. "Re-framing the 'Underclass' Debate." In Michael Katz (ed.), *The "Underclass" Debate.* Princeton, NJ: Princeton University Press.

Kędziorek, Piotr. 1996. "Chłopskie zrzędzenie," *Konteksty. Polska Sztuka Ludowa* 1, 2.

Kideckel, David. 2002. "The Unmaking of an East European Working Class." In C. Hann (ed.), *Postsocialism: Ideals, Ideologies and Practices in Eurasia.* London: Routledge.

———. 2008. *Getting by in Postsocialist Romania: Labor, the Body, and Working-Class Culture.* Bloomington: Indiana University Press.

Kisielewska, Anna. 1970 "Wojciech Rachwał, płanetnik z Przysietnicy." In R. Górki and J. Krzyżanowski (eds.), *Między dawnymi a nowymi laty. Studia folklorystyczne.* Wrocław: Wyd. Ossolineum.

Klein, Melanie. 1987. "Mourning and Its Relation to Manic-depressive States." In J. Mitchell (ed.), *The Selected Melanie Klein,* New York: The Free Press.

Kleszcz, Irena. 2004. "Wykorzystanie ukrytej obserwacji uczestniczącej w badaniu stylu życia szarej strefy," *Kultura i Społeczeństwo* 2.

Kłopot, Stanisław Witold. 1997. "Społeczno-kulturowe aspekty przekształceń struktury gospodarczej rejonu wałbrzysko-noworudzkiego." In L. Skiba (ed.), *Zagłębie węglowe w obliczu restrukturyzacji. Studia i materiały.* Wrocław: Wydawnictwo Silesia.

Kłoskowska, Antonina. 2002. "Przedmowa." *Wzory kultury, Ruth Benedict.* Warsaw: Wydawnictwo Literackie Muza.

Kmita, Jerzy. 1985. *Kultura i poznanie.* Warsaw: PWN.

Kocik, Lucjan. 2000. *Między przyrodą, zagrodą i społeczeństwem. Społeczno-kulturowe problemy ekologii wsi i rolnictwa.* Krakow: Wydawnictwo UJ.

———. 2001. *Eurosceptycyzm i trauma polskiej wsi.* Krakow: Universitas.

Kolberg, Oskar. 1962. *Lud ... [Dzieła wszystkie].* Wrocław, Poznań: PTL.

Kolbuszewski, Jacek. 1988. "Oswajanie krajobrazu. Z problematyki integracji kulturowej na ziemiach odzyskanych." In D. Simonides (ed.), *Symbolika regionów. Studia etnologiczno-folklorystyczne.* Opole: Instytut Śląski.

Kopytoff, Igor. 1986. "The Cultural Biography of Things." In A. Appadurai (ed.), *The Social Life of Things: Commodities in Cultural Perspective.* Cambridge: Cambridge University Press.

Kõresaar, Ene. 2003. "Studies on Socialist and Post-Socialist Everyday Life," *Pro Ethnologia* 16.

Korzeniewska, Katarzyna. 2002. "Biedni (i) emeryci: o ekonomicznej zależności biednych rodzin od pomocy z zewnątrz i o 'underclass' po polsku." In K. Korzeniewska and E. Tarkowska (eds), *Lata tłuste, lata chude ... Spojrzenie na biedę w społecznościach lo kalnych.* Warsaw: IFiS PAN.

Kot, Elżbieta. 2006. *Obserwacje i zapiski pogodowe na Podlasiu jako próba uporządkowania zmieniającego się świata.* Workshop piece, Warsaw University Institute of Ethnology and Cultural Anthropology.

Kowalak, Tadeusz. 1988. "Podstawowe pojęcia. Definicje." *Marginalność i marginalizacja społeczna.* Warsaw: Elipsa.

Kowalewski, Maciej. 2004. "Mity i legendy miast Dzikiego Zachodu," *Opcit* 6, 7.

Kowalski, Piotr. 2000. *Zwierzoczłekoupiory, wampiry i inne bestie.* Kraków: Wydawnictwo UJ.

Kozak, Marek. 2005. "Polska regionalna: bezrobocie i bieda." In M. Jarosz (ed.), *Wygrani i przegrani polskiej transformacji.* Warsaw: PWN.

Kracik, Jan. 1991. *Pokonać czarną śmierć. Staropolskie postawy wobec zarazy.* Kraków: Wydawnictwo M.

Kubiak, Anna. 1997. *Delicje i lewa ręka Kryszny.* Warsaw: Wydawnictwo IFiS.

Kula, Marcin. 2002. *Nośniki pamięci historycznej.* Warsaw: Wydawnictwo DIG.

Kuligowski, Waldemar. 2001. *Antropologia refleksyjna. O rzeczywistości tekstu.* Poznań: Wydawnictwo Poznańskie.

Kurtz, Ernest. 2007. *Shame & Guilt,* New York: iUniverse

Łapińska-Tyszka, Krystyna. 1995. "Bezrobocie wśród mieszkańców wsi." In B. Fedyszak-Radziejowska (ed.), *Wieś i jej mieszkańcy. Zróżnicowania, postawy i strategie zachowań.* Warsaw: IRWiR.

Laskowska-Otwinowska, Justyna. 1998. "Głód w kulturze tradycyjnej i życiu współczesnej wsi. Próba analizy materiałów terenowych w perspektywie porównawczej," *Kultura i Społeczeństwo* 2.

———. 2002. "Elementy kultury romskiej jako źródło marginalizacji oraz bogacenia się Romów polskich." In K. Korzeniewska and E. Tarkowska (eds.), *Lata tłuste, lata chude. Spojrzenia na biedę w społecznościach lokalnych.* Warsaw: IFiS PAN.

Lazar, Imre, and Luse, Agita (eds.). 2007. *Cosmologies of Suffering in Societies of Transition.* Cambridge: Cambridge Scholars Press.

Leacock, E. B. (ed.). 1971. *The Culture of Poverty: A Critique.* New York: Simon and Schuster.

Ledeneva, Alena. 1998. *Russia's Economy of Favours; Blat, Networking and Informal Exchange.* Cambridge: Cambridge University Press.

Leder, Andrzej. 2002. *Paradoks a filozofia. Niesamoistność człowieka w Grecji archaicznej.* Manuscript. IFiS PAN.

Lederman, Rena. 1990. "Pretexts for Ethnography: On Reading Field Notes." In R. Sanjek (ed.), *Field Notes: The Makings of Anthropology.* Ithaca, NY, and London: Cornell University Press.

Lee, Richard. 1968. "What Hunters Do for a Living, Or, How to Make out on Scarce Resources." In R. Lee and I. De Vore (eds.), *Man The Hunter*. Chicago: Aldine.

Lepianka, Dorota. 2002. "Czym jest wykluczenie społeczne? Wprowadzenie do europejskich debat na temat ekskluzji," in *Kultura i Społeczeństwo* 4.

Lévi-Strauss, Claude. 1994. *The Savage Mind*. Oxford: Oxford University Press.

Lewis, Oscar. 1968. *La Vida*. Vintage Books.

―――. 1970. "The Culture of Poverty," *Anthropological Essays*. New York: Random.

Libera, Zbigniew. 1997. *Mikrokosmos, makrokosmos i antropologia ciała*. Tarnów.

Lipko, Tomasz. 2003. "Miasto się rozbiera," *Polityka* 50.

―――. 2004. "Nurkowanie ekstremalne," *Polityka* 16.

Lister, Ruth. 2004. *Poverty*. Cambridge: Polity Press.

Lister, Ruth, and Peter Beresford. 2000. "Where Are 'the Poor' in the Future of Poverty Research?" In J. Bradshaw and R. Sainsbury (eds.), *Experiencing Poverty*. Aldershot: Ashgate.

Low, Setha M. 2001[1994]. "Embodied Metaphors: Nerves as Lived Experience." In Thomas Csordas (ed.), *Embodiment and Experience: The Existential Ground of Culture and Self*. London: Cambridge University Press.

Łukasiewicz, Juliusz. 1992. "Wpływ urodzajów na poziom życia społeczeństwa polskiego w latach 1820–1860." In J. Szytełło (ed.), *Nędza i dostatek na ziemiach polskich od średniowiecza po wiek XX*. Warsaw: Semper.

Mach, Zdzisław. 1998. *Niechciane miasta: Migracja i tożsamość społeczna*. Kraków: Universitas.

Maciejewska-Mroczek, Ewa. 2006. „Marsz do lekcji!" *Opcit* 2.

Mahler, Fred. 1993. "Maldevelopment and Marginality." In J. Danecki (ed.), *Insights into Maldevelopment: Reconsidering the Idea of Progress*. Warsaw: University of Warsaw Press.

Malewska, Anna. 2004. "Tradycja stosowania pojęcia dyskurs i jego przy datność w antropologii współczesności," *Etnografia Polska* 1, 2.

Malinowski, Bronisław. 2002. *Argonauts of the Western Pacific*. London: Routledge.

Małkiewicz, Andrzej. 1997. "Robotnicy Wałbrzycha wobec wydarzeń październikowych 1956 roku," *Polska 1944/45–89. Studia i materiały* 3. Warsaw: Instytut Historii PAN.

Markiewicz, Władysław. 1960. *Przeobrażenia świadomości narodowej reemigrantów polskich z Francji*. Poznań: Wydawnictwo Poznańskie.

Marmuszewski, Stanisław. 1998. "Bogactwo i ubóstwo—dwa motywy potocznego myślenia," *Kultura i Społeczeństwo* 2.

Marody, Mirosława. 1991a. "Działania jednostki a system społeczny." In M. Marody (ed.), *Co nam zostało z tych lat?* London: Aneks.

―――. 1991b. "Jednostka w systemie realnego socjalizmu." In M. Marody (ed.), *Co nam zostało z tych lat?* London: Aneks.

―――. 2002. "Trzy Polski—instytucjonalny kontekst strategii dostosowawczych." *Wymiary życia społecznego. Polska na przełomie XX i XXI wieku*. Warsaw: Wydawnictwo Naukowe Scholar.

Marx, Karl. 1992 [1907]. *Capital. Vol. 3: A Critique of Political Economy.* London: Penguin Books.

Mathews, Gordon. 2000. *Global Culture/Individual Identity: Searching for Home in the Cultural Supermarket.* London: Routledge.

Mauss, Marcel. 2000. *The Gift: The Form and Reason for Exchange in Archaic Societies.* New York: W. W. Norton.

———. 2006. "Techniques of the Body." *Techniques, Technology and Civilisation.* New York: Durkheim Press.

Mazurek, Małgorzata. 2005. *Socjalistyczny zakład pracy. Porównanie fabrycznej codzienności w PRL i NRD u progu lat 60.* Warsaw: Wydawnictwo Trio.

Mencwel, Andrzej. 2002. "Przyczyniać się pomału." In G. Godlewski et al. (eds.), *Animacja kultury. Doświadczenie i przyszłość.* Warsaw: IKP UW.

Mende, Michael. 1997. "'De-industrialization' and 'Re-engineering': New Patterns of Industrial Identity in Their Relations to the Industrial Heritage." In *Historyczne okręgi przemysłowe w okresie deindustrializacji.* Collective work. Wrocław: Instytut Historii Architektury, Sztuki i Techniki Politechniki Wrocławskiej.

Merleau-Ponty, Maurice. 1964. "Eye and Mind." *The Primacy of Perception and Other Essays.* Evanston, IL: Northwestern University Press.

———. 1965. "Fenomenologia i egzystencja." In L. Kołakowski and K. Pomian (eds.), *Filozofia egzystencjalna.* Warsaw: PWN.

———. 1969. *The Visible and the Invisible.* Evanston, IL: Northwestern University Press.

———. 1973. *The Prose of the World.* Evanston, IL: Northwestern University Press.

———. 2002. *Phenomenology of Perception.* London and New York: Routledge Classics.

Merton, Robert K. 1968. *Social Theory and Social Structure*, London and New York: The Free Press.

Michalkiewicz, Stanisław (ed.). 1993. *Wałbrzych. Zarys monografii miasta na tle regionu.* Wrocław: Wydawnictwo Silesia.

Michera, Wojciech. 1994. "Śmierć Jasia i Małgosi," *Konteksty. Polska Sztuka Ludowa* 3, 4.

Mierzejewski, Marcin. 2006. *Metamorfozy. Praktyki postępowania ze śmieciem w trzech podlaskich gminach.* Laboratory work prepared under my guidance, Warsaw University Institute of Ethnology and Cultural Anthropology.

Migasiński, Jacek. 1995. *Merleau-Ponty.* Warsaw: Wiedza Powszechna.

Mogilnicka, Krystyna. 2005. *Czarne jest czarne, białe jest białe. O górniczej metaforyzacji czerni i bieli.* Workshop paper, Warsaw University Institute of Polish Culture.

Mogilnicka, Krystyna, and Weronika Plińska. 2005. *Materiały z warsztatów badawczych w Wałbrzychu 2004–2005.* Computer printout at the Warsaw University Institute of Polish Culture.

Monografia KWB. 2000. *Kopalnia Węgla Brunatnego Bełchatów.* Bełchatów.

Morcinek, Gustaw. 1981. "Biedaszyby na Śląsku." *Z czarnego kraju. Górny Śląsk w reportażu międzywojennym, praca zbiorowa.* Katowice: Śląski Instytut Naukowy.

Mosse, David. 2006. "Anti-social anthropology? Objectivity, objection, and the ethnography of public policy and professional communities," *Journal of the Royal Anthropological Institute* 4.

Mróz, Lech, and Jerzy S. Wasilewski. 2003. "Regressing to Nature, Revising Tradition, Building Ethnicity: A Case of the Reindeer-breeders of the Mongolian Taiga." In L. Mróz and Z. Sokolewicz (eds.), *Betwen Tradition and Post-modernity: Polish Ethnography at the Turn of the Millennium.* Warsaw: Studia Ethnologica DiG.

Mrozek, Wanda. 1987. *Górnośląska rodzina robotnicza w procesie przeobrażeń.* Katowice: Śląski Instytut Naukowy.

———. 1988. "Tradycyjna rodzina górnicza—jej cechy społeczne i kierunki przeobrażeń." In D. Simonides (ed.), *Górniczy stan w wierzeniach, obrzędach, humorze i pieśniach.* Katowice: Śląski Instytut Naukowy.

Murawski, Krzysztof. 1999. *Państwo i społeczeństwo obywatelskie: wybrane problemy rozwoju demokracji w Polsce 1889–1977.* Krakw: WAM.

Murzynowska, Dorota, and Weronika Plińska. 2006. *Ochotnicza Straż Pożarna w Ostałówku—klub kultury.* Ethographic work prepared under my guidance, Warsaw University Institute of Polish Culture.

Myrdal, Gunnar. 1962. *Challenge to Affluence.* New York: Pantheon.

Myśmy ustanowili przyrodę. 1994. "A Conversation: Aleksander Jackowski, Wiesław Myśliwski and Roch Sulima," *Konteksty. Polska Sztuka Ludowa* 3, 4.

Niewiadomski, Donat. 1999. *Orka i siew. O ludowych wyobrażeniach agrarnych.* Lublin: Polihymnia.

Niżnik, Józef. 1979. *Przedmiot poznania w naukach społecznych.* Warszawa: Państwowe Wydawnictwo Naukowe.

Nora, Pierre. 1989. "Between Memory and History: Les Lieux de Memoire," *Representations* 26.

Obeyesekere, Gananath. 1990. *The Work of Culture: Symbolic Transformation in Psychoanalysis and Anthropology.* Chicago and London: University of Chicago Press.

Ogburn, William F. 1964. *On Culture and Social Change.* Chicago and London: Chicago University Press.

Olędzki, Jacek. 1971. *Kultura artystyczna ludności kurpiowskiej.* Wrocław: Ossolineum / Wyd. PAN.

———. 1991. *Murzynowo. Znaki istnienia i tożsamości kulturalnej mieszkańców wioski nadwiślańskiej XVIII–XX w.* Warsaw: Wydawnictwo UW.

———. 1994. "Filodzoon, czyli ciesząca się życiem. O kulturze wierzby," *Konteksty. Polska Sztuka Ludowa* 3/4.

———. 1999. *Ludzie wygasłego wejrzenia.* Warsaw: Wydawnictwo Akademickie Dialog.

Olick, Jeffrey K., and Joyce Robbins. 1998. "Social Memory Studies: from "Collective Memory" to the Historical Sociology of Mnemonic Practices," *Annual Review of Sociology* 24.

Ong, Walter J. 2002. *Orality and Literacy.* New York: Routledge.

Ortega y Gasset, José. 1994. *The Revolt of the Masses.* New York: W. W. Norton.
Ottenberg, Simon. 1990. "Thirty Years of Field Notes: Changing Relationship to the Text." In R. Sanjek (ed.), *Field Notes: The Makings of Anthropology.* Ithaca, NY, and London: Cornell University Press.
Palacz, Rafał. 2000. "Kiedy się zapadniemy?" *Gazeta Wrocławska [Wałbrzych],* 71.
Palska, Hanna. 1998. "'Beznadziejny proletariusz' w pamiętnikach. Kilka uwag o niektórych uwarunkowaniach nowej biedy," *Kultura i Społeczeństwo* 2.
Palska, Hanna, and Joanna Sikorska. 2000. "'Żadnych, żadnych możliwości ... Nie ma wyjścia z tej sytuacji ...' Wielkomiejska bieda, uzależnienie i niemoc." In E. Tarkowska (ed.), *Zrozumieć biednego. O dawnej i obecnej biedzie w Polsce.* Warsaw: Typografia.
Pałubicka, Anna. 1990. *Kulturowy wymiar ludzkiego świata obiektywnego.* Poznań: Wydawnictwo Naukowe UAM.
Panter-Brick, Catherine, Robert H. Layton, and Peter Rowley-Conwy. 2001. "Lines of Enquiry." In C. Panter-Brick, R. Layton, and P. Rowley-Conwy (eds.), *Hunters-Gatherers: An Interdisciplinary Perspective.* Cambridge: Cambridge University Press.
Parsons, Talcott. 2007. *Social Structure and Personality.* New York: The Free Press.
Pawłowski, Rafał. 2004. "Biedaszyby w Wałbrzychu. Historia," *Tygodnik Wałbrzyski* 7.
Pearce, Susan. 1995. *On Collecting: An Investigation into Collecting in the European Tradition.* London: Routledge.
Pedersen, Morten A. 2001. "Totemism, Animism and North Asian Indigenous Ontologies," *Royal Anthropological Institute* 7.
Pels, Peter. 1998. "The Spirit of Matter: On Fetish, Rarity, Fact and Fancy." In P. Spyer (ed.), *Border Fetishism: Material Objects in Unstable Spaces.* London: Routledge.
Pieniążek, Krystyna. 1990. "Rolnicy indywidualni i rynek." In Z. Hemmerling (ed.), *Wieś polska 1944–1989. Wybrane problemy podmiotowości społecznej, życia politycznego, ekonomicznego, oświatowego, kulturalnego i religijnego.* Warsaw: Instytut Nauk Politycznych UW.
Pieniążek, Wojciech, and Grażyna Jaworska. 1995. *Konteksty ekonomicznego myślenia. Wolny rynek na wsi z punktu widzenia antropologa.* Warsaw: IRiGŻ.
Pine, Francis. 1993. "'The Cows and Pigs Are His, the Eggs Are Mine': Women's Domestic Economy and Entrepreneurial Activity in Rural Poland." In C. Hann (ed.), *Socialism: Ideals, Ideologies, and Local Practice.* London and New York: Routledge.
———. 2002. "Retreat to the Household? Gendered Domains in Post-socialist Poland." In C. Hann (ed.), *Postsocialism: Ideals, Ideologies and Practices in Eurasia.* London: Routledge.
Piotrowski, Sławomir. 2004. *Przetrwać . . . lecz nie za wszelką cenę. O lękach społecznych zbieraczy poligonowego złomu i niewypałów.* Computer printout at the Warsaw University Institute of Polish Culture.

Pisarzewski, Tomasz. 2006. *Przemiany życia społecznego w Ostałówku k. Szy-dłowca.* Ethographic workshop, paper prepared under my guidance, Warsaw University Institute of Polish Culture.

Plińska, Weronika. 2005. "Górnicza tragedia." Computer printout at the Warsaw University Institute of Polish Culture.

————. 2006. *Materiały z warsztatów etnograficznych w Ostałówku k. Szydłowca.* Computer printout at the Warsaw University Institute of Polish Culture.

Podgórski, Jarosław. 1996. "Ubóstwo subiektywne." In T. Panek (ed.), *Ubóstwo w świetle badań budżetów domowych.* Warsaw: GUS.

Pokropek, Agnieszka. 1993. "Sen—brat śmierci," *Konteksty. Polska Sztuka Ludowa* 3, 4.

Pomian, Krzysztof. 1990. *Collectors and Curiosities: Paris and Venice 1500–1800.* Cambridge: Polity Press.

Rabinow, Paul. 1977. *Reflections on Fieldwork in Morocco.* Berkeley: University of California Press.

————. 1996. "Representations Are Social Facts: Modernity and Post-Modernity in Anthropology." *Essays on the Anthropology of Reason.* Princeton, NJ: Princeton University Press.

Rakowski, Tomasz. 2006a. "Zwischen Sammeleifer und Archäologie. Die Erfahrung von Geschichte und Gegenwart bei degradierten Gemeinscha ften in den polnischen Westgebieten (am Beispiel von Waldenburg und Umgebung) [Between Gathering and Archaeology: The Experience of the Past and Present in Degraded Societies in Poland in the Recovered Lands]." In P. Loew, C. Pletzing, and T. Serrier (eds.), *Wiedergewonne Geschichte. Zur Aneignung von Vergangenheit in den Zwischenräumen Mitteleuropas [Recovered History: Assimilating the Past in Central European Spheres of Mutual Interchange in the 19th and 20th Centuries].* Wiesbaden: Harrasowitz Verlag.

————. 2006b. 'Body and Fate: The Pension as a Practice of Social Remembering', *Anthropological Journal on European Culture 1.*

Redliński, Edward. 1975. *Konopielka.* Warsaw.

Rejniak, Agnieszka. 2002. "Nowoczesność i 'upadek doświadczenia' według Waltera Benjamina," *Kultura Współczesna* 3, 4.

Ricoeur, Paul. 1981. *The Model of the Text: Meaningful Action Considered as a Text in Hermeneutics and the Human Sciences.* Cambridge: Cambridge University Press.

————. 1989. *Język, tekst, interpretacja.* Warsaw: PIW.

Robotycki, Czesław. 1998. "Natura versus kultura. Stary problem w zielonym opakowaniu." *Nie wszystko jest oczywiste. Antropologia zjawisk kultury potocznej.* Kraków: Wydawnictwo UJ.

———— (ed.). 2001. "PRL z pamięci," *Zeszyty Naukowe UJ "Prace Etnograficzne"* 36.

————. 2003. "Pamięć PRL. Antropolog wobec dooewiadczenia własnej kultury," *Konteksty. Polska Sztuka Ludowa* 3, 4.

Rodak, Paweł. 2004. *Dziennik osobisty: praktyka, przedmiot, tekst.* Computer printout at the Warsaw University Institute of Polish Culture.

Rosner, Andrzej. 2000a. "Środki utrzymania ludności wiejskiej." In X. Dolińska and E. Wosik (eds.), *Chłop, rolnik, farmer? Przystąpienie Polski do Unii Europejskiej—nadzieje i obawy polskiej wsi.* Warsaw: ISP.

———. 2000b. "Bezrobocie na wsi i w rolnictwie." In X. Dolińska and E. Wosik (eds.), *Chłop, rolnik, farmer? Przystąpienie Polski do Unii Europejskiej—nadzieje i oba wy polskiej wsi.* Warsaw: ISP.

——— (ed.). 2002. *Wiejskie obszary kumulacji barier rozwojowych.* Warsaw: IRWiR.

Rothenbuler, Eric. 2003. *Komunikacja rytualna. Od rozmowy codziennej do ceremonii medialnej.* Kraków: Wydawnictwo UJ.

Rychard, Andrzej, and Michał Federowicz (eds.). 1993. *Społeczeństwo w transformacji. Ekspertyzy i studia.* Warsaw: IFiS PAN.

Sadowski, Andrzej. 2001. *Społeczne problemy miejscowości północno-wschodniej Polski w procesie transformacji.* Białystok: Wydawnictwo Uniwersytetu w Białymstoku.

Sahlins, Marshall. 2000. "The Original Affluent Society." *Culture in Practice: Selected Essays.* New York: Zone.

Sánchez-Pardo, Esther. 2003. *Cultures of the Death Drive: Melanie Klein and Modernist Melancholia.* Durham, NC, and London: Duke University Press.

Sanjek, Roger (ed.). 1990a. *Field Notes: The Makings of Anthropology.* Ithaca, NY, and London: Cornell University Press.

———. 1990b. "On Ethnographic Validity." In R. Sanjek (ed.), *Field Notes: The Makings of Anthropology.* Ithaca, NY, and London: Cornell University Press.

Schechner, Richard. 2000. "Ulica jest sceną." *Przyszłość rytuału.* Warsaw: Oficyna Wydawnicza Volumen.

Scott, James C. 1990. *Domination and the Arts of Resistance: Hidden Transcripts.* New Haven, CT, and London: Yale University Press.

Segal, Hanna. 1991. *Dream, Phantasy and Art.* London: Routledge.

"Sfera ubóstwa w Polsce". 1998. *Studia i Analizy Statystyczne.* Warsaw: GUS.

Shäuble, Michaela. 2006. "Imagined Suicide: Self-sacrifice and the Making of Heroes in Post-War Croatia," *Anthropology Matters Journal* 1.

Shäuble, Michaela, Tomasz Rakowski, and Włodzimierz Pessel. 2006. "Doing Fieldwork in Eastern Europe: Introduction," *Anthropology Matters Journal* 1.

Shelton, Anthony. 2001. "Introduction: The Return of the Subject." In A. Shelton (ed.), *Collectors: Expressions of Self and Other.* London: The Horniman Museum and Gardens.

Sikorska, Joanna. 1999. *Konsumpcja: warunki, zróżnicowania, strategie.* Warsaw: IFiS PAN.

Simmel, Georg. 1964. *The Sociology of Georg Simmel.* Translated, edited, and with an introduction by Kurt H. Wolff. New York: The Free Press.

Simonides, Dorota (ed.). 1984. *Bery to nie tylko gruszki, czyli rzecz o humorze śląskim.* Opole: Instytut Śląski.

——— (ed.). 1988a. *Górniczy stan w wierzeniach, obrzędach, humorze i pieśniach.* Katowice: Śląski Instytut Naukowy.

―――. 1988b. "Humor górniczy." In D. Simonides (ed.), *Górniczy stan w wierzeniach, obrzędach, humorze i pieśniach.* Katowice: Śląski Instytut Naukowy.

Skiba, Ludwik. 1979. *Dolnośląskie Zagłębie Węglowe w organizmie gospodarczym PRL.* Warsaw, Wrocław: PWN.

―――. 1997a. "Wstęp." In L. Skiba (ed.), *Zagłębie węglowe w obliczu restrukturyzacji. Studia i materiały.* Wrocław: Wydawnictwo Silesia.

―――. 1997b. "Deindustrializacja bez reindustrializacji." In L. Skiba (ed.), *Zagłębie węglowe w obliczu restrukturyzacji. Studia i materiały.* Wrocław: Wydawnictwo Silesia.

―――. 1997c. "Zakres restrukturalizacji a delimitacja lokalnego rynku pracy." In L. Skiba (ed.), *Zagłębie węglowe w obliczu restrukturyzacji. Studia i materiały.* Wrocław: Wydawnictwo Silesia.

Smelser, Neil. 2004. "Psychological and Cultural Trauma." In J. C. Alexander et al. (eds.), *Cultural Trauma and Collective Identity.* Berkeley, Los Angeles, and London: University of California Press.

Smerd, Krystyna. 2004. "Katastrofa," *Tygodnik Wałbrzyski* 7.

Sommer, Manfred. 2003. *Zbieranie. Próba filozoficznego ujęcia.* Warsaw: Oficyna Naukowa.

Sorokin, Pitirim. 1943. *Man and Society in Calamity: The Effects of War, Revolution, Famine and Pestilence upon the Human Mind, Behavior, Social Organization and Cultural Life.* New York: E. P. Dutton & Co.

Spieralska, Beata. 2004. "Dach nad głową. Pojęcie 'domu' w językach indoeuropejskich," *Konteksty. Polska Sztuka Ludowa* 1, 2.

Spyer, Patricia (ed.). 1998. *Border Fetishism: Material objects in unstable spaces.* London: Routledge.

Stanaszek, Alina. 2004. "Bieda (z) pracy, czyli o biednych pracujących we współczesnym świecie," *Kultura i Społeczeństwo* 2.

Staniszkis, Jadwiga. 1976. "Struktura jako rezultat procesów adaptacyjnych." In W. Morawski (ed.), *Organizacje. Socjologia struktur, procesów, ról.* Warsaw: PWN.

Stewart, Susan. 1984. *On Longing: Narratives on the Miniature, the Gigantic, the Souvenir, the Collection.* Baltimore, MD: The John Hopkins University Press.

Strathern, Mary. 1988. *The Gender of the Gift: Problems with Women and Problems with Society in Melanesia.* Berkeley: University of California Press.

Stomma, Ludwik. 1986. *Antropologia kultury wsi polskiej XIX w.* Warsaw: Wydawnictwo PAX.

Styk, Józef. 1994. "Aksjologia chłopskiej migracji." In I. Machaj and J. Styk (eds.), *Stare i nowe struktury społeczne w Polsce, vol. 1: Miasto.* Lublin: Wydawnictwo: UMCS.

Sułek, Antoni. 2005. "Badania w Marienthalu (1931–1932) i współczesne im badania nad bezrobociem w Polsce," *Kultura i Społeczeństwo* 2.

Sulima, Roch. 1980. "Posłowie." In E. Michalska, *Chylą się dni moje.* Warsaw: Ludowa Spółdzielnia Wydawnicza.

————. 1992a. "Między płaczem a milczeniem." *Słowo i etos. Szkice o kulturze*. Kraków: Wydawnictwo Galicja.

————. 1992b. "Narodziny chłopskiej Księgi." *Słowo i etos. Szkice o kulturze*. Kraków: Wydawnictwo Galicja.

————. 1995. "Rekonstrukcje i interpretacje. Polska folklorystyka dzisiaj." In D. Simonides (ed.), *Folklorystyka. Dylematy i perspektywy*. Opole: Uniwersytet Opolski.

————. 1997. "Między oralnością a piśmiennością. Strategia kolekcjonera a ludowa kultura rękopisu (XIX–XX wiek)," *Mazowieckie Studia Humanistyczne* 1.

————. 2000. *Antropologia codzienności*. Kraków: Wydawnictwo UJ.

————. 2003. "O rytualnych formach komunikacji społecznej," *Przegląd Humanistyczny* 6: 133–139.

Sulimski, Janusz. 1992. *Wzory egzystencji ludności wiejskiej w Małopolsce*. Warsaw: IRWiR.

Szacki, Jerzy. 2002. *Historia myśli socjologicznej*. Warsaw: PWN.

Szacki, Piotr. 2003. "Pamiętać," *Konteksty. Polska Sztuka Ludowa* 3, 4.

Szafraniec, Krystyna. 2002. "Polskie residuum systemowe, czyli pytanie o rolę wsi i chłopów w procesach przekształceń ustrojowych," *Kultura i Społeczeństwo* 4.

Szanciło, Anna. 2005. *O żarcie w społecznościach pogórniczych. Materiały z warsztatowych badań terenowych w Wałbrzychu*. Computer printout at the Warsaw University Institute of Polish Culture.

Szarota, Tomasz. 1995. "Życie codzienne w peerelu—propozycja badawcza," in *Polska 1944–1989. Studia i Materiały* 1. Warsaw: IH PAN.

Szczepański, Jan. 1973. *Zmiany społeczeństwa polskiego pod wpływem uprzemysłowienia*. Warsaw: Instytut Wydawniczy CRZZ.

Szczurowska, Magdalena. 2004. "Wojna prawa z bezprawiem," *Dolnośląska Solidarność* 3.

Szpak, Ewelina. 2006. *Między osiedlem a zagrodą. Życie codzienne mieszkańców PGR-ów*. Warsaw: Wydawnictwo Trio.

Szpakowska, Małgorzata. 2003. *Chcieć i mieć. Samowiedza obyczajowa w Polsce czasu przemian*. Warsaw: W.A.B.

Sztompka, Piotr. 2000. *Trauma wielkiej zmiany: społeczne koszty transformacji*. Warsaw: ISP PAN.

————. 2004. "The Trauma of Social Change: a Case of Post-communist Societies." In J. C. Alexander et al. (eds.), *Cultural Trauma and Collective Identity*. Berkeley, Los Angeles, and London: University of California Press.

Szulc, Adam. 1996. "Ubóstwo materialne w Polsce w latach 1990–1994." In T. Panek (ed.), *Ubóstwo w świetle badan budżetów domowych*. Warsaw: GUS.

Szytełło, Jan (ed.). 1992. *Nędza i dostatek na ziemiach polskich od średniowiecza po wiek XX*. Warsaw: Semper.

Świątkiewicz, Wojciech. 1983. "Kultura a patologia społeczna." In J. Wódz (ed.), *Patologia społeczna w starych dzielnicach mieszkaniowych miast Górnego Śląska*. Katowice: Śląski Instytut Naukowy.

Tarkowska, Elżbieta. 1993a. "Temporalny wymiar przemian zachodzących w Polsce." In A. Jawłowska, M. Kempny, and E. Tarkowska (eds.), *Kulturowy wymiar przemian społecznych.* Warsaw: Wydawnictwo IFiS PAN.

———. 1993b. "Zmieniająca się rzeczywistość społeczna jako szczególna sytuacja badawcza," *Kultura i Społeczeństwo* 3.

———. 1997. "Nierówna dystrybucja czasu—nowy wymiar zróżnicowania społeczeństwa polskiego." In H. Domański and A. Rychard (eds.), *Elementy nowego ładu.* Warsaw: IFiS PAN.

———. 2000a. "Bieda, historia i kultura." In E. Tarkowska (ed.), *Zrozumieć biednego. O dawnej i obecnej biedzie w Polsce.* Warsaw: Typografia.

———. 2000b. "Styl życia biednych rodzin w przeszłości i w teraźniejszości: charakterystyka badań." In E. Tarkowska (ed.), *Zrozumieć biednego. O dawnej i obecnej biedzie w Polsce.* Warsaw: Typografia.

———. 2000c. "O dawnej i obecnej biedzie w Polsce." In E. Tarkowska (ed.), *Zrozumieć biednego. O dawnej i obecnej biedzie w Polsce.* Warsaw: Typografia.

———. 2000d. "Bieda dawna i nowa: historie rodzin." In E. Tarkowska (ed.), *Zrozumieć biednego. O dawnej i obecnej biedzie w Polsce.* Warsaw: Typografia.

———. 2000e. "Bieda popegeerowska." In E. Tarkowska (ed.), *Zrozumieć biednego. O dawnej i obecnej biedzie w Polsce.* Warsaw: Typografia.

———. 2002. "Koniec pegeerowskiego świata w wypowiedziach byłych pracowników PGR-u "Owczary"." In K. Korzeniewska and E. Tarkowska (eds.), *Lata tłuste, lata chude ... Spojrzenie na biedę w społecznościach lokalnych.* Warsaw: IFiS PAN.

———. 2003. *Problem ubóstwa w Polsce.* Computer printout of a lecture delivered for the "Problem of Poverty in Poland" conference (Greifswald, Germany, 10–12 December).

Tarkowska, Elżbieta, and Jacek Tarlowski. 1994. "'Amoralny familizm' czyli o dezintegracji społecznej w Polsce lat osiemdziesiątych." In J. Tarkowski (ed.), *Socjologia świata polityki. Władza i społeczeństwo w systemie autorytarnym* 1. Warsaw: IFiS PAN.

"There's Work in Poland" ["Jest praca w Polsce"]. 2006. *Gazeta Wyborcza,* 7 September, no 209.5216.

Thomas, Wiliam, and Florian Znaniecki. 2010. *The Polish Peasant in Europe and America: Monograph of an Immigrant Group* 5. Charleston: Nabu Press.

Thompson, Paul. 2000. *The Voice of the Past: Oral History.* Oxford: Oxford University Press.

Tokarska, Joanna, Jerzy S. Wasilewski, and Magdalena Zmysłowska. 1982. "Śmierć jako organizator kultury," *Etnografia Polska* 26.

Tokarska-Bakir, Joanna. 1995. "Dalsze losy syna marnotrawnego. Projekt etnografii nieprzezroczystej," *Konteksty. Polska Sztuka Ludowa* 1.

———. 1996. "Obrazki z wystawy 'Ponowoczesność okolic Przemyśla,'" *Regiony* 2.

———. 1997. *Wyzwolenie przez zmysły. Tybetańskie koncepcje soteriologiczne.* Wrocław: Monografie FNP.

————. 1999a. "'Ślepy bibliotekarz'. O pisemnym wymiarze ustności,'" *Konteksty. Polska Sztuka Ludowa* 1,2.

————. 1999. "Zagadka o sześciu łabędziach," *Res Publica Nowa* 9.

————. 2000. *Obraz osobliwy. Hermeneutyczna lektura źródeł etnograficznych.* Krakow: Universitas.

Tomasik, Wojciech. 1999. *Inżynieria dusz. Literatura realizmu socjalistycznego w planie "propagandy monumentalnej."* Wrocław: Monografie FNP.

Tomicka, Joanna, and Ryszard Tomicki. 1975. *Drzewo życia. Ludowa wizja świata i człowieka.* Warsaw: LSW.

Tomicki, Ryszard. 1973. "Tradycja i jej znaczenie w kulturze chłopskiej," *Etnografia Polska* 27, vol. 1.

Tonkin, Elizabeth. 1992. *Narrating Our Past: The Social Construction of Oral History.* Cambridge: Cambridge University Press.

Torański, Błażej. 2000. "Wykupić Faustynów, czyli stan zawieszenia," *Rzeczpospolita* 57.

Townsend, Peter. 1979. *Poverty in the United Kingdom.* London: Allen Lane and Penguin Books.

Trosiak, Cezary. 2000. "Kaława a 'bunkry'. Z badań nad stosunkiem społeczności lokalnej do poniemieckiego zabytku." In Z. Mazur (ed.), *Wspólne dziedzictwo? Ze studiów nad stosunkiem do spuścizny kulturowej na Ziemiach Zachodnich i Północnych.* Poznań: Instytut Zachodni.

Trusewicz, Iwona. 2004. "Zbieracze poszli w las," *Rzeczpospolita* 99.

Turnbull, Collin. 1987. *The Forest People.* New York: Touchstone Press.

Turner, Victor W. 1969. *The Ritual Process: Structure and Anti-structure.* Chicago: Aldine.

————. 1982. *From Ritual to Theatre: The Human Seriousness of Play.* New York: Performing Arts Journal Publications.

————. 1990. "Are There Universals of Performance in Myth, Ritual and Drama?" In R. Schechner and W. Appel (eds.), *By Means of Performance: Intercultural Studies of Theatre and Ritual.* Cambridge: Cambridge University Press: 8–18.

Tyler, Stephen. 1986. "Post-Modern Ethnography: From the Document of the Occult to the Occult Document." In J. Clifford, and G. Marcus (eds.), *Writing Culture: The Poetics and Politics of Ethnography.* Berkeley, Los Angeles, and London: University of California Press.

Tymiński, Maciej. 2002. "Funkcjonowanie klik w zakładach przemysłowych (1950–1970)," *Kultura i Społeczeństwo* 4.

Urbanek, Mariusz. 1998. "Martwe szyby," *Polityka* 33.

"Unemployment Will Fall" ["Bezrobocie będzie jeszcze bardziej spadać"]. 2006. *Gazeta Wyborcza,* 17 August, no. 191.5198.

Valentine, Charles. 1968. *Culture and Poverty: Critique and Counter-proposals.* Chicago: University of Chicago Press.

van Gennep, Arnold. 1961. *The Rites of Passage.* Chicago: University of Chicago Press.

Verdery, Katherine. 1996. *What Was Socialism and What Comes Next?* Princeton, NJ: Princeton University Press.

Vigarello, Georges. 2008. *Concepts of Cleanliness: Changing Attitudes in France since the Middle Ages*. Cambridge: Cambridge University Press.

Wagner, Mathias. 2003. *Postrzeganie problemu polskiej biedy w mediach niemieckich*. Computer printout of a lecture delivered for "Problem of Poverty in Poland" conference. (Greifswald, Germany, 10–12 December).

Wałbrzych. Historia—współczesność—perspektywy. 1970. Collective work. Wrocław, Warsaw, and Kraków: Ossolineum.

Warzywoda-Kruszyńska, Wielisława. 1998. "Wielkomiejscy biedni—formująca się underclass? Przypadek klientów pomocy społecznej," *Kultura i Społeczeństwo* 2.

——— (ed.). 1999. *(Życie) na marginesie wielkiego miasta*. Łódź: Instytut Socjologii UŁ.

Washington, John, Ian Paylor, and Jennifer Harris. 2000. "Poverty Studies in Europe and the Evolution of the Concept of Social Exclusion." In J. Bradshaw and R. Sainsbury (eds.), *Experiencing Poverty*. Aldershot: Ashgate.

Wasilewski, Jacek. 1986. "Społeczeństwo polskie, społeczeństwo chłopskie," *Studia Socjologiczne* 1.

Wasilewski, Jerzy S. 1980. "Podarować—znaleźć—zgubić—zbłądzić. Niektóre kategorie języka symbolicznego związane z opozycją życie—śmierć," *Etnografia Polska* 27, vol. 1.

———. 1989. *Tabu a paradygmaty etnologii*. Warsaw: Wydawnictwo UW.

Watson, Mark. 1997. "Historic Industrial Regions in Times of De-industrialization." In collective work, *Historyczne okręgi przemysłowe w okresie deindustrializacji*. Wrocław: Instytut Historii Architektury, Sztuki i Techniki Politechniki Wrocławskiej.

Watson, Tony J. 1987. *Sociology, Work and Industry*. London and New York: Routledge.

Wawrzyniak, Joanna. 2006. "Die Westgebiete in der Ideologie des polni schen Kommunismus Symbolik Und Alltag am Beispiel der Soldatensiedler [The Recovered Territories in the Ideology of Polish Communism: Symbolism and the Everyday, the Example of the Military Settlers]." In P. Loew, C. Pletzing, and T. Serrier (eds.), *Wiedergewonne Geschichte. Zur Aneignung von Vergangenheit in den Zwischenräumen Mitteleuropas [History Regained: Assimilating the Past in Central European Regions of Mutual Interchange in the 19th and 20th Centuries]*. Wiesbaden: Harrasowitz Verlag.

Weber, Max. 1978. *Economy and Society: An Outline of Interpretive Sociology*. Berkeley: University of California Press.

———. 1993. "Asceticism and the Spirit of Capitalism." *Art in Theory*. Oxford and Malden, MA: Blackwell Publishing.

Węgrzynowska, Maria. 2006. *Próba oswojenia przestrzeni—bloki mieszkalne na podlaskiej wsi*. Laboratory work prepared under my guidance, Warsaw University Institute of Ethnology and Cultural Anthropology.

Weiner, January. 1999. "Ekokalipsa," *Znak* 12.

Weiss, Gail, and Honi Fern Haber. 1999. *Perspectives on Embodiment: The Intersection of Nature and Culture*. London and New York: Routledge.

Wieczorkiewicz, Anna. 1996. "O funkcji i retoryce wypowiedzi muzealnej," *Konteksty. Polska Sztuka Ludowa* 1, 2.

Wieruszewska-Adamczyk, Maria. 1971. "Sankcje systemu kontroli społecznej wobec rodziny wiejskiej na przykładzie dwóch wybranych wsi powiatu bełchatowskiego," *Łódzkie Studia Etnograficzne* 13.

Wierzbicka, Liliana. 1999. "Restrukturyzacja przemysłu węglowego i likwidacja bezrobocia w okręgu wałbrzyskim w latach 1994–1998. Doświadczenia samorządu wałbrzyskiego, osiągnięcia, problemy rozwiązane i trudności," *Dolny Śląsk* 6.

Wilkin, Jerzy. 1988. "Reakcja chłopów na politykę rolną państwa w perspektywie historycznej," *Kultura i Społeczeństwo* 4.

———. 2000. "Zagubiona wieś—miejsce polskiej wsi i rolnictwa w polityce państwa w latach dziewięćdziesiątych." In K. Gorlach and A. Pyć (eds.), *Węzłowe kwestie społeczne wsi polskiej u progu XXI wieku*. Kraków: Instytut Socjologii UJ.

Wilson, William J. 1987. *The Truly Disadvantaged: The Inner City, the Underclass, and Public Policy*. Chicago: University of Chicago Press.

Winnicott, Donald W. 1971. *Playing and Reality*. London: Routledge.

Wolf, Eric R. 1982. *Europe and the People Without History*. Berkeley and Los Angeles: University of California Press.

Wódz, Jacek. 1989. *Problemy patologii społecznej w mieście*. Warsaw: PWN.

Wódz, Kazimiera. 1994. "Underclass w starych dzielnicach przemysłowych miast Górnego Śląska." In I. Machaj and J. Styk (eds.), *Stare i nowe struktury społeczne w Polsce*, vol. 1. Lublin: UMCS.

Wojsławowicz, Ewa. 2006. *Wstyd w pogórniczych społecznoœciach Wałbrzycha i Boguszowa*. Workshop paper, Warsaw University Institute of Polish Culture.

Woroniecka, Grażyna. 2002. "'Kozioł ofiarny' Rene Girarda w perspektywie poststrukturalnej," *Kultura Współczesna* 1, 2.

Woźniak, Andrzej (ed.). 1982. *Tradycyjna kultura robotnicza Żyrardowa*. Warsaw: MOBN.

Wyka, Anna. 1993. *Badacz społeczny wobec doświadczenia*. Warsaw: IFiS PAN.

Wyka, Kazimierz. 1984. "Gospodarka wyłączona." *Życie na niby. Pamiętnik po klęsce*. Kraków, Wrocław: Wydawnictwo Literackie.

Yates, Frances. 2010. *The Art of Memory*. London: Routledge.

Zacharzewski, Jerzy (ed.). 1996. *Wypadki przy pracy w polskich kopalniach węgla kamiennego w latach 1946–1995*. Kraków: Wydawnictwo AGH.

Zadrożyńska, Anna. 1968. "Fenomenologiczna koncepcja historii i kultury. Zastosowanie w polskich badaniach etnograficznych," *Etnografia Polska* 12.

Zając, Paweł. 2004. "'Nadprzyrodzone' w kulturze ludowej," *Literatura Ludowa* 4, 5.

Zalewska, Danuta (ed.). 1996. *Kultura ubóstwa—kultura przetrwania*. Wrocław: Wydawnictwo Uniwersytetu Wrocławskiego.

Żarnowski, Janusz. 1992. "Bieda i dostatek 1918–1939." In J. Szytełło (ed.), *Nędza i dostatek na ziemiach polskich od średniowiecza po wiek XX*. Warsaw: Semper.

Zawadzka, Anna. 2005. "Bezrobotni z dwudziestolecia międzywojennego i z końca wieku. Problemy, postawy, narracje. Analiza 'Pamiętników bezrobotnych,'" *Kultura i Społeczeństwo* 2.

Zawadzki, Bohdan, and Paul Lazarsfeld. 1993. "Psychologiczne konsekwencje bezrobocia," *Kultura i Społeczeństwo* 2.

Zawilski, Apoloniusz. 1967. *Bełchatów i jego historyczne awanse*. Łódź: Wydawnictwo Łódzkie.

Zięba, Joanna. 2004. 742 notebooks of Janina Turek. Computer printout in the Warsaw University Institute of Polish Culture.

Zimniak-Hałajko, Marta. 2000. "Obserwacja uczestnicząca: metodologia badań a przedmiot poznania." In S. Bednarek and K. Łukasiewicz (eds.), *Wiedza o kulturze polskiej u progu XXI wieku*. Wrocław: Wydawnictwo Silesia.

Zinserling, Irena. 2002. "Bezradność społeczna, bezradność wyuczona." *Jednostka i społeczeństwo. Podejście psychologiczne*. Gdańsk: Gdańskie Wydawnictwo Psychologiczne.

Žižek, Slavoj. 2000. "Melancholy and the Act," *Critical Inquiry* 26, summer 4: 657–681.

Znaniecki, Florian. 1973. *Socjologia wychowania*, vol. 2. Warsaw: PWN.

Zowczak, Magdalena. 1993. "Zagłada światów. Między mitologią lokalną a Biblią," *Konteksty. Polska Sztuka Ludowa* 3, 4.

Zubelewicz, Emil. 2005. *Bezprawie biedaszybów. O zwyczaju społeczności Wałbrzycha i Boguszowa*. Workshop paper, Warsaw University Institute of Polish Culture.

Index

www.ingramcontent.com/pod-product-compliance
Lightning Source LLC
Chambersburg PA
CBHW070907030426
42336CB00014BA/2321